Echoes of Dervock

The Dervock Legacy, Volume 1

Angeline Gallant

Published by Angeline Gallant, 2024.

While every precaution has been taken in the preparation of this book, the publisher assumes no responsibility for errors or omissions, or for damages resulting from the use of the information contained herein.

ECHOES OF DERVOCK

First edition. October 8, 2024.

Copyright © 2024 Angeline Gallant.

ISBN: 979-8227782779

Written by Angeline Gallant.

Also by Angeline Gallant

A Dragon's Diary
Dreaming of Dragons

Calling Her Heart
Whisper of the Heart
No Turning Back
Forsake Me Not
Hear My Cry

FORGET ME NOT
Victoria, Ontario's Babies 1894 - 1895

Guardian of the Heart
Fallen Petals

Keeper Of Secrets
A Lady's Secret

Midnight's Awakening
Heart of the Storm
Walking Through The Storm
Walking Through The Storm
Heart of the Storm

Secrets of the Underworld
Deklan's Dragons

Tell My Story Collection
Tell My Story: Germany 1851
Tell My Story: England 1852

The Dervock Legacy
Echoes of Dervock

The Grave Whisperer
Cataraqui United Church Cemetery
Wedding Bells in Kingston, Ontario, Canada 1923
St. Paul's Anglican Churchyard Kingston, Ontario, Canada A-B
St. Paul's Anglican Churchyard, Kingston, Ontario, Canada C - D
St. Paul's Anglican Churchyard, Kingston, Ontario, Canada G - H
St. Paul's Anglican Churchyard, Kingston, Ontario, Canada J - N
St. Paul's Anglican Churchyard, Kingston, Ontario, Canada O - R

St. Paul's Anglican Churchyard, Kingston, Ontario, Canada S - T
St. Paul's Anglican Churchyard, Kingston, Ontario T - Z
Small Graveyards & Burial Grounds: Kingston, Ontario, Canada
Cataraqui United Church Cemetery 1
Cataraqui United Church Cemetery 2
Cataraqui United Church Cemetary 3
Cataraqui United Church Cemetery 4
Cataraqui United Church Cemetery 5
Beth Israel Cemetery
Cataraqui United Church Cemetery 6

The Wolf Whisperer Series
Journey of the Heart
Cry of a Warrior
Wolf Whisperer volumes 1 & 2
The Wolf Whisperer volumes 1 & 2

Timeless Whispers of Dervock Saga
Secrets of Dervock

Standalone
Winds of Change vol 1-3

Watch for more at https://www.goodreads.com/author/show/ 19703964.Angeline_Gallant.

Table of Contents

JOHN McLEESE[1] 1
Likely Physical Description of John McLeese, Sr. 2
Life in Carrowreagh and Derrykeighan, County Antrim in the Late 18th to Early 19th Century | Agricultural Lifestyle: 4
Community and Social Life: 5
JOHN (McALEESE) McLEESE II[2] 24
JANE (UNKNOWN) McLEESE[3] 53
ANN ADAMS[4] 79
DANIEL ADAMS[5] 81
DANIEL ADAMS[6] 85
SAMUEL ALLEN ESQ.[7] 96
FRANCES (HIGGINSON) ALLEN[8] 117
DR. SAMUEL ALLEN M.D.[9] 138
MILLICENT MARY (BENNING) ALLEN[10] 169
VEN. CONWAY BENNING LL.D.[11] 201
ANN (ELLIS) BENNING[12] 287
JAMES BENNING[13] 367
ELEANOR (BENNING) DALWAY[14] 396
ELIZABETH BOYD[15] 417
GEORGE BOYD[16] 421
JEAN (GORDON) BOYD[17] 439
JOSEPH ANDERSON[18] 443
WILLIAM DUNLOP[19] 458
SARAH (UNKNOWN) BARRY[20] 461

JOHN McLEESE[1]

Name: John McLeese, Sr.
Birthplace: Carrowreagh, County Antrim, Ireland
Date of Birth: 1749
Residence: Spent his entire life in County Antrim, primarily in the villages of Carrowreagh and Derrykeighan
Date of Death: September 5, 1814
Occupation: Likely a farmer or tradesman, working the land in rural County Antrim
Religion: Presbyterian (common in the Ulster region during this time, especially among Scottish-descended settlers)
Personality: Stoic, hardworking, and community-focused, John was the type of man shaped by the rural life of 18th-century Ireland, dedicated to his family and the rhythms of the land. He likely had a strong sense of loyalty to his Protestant faith and a cautious, perhaps skeptical, attitude toward political upheaval and change.

Likely Physical Description of John McLeese, Sr.

Height: Average for the time, likely around 5'6"–5'8" (men during this period were generally shorter than today due to diet and health factors).

Build: Sturdy and muscular from years of physical labor on the farm. His hands would have been calloused from working the land, and his body weathered from a lifetime of outdoor work in the fields.

Hair: As a young man, John likely had dark brown or black hair, common among the Scots-Irish population in Ulster. By the time of his death, his hair would have been streaked with grey or entirely grey, possibly thinning at the temples.

Eyes: Blue or grey eyes would have been a typical feature in the region. His gaze would have been keen, showing both the weariness of a hardworking life and the quiet wisdom of experience.

Complexion: Fair-skinned but weathered by years of sun exposure. His face would have likely been lined with wrinkles from working outdoors. He may have had ruddy cheeks, a common trait among those who spent long days in the elements.

Clothing: John would have worn simple, functional clothing suited for farm work. Likely made of wool or linen, his daily attire would include breeches, a long-sleeved shirt, and a waistcoat. In colder months, he might have worn a woolen coat and a cap to keep warm. His shoes would have been sturdy but well-worn from constant use on rough terrain.

ECHOES OF DERVOCK

Life in Carrowreagh and Derrykeighan, County Antrim in the Late 18th to Early 19th Century

Agricultural Lifestyle:

John's life would have revolved around farming. County Antrim's rural economy was based largely on agriculture, particularly growing crops like potatoes and oats, and raising livestock such as cattle and sheep. As a farmer, John's daily routine would be dictated by the seasons—planting in the spring, tending the fields and animals during the summer, and harvesting in the fall. Winter was a quieter time but still involved tending to livestock and repairing tools and buildings for the coming year. The work was demanding and relentless, leaving little time for leisure.

Community and Social Life:

Life in rural County Antrim was closely tied to the local Presbyterian church, which acted as both a religious and social hub. John would have attended services every Sunday, bringing his family with him. The church would have been an important part of his life, offering not just spiritual guidance but also a sense of community. Outside of church, social events in rural areas were few and far between but might include seasonal fairs or gatherings to mark important events like harvest time.

The village of Derrykeighan, where John lived later in life, was a small, tight-knit community. Everyone would have known each other, and there was likely a strong sense of mutual reliance, especially in times of hardship. Neighboring families would help each other with the harvest or during difficult winters, and John would have been an active part of this local support network.

Political Climate:

John lived through some of the most turbulent years in Irish history, particularly the Irish Rebellion of 1798 and the tensions between Catholics and Protestants that it exacerbated. As a Protestant in County Antrim, John likely identified with the Protestant Ascendancy, and while he might not have been a wealthy landowner, his position as a Protestant would have afforded him more social and economic security than his Catholic neighbors. However, the fear of unrest and violence would have been a constant in his life during these years.

Though removed from the center of rebellion activity, rural areas like Carrowreagh and Derrykeighan would have been impacted by the general atmosphere of tension. John likely viewed the rebellion with a mix of fear and pragmatism, focusing more on protecting his family and community than on political causes. In the aftermath, the consolidation of British rule in Ireland through the Act of Union in 1801 would have further entrenched his loyalty to the status quo, though he might also have harbored a growing concern for the political future of the region.

As a 3-year-old living in Carrowreagh, County Antrim, Ireland in 1749, when Benjamin Franklin conducted his famous kite experiment and determined that lightning was electrical, John McLeese Sr. would have been too young to fully grasp or react to the scientific significance of the discovery. At that age, his world would have primarily revolved around his immediate surroundings: his family, the farm, and the rural life of his small community.

However, news of Franklin's experiment likely would have reached Ireland gradually over time, likely through local clergy, educated members of the community, or traveling merchants. Since Franklin's work was groundbreaking and stirred excitement across the scientific community, by the time John was older (perhaps in his early teens), he would have been more aware of the concept.

How It Might Have Affected Him:

1. Religious and Superstitious Interpretations:

Growing up in the mid-18th century, people in rural Ireland still had a strong connection to religious and superstitious beliefs, especially about natural phenomena like thunderstorms. Lightning was often viewed as a sign of God's power, and many believed it was a form of divine punishment or warning. Franklin's discovery that lightning was electrical may have been met with skepticism or even discomfort among John's family and neighbors, as it challenged these long-held beliefs.

As John grew older, he might have found himself caught between these traditional views and the growing influence of scientific discoveries. This tension between faith and science was a significant part of life in this era, and John might have been fascinated by the idea that such a powerful force as lightning could be understood and even potentially controlled by human knowledge.

2. Rural Influence:

In rural County Antrim, practical applications of electricity were not immediately apparent. Farming communities like John's were focused on survival, growing crops, and tending livestock. The idea of electricity as a scientific force would have seemed distant and abstract. However, as he matured and heard more about these discoveries, John might have viewed it with a mix of awe and curiosity, wondering how such knowledge could ever affect his daily life.

3. Connection to the Wider World:

John, like many rural farmers in the 18th century, would have lived in a relatively isolated environment. News of Franklin's discoveries may have provided a window into a rapidly changing world, reminding John of the advancements happening far from his small community. While it may not have had an immediate impact on his day-to-day existence, such events would have contributed to a growing awareness that the world was larger than his village and that science and progress were beginning to reshape society.

John's Potential Reaction as an Adult:

By the time John McLeese reached adulthood, Franklin's experiments with electricity and the lightning rod would have been more widely known. Practical inventions like the lightning rod, which Franklin created in 1752, would have had a tangible impact on the way people in rural Ireland thought about lightning and storms. In farming communities, where lightning strikes could easily cause fires, the introduction of the lightning rod might have been seen as a valuable and potentially life-saving innovation.

As a pragmatic farmer, John might have embraced the lightning rod and the concept of harnessing electricity, seeing it as a practical tool to protect his home and family from the dangers of lightning. He may have heard about local churches or wealthy landowners installing lightning rods to protect buildings and might have been impressed by this newfound ability to "tame" nature.

Summary:

In summary, as a 3-year-old in 1749, John McLeese Sr. would not have been directly affected by Benjamin Franklin's discovery that lightning is electrical. However, as he grew older, he would have been exposed to the broader implications of this discovery through the gradual spread of scientific knowledge. By adulthood, he likely viewed it with a mix of curiosity, awe, and pragmatism, understanding that while scientific advancements like the lightning rod were remarkable, they were also useful tools in the practical world of farming and rural life in County Antrim.

When the Industrial Revolution began in 1760, John McLeese Sr., at 11 years old, would have been living in rural Carrowreagh, County Antrim, Ireland, where life was still dominated by agricultural rhythms and traditional rural practices. The immediate effects of industrialization would have taken time to reach the remote farming communities of Northern Ireland, so John may not have seen its influence in his everyday life at first. However, as he grew older and the Revolution progressed, he would have inevitably been affected by its ripple effects.

How He Might Have Reacted at 11 Years Old:

1. Limited Immediate Awareness:

At the age of 11, John's world would have been focused on helping his family with daily farming chores and learning skills necessary for rural life. The Industrial Revolution initially took root in urban areas of Britain, particularly in England, where factories and mechanized production began transforming the textile and manufacturing industries. In the rural areas of County Antrim, such developments would have felt distant and might not have been a primary concern for John or his community at this stage.

As an 11-year-old boy, John would have had little direct knowledge of the technological changes taking place in factories, though he might have heard whispers of it from travelers, merchants, or local priests who had a broader awareness of world events. It's possible he could have reacted with curiosity or indifference, depending on how much the idea of machinery or mass production entered his rural world.

2. Connection to Farming:

John would have primarily lived in an agrarian environment where farming practices were passed down through generations. While the Industrial Revolution would revolutionize agriculture as well, with advancements in tools and techniques (like the introduction of threshing machines), these changes would come later. At 11, he would still be working with traditional hand tools, and the idea of industrial machinery transforming farming would have seemed foreign or even unnecessary at the time.

His life would have centered around the land and seasons, and the impact of industrial advancements on the urban working class, such as factories or coal mines, would have been outside of his daily experience.

HOW THE INDUSTRIAL Revolution Affected Him Over Time:

1. Economic Impact on Rural Life:

As John grew older, the effects of the Industrial Revolution would gradually become more apparent in his rural community. Although Ireland did not industrialize as quickly as England and Scotland, by the late 18th and early 19th centuries, industrialization began to influence agriculture and the local economy. New tools, such as seed drills and threshing machines, made farming more efficient, allowing for greater crop yields and the expansion of markets.

John might have witnessed local farmers adopting these new technologies, or he may have found himself adjusting to the introduction of more mechanized farming methods, which could have brought changes to the rural economy of County Antrim. This could have been both a source of excitement and anxiety, as traditional methods of farming were deeply rooted in the community.

2. Urban Migration and Social Change:

With industrialization, many rural families began migrating to cities in search of work in factories, particularly in places like Belfast, where the linen industry became prominent. While John and his family might have remained in Carrowreagh, it's likely that they saw neighbors or relatives move to urban centers for better economic opportunities. This migration would have changed the social fabric of rural communities, making them less insular as more people were exposed to city life and industrial jobs.

John, as a farmer, might have felt conflicted by these changes—on one hand, the lure of better opportunities in urban areas, and on the other, the strong connection to the land and traditional farming ways.

3. Impact on Daily Life:

By the late 18th century, the Industrial Revolution brought new consumer goods, like manufactured textiles, iron tools, and other items, into rural areas. John may have noticed the growing availability of cheaper, mass-produced goods in local markets, a stark contrast to the handcrafted items his family and neighbors had relied on. These new products could have made certain aspects of life more convenient, but they also represented a shift away from the self-sufficiency that rural families like John's were accustomed to.

It's possible that John viewed these changes with a degree of caution, recognizing the benefits of new tools and materials but also wary of how industrialization might undermine traditional ways of life.

4. Cultural Shifts:

Industrialization also led to cultural changes as urban life became more prominent, and class distinctions sharpened between wealthy industrialists and the working class. In Northern Ireland, tensions between the Protestant and Catholic communities were further exacerbated by economic and social changes brought by industrialization, and John may have witnessed or heard about labor disputes and social unrest, especially in cities like Belfast.

As a rural Protestant, John would have been influenced by these tensions and the ways industrialization affected Protestant and Catholic communities differently. He may have grown more aware of the broader economic disparities and the political changes taking place in Ireland.

IN SUMMARY:

While John McLeese Sr. wouldn't have experienced the full effects of the Industrial Revolution until he was older, the technological, economic, and social changes it brought would have gradually filtered into his world in rural Carrowreagh, County Antrim. As a young boy, he might have reacted with curiosity or indifference to distant talk of machines and factories, but by the time he reached adulthood, he would have seen how industrialization altered the fabric of Irish life.

The availability of new tools and goods, the migration of people to cities, and the overall shift in economic opportunities likely affected John in ways both practical and cultural, shaping his view of the world as it transformed around him. He would have had to navigate these changes while still holding onto the values of hard work, family, and community that were central to rural life in County Antrim during this time.

At 34 years old, John McLeese Sr. would have likely responded to the news of the first successful hot air balloon flight in 1783 with a mixture of curiosity, awe, and possibly skepticism. Living in rural Carrowreagh, County Antrim, Northern Ireland, John would not have witnessed the event firsthand, but word of the achievement would have spread across Europe, eventually reaching even remote areas like his.

Likely Response to the Hot Air Balloon Flight:

1. Curiosity and Fascination:

The concept of human flight would have been groundbreaking and almost magical to John. While he lived in a world defined by horse-drawn carts, ships, and traditional farming methods, the idea of humans ascending into the sky in a balloon would have sounded like something out of legend. John may have been captivated by the very notion that humans could now mimic birds and leave the earth for the skies, a concept unimaginable for most people of his era. He would likely have followed any news or gossip about the hot air balloon with keen interest, wondering how such a feat was even possible.

2. Skepticism:

In rural Northern Ireland, such scientific advancements might have been met with some degree of skepticism. Given that much of John's world was still dominated by agriculture and traditional beliefs, some in his community might have questioned whether the reports were true or dismissed them as fanciful exaggerations. John himself could have been skeptical at first, particularly if the idea of human flight seemed unnatural or dangerous to him.

He may have also wondered how reliable or practical such a new invention could be. In his agricultural world, technological innovations were valued for their practicality—helping with farming, transportation, or trade—and the idea of flying in a balloon might have seemed too far removed from everyday life to be immediately relevant.

3. Religious and Cultural Reflection:

As a Protestant living in a deeply religious society, John may have also viewed the achievement through a spiritual or moral lens. Some people at the time may have felt that human flight was an unnatural challenge to the order of God's creation, as mankind was meant to stay on the ground. John might have pondered whether such an invention was in accordance with divine will or whether it represented dangerous human hubris.

Impact on John's Life and Perception of the World:

1. Expanding Horizons:

News of the hot air balloon's success would have expanded John's view of what was possible in the world. While he may not have directly experienced technological advances in his everyday rural life, the hot air balloon represented a new age of scientific exploration and innovation. It would have broadened his sense of the potential for human achievement, even if it seemed distant from his own daily experiences as a farmer.

This event would have been part of a growing awareness of how the world was changing, as other developments like the Industrial

Revolution and scientific discoveries were becoming more widespread. Although rural Northern Ireland remained largely untouched by industrialization at that time, John would have realized that new technologies were gradually transforming society, even if they weren't immediately affecting his life.

2. Influence on Travel and Communication:

While hot air ballooning was in its infancy, it symbolized the beginning of a new era of transportation and communication. John may have thought about the potential future impact of such innovations on travel, although the hot air balloon itself wouldn't have revolutionized transportation for many years. The idea that the world was becoming smaller through quicker, more efficient travel would have sparked John's imagination, even if it was something far removed from his rural life at that point.

3. Community Conversations:

In rural Carrowreagh, the news of the hot air balloon flight would have been a topic of conversation in the local community. Farmers, laborers, and townsfolk would likely have gathered to discuss this incredible feat. John, as a member of this tight-knit farming community, would have participated in these conversations, sharing stories or opinions on the balloon flight and hearing others' reactions.

He may have been struck by the different reactions in his community—some people might have been excited about the possibilities of human flight, while others were more conservative in their views, considering it an unnecessary or even dangerous development.

In Summary:

John McLeese Sr.'s response to the successful hot air balloon flight in 1783 at 34 years old would likely have been a mixture of awe, curiosity, and skepticism. Living in rural County Antrim, far removed from the centers of scientific and technological advancement, he would have seen the event as something extraordinary but disconnected from his daily reality. The concept of humans flying would have felt like a distant marvel, perhaps discussed with wonder among his neighbors but unlikely to affect his agricultural life in any tangible way.

The event, however, would have contributed to John's growing awareness that the world around him was rapidly changing. It would have reinforced the idea that new inventions and scientific advancements were reshaping human understanding of the world, even if the practical benefits of such changes had not yet reached his rural life in Northern Ireland.

At 49 years old, John McLeese Sr. would have experienced a complex range of reactions and impacts from the Irish Rebellion of 1798, an event that occurred during a period of significant social and political upheaval in Ireland.

Reaction to the Irish Rebellion:

1. Shock and Concern:

John, living in the rural village of Carrowreagh, would have likely been shocked by the news of the rebellion, which was a major uprising against British rule. Although Carrowreagh was a relatively remote area, the violence and unrest of the rebellion would have had ripple effects throughout Ireland, reaching even his community. The disruption of traditional life and the potential for violence would have caused concern and fear among the local population.

2. Sympathy or Opposition:

Given the nature of the rebellion, John's reaction would have been influenced by his personal views and circumstances. As a farmer in County Antrim, he might have had mixed feelings. On one hand, he might sympathize with the rebels' desire for greater autonomy and reform, especially if he experienced hardships or felt disenfranchised by British rule. On the other hand, he could have been wary of the rebellion's potential to lead to further instability and violence, which could disrupt his daily life and endanger his family.

3. Practical Concerns:

For someone of John's age and occupation, the immediate concern would have been the practical implications of the rebellion. His priority would be to ensure the safety of his family and the security of his property. The rebellion could lead to interruptions in trade, shortages of goods, and possible threats of violence or looting. As a farmer, he would be concerned about the impact of the unrest on his crops and livestock.

Impact on John's Life:

1. Increased Tensions:

The rebellion would have heightened tensions within his community. Carrowreagh, though small and rural, would not have been immune to the broader political currents affecting Ireland. John would have had to navigate the heightened sense of fear and uncertainty that came with the rebellion, which could strain community relations and disrupt daily life.

2. Economic Disruption:

The rebellion's impact on trade and commerce would have likely affected John's agricultural activities. Disruptions in transport and trade could have led to difficulties in selling his produce or acquiring necessary supplies. This would have compounded the challenges of maintaining his farm and supporting his family during a period of economic instability.

3. Political Awareness:

The events of the rebellion might have increased John's political awareness. Even if he remained largely focused on his farming life, the rebellion would have highlighted the broader struggles for political reform and autonomy in Ireland. John might have become more engaged in local discussions about political and social change, even if he did not actively participate in political movements.

4. Personal Reflection:

At 49, John would be at a reflective stage of his life, contemplating his role in the changing world around him. The rebellion would prompt him to think about the future of his family and community, and how the ongoing struggle for Irish autonomy might affect the generations to come. The uncertainty and upheaval could lead him to ponder the stability of his own life and the legacy he wishes to leave behind.

In Summary:

John McLeese Sr.'s reaction to the Irish Rebellion of 1798 at age 49 would have been shaped by a mix of shock, concern, and practical considerations. As a rural farmer in County Antrim, he would have been affected by the broader instability and economic disruptions caused by the rebellion. While he might have had sympathies towards the rebels' cause, the immediate impact on his daily life and the safety of his family would have been his primary concern. The rebellion would have made him more aware of the political and social changes happening in Ireland, influencing his perspectives on the future of his community and his role within it.

At 51 years old in 1800, John McLeese Sr. would have experienced the introduction of left and right specific shoes by William Young with a mix of curiosity and practical consideration. Here's how he might have reacted and been affected:

Reaction to the Invention:

1. Curiosity and Interest:

John, being a practical man with an interest in improvements that could affect his daily life, would likely have been intrigued by the idea of shoes designed specifically for left and right feet. This was a significant innovation, as footwear at the time was typically made with a more uniform shape, often leading to discomfort.

2. Practical Evaluation:

As a farmer who spent a lot of time on his feet, John would have been interested in how this new design could affect his comfort and functionality. The idea of shoes that better matched the natural shape of the feet might have been appealing to him, especially if it promised greater comfort and better support.

3. Skepticism or Acceptance:

While John might have been curious, he could also have been skeptical about the practicality and cost of adopting this new type of footwear. Rural areas like Carrowreagh were not always quick to adopt new technologies, especially if they came at a higher cost. John would need to weigh the benefits against his budget and the availability of these specialized shoes.

Impact on John's Life:

1. Improved Comfort:

If John chose to adopt this innovation, he would likely have experienced improved comfort while working. Shoes designed for the specific shape of each foot would reduce discomfort and potentially prevent foot-related issues, which could be especially beneficial given his active lifestyle.

2. Economic Considerations:

Depending on the cost and availability of these new shoes, John might have faced some economic impact. If the shoes were more expensive than standard ones, he would need to consider whether the investment was justified by the benefits. In rural areas, new inventions often took time to become widespread due to economic constraints.

3. Social Influence:

The introduction of such innovations could also affect social perceptions. If John adopted these new shoes and found them beneficial, he might share his experiences with others in his community, potentially influencing them to consider similar improvements. His endorsement of the shoes could serve as a form of social proof for others to follow.

4. Legacy of Innovation:

John's reaction to such innovations would reflect his broader attitude toward progress and change. His acceptance of improved footwear would demonstrate an openness to advancements that enhance quality of life, which would be consistent with a practical and resilient character. This mindset might also influence how he approached other innovations or changes in his later years.

In Summary:

John McLeese Sr.'s response to the introduction of left and right specific shoes in 1800 would likely be a combination of curiosity and practical assessment. As a man who valued comfort and practicality, he would appreciate the potential benefits of improved footwear but would need to consider the economic implications. The impact on his daily life would include improved comfort and possibly a greater willingness to adopt new technologies if they proved beneficial. His response to this innovation would reflect his practical nature and openness to progress.

When John McLeese Sr. died in Derrykeighan, County Antrim, on September 5, 1814, life in the area would have been shaped by several historical, social, and economic factors. Here's an overview of what life would have been like for John at that time:

Economic and Social Context:

1. Agricultural Economy:

By 1814, the local economy in County Antrim was predominantly agricultural. Farming would have been the primary occupation, with many people engaged in subsistence farming. John McLeese Sr., having spent his life in Carrowreagh and Derrykeighan, would have been accustomed to working the land, growing crops, and raising livestock. The agricultural methods were still relatively traditional, with many farmers using manual labor and basic tools.

2. Impact of the Napoleonic Wars:

The early 19th century was a time of significant political and economic upheaval due to the Napoleonic Wars (1803–1815). The conflict affected trade and led to economic challenges, including food shortages and inflation. Rural communities like Derrykeighan would have felt the effects of these disturbances, with fluctuating prices for goods and increased hardship for farmers.

3. Technological and Social Change:

The Industrial Revolution, which began in Britain in the late 18th century, was beginning to have an impact on Ireland. Although County Antrim was not as industrialized as other parts of Britain, changes were starting to trickle into rural areas. This included innovations in agriculture, such as improved plowing methods and the introduction of new tools and machinery, which could have influenced John's farming practices.

4. Community Life:

Derrykeighan would have been a small, close-knit community. Social life would have revolved around local events, church services, and communal activities. As a respected member of the community, John would have been involved in local affairs and known for his contributions to the village life.

Physical Environment:

1. Rural Landscape:

The landscape of County Antrim in 1814 would have been characterized by rolling hills, farmland, and small villages. Derrykeighan, being a rural area, would have had a picturesque but modest setting, with stone cottages, farmhouses, and fields. The natural beauty of the area, with its lush green fields and rugged terrain, would have been a constant feature of John's daily life.

2. Living Conditions:

Living conditions in rural Ireland during this period were modest by modern standards. Homes were typically simple, with thatched or slate roofs, and were furnished with basic necessities. Heating was provided by a central hearth or stove, and cooking was done over an open fire. Despite the simplicity, homes were often well-kept and reflective of the local customs and traditions.

Personal Impact:

1. Health and Well-being:

By 1814, John would have been experiencing the physical effects of aging. Rural life, characterized by hard manual labor and exposure to the elements, would have taken a toll on his health. Despite this, John's resilience and long years of work would likely have earned him respect and a degree of comfort in his final years.

2. Legacy:

As he neared the end of his life, John would have been reflecting on his contributions to his family and community. His legacy would have been marked by his work ethic, his role in local affairs, and his influence on the next generation. His death in Derrykeighan would have been a significant event for his family and the local community, marking the end of an era in their lives.

In Summary:

Life for John McLeese Sr. in Derrykeighan, County Antrim, in 1814 was shaped by the agricultural economy, the impacts of the Napoleonic Wars, and the gradual influence of industrial changes. His days would have been filled with the routine of farm work and the rhythms of rural life. Despite the challenges, his role in the community and the natural beauty of his surroundings would have provided a sense of fulfillment and connection to his land and people. His death marked the end of a significant chapter in both his family's and community's history.

Here's a suggested genealogy travel itinerary to honor the life of John McLeese Sr. This itinerary will take you through significant locations related to his life and legacy, providing a meaningful and memorable experience.

Day 1: Arrival in Belfast, Northern Ireland
- Morning: Arrive in Belfast International Airport.
- Afternoon: Check into your hotel and rest after your journey.
- Evening: Enjoy a welcome dinner at a local restaurant and explore Belfast's vibrant city center.

Day 2: Belfast to Dervock
- Morning: Drive from Belfast to Dervock (approximately 1.5 hours).
- Afternoon: Visit the Derrykeighan Graveyard on Castlecat Road, Dervock. Spend time at the memorial of John McLeese Sr. and reflect on his life and legacy

https://www.findagrave.com/cemetery/2580387/derrykeighan-old-church-graveyard

https://billiongraves.com/grave/John-McLeese-Sr/41160966

- EVENING: EXPLORE the village of Dervock and have dinner at a local pub.

Day 3: Exploring Dervock and Surroundings
- Morning: Visit the Ballymoney Museum to learn more about the local history and the families buried in Derrykeighan Graveyard https://www.causewaycoastandglens.gov.uk/see-do/arts_museums/museums-services/ballymoney-museum/ballymoney-heritage/old-graveyards/derrykeighan-graveyard

https://billiongraves.com/cemetery/Derrykeighan-Old-Cemetery/306746

- EVENING: RETURN TO your accommodation and enjoy a relaxing evening.

Day 4: Ancestral Research and Local Exploration

- Morning: Visit the Causeway Coast and Glens Borough Council to access local archives and records for further genealogical research https://www.causewaycoastandglens.gov.uk/see-do/arts_museums/museums-services/ballymoney-museum/ballymoney-heritage/old-graveyards/derrykeighan-graveyard

- AFTERNOON: EXPLORE the beautiful Causeway Coast, including the Giant's Causeway and Dunluce Castle.
- Evening: Dinner at a coastal restaurant with views of the Atlantic Ocean.

Day 5: Cultural Immersion in Belfast

- Morning: Return to Belfast.
- Afternoon: Visit the Ulster Museum and the Botanic Gardens.
- Evening: Enjoy a traditional Irish music session at a local pub.

Day 6: Departure

- Morning: Check out of your hotel and head to Belfast International Airport for your departure.

This itinerary combines genealogical research with cultural and historical exploration, providing a comprehensive and enriching experience.

JOHN (McALEESE) McLEESE II[2]

Character Profile: John McLeese II (c. 1780 – January 29, 1869)

Full Name: John McLeese II (also known as John McAleese Jr.)

Birth: Around 1780, Carrowreagh, County Antrim, Ireland

Death: January 29, 1869, Bonnycastle, County Antrim, Ireland

Burial: Likely in a local cemetery in Bonnycastle, County Antrim

Family:

- Spouse: Mollie McLaughlin
- Children:
- Daniel McLeese (b. 1810)
- Margaret Bridget McLeese (later McLaughlin) (b. 1823)

Physical Description:

Appearance:

- Height and Build: John McLeese II would have likely been of average height for the period, around 5'7" to 5'10". His build would have been robust, reflecting the hard labor and active lifestyle of rural 19th-century Ireland.

- Face and Features: As a man in his late 50s and early 60s by the time of his death, he would have had a weathered face with signs of aging, including wrinkles and possibly some gray in his hair. His complexion would have been tanned and rugged from years of working outdoors.

- Hair and Eyes: His hair, which may have started as brown, would have grayed with age. His eyes, likely a shade of blue or gray, would reflect a life of hard work and experience.

- Attire: John would have worn practical and sturdy clothing suitable for rural work, including woolen shirts, vests, and trousers, often topped with a coat or jacket. His clothing would have been functional, reflecting the modest, agrarian lifestyle of the time.

Attributes and Character:

Work Ethic and Skills:

- Agricultural Expertise: Following in the footsteps of his father, John McLeese II would have been well-versed in farming and land management. His skills would have been essential for maintaining the family farm and adapting to the changing agricultural practices of the early 19th century.

- Resilient and Hardworking: His resilience would be a hallmark of his character, shaped by a life of labor and the economic pressures of the time. His ability to manage the farm and provide for his family demonstrates his hardworking nature.

Family and Community Life:

- Devoted Family Man: John's marriage to Mollie McLaughlin and his role as a father to Daniel and Margaret Bridget highlight his commitment to his family. His efforts would have been focused on ensuring the well-being and success of his children.

- Community Involvement: Living in a small rural community, John would have been an integral part of local life, participating in communal activities and contributing to the social fabric of Bonnycastle and the surrounding area.

Impact of Historical Context:

- Economic and Social Changes: By the time of John McLeese II's adulthood, Ireland was experiencing significant changes due to the Industrial Revolution. Although rural areas like County Antrim were less affected by industrialization, John would have seen advancements in agriculture and local industries that influenced his farming practices and community life.

- Political Climate: During John's lifetime, Ireland was also experiencing political shifts, including the aftermath of the Irish Rebellion of 1798 and the Act of Union in 1801. These events would have impacted his life and community, affecting everything from economic conditions to political sentiment.

Legacy:

- Family Continuity: John's legacy would be reflected in his children, especially in the way he raised them and prepared them for their future. His son Daniel and daughter Margaret Bridget would carry forward the values and skills imparted by John.

- Local Influence: As a respected member of his community, John McLeese II's contributions to local life and his role as a father and farmer would have cemented his place in the history of Bonnycastle and County Antrim.

Summary:

John McLeese II was a resilient and hardworking individual shaped by the agrarian life of early 19th-century County Antrim. His physical appearance and character would reflect a life of labor and dedication to his family and community. Despite the broader changes occurring in Ireland during his lifetime, John's steadfast nature and commitment to his family ensured his lasting impact on his descendants and local community.

Life in Carrowreagh, County Antrim, Ireland (circa 1780)

Geography and Settlement:

- Location: Carrowreagh is a small rural settlement in County Antrim, Northern Ireland. The landscape is characterized by rolling hills, farmland, and scattered woodlands, typical of the region's pastoral scenery.

- Agriculture: The primary economic activity in Carrowreagh would have been agriculture. The fertile soil was ideal for growing crops such as oats, barley, and potatoes, while livestock farming was also common. Farmers like John McLeese Sr. and Jr. would have worked the land, managing crops and animals.

Community and Social Life:

- Population: Carrowreagh would have been a small, tight-knit community with a limited population. Social interactions were often centered around local gatherings, including church services, fairs, and market days.

- Religion: The predominant religion in the area was likely Protestant, with the majority of the local population adhering to the Church of Ireland (Anglican) or Presbyterian denominations. Religious services and church activities played a central role in community life.

- Housing: Homes in Carrowreagh during this period were typically simple, stone-built cottages with thatched or slate roofs. They were modest but functional, providing basic shelter for families engaged in agricultural work.

Economy and Work:

- Farming: Farming was the backbone of the local economy. Families worked small plots of land, growing staple crops and raising animals for food and trade. Agricultural techniques were traditional, relying on manual labor and basic tools.

- Local Trades: In addition to farming, there may have been a few local tradespeople, such as blacksmiths, weavers, and carpenters, providing essential services to the community.

Daily Life and Challenges:

- Living Conditions: Life in Carrowreagh would have been characterized by hard work and subsistence living. Families worked long hours to maintain their farms and support themselves. Living conditions were modest, with little access to modern conveniences.

- Education: Formal education was limited, especially in rural areas. Children often received basic instruction at local schools or from private tutors. Education was generally geared towards practical skills and religious instruction.

- Health and Medicine: Medical care was rudimentary, with reliance on traditional remedies and herbal treatments. Access to professional medical care was limited, and health issues could significantly impact daily life.

Historical Context:

- Political Climate: In 1780, Ireland was under British rule, and the political landscape was marked by tensions between the Irish and the British government. The period saw increasing calls for legislative reform and greater autonomy for Ireland.

- Economic Pressures: The late 18th century was a time of economic hardship for many rural communities. Agricultural work was challenging, and economic pressures from rising rents and taxes could strain local families.

Summary:

In 1780, Carrowreagh, County Antrim, was a small, rural community where agriculture was the primary livelihood. Life was marked by hard work, modest living conditions, and strong community ties. Daily life revolved around farming, local trades, and religious practices, with limited access to formal education and medical care. The broader political and economic context of Ireland during this period would have influenced local life, adding to the challenges faced by families like the McLeeses.

At the age of 3, John McLeese Jr. would have been too young to comprehend the significance of the hot air balloon's first successful flight in 1783. However, here's a look at how this event might have influenced him indirectly, as he grew up:

Early Reaction and Immediate Impact

- Limited Direct Awareness: As a toddler, John would not have been aware of or understood the implications of the hot air balloon flight. Such innovations were more likely to be discussed by adults and were not immediately relevant to rural life in Carrowreagh.

Long-term Impact and Cultural Context

- Curiosity and Innovation: As John grew older, the concept of flight might have sparked curiosity and wonder. The flight of the hot air balloon was one of the early achievements in aviation and symbolized the spirit of innovation and exploration. Such advancements could have inspired him or those around him, fueling an interest in new technologies or ideas.

- Gradual Technological Influence: Although the immediate impact in rural areas would have been minimal, the broader technological progress over time could have influenced local attitudes towards innovation. By the time John was an adult, he might have been aware of the advances in science and technology, including improvements in transportation and communication, which could have affected his views on progress.

Broader Historical Context

- Scientific Curiosity: Growing up during a period of significant scientific and technological advancements, including the Industrial Revolution, John might have been influenced by the general atmosphere of innovation and progress. The success of the hot air balloon was part of a larger trend of scientific exploration that characterized the late 18th and early 19th centuries.

- Local Impact: While the hot air balloon itself didn't directly impact daily life in Carrowreagh, the era's technological advancements gradually affected rural communities. Improved transportation and communication methods, influenced by the spirit of innovation, could have reached Carrowreagh over time, affecting John's life in indirect ways.

In Summary

While John McLeese Jr. would not have directly reacted to or been influenced by the hot air balloon flight at the age of 3, the broader context of technological and scientific advancements during his lifetime would have contributed to a general atmosphere of curiosity and progress. As he grew up, these advancements would have shaped the world around him, influencing his environment and potentially inspiring a sense of wonder and appreciation for innovation.

At 17 years old during the Irish Rebellion of 1798, John McLeese Jr. would have been at an age where he was becoming more aware of and involved in the political and social upheavals of his time. Here's how the rebellion might have affected him:

Immediate Reaction

- Personal Impact: Living in Carrowreagh, a rural area in County Antrim, John would have likely experienced the rebellion's effects through the broader context of local disturbances and the atmosphere of unrest. The rebellion, primarily centered in more populous areas, would have caused anxiety and uncertainty even in rural communities.

- Family and Community: If local communities were involved in the rebellion or faced repercussions from it, John might have witnessed changes in his family's daily life and the stability of his community. He could have seen disruptions in trade, changes in local governance, or tensions between different groups in the area.

Emotional and Social Effects

- Sense of Unrest: The rebellion aimed to end British rule in Ireland and establish an independent Irish Republic. The ideals and actions of the rebels, who were seeking greater political and social freedoms, might have inspired John or elicited strong opinions about the political situation in Ireland.

- Impact on Views: The rebellion's suppression and subsequent actions by the British government, such as increased military presence and punitive measures, might have influenced John's views on politics, governance, and rebellion. He could have developed a sense of sympathy for the rebels or a stronger alignment with loyalist perspectives, depending on his family's and community's stance.

Long-Term Effects

- Cultural and Political Climate: The aftermath of the rebellion brought about significant changes, including the Act of Union in 1801, which merged Ireland with Great Britain to form the United Kingdom. These political changes would have influenced John's life as he entered adulthood. The socio-political landscape of Ireland shifted, and the effects of the rebellion would have been felt in various ways, including economic changes, shifts in local governance, and evolving social dynamics.

- Historical Reflection: John's experiences and reflections on the rebellion might have shaped his understanding of Irish history and his position within it. As he grew older, he could have viewed the rebellion as a pivotal moment in Ireland's struggle for self-determination, influencing his perspective on Irish identity and politics.

In Summary

At 17, John McLeese Jr. would have been affected by the Irish Rebellion of 1798 through a combination of personal, familial, and community impacts. While he might not have been directly involved, the rebellion's repercussions would have influenced his perceptions of political and social issues, shaping his views as he matured into adulthood.

In 1809, John McLeese Jr., at 28, and Jane, at 21, would have experienced a wedding reflecting early 19th-century Irish customs. Here's a look at what their wedding might have been like and what they might have worn:

Wedding Ceremony and Celebration

- Venue: Their wedding would likely take place in a local church, given the prominence of religious ceremonies in rural

Ireland at the time. A small, modest parish church in Carrowreagh or a nearby town would have been a typical setting. The ceremony would be straightforward and focused on the religious aspects, with a local clergyman officiating.

- Guests: The guest list would include close family, friends, and possibly neighbors. Given the small size of rural communities, the gathering would be intimate, with a focus on the immediate social circle.

- Reception: After the ceremony, a simple reception or gathering would follow. This could take place at the bride's or groom's family home, or in a local hall or community space. Food and drink would be homemade, including traditional fare like bread, cheese, meats, and seasonal vegetables, often accompanied by ale or homemade spirits.

- Traditions: Customs such as a wedding breakfast (a light meal following the ceremony) would be customary. Dancing, singing, and storytelling could be part of the celebration, with local folk traditions and music contributing to the festive atmosphere.

Attire

- Bride: Jane's wedding attire would reflect the styles of the early 19th century. She might wear a gown made of simple fabrics such as muslin or cotton, often in white or a soft pastel color. The dress would have a high waistline, empire style, with short puffed sleeves and a low neckline. Accessories might include a simple bonnet or a ribbon, and a modest veil or headdress. The gown would be relatively plain, reflecting the more understated and practical fashion of the time, especially in rural settings.

- Groom: John would wear a dark wool suit, consisting of a tailcoat, waistcoat, and trousers. His clothing would be tailored but not overly elaborate, reflecting his status as a rural tradesman or farmer. A white or light-colored cravat or neckerchief would complete the ensemble, and he might wear a simple hat such as a top hat or a beaver hat.

Cultural and Social Context

- Economic and Social Status: Given John's likely occupation and the rural setting, their wedding would be modest, reflecting the economic realities of the time. It would be a practical affair, focused on the union of two families and their community connections.

- Marriage Customs: Marriages were often arranged or influenced by familial and community considerations. The ceremony and celebrations would emphasize family, local customs, and community bonds rather than extravagant displays.

Overall, John and Jane's wedding in 1809 would have been a simple yet meaningful occasion, marked by traditional ceremonies and practical attire. The focus would be on the solemnity of the union and the celebration of their new life together within their close-knit community.

When John McLeese Jr. was 30 years old and living in Ballymoney, County Antrim, in 1810, his life would have been shaped by the social, economic, and political context of early 19th-century Ireland. Here's a look at what his life might have been like at that time and how the birth of his son, Daniel, would have affected him:

John's Life in 1810

- Occupation: By 1810, John might have been engaged in agriculture or a local trade. Ballymoney was a market town, and his work could have involved farming, local trades, or possibly small-scale industry. Economic activities would have been influenced by the ongoing effects of the Napoleonic Wars, which caused economic strain and inflation.

- Living Conditions: John's living conditions would reflect the rural setting of Ballymoney. His home would likely be a modest, single-story structure with thatched or slate roofing, simple furnishings, and basic amenities. Life would be centered around hard work, community ties, and family.

- Community and Social Life: Ballymoney, being a market town, would have had a close-knit community with a mix of rural and small-town influences. Social activities would include local fairs, market days, and gatherings at the parish church. Community life would be important, with strong connections to neighbors and local traditions.

Impact of Daniel's Birth

- Emotional and Personal Impact: The birth of Daniel in 1810 would have been a significant event in John's life. As a father, John would experience a profound sense of joy and responsibility. The arrival of a son would bring hope for the future and the continuation of the family line. John's role as a father would deepen his sense of purpose and commitment to providing for his family.

- Family Dynamics: The addition of a child would influence family dynamics, with John and his wife, Jane, adjusting to the demands of parenthood. Their home life would become more focused on the care and upbringing of Daniel. This would also impact John's daily routines, work schedule, and responsibilities.

- Social and Economic Effects: The birth of a son could have implications for John's social standing and economic planning. In early 19th-century rural Ireland, having a male heir was often seen as essential for continuing the family lineage and contributing to the labor force. John would likely view Daniel's birth as both a personal blessing and a practical asset for future work and support.

- Community Reactions: In the close-knit community of Ballymoney, the birth of a child would be celebrated with family and friends. Neighbors might offer congratulations and support, and local customs surrounding childbirth and infant care would be observed. John's status as a father would be recognized and respected within the community.

Overall, the birth of Daniel in 1810 would have brought significant emotional joy and practical considerations to John's life. It would mark a new chapter in his family life, affecting his daily routines, social interactions, and future aspirations.

At 34 years old in 1815, John McLeese Jr. would have likely had a range of reactions to the defeat and exile of Napoleon Bonaparte, reflecting the broader geopolitical context and its impact on his personal and community life in County Antrim, Ireland.

Reaction to Napoleon's Defeat

1. Relief and Optimism: The defeat of Napoleon would have been seen as a relief by many in Britain and Ireland, as it marked the end of years of conflict and instability brought about by the Napoleonic Wars. John might have felt a sense of optimism and hope for a period of peace and stability following years of uncertainty.

2. Interest in European Affairs: While John was living in a rural area, he would have been aware of the major political and military events of the time through local news and discussion. The defeat of a figure as prominent as Napoleon would have been a topic of conversation, and John might have engaged in discussions about the implications for Europe and Britain.

Effects on John's Life

1. Economic Impact: The end of the Napoleonic Wars had significant economic repercussions. For many, it meant the end of wartime economic measures and potentially a return to peacetime economic activities. John might have experienced changes in local trade, agriculture, or market conditions as the economy adjusted to peacetime stability.

2. Social and Political Climate: Napoleon's defeat contributed to the reshaping of European political boundaries and alliances. In

Ireland, this period also saw the continuation of political unrest and demands for reform. John's reaction might have included a heightened awareness of political developments and their impact on Ireland's relationship with Britain.

3. Personal Reflection: On a personal level, John might have reflected on the broader changes occurring in Europe and their implications for his own life and family. The end of a major conflict could have prompted him to think about the future and the potential for improvements in his own circumstances and those of his community.

4. Community Impact: The local community in Carrowreagh would have been affected by the broader political and economic changes. John might have witnessed changes in local attitudes, celebrations or gatherings related to the news, and shifts in local leadership or governance.

Overall, John McLeese Jr.'s reaction to Napoleon's defeat and exile would have been shaped by his understanding of the broader political context and its implications for his community and personal life. The end of the Napoleonic Wars marked a significant shift in European and British history, influencing economic conditions, political dynamics, and societal attitudes, all of which would have impacted John in various ways.

John McLeese Jr., at 34 years old, would have experienced profound emotional and practical impacts following the death of his father, John McLeese Sr., on September 5, 1814. Here's how the death of his father might have affected him:

Emotional Impact

- Grief and Loss: The death of his father would have been deeply affecting for John Jr. Losing a parent is a significant emotional blow, and John Jr. would likely have gone through a period of mourning and sadness. His father's death would evoke memories of their shared experiences and highlight the finality of his father's presence in his life.

- Reflection on Legacy: John Jr. might have reflected on his father's legacy and the life they had shared. This could include contemplating the values, teachings, and family traditions his father had imparted. It would also be a time to think about how to honor and continue his father's legacy in his own life and the lives of his children.

Practical Impact

- Family Responsibilities: As the eldest son, John Jr. would have likely felt an increased sense of responsibility towards his family, especially if his father had been a key provider or decision-maker. This might involve taking on more responsibilities within the family home or farm, ensuring that the family's needs were met in the wake of his father's passing.

- Financial Considerations: Depending on the estate and financial situation left by his father, John Jr. might have had to manage or settle financial matters, such as debts, property inheritance, or the division of assets among family members. This could have included managing the family farm or other business interests.

- Community and Social Role: In a small community like Derrykeighan, the death of a prominent local figure like John Sr. would be felt widely. John Jr. might have been involved in organizing or participating in the funeral arrangements and would likely have received support and condolences from the local community. His role in the community might have been affected as he adjusted to his new responsibilities.

Impact on Personal Life

- Family Dynamics: John Jr.'s relationship with his own family, including his wife Jane and their children, could have been influenced by the loss. He would need to balance his grief with his duties as a father and husband, which might also affect his emotional well-being and family dynamics.

- Future Outlook: The loss of his father might prompt John Jr. to reassess his own life goals and plans. He might feel a heightened sense of urgency to secure his family's future and establish a stable legacy for his children.

Overall, the death of his father would have had a significant impact on John McLeese Jr. emotionally and practically. It would be a period of adjustment and reflection, with a shift in responsibilities and a deeper contemplation of his role within the family and community.

At 40 years old, in 1821, John McLeese Jr. would likely have had a range of emotions and reactions to the birth of his daughter, Jane. Here's how the birth might have affected him:

Reaction to the Birth of His Daughter

1. Joy and Pride: As a father of young children, John would have likely experienced a deep sense of joy and pride with the birth of his daughter. Having a new child, particularly a daughter, would have been a significant and happy event for him and his family.

2. Reflection on Family Legacy: At 40, John would have been reflecting on his role as a father and the legacy he was building for his children. The birth of Jane would have reinforced his commitment to providing for and raising his family, continuing the legacy of his own father and shaping the future of his children.

3. Increased Responsibility: With the arrival of a new child, John would have felt an increased sense of responsibility. Supporting a growing family required more resources and attention, which would have added to his existing responsibilities as a husband and father.

Effects on John's Life

1. Strengthened Family Bonds: The birth of Jane would have likely strengthened family bonds, bringing John and his wife Jane

(his spouse) closer together in their shared responsibilities and joys of parenting.

2. Adjustment to Daily Life: John's daily life would have adjusted to accommodate the needs of a newborn. This might have included changes in his routine and additional responsibilities around the home and farm.

3. Emotional Impact: The arrival of a daughter could have deepened John's emotional connection to his family, fostering a sense of fulfillment and nurturing his paternal instincts. It would have brought renewed purpose and joy to his life, enhancing his overall well-being.

4. Community and Social Standing: In the context of early 19th-century rural Ireland, the birth of a daughter would be a welcomed addition to the family. John's standing in the community might have been positively affected by the growing family, and the birth could have been a point of social engagement with neighbors and extended family.

In summary, John McLeese Jr.'s reaction to the birth of his daughter Jane would have been marked by joy, pride, and an increased sense of responsibility. The birth would have reinforced his role as a father, impacting his family dynamics and personal sense of fulfillment.

When John McLeese Jr. was 43 years old and his daughter Margaret Bridget was born in County Antrim in 1823, his reaction and the impact on his life would likely have been as follows:

Reaction to the Birth of Margaret Bridget

1. Joy and Contentment: John would have experienced significant joy and contentment with the birth of his daughter. As a father, welcoming a new child into the family would have been a source of happiness and pride. Having a daughter would also have been seen as a blessing, enriching his family life.

2. Sense of Fulfillment: At 43, John might have felt a sense of fulfillment in seeing his family grow. The arrival of Margaret Bridget would add to his sense of accomplishment and continuity, reinforcing his role as a provider and protector.

3. Emotional Bonding: John would likely have formed a strong emotional bond with Margaret Bridget. His paternal instincts would drive him to nurture and care for her, and the joy of a new child would bring warmth and affection into his life.

Effects on John's Life

1. Increased Responsibility: The birth of Margaret Bridget would have introduced additional responsibilities for John. As a father of multiple children, he would have had to balance his work, family duties, and the care of his growing household. This would have added to his workload but also strengthened his commitment to his family's well-being.

2. Changes in Family Dynamics: The arrival of a new child would affect the dynamics within the family. John and his wife Jane would need to adapt to the needs of their new daughter while continuing to care for their other children. The family's routines and interactions would shift to accommodate Margaret Bridget.

3. Social and Community Impact: In early 19th-century County Antrim, the birth of a daughter would be celebrated within the local community. John's standing in the community might have been positively impacted, and the event could have been a point of social interaction with neighbors and extended family.

4. Personal Reflection: At 43, John might have reflected on his life and the legacy he was creating for his children. The birth of Margaret Bridget would have reinforced his focus on providing a stable and nurturing environment for his family, shaping his aspirations for their future.

Overall, John McLeese Jr.'s reaction to the birth of Margaret Bridget would have been characterized by joy and a deep sense of fulfillment. The arrival of his daughter would have strengthened family bonds, introduced new responsibilities, and impacted his role within his family and community.

When John McLeese Jr. was 45 years old and his final child, John McLeese III, was born in 1825, his reaction and the impact on his life would likely have been as follows:

Reaction to the Birth of John McLeese III

1. Joy and Excitement: John would have felt considerable joy and excitement at the birth of his last child. Even at 45, the arrival of a new child would bring renewed energy and happiness to his life. The birth of a son would have been particularly significant, as it would ensure the continuation of the family name and lineage.

2. Pride: As a father, John would likely have felt proud to welcome another son into the family. This would reinforce his role as a patriarch and provide him with a sense of accomplishment in raising his children.

3. Strengthened Family Bonds: The birth of John McLeese III would likely have strengthened family bonds, bringing the family closer together. John and his wife Jane would have shared in the joy of their new child's arrival and would have worked together to integrate him into the family dynamic.

Effects on John's Life

1. Increased Responsibility: At 45, John would have experienced increased responsibility with the birth of his final child. Balancing his existing duties and responsibilities while caring for a newborn would have added to his workload. This might have required adjustments in his daily routine and work schedule.

2. Reflective Outlook: John might have become more reflective about his life and legacy. The arrival of a final child could prompt thoughts about his role as a father, his aspirations for his children, and the legacy he hoped to leave behind.

3. Family Dynamics: The dynamics within the McLeese household would have shifted with the introduction of a new baby. John would need to manage the needs of his growing family, including his older children, while attending to the needs of John III.

4. Community Perspective: In early 19th-century County Antrim, the birth of a new child would be a noteworthy event in the community. The arrival of John McLeese III might have been celebrated locally, enhancing John's standing within his social circle.

5. Long-Term Impact: As John approached his late 40s, having a newborn could affect his long-term planning. He would need to consider the future needs of his family, including provisions for his children's education and well-being as he aged.

Overall, John McLeese Jr.'s reaction to the birth of his final child would have been one of joy, pride, and renewed purpose. The impact on his life would include increased responsibilities, a deeper reflection on his legacy, and adjustments in family dynamics.

At 48 years old, John McLeese Jr. faced immense personal loss in 1828 with the deaths of his wife Jane, his son John McLeese III, and the subsequent burial of his family members alongside his father in the Dervock cemetery. His reaction and the effects on him would have been profound:

Reaction

1. Deep Grief and Mourning: John would have been overwhelmed by intense grief and mourning. Losing his wife and a young child within the same year would have been devastating. The emotional toll of such a loss would have been significant, affecting his mental and emotional well-being deeply.

2. Sense of Loss and Loneliness: The combined loss of Jane and his son would likely have left John feeling profoundly lonely. As he

was approaching the later years of his life, the deaths of his closest family members would have accentuated his sense of isolation.

3. Burden of Responsibilities: With the passing of his wife and son, John would have been faced with the immediate and practical challenges of arranging their burials, which would have added to his emotional strain. Erecting a monument to his father while dealing with these losses would have been a significant emotional burden.

4. Reflective and Contemplative: John might have become more reflective about his own mortality and the meaning of life. The loss of loved ones often prompts a person to contemplate their own life's purpose and legacy.

Effects on John

1. Emotional and Psychological Impact: The deaths of his wife and young child would have likely led to a period of profound sadness and potentially depression. John might have found it difficult to cope with daily activities and responsibilities due to the overwhelming grief.

2. Changes in Family Dynamics: The loss of his immediate family members would have altered the dynamics within his household and community. John would have needed to adjust to the absence of Jane's support and the companionship of his young son.

3. Physical and Health Impact: The stress and grief from such losses could have impacted John's physical health. Emotional stress often manifests in physical ailments, which might have affected John's well-being and possibly his ability to manage his affairs effectively.

4. Legacy and Memorialization: Erecting a monument to his father and burying his wife and son with his father would have been an attempt to honor and preserve the memory of his loved ones. This act would have been a significant emotional gesture,

reflecting his deep sense of loss and his desire to commemorate his family's legacy.

5. Community Impact: John's loss would likely have been felt within his local community, where such events would be significant. He might have received sympathy and support from neighbors and friends, though the emotional and personal impact would remain deeply personal.

Overall, John McLeese Jr.'s reaction to the deaths of his wife and son would have been marked by profound grief, loneliness, and a deep sense of loss. The impact on his life would involve emotional distress, changes in daily routines, and a reflective consideration of his legacy and future.

At 59 years old in 1839, when photography became publicly available, John McLeese Jr. would likely have had a range of reactions and experiences regarding this new technology:

Reaction

1. Curiosity and Fascination: John, being a man of his time, would have likely been intrigued by the invention of photography. The ability to capture and preserve images of people and places would have seemed like a remarkable and innovative development.

2. Skepticism or Reservation: Depending on his personality and openness to new technology, John might also have been somewhat skeptical about the practical applications and reliability of photography. He may have viewed it as an intriguing novelty rather than a transformative tool.

3. Interest in Preservation: Given that John experienced significant personal loss, the advent of photography might have appealed to him as a means of preserving the likenesses of family members and important moments. This could have offered him a new way to keep memories of his loved ones alive.

Effects

1. Emotional Impact: The ability to have a visual representation of family members and significant events might have provided John with a sense of comfort and connection. It could have been especially meaningful for him as he had recently lost several family members. The prospect of having their likeness captured and preserved could have been emotionally significant.

2. Social and Cultural Impact: Photography's public availability would have slowly begun to change how people recorded and remembered their lives. John, as a member of a rural community, might have been exposed to this change gradually. He could have been among the early adopters in his area or remained indifferent depending on his circumstances.

3. Legacy and Memory Preservation: The introduction of photography could have influenced how John thought about legacy and memory. If he or his surviving family members chose to have their portraits taken, it would have added a new dimension to how they preserved their personal and familial history.

4. Adaptation to New Technology: John might have witnessed or heard about the practicalities and limitations of early photography, such as the long exposure times and the cumbersome equipment. His reaction to these aspects would have depended on his interest in embracing or resisting new technologies.

Overall, John's reaction to the advent of photography would likely have been a mix of curiosity, potential skepticism, and emotional appreciation. The technology could have offered him a new way to preserve memories and connect with his past, potentially impacting how he viewed and engaged with the changing world around him.

At the age of 65, John McLeese Jr. would have faced significant changes due to the onset of the Great Famine (1845-1852) and the resulting mass Irish immigration. Here's how he might have reacted and been affected:

Immediate Reactions

1. Economic Hardship:

- Personal Impact: John would likely have been deeply concerned about the immediate effects of the famine on his own livelihood. With agriculture being the primary source of income and sustenance, the failure of the potato crop would have led to severe food shortages. This would directly affect his ability to feed himself and his family.

- Community Impact: As a member of a rural community, John would have witnessed the widespread suffering of his neighbors. The famine's impact on local agriculture would have led to increased poverty, illness, and potentially higher death rates in his community.

2. Emotional Response:

- Despair and Anxiety: The famine would have caused significant distress. John would likely have felt a deep sense of despair and anxiety about the future, both for himself and for the community. The loss of the potato crop would have been a traumatic event, given its central role in his diet and economy.

Effects on Daily Life

1. Farming and Food:

- Crop Failure: The potato blight would have led to failed crops, affecting his ability to grow food and generate income. John might have had to rely on other, less reliable food sources and possibly faced hunger or malnutrition.

- Economic Strain: The economic strain from failed crops would have made it difficult for him to sustain his household and maintain any land he owned. He might have been forced to seek alternative means of subsistence or assistance.

2. Community and Social Effects:

- Increased Emigration: The famine led to a wave of emigration as many Irish people sought better opportunities abroad. John might have seen friends, relatives, or neighbors leave for countries like the United States, Canada, or Australia. This would have brought a sense of loss and potentially left a void in the local community.

- Social Strains: The economic and social strains of the famine might have led to increased community tensions. John could have been involved in local efforts to support those in need, but the overall atmosphere would likely have been one of hardship and desperation.

Long-term Impact

1. Health and Well-being:

- Physical Health: At 65, John would have been more vulnerable to the effects of malnutrition and illness resulting from the famine. His ability to work and maintain his health would have been compromised.

- Emotional Toll: The emotional toll of witnessing widespread suffering and the loss of many community members would have been significant. The long-term impact on his mental health could include increased anxiety, depression, or a sense of helplessness.

2. Legacy and Memory:

- Family Legacy: The famine's impact on his family's livelihood would have been a defining moment in their history. John's experiences during this time might have influenced how he talked about or remembered these events, shaping the legacy he left to his children and future generations.

- Community Memory: As a local figure, John would have contributed to the collective memory of the famine within his community. His experiences and actions during this time would be remembered as part of the broader narrative of the Great Famine's impact on rural Ireland.

Summary

At 65 years old, John McLeese Jr. would have been deeply affected by the Great Famine and the mass emigration it prompted. The immediate economic hardship, emotional distress, and long-term impacts on his health and community life would have been profound. The famine would have reshaped his daily existence, leaving him to navigate the challenges of a dramatically changing environment.

At the age of 89, John McLeese Jr.'s life in Carrowreagh, County Antrim in 1869 would have been shaped by several factors, reflecting the historical context and the personal experiences of his later years.

Daily Life

1. Health and Mobility:

- Physical Health: By this age, John would likely have experienced the typical physical ailments associated with old age, such as arthritis, reduced mobility, and general frailty. He might have required assistance with daily tasks and relied on the support of family members.

- Care: Local community and family support would have been crucial. His wife, Jane, had passed away earlier, so John might have been living with one of his children or other relatives who would help care for him.

2. Living Conditions:

- Home: He would have continued to live in Carrowreagh, possibly in a home that had been adapted over the years to meet his needs. The house would reflect the rural and somewhat modest lifestyle of the time, with basic amenities.

- Community: Life in Carrowreagh would have remained relatively unchanged in terms of its rural, agricultural nature, but with the gradual introduction of new technologies and changes in agricultural practices.

Historical Context

1. Industrial and Technological Changes:

- Industrial Revolution: By 1869, the Industrial Revolution had significantly transformed Ireland, though rural areas like Carrowreagh would have seen slower changes. Improvements in transportation, such as railways, and advances in agriculture would have started to influence local life.

- Photography and Communications: The invention of photography in 1839 and advancements in communications would have marked significant technological progress. John would have been aware of these developments, although their impact on daily rural life would have been less direct.

2. Political and Social Climate:

- Irish Society: The mid-19th century in Ireland was marked by social and political changes, including ongoing discussions about land reform and Irish nationalism. The aftermath of the Great Famine continued to affect the social and economic landscape, with ongoing challenges related to poverty and emigration.

- Local Impact: In Carrowreagh, John would have witnessed the effects of these broader changes, though his direct involvement in political or social movements would have been limited by his age and rural location.

Personal Legacy

1. Family:

- Children and Grandchildren: John would likely have been surrounded by his children and possibly grandchildren, providing him with family support and companionship. His family's presence would have been a source of comfort and stability.

- Legacy: John's long life would have been viewed with respect and reverence within his family and community. His experiences, including the hardships of the Great Famine and the changes brought by the Industrial Revolution, would have been part of the family narrative passed down to future generations.

2. Community Standing:

- Local Role: As an elder in his community, John might have been seen as a respected figure with a wealth of experience. His long life would have made him a repository of local history and traditions.

- End of an Era: John's death in 1869 marked the end of his personal era, but it also symbolized the closing of a chapter in the history of Carrowreagh, with the transition to a new generation that would face different challenges and opportunities.

Summary

At 89, John McLeese Jr.'s life in Carrowreagh would have been marked by the challenges of old age and the gradual changes brought by industrialization and social developments. His life would have been deeply intertwined with his family and local community, reflecting a legacy shaped by both personal experiences and broader historical events. His final years would have been characterized by a blend of traditional rural life and the early impacts of modern technological and social changes.

Here's a suggested genealogy travel itinerary to honor the life of John McLeese II. This itinerary will take you through significant locations related to his life and legacy, providing a meaningful and memorable experience.

Day 1: Arrival in Belfast, Northern Ireland

• Morning: Arrive in Belfast International Airport.

• Afternoon: Check into your hotel and rest after your journey.

• Evening: Enjoy a welcome dinner at a local restaurant and explore Belfast's vibrant city center.

Day 2: Belfast to Ballycastle

• Morning: Drive from Belfast to Ballycastle (approximately 1.5 hours).

• Afternoon: Visit Bonamargy Friary, a historical site in Ballycastlehttps://discovernorthernireland.com/things-to-do/

bonamargy-friary-p675001. Explore the ruins and learn about the local history.

• Evening: Check into your accommodation in Ballycastle and enjoy dinner at a local restaurant.

Day 3: Exploring Ballycastle

• Morning: Visit the Ballycastle Museum to learn more about the local history and the families who lived in the areahttps://www.ireland.com/en-us/destinations/regions/ballycastle/.

• Afternoon: Take a walk along the Ballycastle Heritage Trail and explore the town's historical landmarkshttps://www.ireland.com/en-us/destinations/regions/ballycastle/.

• Evening: Enjoy a relaxing evening at your accommodation.

Day 4: Derrykeighan Graveyard and Surroundings

• Morning: Drive to Derrykeighan Graveyard on Castlecat Road, Dervock (approximately 20 minutes from Ballycastle). Spend time at the memorial of John McLeese II and reflect on his life and legacyhttps://www.findagrave.com/cemetery/2580387/derrykeighan-old-church-graveyard.

• Afternoon: Visit the Causeway Coast and Glens Borough Council to access local archives and records for further genealogical researchhttps://www.causewaycoastandglens.gov.uk/see-do/arts_museums/museums-services/ballymoney-museum/ballymoney-heritage/old-graveyards/derrykeighan-graveyard.

• Evening: Return to Ballycastle and have dinner at a local pub.

Day 5: Exploring the Causeway Coast

• Morning: Visit the Giant's Causeway, a UNESCO World Heritage site, and enjoy the stunning coastal scenery.

• Afternoon: Explore Dunluce Castle, a medieval castle with a rich historyhttps://discovernorthernireland.com/things-to-do/dunluce-castle-p675011.

- Evening: Dinner at a coastal restaurant with views of the Atlantic Ocean.

Day 6: Cultural Immersion in Belfast
- Morning: Return to Belfast.
- Afternoon: Visit the Ulster Museum and the Botanic Gardens.
- Evening: Enjoy a traditional Irish music session at a local pub.

Day 7: Departure
- Morning: Check out of your hotel and head to Belfast International Airport for your departure.

This itinerary combines genealogical research with cultural and historical exploration, providing a comprehensive and enriching experience.

JANE (UNKNOWN) McLEESE[3]

Jane McLeese, born in 1788, would have lived through a period of significant change in fashion and social norms in Ireland. Here's a likely description of her appearance and attire, along with some context about her life and style:

Physical Appearance

1. General Features:

- Complexion: Jane would likely have had a fair complexion, typical of Irish women of the time, often showing signs of exposure to the elements, given the rural setting.

- Hair: Her hair might have been dark brown or auburn, styled according to the fashion of the early 19th century. Women often wore their hair pulled back into simple buns or low chignons, sometimes adorned with ribbons or modest accessories.

- Face and Build: She would have had a robust build, influenced by the hard work of rural life. Her face would have shown the signs of her years and the challenges she faced, including the stress of her early death.

Attire

1. Early 19th-Century Fashion:

- Dress Style: During Jane's lifetime, women's fashion transitioned from the Empire style (characterized by high waistlines just under the bust) to more fitted and structured dresses with lower waistlines by the 1820s. She would have worn dresses made of lightweight fabrics like muslin or cotton during the earlier part of the century, transitioning to heavier fabrics like wool or velvet in the 1820s.

- Colors and Fabrics: Her clothing would have been practical for rural life, likely in muted colors and durable fabrics. Common colors for women's dresses included shades of blue, green, and brown. Fabric choices were influenced by affordability and practicality, with wool and linen being common.

2. Accessories:

- Headwear: Jane might have worn a simple bonnet or a cap, typical for women in rural Ireland. Bonnets were often made of fabric or straw and were used to protect the face from the sun and weather.

- Shoes: Her footwear would have been practical, likely sturdy leather shoes suitable for walking and daily activities.

- Outerwear: For colder weather, she would have worn a shawl or a woolen cloak. These were essential for warmth and could be quite decorative, depending on her financial means.

Social Context

1. Marriage and Family Life:

- Marriage: Jane married John McLeese Jr. in 1809 at the age of 21. Her attire for the wedding would have been a reflection of the modest and practical style of the time, with simple, elegant designs.

- Family Life: Jane's life was marked by significant family responsibilities, including raising children. Her attire would have been practical and suited to her daily tasks, reflecting the practical needs of a rural woman.

2. Death and Burial:

- Final Resting Place: Jane's burial in the same grave as her father-in-law, John McLeese Sr., and her young son, John McLeese III, indicates a strong family connection. The grave would have been marked by a simple headstone or monument, in keeping with the modesty of the time.

Summary

Jane McLeese, born in 1788, would have dressed in the practical and modest styles of early 19th-century Ireland. Her clothing would have been characterized by simplicity and durability, reflecting both her rural lifestyle and the prevailing fashion trends of her time. Despite the changing fashions, her attire would have remained practical and suited to her role as a wife and mother in a rural community. Her final years would have seen her wearing clothing typical of the early 1820s, which emphasized practicality and modesty.

Jane's early life, beginning in 1788 in Ireland, would have been shaped by various socio-economic and political factors. Here's an overview of what life would have been like during that period:

Social and Economic Context

1. Post-Revolutionary Ireland:

- Political Climate: Ireland was under British rule, and the late 18th century was a period of significant political tension. The Irish Rebellion of 1798 had recently ended, and the Act of Union in 1801 had created the United Kingdom of Great Britain and Ireland, merging the Irish and British parliaments.

- Social Hierarchy: The society was largely rural and agrarian, with a rigid class structure. The majority of the population were small tenant farmers or laborers, working under the influence of landlords.

2. Economic Conditions:

- Agriculture: The economy was predominantly agricultural. Farming techniques were basic, and life was heavily influenced by the seasonal cycles of planting and harvesting. The land was often rented from landlords, and many families faced economic hardships.

- Livelihood: Families relied on subsistence farming. Women were involved in household tasks, such as spinning and weaving, while men worked the fields. The early 19th century saw limited industrial development in rural areas.

Daily Life and Culture

1. Family and Social Structure:

- Family Life: Families were typically large, and extended families often lived together. The roles within the household were clearly defined, with women managing domestic tasks and men handling agricultural work.

- Community: Rural communities were close-knit, with local events and gatherings playing a crucial role in social life. Church services and market days were significant social occasions.

2. Housing and Living Conditions:

- Housing: Homes were simple, often made of stone or wattle and daub with thatched roofs. Interiors were basic, with a central hearth for cooking and heating.

- Living Conditions: The standard of living was modest. Most homes had minimal furniture and relied on basic amenities. Access to goods and services was limited, with local markets being the primary source of supplies.

Fashion and Customs

1. Clothing:

- Women's Fashion: Women's clothing was practical and modest. Common attire included long dresses, petticoats, and shawls. Fabrics were often wool, linen, or cotton, and clothing was handmade.

- Men's Fashion: Men wore simple shirts, waistcoats, and breeches or trousers. Workwear was practical and durable.

2. Customs:

- Festivals and Traditions: Traditional Irish festivals and customs were observed, including seasonal celebrations and local fairs. Folk music and dance were integral to community life.

- Religious Practices: Religion played a central role, with the majority of the population being Roman Catholic. Church attendance was a significant part of daily life.

Summary

In 1788, Ireland was a rural and agrarian society with a complex political and social landscape. Life for Jane would have been characterized by traditional farming practices, a strong sense of community, and a modest standard of living. The economic hardships and social constraints of the time would have influenced her daily life, shaping her experiences as a young woman growing up in Ireland.

At 10 years old during the Irish Rebellion of 1798, Jane would have been a child living in a turbulent period of Irish history. Here's how the rebellion might have affected her and how she might have reacted:

Impact on Jane

1. Emotional and Psychological Impact:

- Fear and Uncertainty: The rebellion brought significant violence and upheaval. Jane, being a child, would likely have experienced fear and confusion as the conflict disrupted daily life. The presence of military forces and the threat of violence would have created a sense of insecurity.

- Loss and Displacement: The rebellion led to widespread suffering, including the destruction of property and loss of life. Jane's family might have been affected by these disturbances, leading to potential displacement or economic hardship.

2. Social and Familial Impact:

- Community Disruption: The rebellion would have caused disruption in her community. Local events and gatherings might have been postponed or canceled due to the conflict, impacting her social interactions and childhood experiences.

- Family Dynamics: If her family was directly affected by the rebellion, it could have led to changes in their living conditions, such as financial strain or relocation. Her parents might have been preoccupied with dealing with the aftermath of the rebellion, affecting the stability of her home life.

3. Educational and Personal Impact:

- Interrupted Education: The rebellion could have interrupted her education. Schools might have closed or been repurposed for other uses, affecting her schooling and learning opportunities.

- Personal Development: The turmoil of the rebellion would have impacted her personal development, potentially shaping her worldview and experiences of authority and conflict. Her childhood would have been marked by the broader societal instability and struggle.

Possible Reactions

1. Curiosity and Confusion:

- As a child, Jane might have been curious about the events occurring around her but unable to fully understand their significance. She might have heard fragments of adult conversations and news, leading to a mix of curiosity and confusion about the rebellion.

2. Emotional Response:

- Her emotional response would likely have included a sense of fear and distress due to the chaos and instability around her. The rebellion's impact on her immediate environment—such as disruptions to normal routines and visible signs of conflict—would have contributed to her emotional experience.

3. Resilience and Adaptation:

- Despite the upheaval, Jane would have adapted to her changing circumstances. Children often show resilience in the face of adversity, and she might have found ways to cope with the disruptions and challenges posed by the rebellion.

Summary

At 10 years old, Jane's reaction to the Irish Rebellion of 1798 would have been influenced by the fear and uncertainty of living through a period of conflict. The rebellion would have disrupted her childhood, impacting her emotional well-being, family life, and education. While she might not have fully understood the complexities of the rebellion, its effects on her community and family would have left a lasting imprint on her early years.

When Jane was 12 years old in 1800, William Young's innovation of designing shoes specifically for left and right feet would have been a notable development, though it might have had a more subtle impact on her daily life compared to larger technological advancements. Here's how Jane might have reacted and how it could have affected her:

Reaction to the Innovation

1. Curiosity and Interest:

- Novelty: As a young girl, Jane would likely have been curious about the new shoe design. This innovation, though not immediately life-changing, would have intrigued her as a practical improvement in everyday items.

- Practical Impact: Jane might have noticed the improvement in comfort and fit that shoes designed for each foot provided. She might have experienced these benefits firsthand if her family was able to acquire the new shoes.

2. Awareness of Practical Benefits:

- Comfort: The introduction of properly fitted shoes would have likely been seen as a positive development. Improved comfort and support from well-designed shoes would have been a tangible benefit that Jane could appreciate.

- Quality: Jane's family might have viewed the new shoes as a sign of progress in craftsmanship and innovation, leading to a greater appreciation for the quality of footwear.

Effects on Her Life

1. Improved Daily Comfort:

- Physical Comfort: Jane would have experienced increased comfort from wearing shoes that fit better. This improvement would have been particularly beneficial in a time when shoes were often handmade and less standardized.

- Reduced Footwear Issues: Better-fitting shoes would have reduced issues such as blisters and foot pain, making everyday activities more comfortable for Jane.

2. Societal and Economic Impact:

- Family Finances: If Jane's family could afford the new shoes, it might have reflected a gradual improvement in their standard of living. However, the initial cost of adopting new footwear designs might have been a consideration for many families.

- Social Status: Wearing well-designed shoes might have also carried a subtle mark of social status, indicating a family's ability to keep up with modern improvements.

3. Long-term Influence:

- Awareness of Innovation: Growing up with the awareness of such innovations might have influenced Jane's views on technology and progress. It could have made her more receptive to future advancements and improvements in daily life.

Summary

At the age of 12, Jane would have reacted to William Young's design of shoes for left and right feet with curiosity and a sense of the practical benefits of improved footwear. The innovation would have enhanced her daily comfort and highlighted advancements in craftsmanship, contributing positively to her quality of life. Although not a revolutionary change, it would have been a noteworthy improvement in her experience of everyday life.

When Robert Fulton built the first commercially successful steamboat in 1807, Jane, at 19 years old, would have likely experienced a mix of curiosity, excitement, and practical considerations. Here's how she might have reacted and how it would have affected her life:

Reaction to the Steamboat Innovation

1. Excitement and Fascination:

- Innovation: The advent of the steamboat was a significant technological advancement that likely sparked interest and excitement. Jane would have been intrigued by this new mode of transportation and its implications for travel and commerce.

- Social Discussions: As news of Fulton's steamboat spread, it would have been a topic of conversation among her family and community, reflecting both the wonder of the invention and its potential impact on daily life.

2. Awareness of Practical Benefits:

- Efficiency: Jane would have recognized the steamboat's potential to revolutionize transportation on waterways, making travel faster and more reliable compared to traditional sail-powered ships.

- Economic Impact: The introduction of steamboats promised to enhance trade and transportation, potentially improving the local economy by facilitating easier and more efficient movement of goods and people.

Effects on Her Life

1. Improved Transportation:

- Travel: While Jane's immediate daily life in rural Ireland might not have been directly impacted by the steamboat, improved transportation links could eventually affect her, especially if she or her family traveled or engaged in trade.

- Access to Goods: Easier transportation could lead to better access to a wider variety of goods and services in her community, contributing to an improved quality of life.

2. Economic and Social Changes:

- Local Economy: The steamboat could influence the local economy by enhancing regional trade. This economic improvement might gradually affect Jane's community, creating more opportunities for commerce and employment.

- Social Impact: As transportation improved, it could lead to greater mobility and exchange between communities, potentially broadening Jane's social and cultural horizons.

3. Influence on Future Generations:

- Awareness of Technological Progress: Growing up during a period of rapid technological advancement, including the steamboat, could influence Jane's view of innovation and progress. She might have become more receptive to future technological changes and advancements.

Summary

At 19 years old, Jane would have likely been fascinated by Robert Fulton's development of the steamboat, recognizing its potential to transform transportation and commerce. While its direct impact on her immediate daily life in rural Ireland might have been limited initially, the broader economic and social changes brought about by such innovations would have influenced her community and, over time, her own experiences and opportunities. The excitement and promise of technological progress during this era would have shaped her outlook and adaptability to future advancements.

When Jane McLeese (née McLaughlin) gave birth to her first child, Daniel, at the age of 22 in 1810, it would have been a life-altering experience for her. Here's how this event likely affected her:

Emotional and Personal Impact:

- Joy and Fulfillment: As a young mother, Jane would have experienced a mix of joy and fulfillment at the birth of her son. In early 19th-century Ireland, the role of a wife and mother was central to a woman's identity, so the arrival of her first child would have been a significant personal milestone.

- Sense of Responsibility: With the birth of Daniel, Jane would have taken on new responsibilities as a mother. In rural Irish communities, mothers played a key role in the upbringing of children, from tending to their basic needs to instilling values and faith.

- Emotional Bonds: The birth of a child likely strengthened Jane's bond with her husband, John McLeese Jr., as they shared the experience of parenthood. The family unit would have become even more central to her life, and her love for her child would have given her a new focus and purpose.

Physical Impact:

- Childbirth and Recovery: Childbirth at that time, without the modern medical care available today, would have been a physically taxing and possibly dangerous event. Jane would have likely relied on midwives or women in the community to help with the birth. The postpartum period would have been a time of rest and recovery, but she would have been expected to return to household duties fairly quickly.

- Health and Nutrition: As a young woman, Jane likely had the strength and resilience to recover from childbirth, though she would have needed proper nourishment and care. In rural areas, families relied on their farms and local resources for food, and breastfeeding would have been the natural choice for feeding the baby, further demanding her physical energy.

Daily Life and Responsibilities:

- Household Duties: Despite the demands of caring for an infant, Jane would still have been responsible for her duties around the home, such as cooking, cleaning, and tending to the farm or garden. In rural County Antrim, wives often worked alongside their husbands in managing the household and agricultural work, making Jane's role essential to the family's survival.

- Support from Extended Family: Jane may have relied on help from extended family members, such as John's father, John McLeese Sr., or her own relatives if they were nearby. In a close-knit community, neighbors or other women in the family would likely have offered assistance during the early days of motherhood.

Social and Religious Influence:

- Community and Social Standing: Having children, particularly a son, would have elevated Jane's standing within the community. In early 19th-century Ireland, a woman's ability to bear and raise children was highly valued, and Jane would have received congratulations and support from friends and neighbors.

- Religious Duty: Baptism and raising the child in the church would have been a major focus for Jane. The religious ceremony would have been important not only for her personal faith but also for maintaining family and community ties. The church played a significant role in everyday life, and ensuring Daniel's spiritual upbringing would have been a key responsibility for Jane.

Long-Term Impact:

- Shaping Family Life: As a mother, Jane's primary focus would have been on raising her children and supporting her husband. The birth of Daniel would have marked the beginning of her journey as a mother, and her future decisions and life choices would likely revolve around her growing family.

- Personal Growth: Becoming a mother at 22 would have caused Jane to mature quickly, as she navigated the challenges and rewards of motherhood. As her family grew, her role as a mother and homemaker would have defined much of her daily life and her contributions to the McLeese household.

In summary, the birth of Daniel would have had a profound effect on Jane, bringing her joy and fulfillment, but also increased responsibilities. As a young mother in a rural community, her life would have revolved around caring for her child, maintaining the household, and supporting her family.

In 1815, when Napoleon Bonaparte was defeated at the Battle of Waterloo and subsequently exiled to Saint Helena, Jane McLeese would have been 27 years old, living in rural Ireland. Her reaction and the effect this historic event had on her would likely have been influenced by several factors, including her location, social standing, and the context of life in Ireland at the time.

Reaction to Napoleon's Defeat:

1. Awareness of the Event: News of Napoleon's defeat would have taken some time to reach rural communities like the one Jane lived in. Information often traveled by word of mouth, newspapers, and through the church or local authorities. Given the global impact of the Napoleonic Wars, Jane would have heard about it, though perhaps not immediately.

2. Relief and Optimism: Napoleon's defeat marked the end of more than a decade of warfare that had affected much of Europe. Although Ireland itself wasn't directly involved in the battles, Irishmen fought in the British army, and the economy and social fabric were impacted by the wars. For Jane and her community, the defeat of Napoleon might have brought a sense of relief, signaling a possible return to peace and stability.

3. Religious and Political Perspective: As a Catholic, Jane might have had mixed feelings about Napoleon. On the one hand, Napoleon was seen by some Catholics as a figure who had re-established the Church's position in France after the French Revolution's anti-clericalism. On the other hand, Ireland's relationship with Britain would have colored her reaction, as Britain played a key role in Napoleon's defeat. Jane may have viewed this victory with a cautious optimism, hoping it would

bring some stability and perhaps even improved conditions for Irish Catholics under British rule.

Effect on Jane's Life:

1. Indirect Economic Impact: The end of the Napoleonic Wars led to economic changes across Europe. For Ireland, and especially rural communities like Jane's, this could mean a temporary improvement in trade or agricultural stability as the demand for goods shifted back to peacetime needs. However, this would be followed by economic hardships in the post-war period, particularly for tenant farmers, as agricultural prices dropped.

2. Impact on Irish-British Relations: The conclusion of the Napoleonic Wars also saw renewed attention to domestic issues within Britain and Ireland. For Jane, this could have meant continuing to live under British rule in a society that was still deeply unequal for Catholics. Though Napoleon's defeat itself didn't directly impact Irish Catholic rights, the post-war era saw growing unrest in Ireland due to ongoing social and political inequality, something Jane and her family would have been affected by.

3. Family and Community Focus: Jane's day-to-day life would have continued to revolve around her family, especially with the birth of her children. While the news of Napoleon's defeat might have been discussed in her community, it would not have dramatically altered her role as a wife and mother in rural County Antrim. Her immediate concerns would have been focused on the survival and well-being of her family, especially in the challenging economic conditions that followed the end of the war.

Cultural and Social Reflection:

1. Pride in Britain's Victory: If Jane had any family members or neighbors who had served in the British military, there may have been a sense of local pride in Britain's victory over Napoleon. The British army recruited Irish soldiers, and news of their involvement

in the defeat of Napoleon would have likely been discussed within her community.

2. Post-War Anxiety: While there may have been initial relief at the end of the wars, the years immediately following Napoleon's defeat were marked by economic downturns, including in agriculture, which would have been relevant to Jane's life. As part of a farming family, she would have been affected by fluctuations in crop prices and the pressures placed on Irish tenant farmers by landlords.

Long-Term Impact:

Napoleon's defeat likely had an indirect impact on Jane's life, primarily through the larger socio-economic changes that followed in Ireland. The post-Napoleonic period saw the seeds of discontent grow in Ireland, leading eventually to movements for Catholic emancipation and political reform. While Jane's life in rural County Antrim may have remained focused on her family and local concerns, the broader changes in Irish society would have influenced the political landscape her children and grandchildren grew up in.

In summary, Jane's reaction to Napoleon's defeat would likely have been one of cautious optimism and relief, tempered by the realities of life in Ireland under British rule. The event would not have directly impacted her day-to-day life, but the larger social and economic consequences of the post-war period would have shaped her experiences in the years to come.

When the bicycle was invented in Germany in 1817 by Karl Drais, Jane McLeese was living in rural County Antrim, Ireland, at the age of 29. The invention of the bicycle, specifically the "Draisine" or "running machine" (an early version of the bicycle without pedals), would not have had an immediate or direct impact on her life, for several reasons:

Limited Access and Information:

1. Distance from Invention: Jane lived in a rural part of Ireland, far from the urban centers of Europe where technological innovations were more readily accessible. News of the invention might not have reached her community quickly, if at all, especially considering that early bicycles were more of a curiosity than a practical tool at first.

2. Economic Considerations: As a farmer's wife, Jane's life was likely focused on her family and daily tasks related to farming. The early versions of the bicycle were expensive and more of a novelty item for the wealthy in continental Europe, making it unlikely that Jane or her community would have had the opportunity to see one, let alone own one.

Potential Reaction:

1. Curiosity or Fascination: If Jane had heard about the invention of the bicycle through local gossip, travelers, or newspapers, she may have been curious or fascinated by the idea of a new mode of transport. However, it likely would have seemed like a distant innovation, not something directly related to her rural lifestyle. The notion of a machine that allowed someone to travel faster on land may have sparked some interest, but it wouldn't have felt immediately relevant.

2. Practical Thinking: Jane's life in rural County Antrim would have been deeply practical, and she likely focused on the daily challenges of managing a household and raising children. In this context, the invention of a bicycle may not have seemed like something that would make her life easier, given that traditional methods like walking or using horses for transport were more practical and established at the time.

Long-Term Impact:

1. Delayed Adoption in Ireland: Bicycles did not become popular or widely used in Ireland until later in the 19th century, long after Jane's lifetime. By the time bicycles became more

accessible and affordable in the 1860s and 1870s, Jane would have been in her 70s. She may have seen or heard of bicycles becoming more common in the years leading up to her death in 1828, but she wouldn't affect her.

When Jane McLeese gave birth to her daughter Jane in 1821, she was 33 years old. Here's how this event might have affected her:

Emotional Impact:

1. Joy and Fulfillment: The birth of a child often brings immense joy and a sense of fulfillment. Jane, having already experienced the joys of motherhood with her other children, would likely have felt a deep emotional connection to her new daughter, enhancing her sense of family and personal achievement.

2. Reflection and Nostalgia: As Jane was 33 years old, the birth of her daughter might have prompted reflections on her own life and experiences as a mother. She might have felt nostalgic for the earlier years of motherhood and appreciated the continuity of her family through her new daughter.

Physical and Practical Effects:

1. Health and Recovery: At 33, Jane would have been managing the physical demands of childbirth and recovery. The birth of a child at this age might have been more challenging than in her earlier years, but Jane's experience as a mother would have helped her navigate this process.

2. Family Dynamics: The arrival of a new baby would have affected family dynamics. Jane would have needed to balance the needs of her newborn with those of her other children. This shift might have led to changes in family routines and responsibilities.

3. Support System: Jane would likely have relied on her husband, John McLeese Jr., and possibly other family members for support during the early days after the birth. The presence of a strong support system would have been crucial for her well-being.

Social and Cultural Context:

1. **Community Role:** In early 19th-century Ireland, the birth of a child was often a communal event, with neighbors and extended family providing support. Jane's daughter's birth would have been celebrated within her community, reinforcing social bonds and her role within the local network.

2. **Motherhood and Status:** As a mother of multiple children, Jane's status within the community would have been enhanced. Children were highly valued, and a growing family would contribute to her social standing and influence in her local area.

Long-Term Impact:

1. **Family Legacy:** Jane's new daughter would have been seen as a continuation of the McLeese family line. The birth of a child at this stage in her life would have reinforced her role in shaping the family's future and legacy.

2. **Emotional Connection:** Jane would have developed a strong emotional bond with her daughter, which would have influenced her relationships with her other children and her approach to parenting.

Conclusion:

The birth of her daughter in 1821 would have been a significant and fulfilling event for Jane McLeese. It would have brought both joy and practical challenges, affecting her family dynamics, health, and role within the community. Jane's experience as a mother and her strong support system would have helped her manage the demands of adding a new child to her family.

When Jane McLeese gave birth to her daughter Margaret Bridget in 1823, at the age of 35, the experience would have had several implications for her:

Emotional Impact:

1. **Joy and Satisfaction:** The birth of a new child typically brings joy and a renewed sense of purpose. Despite her age, Jane would

have likely felt immense joy and satisfaction in welcoming another daughter into the family.

2. Reflection on Aging: At 35, Jane might have been more acutely aware of the challenges associated with having children later in life. This could have led to reflections on her age and its impact on her health and energy levels.

Physical and Health Considerations:

1. Health Risks: Childbirth at 35 was considered advanced age for the period, potentially carrying higher risks for both mother and child. Jane would have needed to take extra care of her health during pregnancy and childbirth, and her recovery might have been more arduous compared to earlier pregnancies.

2. Recovery and Fatigue: The physical demands of childbirth and recovery could have been more taxing. Jane may have experienced increased fatigue and required more support from her family and community.

Family Dynamics:

1. Balancing Responsibilities: With several children already in the family, Jane would have needed to balance the demands of a newborn with the needs of her older children. This could have altered family routines and dynamics.

2. Impact on Older Children: The birth of Margaret Bridget might have influenced her relationships with her older siblings, potentially fostering new bonds or creating shifts in family roles and responsibilities.

Social and Cultural Context:

1. Community Support: In early 19th-century Ireland, the birth of a child was often a communal event. Jane would have received support and congratulations from her community, reinforcing her role within the local social structure.

2. Perceptions of Age: While 35 was relatively old for childbirth in the early 19th century, having a healthy child would

have been seen as a positive outcome. Jane's age might have been a topic of discussion, but her successful delivery would likely have been celebrated.

Long-Term Impact:

1. Family Legacy: The birth of Margaret Bridget would have contributed to the continuation of the McLeese family line. Jane's role as a mother would have continued to be central to her identity and responsibilities.

2. Personal Reflection: Jane might have reflected on her role as a mother and the future of her family, especially considering the challenges associated with childbirth at an older age. Her experiences would have shaped her approach to parenting and family life.

Conclusion:

The birth of Margaret Bridget in 1823 would have been a significant event for Jane McLeese. Despite the challenges associated with having a child at 35, Jane would have experienced both joy and fulfillment. The arrival of her daughter would have had implications for her health, family dynamics, and social standing, while also reinforcing her role in her family and community.

When Jane McLeese gave birth to her last child, John McLeese III, in 1825 at the age of 38, several factors would have influenced her experience:

Emotional Impact:

1. Joy and Fulfillment: Despite the challenges of having a child at a later age, Jane likely felt joy and a sense of fulfillment in bringing another child into the world. Each new birth would have reinforced her role as a mother and the continuation of her family line.

2. Possible Anxiety: Given her advanced age for childbirth at that time, Jane might have experienced anxiety about potential

health risks for herself and the baby. Concerns about her ability to care for a newborn while managing her other responsibilities could have been significant.

Physical and Health Considerations:

1. Health Risks: At 38, Jane would have faced higher risks during pregnancy and childbirth. The medical knowledge and practices of the period offered limited support for advanced maternal age, so Jane would have needed to be particularly cautious about her health.

2. Recovery: Recovery from childbirth could have been more challenging. Jane's physical strength and energy levels might have been impacted, requiring more time and support to regain her health and manage her household.

Family Dynamics:

1. Balancing Responsibilities: With multiple children, Jane would have needed to juggle the demands of a newborn with those of her older children. This balancing act would have required significant effort and adjustment in family routines.

2. Influence on Older Siblings: John McLeese III's arrival would have impacted the dynamics among his older siblings. He might have been welcomed warmly or might have changed the roles and interactions within the family.

Social and Cultural Context:

1. Community Support: In early 19th-century Ireland, the birth of a child was a communal event, and Jane would likely have received support and congratulations from her neighbors and community members. This support would have been important for her physical recovery and emotional well-being.

2. Perceptions of Age: Although 38 was considered advanced age for childbirth at the time, successful delivery of a healthy baby would have been a positive outcome, and Jane's resilience would have been admired within her community.

Long-Term Impact:

1. Family Legacy: The birth of John McLeese III would have been a crucial event for ensuring the continuation of the McLeese family name and legacy. Jane's role as a mother would have remained central to her identity and her family's future.

2. Personal Reflection: Jane might have reflected on her journey as a mother, particularly in light of having a child at an older age. This reflection could have influenced her approach to parenting and her hopes for her children's futures.

Conclusion:

Jane's experience of having her last child, John McLeese III, at 38 years old would have been shaped by a mix of joy, concern, and practical challenges. While the birth would have been a significant source of happiness, the risks associated with advanced maternal age would have been a concern. Jane's resilience and the support of her family and community would have played a key role in managing the demands of this later-life childbirth and ensuring the well-being of her family.

When John Walker invented the first friction matches in 1826, Jane McLeese, at 38 years old, would have likely experienced a range of reactions and effects from this new invention:

Reaction:

1. Curiosity and Interest: Jane, as a homemaker managing a household, would have been intrigued by the convenience of friction matches. The ability to light fires more easily than with flint and steel would have piqued her interest.

2. Practical Appreciation: Given the challenges of starting fires with traditional methods, Jane would have appreciated the simplicity and efficiency of matches. They would have represented a significant improvement in daily life, making it easier to light stoves, hearths, and lamps.

Impact on Daily Life:

1. Increased Convenience: Matches would have made lighting fires more straightforward and less labor-intensive. Jane's daily routine would benefit from the reduced effort and time needed to start fires for cooking and heating.

2. Safety Improvements: Matches were safer and more reliable compared to older methods like using flint and steel or chemical fire starters. This improvement would have enhanced safety in the household, reducing the risk of accidental fires caused by more cumbersome fire-starting methods.

3. Economic and Social Implications: The introduction of matches might have influenced the local economy and Jane's household expenses. Matches would have been more affordable and accessible compared to other fire-starting methods, potentially saving money in the long run.

Long-Term Effects:

1. Cultural Shift: Matches contributed to a cultural shift in how people approached fire-starting and daily chores. Jane would have witnessed the gradual transition from traditional methods to the more modern convenience of matches, reflecting broader changes in household technology.

2. Adaptation to New Technology: Jane's adaptation to using matches would have mirrored broader societal changes as new technologies became integrated into everyday life. This adaptation would have influenced her approach to household management and her role within the family.

Conclusion:

Jane McLeese's reaction to John Walker's invention of friction matches in 1826 would have been one of practical appreciation and interest. The convenience and safety provided by matches would have significantly impacted her daily life, improving household tasks and contributing to a shift towards more modern methods of fire-starting. The invention would have been seen as a welcome advancement in her household management and daily routines.

The death of her young son John McLeese III and her own passing in 1828 would have been devastating for Jane. Here's how these events likely affected her:

Emotional Impact:

1. Grief and Loss: The death of her child at such a young age would have caused immense sorrow and emotional distress. As a mother, Jane would have felt a profound sense of loss and mourning.

2. Health and Well-being: The combination of grieving her son and facing her own declining health could have been overwhelming. In the early 19th century, the stress and physical toll of such events could significantly impact an individual's health.

Impact on Her Life and Family:

1. Family Dynamics: Jane's death, alongside her son's, would have left John McLeese Jr. and their surviving children, Daniel and Margaret Bridget, in a state of grief. This would also place additional responsibilities on John and other family members.

2. Legacy and Memory: The decision to bury Jane and her son in the same grave as her father-in-law indicates a desire to keep family bonds strong even in death. The shared grave would symbolize the family's close ties and the lasting impact of their loss.

3. Practical Matters: In 1828, the passing of a family member would require immediate practical arrangements, including funeral preparations and settling of affairs. Jane's death would have left John with the task of managing these responsibilities while grieving.

Historical Context:

1. Burial Practices: During this period, it was common for families to be buried together in the same grave or family plot. This

practice reflected the importance of family unity in death, as well as the prevailing cultural and religious attitudes towards burial.

2. Community Support: Jane's death would have elicited sympathy and support from the local community in Dervock. Community support would have been crucial in helping John and his surviving children cope with their loss.

Conclusion:

Jane's death at 40, just after losing her young son, would have been a period of deep personal grief and hardship. Her passing, along with the burial arrangements, reflects the close family ties and the emotional impact of her death on those left behind. The support of her community and the memory of her family would have been central to the family's coping process during this difficult time.

Here's a suggested genealogy travel itinerary to honor the life of Jane McLeese. This itinerary will take you through significant locations related to her life and legacy, providing a meaningful and memorable experience.

Day 1: Arrival in Belfast, Northern Ireland

- Morning: Arrive in Belfast International Airport.
- Afternoon: Check into your hotel and rest after your journey.
- Evening: Enjoy a welcome dinner at a local restaurant and explore Belfast's vibrant city center.

Day 2: Belfast to Dervock

- Morning: Drive from Belfast to Dervock (approximately 1.5 hours).
- Afternoon: Visit the Derrykeighan Graveyard on Castlecat Road, Dervock. Spend time at the memorial of Jane McLeese and reflect on her life and legacy.
- Evening: Explore the village of Dervock and have dinner at a local pub.

Day 3: Exploring Dervock and Surroundings

- Morning: Visit the Benvarden Gardens, a beautiful historical garden near Ballymoney
  https://www.benvarden.co.uk/

- AFTERNOON: TAKE A guided tour of the Derrykeighan Old Church Graveyard and see the old headstones and ruins.
- Evening: Return to your accommodation and enjoy a relaxing evening.

Day 4: Ancestral Research and Local Exploration
- Morning: Visit the Causeway Coast and Glens Borough Council to access local archives and records for further genealogical research.
- Afternoon: Explore the beautiful Causeway Coast, including the Giant's Causeway and Dunluce Castle
  https://discovernorthernireland.com/things-to-do/dunluce-castle-p675011

- EVENING: DINNER AT a coastal restaurant with views of the Atlantic Ocean.

Day 5: Cultural Immersion in Belfast
- Morning: Return to Belfast.
- Afternoon: Visit the Ulster Museum and the Botanic Gardens.
- Evening: Enjoy a traditional Irish music session at a local pub.

Day 6: Departure
- Morning: Check out of your hotel and head to Belfast International Airport for your departure.

This itinerary combines genealogical research with cultural and historical exploration, providing a comprehensive and enriching experience.

ANN ADAMS[4]

1. Appearance and Clothing:
   - Age and Stature: Ann Adams, if she were a close relative like Daniel Adams's mother, might have been in her 30s or 40s at the time of her death in the mid-18th century.
   - Clothing: She would have worn typical 18th-century women's attire, which included a shift or chemise as an undergarment, a petticoat, a gown or dress (often made from wool or linen), and a shawl or apron for additional warmth and practicality. Her clothing would have been modest and practical, suited for rural life.

2. Health and Personal Care:
   - Health: Life in the 18th century came with many health challenges, so Ann might have faced health issues common to the time, such as illnesses with limited medical intervention.
   - Personal Care: Her personal care would include maintaining cleanliness with available resources, and her grooming would be modest, likely involving a simple hairstyle, often kept under a bonnet or cap.

3. Burial and Grave:
   - Burial Practices: Ann Adams's burial alongside Daniel Adams suggests they were closely related. The grave would likely be marked with a simple headstone or grave marker, which might include her name, date of death, and possibly a brief inscription.

- Family Significance: Sharing a grave with Daniel indicates a strong familial bond, possibly a parent-child relationship or close kin.

4. Historical Context:

- Rural Life: In the mid-18th century in rural Ireland, daily life was characterized by agrarian activities and close-knit communities. Ann's life would have involved managing household tasks, possibly assisting with farming, and participating in community events.

- Community and Family: Given the importance of family and community in this era, her role in the family would have been significant, contributing to both household management and social responsibilities.

Summary:

Ann Adams, buried with Daniel Adams, would have led a life typical of the 18th-century rural Irish community. Her appearance and clothing would reflect the period's modest and practical styles. Her burial alongside Daniel emphasizes their familial connection, and her life would have been influenced by the challenges and community-centered life of that era.

DANIEL ADAMS[5]

Given Daniel Adams' time period and location (Devrock, County Antrim, Ireland) in the mid-18th century, here's a likely description of what he might have looked like:

Physical Appearance:

1. Facial Features: As a child born in 1739, Daniel would likely have had a delicate, youthful appearance with a soft face typical of a young child of that era. His features would have been shaped by the genetic traits of his parents, possibly including a fair complexion and light hair, which were common in Ireland at the time.

2. Hair: Children's hairstyles in the 18th century varied, but young boys often had their hair cut short or styled in soft curls. Daniel may have had light brown or blonde hair, as lighter hair colors were more common among Irish children.

3. Clothing: During the mid-18th century, children's clothing was similar to that of adults but scaled down. For a boy of his age, Daniel would have worn simple garments such as a linen or woolen shirt, breeches, and possibly a small jacket. His clothing would have been practical and made from durable materials suitable for everyday life in rural Ireland.

4. Health and Stature: Given that he passed away at the age of 13, Daniel may have been slender and not fully developed in stature. The health conditions of the time, including limited access to medical care and nutrition, might have affected his growth and overall health.

Contextual Factors:

1. Historical Influence: The period was marked by rural and relatively simple lifestyles. Daniel's appearance would reflect the modesty and practicality of the time, with clothing and personal grooming kept minimal due to economic and social constraints.

2. Cultural Context: In 18th-century Ireland, children from rural areas often had a rustic and unadorned appearance. Their clothing would typically be functional, and their overall look would be indicative of the agricultural and agrarian lifestyle prevalent in the region.

Summary:

Daniel Adams, born in 1739 and passing away in 1752, would likely have had a youthful, delicate appearance with short, simple hair and modest clothing typical of the mid-18th century in Ireland. His physical look would be reflective of the rural lifestyle and the health conditions of the time.

In 1739, Ireland was under British rule and experienced a range of social, economic, and political conditions. Here's a snapshot of life in Ireland during that year:

Social and Economic Life:

1. Agrarian Economy:

- Farming: Most people in Ireland lived in rural areas and were engaged in agriculture. The economy was largely agrarian, with people farming the land to produce crops and raise livestock.

- Land Ownership: Land ownership was a significant factor in social status, and the majority of land was controlled by Anglo-Irish landlords, while the majority of the population were tenant farmers.

2. Living Conditions:

- Housing: People lived in simple, one-story cottages made of stone or wattle and daub with thatched roofs. Homes were basic, with a central hearth for cooking and heating.

- Daily Life: Life was centered around farming and local community activities. Most households were self-sufficient, growing their own food, and producing clothing and tools.

3. Social Structure:

- Class Division: There was a clear division between the Anglo-Irish upper class and the Irish peasantry. The Anglo-Irish were often Protestant landowners, while the majority of the population was Catholic.

- Community: Social life revolved around local markets, fairs, and religious events. Communities were tight-knit, and people relied on each other for support.

4. Political and Religious Context:

- British Rule: Ireland was governed by the British Parliament and had limited self-governing powers. Tensions between the Irish and British authorities were common, with various movements advocating for greater Irish autonomy.

- Religious Tensions: The religious divide between the Protestant minority and the Catholic majority created social and political tensions. Penal laws that discriminated against Catholics were in place but were gradually being relaxed over time.

5. Economic Developments:

- Trade: The early 18th century saw some improvements in trade and industry, although Ireland remained largely agrarian. Irish trade was growing, particularly in linen production and export.

- Infrastructure: Infrastructure improvements, such as road building, were slowly advancing, but many rural areas remained isolated.

6. Education and Culture:

- Education: Education was limited, with few formal schools, particularly in rural areas. Most learning occurred informally within families or through religious institutions.

- Culture: Irish culture was rich in oral traditions, including storytelling, music, and dance. Folk traditions were strong, and the Irish language was widely spoken in many regions.

Summary:

In 1739, Ireland was predominantly rural and agrarian, with a clear social divide between the Anglo-Irish and the Irish peasantry. Daily life was centered around farming, community activities, and religious observances. Political and religious tensions existed due to British rule and the religious divide, while gradual economic developments and cultural traditions shaped the lives of its people.

DANIEL ADAMS[6]

Daniel Adams (1729-1809) - Description and Context
Physical Appearance:
Daniel Adams, born in 1729, would likely have had a robust and practical appearance typical of the time. He might have had:

- Height and Build: A moderately tall and sturdy build, reflecting the physical labor and outdoor activities common in 18th-century Ireland.

- Facial Features: A weathered face with rugged features, possibly with a strong jawline and prominent cheekbones. His hair might have been dark, turning grey as he aged.

- Attire: For much of his life, he would have worn practical clothing such as woolen breeches, linen shirts, and simple woolen coats, with a wide-brimmed hat for sun protection. By the early 19th century, his attire might have included more formal garments like a frock coat or waistcoat.

Life at the Time of His Birth:

- Rural Ireland: Daniel was born in 1729 in rural Ireland, a time when the country was predominantly agricultural. Life was centered around farming and local communities, with most people living in small villages or isolated farms.

- Economic Conditions: The Irish economy was largely agrarian, with subsistence farming being the norm. Many families struggled with poverty and subsistence living, and the rural landscape was characterized by small plots of land, stone cottages, and simple farming tools.

- Political and Social Context: The 18th century in Ireland was marked by complex political dynamics, including tensions between the Catholic majority and the Protestant ruling class. The period saw frequent political strife and changes in land ownership, impacting the daily lives of rural inhabitants.

- Social Life: Community life was closely knit, with social activities revolving around local markets, fairs, and religious events. Traditional customs and folk practices were integral to daily life.

Daniel Adams would have lived through significant historical changes, including the agricultural developments and social shifts of the late 18th and early 19th centuries. His life would have been shaped by the evolving political landscape, economic challenges, and the gradual modernization of Ireland.

Benjamin Franklin determined that lightning was electrical in 1752. If Daniel Adams was 23 years old in 1752, here's how he might have reacted to Franklin's discovery:

Reaction and Impact on Daniel Adams (born 1729):

1. Curiosity and Interest: At 23, Daniel would likely have been curious and intrigued by Franklin's discovery. As a young adult, he might have been particularly interested in scientific advancements and new ideas. The revelation that lightning was electrical would have been seen as a groundbreaking development in understanding natural phenomena.

2. Local Impact: In rural Ireland, access to the latest scientific knowledge might have been limited. However, if Daniel had access to newspapers or other sources of information, he might have learned about Franklin's work. This discovery would have been a topic of conversation among educated circles and in communities interested in science.

3. Effect on Daily Life: While the immediate practical effects of Franklin's discovery might not have been directly felt in Daniel's daily life, the broader impact on science and technology would

have eventually influenced society. The understanding of electricity would lead to further technological advancements and innovations over time.

4. Intellectual Influence: The knowledge of electricity being a natural phenomenon rather than a mystical or purely physical force might have influenced Daniel's view of science and the natural world. It could have contributed to a growing interest in scientific exploration and understanding.

5. Potential for Future Impact: Although Franklin's work was theoretical at the time, it laid the groundwork for future developments in electrical engineering and technology. Daniel's awareness of these advancements might have sparked an interest in science and technology, impacting his outlook on progress and innovation.

Overall, Daniel's reaction to Franklin's discovery would likely have been one of fascination and interest, contributing to his broader understanding of science and the natural world, even if its direct impact on his daily life was minimal at the time.

When the Industrial Revolution began in 1760, Daniel Adams, at 31 years old, would have experienced both the immediate changes and the broader impacts of this transformative period. Here's how it might have affected him:

Reaction:

1. Curiosity or Skepticism: Depending on his occupation and education, Daniel might have been curious about the technological advancements, such as new machinery and methods of production. Alternatively, he might have been skeptical or resistant, especially if he felt threatened by the changes.

2. Interest in Innovation: If Daniel was involved in agriculture or crafts, he might have shown interest in how new technologies could improve efficiency. The introduction of mechanized farming tools, for example, could have intrigued him.

3. Concern Over Social Changes: As the Industrial Revolution also brought significant social changes, Daniel might have been concerned about the impact on traditional ways of life and the challenges faced by rural communities.

Effects:

1. Economic Impact: If Daniel was engaged in traditional farming or artisan work, he might have experienced economic shifts due to the increasing prevalence of factory-produced goods. The competition from cheaper, mass-produced items could have affected his livelihood.

2. Social Disruption: The changes brought about by the Industrial Revolution, including urbanization and shifts in labor patterns, might have disrupted his community. This could include shifts in local economies, migration patterns, and social structures.

3. Technological Adoption: Depending on his openness to new technologies, Daniel might have adopted some innovations, such as improvements in agricultural techniques or tools. This could have influenced his productivity and daily life.

4. Cultural Impact: The Industrial Revolution also led to changes in cultural practices and norms. Daniel might have observed changes in social interactions, working conditions, and community life as industrialization progressed.

5. Health and Living Conditions: Industrialization often led to improved living standards in terms of access to goods and services, but it also introduced new health challenges, such as pollution and poor working conditions in factories. Daniel's health and quality of life could have been affected by these changes.

In summary, Daniel's reaction to the Industrial Revolution would likely have been a mix of curiosity, concern, and adaptation. The effects on his life would have been multifaceted, impacting his economic situation, social environment, and potentially leading to significant changes in his lifestyle and community dynamics.

Here's how Daniel Adams, at 55 years old in 1784, might have reacted to and been affected by the first successful hot air balloon flight:

Reaction:

1. Amazement and Fascination: As a person of his time, Daniel Adams would likely have been amazed by the hot air balloon's flight. The ability to float in the air would have been a dramatic and wondrous sight, especially in an era without modern aviation.

2. Interest in Technological Progress: The event might have piqued his interest in new technologies and scientific advancements. It could have led to curiosity about the principles of aerodynamics and the science behind ballooning.

3. Social and Community Impact: In his rural community, news of such a remarkable event would have been a topic of conversation. Daniel might have shared his thoughts and discussed the implications with his peers, adding to the local dialogue about scientific progress.

Effects:

1. Broader Perspective on Innovation: The successful flight might have broadened Daniel's perspective on technological possibilities. While it might not have had a direct impact on his daily life, it would have contributed to a sense of excitement about the future and the potential for new inventions.

2. Cultural Influence: The event would likely have been viewed as a symbol of the advancing age of exploration and innovation. It could have influenced local attitudes towards scientific advancements and encouraged a more progressive mindset within his community.

3. Limited Practical Impact: Given his rural location and age, Daniel would not have had direct interaction with ballooning technology. However, the flight might have indirectly affected his

view of the world, making him more aware of and interested in scientific advancements and their implications for society.

At 69 years old during the Irish Rebellion of 1798, Daniel Adams would have been in a significant phase of his life, possibly experiencing the rebellion as an older adult with considerable life experience. Here's how he might have reacted and how it could have affected him:

Reaction:

1. Concern and Anxiety: Given his age and likely life stage, Daniel would have been concerned about the instability and conflict arising from the rebellion. Such events could threaten the safety and security of his community and his own well-being.

2. Personal Impact: As a member of a rural community, Daniel might have felt personally impacted by the rebellion's upheaval. While he might not have been directly involved, the general unrest and potential violence could have affected him and his family.

3. Reflective Response: At his age, Daniel might have viewed the rebellion through a historical lens, reflecting on past events and their similarities to current struggles. His perspective would likely be shaped by his understanding of previous uprisings and political movements.

Effects:

1. Emotional Strain: The rebellion would have caused emotional strain and anxiety due to the potential for violence and disruption. Daniel would likely have been worried about the safety of his family and the impact of the rebellion on his local community.

2. Community Relations: The rebellion might have affected Daniel's relations within the community. Depending on his political or religious affiliations, he might have found himself at odds with others who held different views.

3. Legacy and Reflection: As an older individual, Daniel might have focused on the legacy and future of Ireland following the rebellion. He might have engaged in discussions about the political and social changes resulting from the uprising, affecting his views on Irish politics and governance.

4. Economic and Social Impact: The rebellion could have had economic implications for local communities, including disruptions to trade and agriculture. This would affect Daniel's economic situation and the general stability of his daily life.

Overall, the Irish Rebellion would have likely been a significant and distressing event for Daniel Adams, shaping his experiences and perceptions of Ireland's political landscape in his later years.

At 71 years old, Daniel Adams would likely have had a mixed reaction to William Young's invention of shoes designed specifically for the left and right foot in 1800. Here's how it might have impacted him:

Reaction:

1. Curiosity and Interest: Given his age and experience, Daniel might have been curious about this new development in footwear. Innovations that improved daily life would have intrigued him, especially if he had been involved in trades or activities where footwear was important.

2. Skepticism or Approval: Depending on his personal disposition, Daniel might have been skeptical about the necessity of such a change or he could have appreciated the practical benefits. Shoes specifically designed for the left and right foot would have been a novel concept at the time, and he might have needed time to adjust to this new idea.

3. Awareness of Improvement: If he had experienced discomfort or difficulty with ill-fitting shoes in the past, he might have seen this invention as a positive advancement. Improved

comfort and fit would have been particularly appreciated by someone of his age, who might have had foot issues.

Effects:

1. Improved Comfort: If Daniel adopted the new design, he might have experienced improved comfort and better-fitting shoes. This could have had a positive impact on his daily life, especially if he was still active and used to walking or working outdoors.

2. Adoption of New Fashion: As an older individual, Daniel might have been less inclined to immediately adopt new trends. However, if the benefits of the new shoe design were demonstrated, he might have eventually made the switch, especially if others in his community began using them.

3. Impact on Social Status and Lifestyle: If Daniel was involved in local social circles or trades where such innovations were discussed, he might have been aware of the broader implications of this invention on fashion and daily life. The adoption of better-fitting shoes might have gradually influenced his view of personal and community improvements.

Overall, Daniel Adams' reaction to the invention of shoes for the left and right foot would likely have been a blend of curiosity, practical consideration, and potential adoption based on the benefits he personally experienced. The innovation would have contributed to a gradual improvement in comfort and fit in footwear, potentially affecting his daily activities and lifestyle positively.

At 78 years old in 1807, when Robert Fulton built the first commercially successful steamboat, Daniel Adams would have likely had a complex and multifaceted reaction:

Reaction:

1. Astonishment and Interest: As an elderly man witnessing a groundbreaking technological advancement, Daniel would probably have been astonished by the arrival of the steamboat.

This innovation represented a significant leap in transportation technology, and such changes would have captured the imagination of someone who had seen the gradual evolution of various technologies over his lifetime.

2. Skepticism or Caution: Given his age and the nature of new technologies, Daniel might have been cautious or skeptical about the practical implications and long-term success of steamboats. Such innovations often took time to become widely accepted and reliable, and he might have had reservations about their immediate impact.

3. Pride and Nationalistic Sentiment: Depending on his personal views and the broader context of his life, Daniel might have felt a sense of pride in seeing such advancements occurring in his lifetime, especially if he saw it as a mark of progress and innovation coming from the United States or Europe, depending on his geographic context.

Effects:

1. Indirect Impact: As a resident of Kilmoile in Ireland, Daniel might not have been directly affected by the steamboat's introduction. However, he could have been aware of its impact on global trade and transportation. The steamboat revolutionized how goods and people were transported, which would have had indirect effects on global markets and possibly even on local economies over time.

2. Awareness of Progress: The advent of the steamboat could have deepened Daniel's appreciation for technological progress and industrialization. He might have reflected on the rapid pace of change and the improvements in transportation that began to shape the modern world.

3. Legacy and Reflection: At his advanced age, Daniel would have witnessed the early stages of the Industrial Revolution and other technological innovations. The arrival of the steamboat

would be seen as part of the broader trend of transformative advancements, reinforcing the notion that he lived through a period of profound change and progress.

In summary, Daniel Adams' reaction to the steamboat would likely have been a mixture of astonishment, interest, and possibly skepticism. While the direct impact on his daily life may have been minimal, the broader implications of such innovations would have contributed to his understanding of technological and industrial progress.

When Daniel Adams passed away in 1809 at the age of 80, his life and surroundings would have reflected a period of significant social and technological change. Here's a snapshot of what his life might have been like:

Lifestyle and Daily Life:

1. Rural Setting: Living in Kilmoile, County Antrim, Daniel would have been accustomed to a rural lifestyle. His daily life would have revolved around agricultural activities, local trade, and community events. The early 19th century was a time when rural communities were relatively self-sufficient, with agriculture being a primary occupation.

2. Economic Conditions: By 1809, Ireland was experiencing the early effects of the Industrial Revolution, but in rural areas like Kilmoile, many traditional farming practices continued. The local economy would have been largely agrarian, with advancements in technology and industry having a slower impact on rural areas.

3. Social Structure: As an elderly man, Daniel would have been regarded with respect within his community. Elders were often seen as repositories of wisdom and experience. His interactions with family and neighbors would likely have been centered around community gatherings and family events.

4. Health and Longevity: At 80 years old, Daniel would have been considered quite elderly. His health might have been

declining, and he would likely have had to rely on traditional remedies and the care of family members for ailments common in old age.

5. Technology and Innovation: Daniel would have witnessed significant technological advancements during his lifetime, including the early stages of the Industrial Revolution, the development of the steam engine, and the introduction of innovations such as the steamboat. These changes would have been gradually making their way into various aspects of life, though rural areas often adopted new technologies more slowly.

6. Family and Community: Daniel would likely have been surrounded by his family and local community in his final years. His burial in Dervock suggests that he was connected to the area and that his final resting place was chosen within his local community's cemetery.

In Summary:

Daniel Adams' life in 1809 was characterized by the transition between traditional rural practices and the early effects of industrialization. As an 80-year-old, he would have experienced the gradual shifts in technology and society while maintaining a primarily agrarian lifestyle. His final years would have been spent in the company of family and community, reflecting the values and customs of early 19th-century rural Ireland.

SAMUEL ALLEN ESQ.[7]

Samuel was born in 1742.

In 1752, when Samuel Allen was 10 years old, Benjamin Franklin's experiments demonstrated that lightning is a form of electricity. Given Samuel's background as a young boy in a rural, agrarian setting, here's how he might have reacted and been affected:

Reaction to Franklin's Discovery

1. Curiosity and Fascination:

- Interest in Science: As a young boy, Samuel might have been intrigued by the idea of electricity and its effects. Franklin's discovery would have been a remarkable and novel concept, potentially sparking an interest in scientific inquiry and natural phenomena.

- Local Knowledge: In a rural area like Lisconnon, news of such scientific advancements might have reached Samuel through local discussions or news from larger towns or cities, though it might have been less immediate compared to urban areas.

2. Impact on His Understanding of Nature:

- New Perspectives: The idea that lightning was a form of electricity would have challenged and expanded Samuel's understanding of the natural world. It would have introduced him to the idea that natural forces could be explained through scientific principles rather than purely religious or superstitious beliefs.

Impact on His Life

1. Educational Influence:

- Inspiration for Learning: If Samuel had access to education or mentors who discussed scientific ideas, Franklin's discovery might have inspired him to pursue knowledge in related fields. Education in rural areas was often limited, but any exposure to scientific ideas could have encouraged him to learn more about science or mathematics.

- Scientific Curiosity: The discovery might have fostered a lifelong curiosity about scientific advancements and innovations, even if Samuel's immediate environment did not provide direct opportunities for scientific exploration.

2. Community and Practical Effects:

- Practical Impact: While the immediate practical impact of Franklin's discovery on a rural farm in Lisconnon might have been minimal, the broader implications of understanding electricity would eventually influence technological advancements and improvements in infrastructure.

- Cultural Impact: As scientific knowledge gradually spread, Samuel's community might have been exposed to new ideas and innovations that were influenced by Franklin's work, affecting various aspects of life, from safety measures to technological developments.

Summary:

As a 10-year-old in 1752, Samuel Allen would likely have been fascinated by the idea that lightning was a form of electricity, though the immediate impact on his rural life would have been limited. However, the discovery could have sparked his interest in science and contributed to a broader cultural awareness of scientific progress, influencing his perspective on the natural world and potentially inspiring future learning or curiosity about scientific advancements.

As an Esquire at 18 years old in 1760, Samuel Allen would have had a different perspective and set of opportunities during the early stages of the Industrial Revolution:

Reactions and Impacts

1. Curiosity and Influence:

- Interest in Technological Developments: Being from a privileged class, Samuel might have been particularly curious about technological advancements. He would have had access to information about new inventions and industrial processes, which could influence his views on progress and innovation.

- Potential Involvement in Industry: While his role as an Esquire primarily involved managing estates and local affairs, Samuel might have considered investing in or overseeing new industrial ventures or businesses, given his social and economic standing.

2. Economic and Social Impact:

- Economic Advantages: The Industrial Revolution brought significant economic changes. As an Esquire, Samuel would likely have had the means to benefit from these changes, possibly investing in emerging industries or new technologies that could increase his wealth and influence.

- Enhanced Social Position: Samuel's elevated social status would have positioned him well to capitalize on the economic opportunities presented by industrialization. His ability to leverage new technologies or investments might further enhance his social and economic standing.

3. Community and Lifestyle Changes:

- Impact on Estate Management: The changes brought about by the Industrial Revolution might have influenced how Samuel managed his estate. Innovations in agriculture and transportation could affect his landholdings, productivity, and the local economy.

- Cultural Shifts: Samuel would have witnessed shifts in community life and cultural practices due to industrialization. His position as an Esquire might have involved adapting to these changes in a way that preserved or enhanced his status within the community.

4. Personal and Family Impact:

- Career and Ambitions: Samuel's career ambitions would likely align with his social standing. He might have explored opportunities to invest in or oversee new industrial enterprises, contributing to his family's wealth and influence.

- Educational and Social Networking: His privileged background would provide him with access to education and social networks that could facilitate his involvement in the broader changes of the Industrial Revolution. This access would be crucial for staying informed and making strategic decisions.

Summary:

At 18, Samuel Allen, as an Esquire, would have been positioned to observe and potentially benefit from the early stages of the Industrial Revolution. His reaction would likely be one of keen interest and strategic adaptation, leveraging his social and economic advantages to capitalize on technological advancements and changes in industry. The Revolution would offer him opportunities to enhance his wealth, status, and influence, while also necessitating adjustments in how he managed his estate and engaged with the evolving community.

When Samuel Allen, Esq. was 38 years old, his only child, Samuel Allen, was born on February 14, 1780. This event would likely have had a profound emotional and social impact on him, given the importance of lineage and heirs in his status as an Esquire. Here's how the birth of his son might have affected him:

Emotional Impact:

- Joy and Pride: Samuel Allen, Esq., as an Esquire and landowner, would have felt immense pride and joy at the birth of a son to carry on the family name and legacy. During this period, having a male heir was especially important for securing family estates and maintaining social standing. The birth of his son would have been a significant milestone in his life.

- Sense of Purpose and Responsibility: With the birth of his only child, Samuel likely felt a renewed sense of purpose in providing for and raising his son to become a respectable figure in society. As an Esquire, there would have been an expectation to groom his son to take over family responsibilities, including property management, social duties, or entering a respected profession.

Impact on His Role as an Esquire:

- Securing the Family Legacy: In an era when family continuity was paramount, the birth of a son would have reassured Samuel Allen, Esq. that his family line would continue. It would have also encouraged him to focus on managing his estate, investments, or any legal responsibilities he had, knowing that one day his son would inherit these responsibilities.

- Education and Preparation for His Son: Samuel would have likely been highly invested in ensuring that his son received the best possible education. Being born into the family of an Esquire, young Samuel Allen would have had access to quality tutors or schools, setting the foundation for his later career as a medical doctor. Samuel, Esq. might have taken an active role in overseeing his son's education and ensuring he developed the skills necessary to succeed in society.

Social Status and Expectations:

- Increased Social Standing: The birth of a male heir would further cement Samuel Allen, Esq.'s standing in society, as producing a son was a key indicator of family success. He might have received congratulations from peers, and the event would likely have been celebrated in local society circles.

- Planning for His Son's Future: Samuel would have started thinking about his son's future, particularly in terms of what career or role in society would be appropriate. Given that his son eventually became a medical doctor, it's possible that Samuel, Esq. supported and encouraged a career in medicine, a highly respected profession at the time.

Long-Term Impact – Seeing His Son Become a Doctor:

- Pride in His Son's Achievements: Samuel Allen, Esq. would have been proud of his son's accomplishments in becoming a medical doctor. At the time, becoming a doctor required a great deal of education and was regarded as an esteemed profession. The fact that his son entered such a field likely reflected well on the family's status and reputation.

- Fulfillment of Legacy: For Samuel Allen, Esq., the fact that his son pursued a professional career would have been a source of fulfillment, knowing that his lineage was contributing to society in a meaningful way.

In summary, the birth of his only child would have been an immensely important event for Samuel Allen, Esq., bringing joy, pride, and a sense of security regarding his family's future. The fact that his son became a medical doctor would have only enhanced that pride, further affirming Samuel's success in raising a capable and respectable heir.

In 1783, when Samuel Allen, Esq. was 42 years old, the successful flight of the first hot air balloon by the Montgolfier brothers would likely have sparked significant interest and curiosity in him. Given his status as an Esquire, Samuel's reaction and the impact on his life could have been as follows:

Reactions and Impact

1. Curiosity and Interest:

- Intellectual Fascination: Samuel, with his privileged access to education and information, would likely have been intrigued by the technological innovation of ballooning. The concept of human flight and advancements in science and engineering would have captured his imagination.

- Social Prestige: Samuel might have seen the hot air balloon as a symbol of progress and innovation. Attending demonstrations or learning about the latest technological achievements could enhance his social status and reputation within his community.

2. Economic and Social Impact:

- Investment Opportunities: The successful flight of a hot air balloon could have sparked interest in new ventures. Samuel might have explored opportunities to invest in or support developments related to ballooning or other technological innovations.

- Networking and Influence: Being an Esquire, Samuel was likely connected to influential circles. His engagement with new technologies could have provided him with social and business connections, enhancing his influence and standing within his community.

3. Personal and Family Impact:

- Enhancing Status: Demonstrating an interest in cutting-edge technology could further establish Samuel as a forward-thinking and progressive figure in society. This would be beneficial for his social standing and personal reputation.

- Educational Influence: Samuel's children or younger family members might also be encouraged to explore scientific and technological pursuits, influenced by his interest in such advancements.

4. Lifestyle and Community Impact:

- Involvement in Innovations: Samuel might have been involved in discussions or local events related to technological advancements. His estate management could also see changes as a result of new innovations in transportation and communication.

- Cultural Engagement: The hot air balloon's success would have contributed to the broader cultural fascination with science and exploration. Samuel's involvement in or support of such interests could align him with contemporary cultural and intellectual movements.

Summary:

At 42 years old, Samuel Allen, Esq. would likely have been captivated by the successful flight of the hot air balloon. His reaction would involve intellectual curiosity and a potential interest in investment opportunities. The balloon's success could enhance his social standing and influence, provide networking opportunities, and contribute to his reputation as a progressive figure. His engagement with such innovations might also positively impact his family's and estate's fortunes, reflecting broader societal shifts in the late 18th century.

In 1783, when Samuel Allen, Esq. was 42 years old, the successful flight of the first hot air balloon by the Montgolfier brothers would likely have sparked significant interest and curiosity in him. Given his status as an Esquire, Samuel's reaction and the impact on his life could have been as follows:

Reactions and Impact

1. Curiosity and Interest:

- Intellectual Fascination: Samuel, with his privileged access to education and information, would likely have been intrigued by the technological innovation of ballooning. The concept of human flight and advancements in science and engineering would have captured his imagination.

- Social Prestige: Samuel might have seen the hot air balloon as a symbol of progress and innovation. Attending demonstrations or learning about the latest technological achievements could enhance his social status and reputation within his community.

2. Economic and Social Impact:

- Investment Opportunities: The successful flight of a hot air balloon could have sparked interest in new ventures. Samuel might have explored opportunities to invest in or support developments related to ballooning or other technological innovations.

- Networking and Influence: Being an Esquire, Samuel was likely connected to influential circles. His engagement with new technologies could have provided him with social and business connections, enhancing his influence and standing within his community.

3. Personal and Family Impact:

- Enhancing Status: Demonstrating an interest in cutting-edge technology could further establish Samuel as a forward-thinking and progressive figure in society. This would be beneficial for his social standing and personal reputation.

- Educational Influence: Samuel's children or younger family members might also be encouraged to explore scientific and technological pursuits, influenced by his interest in such advancements.

4. Lifestyle and Community Impact:

- Involvement in Innovations: Samuel might have been involved in discussions or local events related to technological advancements. His estate management could also see changes as a result of new innovations in transportation and communication.

- Cultural Engagement: The hot air balloon's success would have contributed to the broader cultural fascination with science and exploration. Samuel's involvement in or support of such interests could align him with contemporary cultural and intellectual movements.

Summary:

At 42 years old, Samuel Allen, Esq. would likely have been captivated by the successful flight of the hot air balloon. His reaction would involve intellectual curiosity and a potential interest in investment opportunities. The balloon's success could enhance his social standing and influence, provide networking opportunities, and contribute to his reputation as a progressive figure. His engagement with such innovations might also positively impact his family's and estate's fortunes, reflecting broader societal shifts in the late 18th century.

When Samuel Allen, Esq., was 58 years old in 1800, William Young designed shoes specifically for the left and right feet, a significant innovation in footwear. Prior to this, shoes were made in identical shapes for both feet, leading to discomfort and inefficiency. Here's how Samuel Allen, Esq., might have reacted to this invention and the effect it could have had on him:

Reaction to the Innovation:

- Curiosity and Interest: As a man of means and social standing, Samuel Allen, Esq., likely had an interest in advancements and inventions that could improve his quality of life. The design of shoes that better fit each foot would have caught his attention, as comfort and practicality in everyday items would have been valued by someone of his position.

- Skepticism or Pragmatism: Initially, Samuel may have been skeptical about the need for such a design, especially if he had lived his entire life wearing symmetrical shoes. However, as an Esquire, he would have likely been open to trying new innovations, especially those that might offer practical benefits.

Effect on His Daily Life:

- Increased Comfort: Upon adopting the use of these new shoes, Samuel would likely have noticed an immediate improvement in comfort. For someone in his position, who might have attended social functions, managed estates, or traveled regularly, more comfortable footwear would have made his daily activities easier and less fatiguing.

- Symbol of Modernity and Status: Having shoes specifically designed for the left and right feet would have been seen as a modern, sophisticated advancement. As an Esquire, Samuel likely prided himself on being at the forefront of modern trends. Owning or wearing these shoes could have become a subtle way of demonstrating his awareness of and participation in contemporary innovations.

Social Impact:

- Influence on Peers: Samuel, being a man of influence and status in his community, might have played a role in spreading awareness of this new shoe design among his peers. His adoption of such an innovation could have encouraged others in his social circle to do the same, further promoting the shift toward more practical and comfortable footwear.

- Access to High-Quality Goods: As a man of wealth, Samuel would have had access to the finest materials and skilled artisans, meaning he could easily afford these new shoes. This would have reinforced his lifestyle, where quality and luxury were important aspects of his social standing.

Health and Longevity:

- Physical Well-being: As someone in his late 50s, Samuel would have been more attuned to the physical discomforts that come with age. The improved design of shoes tailored to each foot might have contributed to better posture and reduced strain on his feet, especially during long walks or prolonged periods of standing. This innovation could have had a subtle but positive impact on his overall health, especially as mobility became more important with age.

Conclusion:

Overall, Samuel Allen, Esq. would have likely welcomed the invention of left- and right-foot-specific shoes, finding them a useful and comfortable improvement in daily life. The innovation may have also served as a symbol of his modern sensibilities and status, while offering practical benefits that would have enhanced his comfort and health as he aged.

When Samuel Allen, Esq. was 65 years old in 1807, Robert Fulton's successful launch of the first commercial steamship would have been a groundbreaking event. This innovation marked the beginning of a new era in transportation and trade. Samuel's reaction and the effect it had on him would have been shaped by his status, wealth, and the broader societal context in Ireland at the time.

Reaction to the Steamship:

- Fascination with Innovation: As an educated and influential man, Samuel Allen, Esq. would likely have been fascinated by the news of such a monumental technological breakthrough. The steamship was a symbol of progress, innovation, and the potential for increased efficiency in transportation, particularly for trade and travel. Samuel, living through the early stages of the Industrial Revolution, would have been aware of how new technologies were shaping the world.

- Pragmatic Interest: As an Esquire, he may have had a keen interest in how steamships could impact economic activities, particularly in Ireland, where trade by sea was critical. The steamship's ability to travel faster and more reliably than wind-powered vessels would have piqued his interest, especially if he had any connections to business or trade.

- Skepticism or Caution: Although intrigued by the steamship, Samuel might have harbored some skepticism about how quickly this new technology would become widespread. Given that he was from an older generation, there could have been some hesitation to immediately embrace such a drastic change in transportation technology.

Effect on His Life:

- Impact on Travel: Although it is unlikely that Samuel, at 65 years old, would have personally taken many long sea voyages, the advent of steam-powered ships opened up new possibilities for faster and more reliable travel, both domestically and internationally. If he were involved in any land or estate management, faster transportation of goods or personal travel could have benefited him directly or indirectly through enhanced business opportunities.

- Economic Implications: Samuel, being a landowner and likely having a role in local economics, could have seen the steamship as a means of stimulating trade, both domestically within Ireland and with neighboring countries. The increased efficiency of transporting goods across the seas could have improved commerce, lowering costs and improving the availability of products. As an Esquire, he would have been concerned with the prosperity of his local economy, and the steamship might have offered a way to promote growth.

- Political and Social Impacts: The steamship represented progress and industrial advancement, which were central themes of the time. Samuel, being a man of status, might have been aware of how new technologies like the steamship were influencing global power dynamics, particularly in the context of Britain's growing empire. Ireland, being part of the United Kingdom at the time, could have benefitted from the expanding global trade routes made possible by steam-powered vessels.

- Impact on the Future of Ireland: For Samuel, living in a period of significant change, the steamship would have represented the future. He may have considered how this new technology could change life for future generations in Ireland, possibly making the country more interconnected with global commerce and enhancing Ireland's strategic importance in trade routes. If Samuel had any foresight, he would have recognized that steamships would eventually play a major role in changing the pace and scope of economic development in Ireland.

Conclusion:

Overall, Samuel Allen, Esq. would have likely reacted to the invention of the commercial steamship with fascination and cautious optimism. The steamship symbolized the technological advances of the age, and as a man who would have seen the effects of the Industrial Revolution on everyday life, he would have understood the potential benefits for transportation, commerce, and communication. While it may not have had a direct and immediate effect on his daily life at 65 years old, the long-term implications of the steamship would have been profound for society, and Samuel would likely have been aware of its significance for future generations.

Samuel Allen, Esq., at 73 years old when Napoleon was defeated and exiled in 1815, would likely have reacted with a combination of relief and reflection. Napoleon's downfall marked the end of a long period of instability in Europe, and its effects would have been felt across Ireland, including by Samuel.

Reaction to Napoleon's Defeat and Exile:

- Relief and Stability: As an Esquire and a man of status in Ireland, Samuel would have welcomed the end of the Napoleonic Wars. The years of conflict had caused uncertainty and disruption across Europe, affecting trade, politics, and the economy. The defeat of Napoleon would have likely brought Samuel a sense of relief, as it signified a return to peace and the stabilization of Europe. Ireland, like other parts of the United Kingdom, had been involved in the war effort, so the cessation of hostilities would have been viewed positively.

- Pride in Britain's Victory: Samuel, as a subject of the British Crown, would likely have felt pride in Britain's role in defeating Napoleon. The British military, under leaders such as the Duke of Wellington, had played a central part in the final defeat of Napoleon at the Battle of Waterloo. Samuel may have admired the military success of his nation, and the victory would have reinforced the global dominance of the British Empire.

- Political and Social Reflections: Napoleon's wars had triggered political upheaval across Europe, and many in the British Isles, including Ireland, feared the spread of revolutionary ideas. Samuel, as part of the upper class, would have been concerned about how these ideas could destabilize the traditional order. With Napoleon defeated and exiled, the threat of revolution spreading further into the British Isles seemed diminished. This would have offered Samuel and others of his social standing a renewed sense of security regarding their position in society.

Effects on Samuel's Life:

- Economic Impact: The end of the Napoleonic Wars meant the removal of blockades and restrictions that had disrupted trade for over a decade. Samuel, as an Esquire, likely had interests in agriculture or land, and the return to peace could have meant an improvement in trade and commerce. With Europe returning to stability, there would have been new opportunities for Irish exports, and Samuel may have benefitted from a growing economy as peacetime returned.

- Social Impact: The Napoleonic era had been a time of great tension and fear, especially for the upper classes, as revolutionary ideas had spread throughout Europe. Napoleon's defeat signified the end of these upheavals, and Samuel might have viewed this as a return to normalcy. With peace restored, social life and local governance could stabilize, and Samuel's role as an Esquire would likely return to more typical, pre-war concerns. The end of war also often brings a sense of renewed community and optimism, which Samuel may have felt in his own circles.

- Political Landscape in Ireland: While Napoleon's defeat restored stability to Europe, Ireland remained a part of the United Kingdom, where the effects of the Act of Union (1801) were still being felt. Samuel, living in this post-union Ireland, would have been affected by the political landscape shaped by British control. The defeat of Napoleon reinforced Britain's global dominance, but the lingering issues of Irish self-governance and Catholic emancipation were still unresolved. Depending on Samuel's political views, he may have seen the defeat of Napoleon as either an opportunity for Ireland to strengthen its ties with Britain or a continuation of British dominance that hindered Irish independence.

Conclusion:

Samuel Allen, Esq. would have reacted to Napoleon's defeat and exile with relief and perhaps a sense of pride in Britain's military success. The return of peace in Europe likely brought stability and economic recovery, which would have had positive effects on Samuel's personal and social life as an Esquire in Ireland. Though the political situation in Ireland remained complex, Napoleon's defeat marked the end of an era of war and uncertainty, ushering in a period of peace that would have influenced Samuel's later years.

At 75 years old, when the bicycle (or "draisine" as it was originally known) was invented in 1817 by Karl Drais, Samuel Allen, Esq., would have likely reacted with a mix of curiosity and mild amusement.

Reaction to the Bicycle's Invention:

- Curiosity about Innovation: As an elderly man of status, Samuel might have been intrigued by this new invention, which allowed for personal transportation in a way that didn't require a horse. He may have viewed it as an interesting innovation, reflecting the growing wave of new technologies emerging during the early 19th century. However, given his age, it is unlikely that Samuel would have seen much practical use for it in his own life, but he might have appreciated its potential for others, particularly younger people.

- Skepticism or Amusement: As someone who grew up in a world where horse-drawn carriages or simply walking were the main forms of transportation, Samuel might have found the idea of a human-powered, two-wheeled vehicle a little amusing or impractical, at least at first glance. It is also possible that he viewed it as a novelty rather than something that would become a widespread means of transportation in the future.

Effect on Samuel's Life:

- Limited Direct Impact: Given his age and social standing, the bicycle's invention would likely not have had a significant direct effect on Samuel's life. As an Esquire, he would have had access to horses and carriages, so the need for a bicycle would have been minimal. Additionally, the early form of the bicycle, the draisine, required significant physical effort to operate, making it less appealing for someone of Samuel's age.

- Impact on Society: While Samuel might not have personally used a bicycle, he could have observed how it began to change local society. The bicycle provided a new mode of transport for the general population, particularly for those who couldn't afford a horse. This development could have been interesting to Samuel as it opened up a new form of mobility for ordinary people. It would have been a small but notable step in the increasing technological innovations of the time.

- Social Mobility and Accessibility: While Samuel likely wouldn't have needed a bicycle for transportation, he might have seen its potential in giving more people access to quicker transport.

This could have had an impact on how people moved between towns and villages, making it easier for tradesmen, laborers, and others to get to places that had previously been difficult to reach on foot.

Conclusion:

Samuel Allen, Esq. would likely have viewed the invention of the bicycle with curiosity, recognizing it as part of the ongoing wave of technological progress, but it would have had little direct impact on his life. He might have appreciated its benefits for younger and more active individuals or those without access to horses, but as a man of advanced age and means, his personal reliance on traditional modes of transportation would likely have remained unchanged. The bicycle would symbolize to him the rapid changes of his time, highlighting how innovation was transforming society, even as he entered his final years.

When Samuel Allen, Esq. passed away on May 4, 1820, at the age of 78, his life would have reflected a combination of dignity, respectability, and adaptation to the social and political changes of late 18th and early 19th century Ireland. Here's what his life might have been like in his final years:

Social Status and Lifestyle:

- Esquire Status: As an Esquire, Samuel held a prominent position in society. Esquires were often landowners, respected members of their communities, and had influence in local affairs. Samuel would have likely enjoyed the privileges of his class, living in relative comfort, possibly on an estate in Lisconnon. His status would have afforded him the best available amenities for his time.

- Respect and Influence: By the time of his death, Samuel would have been a respected elder in his community. His role as an Esquire likely meant that he played a part in local governance or legal matters, providing leadership and judgment on important local issues. Even in his later years, his opinions would have been valued, and his presence at community events or meetings would have carried weight.

Family Life:

- Marriage and Fatherhood: Samuel was married to Frances, and their only child, Samuel Allen Jr., was born in 1780. His son grew up to become a medical doctor, a prestigious profession. Samuel would have been proud of his son's achievements, as having a son in such a respectable and educated field would have brought further honor to the family. By 1820, his son would have been a well-established figure, possibly living nearby or visiting often, providing Samuel with the comfort of knowing his lineage and name would continue.

- Family Legacy: As Samuel aged, he would have been focused on ensuring that his family legacy remained intact. He may have spent his later years organizing his estate, securing his land, and ensuring that his family would continue to prosper after his passing.

Health and Old Age:

- Physical Health: At 78 years old, Samuel was elderly by the standards of the time. While life expectancy in the early 19th century was much lower, those who reached Samuel's age would often deal with age-related health issues, such as arthritis, decreased mobility, or general frailty. However, given his status and wealth, Samuel would have had access to the best medical care available at the time, possibly from his own son, Samuel Jr., the doctor.

- Reflections on Life: In his final years, Samuel may have spent time reflecting on the dramatic changes he had witnessed during his life. From the Industrial Revolution to political upheavals in Ireland, including the 1798 Rebellion, Samuel had seen a world in flux. While his own life was relatively stable due to his class, the broader societal changes would not have escaped his notice.

Political and Social Environment:

- Post-Rebellion Ireland: Samuel passed away only 22 years after the Irish Rebellion of 1798, a significant event in Irish history that aimed to end British rule and establish an independent Ireland. While Samuel, as an Esquire, may have been more conservative and loyal to the Crown, the rebellion would have affected the social and political climate in which he lived. The years following the rebellion saw increased tension between Irish Catholics and Protestants, and the Act of Union in 1801 had united Ireland with Britain. Samuel likely lived through a period of uncertainty and adjustment in the wake of these political changes.

- Changing Economy: The Industrial Revolution had been underway for decades, and Samuel would have witnessed its effects on Irish society. While rural areas like Lisconnon may not have been as industrialized as urban centers, there was likely a growing awareness of the changing economy, with increasing mechanization and shifts in labor patterns. As a landowner, Samuel would have been mindful of how these changes impacted agriculture, trade, and the local workforce.

Religious Life:

- Religious Observance: Ireland in the early 19th century was deeply religious, and Samuel's life would have been shaped by this. While we do not know his specific religious affiliation, it is likely that, as an Esquire, he was either Anglican or Presbyterian, both of which were common among the upper classes in Ulster. Regular church attendance, participation in religious festivals, and community leadership roles in the church would have been significant aspects of his life.

Death and Burial:

- Community Mourning: Samuel's death at the age of 78 would have been marked with respect by his family and community. As a well-regarded figure, his passing likely led to a formal funeral service attended by family, friends, and neighbors.

Given his Esquire status, his funeral would have been more elaborate than those of lower classes, with a procession and burial in a prominent local cemetery, Dervock, where he is interred alongside his wife, Frances, and their son, Samuel Jr.

- Burial in Dervock: Dervock, where he is buried, is a small town with historical significance, and it would have been fitting for someone of Samuel's standing to be buried in a well-maintained, local cemetery. His grave would have served as a symbol of the family's prestige and legacy in the community.

Conclusion:

When Samuel Allen, Esq., passed away in 1820, he likely did so as a respected and accomplished figure in his community. His life had been shaped by a rapidly changing world, from the Industrial Revolution to political unrest in Ireland, and he had adapted to these changes while maintaining his family's status and ensuring their legacy. His family, particularly his son Samuel Jr., would have continued to honor his memory and the values he upheld.

FRANCES (HIGGINSON) ALLEN[8]

Frances Higginson, born in 1735, the future wife of Samuel Allen, Esq., likely had the appearance and style typical of an upper-class woman of her time and station. While her specific physical characteristics are unknown, we can infer certain aspects of her appearance based on her class, the era, and common traits of women in her region.

Physical Appearance:

- Complexion: Given that Frances was from the upper class, she likely had a pale complexion, as fair skin was highly prized in the 18th century, especially among those who could afford to avoid outdoor labor. Pale skin was seen as a sign of wealth and refinement.

- Hair: Women of the time often had their natural hair color emphasized by fashionable wigs or elaborate hairstyles. If she followed the trends of the day, Frances might have had light to dark brown hair, possibly curled or powdered white, as was popular in the mid-18th century. Wigs were common, and powdered hairstyles were a status symbol, so it's possible Frances would have styled her hair elaborately for special occasions.

- Eyes: While there is no record of her specific eye color, blue, green, or brown eyes were all common in Ireland. As an upper-class woman, her eyes would have been framed by carefully applied cosmetics, enhancing their shape and size.

- Build: Frances would likely have had a figure that was shaped by the fashion of the time. The 18th-century ideal was a fuller, more rounded figure, with a narrow waist. Corsets were commonly worn, so she may have had a pronounced hourglass shape, at least when dressed in her formal attire.

Fashion and Style:

- Clothing: As a woman of status, Frances would have worn elegant dresses made from fine fabrics such as silk, satin, and wool. Her clothing would have been designed to reflect her social standing, with rich colors like deep blues, greens, or burgundies that were available only to those who could afford high-quality dyes.

In the 18th century, women's dresses often had fitted bodices with wide skirts supported by petticoats and hoops, particularly for formal occasions. The neckline was usually low, and the sleeves were often elbow-length with ruffles or lace. Her day-to-day attire may have been simpler but still reflected the style and grace of her class.

- Accessories: Frances would have likely worn accessories such as lace caps, gloves, and jewelry. Pearls or precious stones were popular among the upper class, and she may have adorned herself with these to signify her wealth and position. Brooches, necklaces, and rings were common adornments for women of her status.

- Grooming: As someone from a prominent family, Frances would have taken care of her personal appearance, as grooming was important for women of the time. She would have likely used simple cosmetics, such as powders for her face, rouges for her cheeks, and perhaps a touch of kohl to darken her eyebrows or lashes. Perfumes or scented oils were also popular among upper-class women to enhance their appeal.

Overall Appearance:

Frances Higginson likely presented herself with the grace and elegance expected of a woman of her social rank. Her appearance, whether at social gatherings, church, or around her home, would have been carefully crafted to reflect her family's status. Though we do not know her specific traits, her fashion, grooming, and accessories would have been typical of an affluent woman in mid-18th century Ireland.

In 1739, when Frances Higginson was 4 years old, the Methodist Church was founded by John Wesley. As a young child from an affluent family, the direct impact of the Methodist movement on her life would likely have been minimal, but it could have influenced her surroundings and community in several ways:

Impact on Frances's Early Life:

1. Social and Religious Environment:

- Religious Influence: Although Frances was very young at the time, her family's religious environment could have been influenced by the rise of Methodism. If her family were part of or influenced by the Evangelical movement, it might have shaped her upbringing and the values she was taught as she grew older.

- Community Impact: In broader terms, Methodism began to gain followers and influence in various communities. This could have affected local social norms, charitable activities, and community values in Ireland, potentially reaching her family's circle.

2. Educational and Moral Values:

- Moral Teachings: The Methodist Church emphasized personal piety, social justice, and education. As Frances grew up, the Methodist influence on educational and moral values might have indirectly affected her environment, even if she was not personally involved with the church.

- Charitable Works: Methodists were known for their charitable work and social reform. If her family was involved in or influenced by these activities, it might have affected their social standing and community interactions.

3. Family Influence:

- Parental Views: If Frances's parents were influenced by the Methodist movement, this could have shaped her early education and values. They might have supported Methodist charitable activities or embraced its teachings in their household.

In summary, while the founding of Methodism in 1739 likely had a limited direct impact on Frances as a young child, it could have influenced her life indirectly through changes in the religious and social climate of her time. As she grew older, the broader influence of Methodism on societal values and community life could have shaped her experiences and the environment she was part of.

In 1752, when Frances Higginson was 17 years old, Benjamin Franklin's discovery that lightning is electrical would have been a significant and intriguing development. Here's how it might have impacted her and how she might have reacted:

Reaction and Impact:

1. Scientific Curiosity:

- Interest in Science: As a young woman of 17, Frances might have been intrigued by the scientific advancements of her time. The concept of electricity being related to lightning would have been a fascinating and somewhat revolutionary idea, potentially sparking her curiosity about science and natural phenomena.

2. Intellectual Climate:

- Educational Influence: Depending on her educational background and social circle, Frances might have been exposed to discussions about Franklin's discoveries through local intellectual or scientific gatherings. This might have influenced her intellectual interests or her views on scientific progress.

3. Practical Implications:

- Safety and Technology: The practical implications of Franklin's discovery, such as improved lightning rods, could have impacted her family and community by increasing safety measures against lightning strikes. This would be a positive, practical outcome of the discovery in everyday life.

4. Cultural Impact:

- Social Discussions: The discovery might have been a topic of conversation among the educated and affluent circles in her community. As a member of such a circle, Frances might have heard about the discovery from family or social acquaintances, which could have shaped her views on science and its role in society.

5. Personal Reflection:

- Impact on Beliefs: If Frances had an interest in science or was involved in discussions about technological progress, Franklin's discovery might have influenced her thinking about the natural world and the capabilities of human understanding and innovation.

In summary, while the direct impact of Franklin's discovery on Frances would depend on her personal interests and social environment, it is likely that she would have been aware of and intrigued by this groundbreaking scientific achievement. It could have influenced her intellectual environment and contributed to her understanding of the world around her.

When Frances Higginson was 25 years old in 1760, the Industrial Revolution was beginning to take shape in Britain. Here's how she might have reacted and been affected by this transformative period:

Reaction and Impact:

1. Social and Economic Changes:

- Economic Shifts: The Industrial Revolution marked the beginning of significant changes in industry and economy. Frances, coming from a background of higher social standing as the future wife of Samuel Allen, Esq, might have observed these changes primarily through economic shifts affecting her family's wealth and social status. The rise of industrialization could have led to changes in trade, production, and the overall economic landscape that impacted her life indirectly.

2. Technological Advancements:

- Awareness of Innovation: Frances might have been aware of new technologies and innovations, such as improvements in machinery, textiles, and transportation. These advancements could have influenced her daily life, including the availability of goods, fashion, and perhaps even the way her family managed their estate.

3. Social Impact:

- Social Changes: The social changes brought about by the Industrial Revolution, including shifts in labor and class structures, might have been evident in her community. As someone in a higher social class, she might have seen both opportunities and challenges arising from these changes, such as the growth of new social classes and changes in societal roles.

4. Lifestyle Adjustments:

- Domestic Life: Industrial advancements could have led to changes in domestic life and household management. Improvements in technology and transportation might have made certain tasks easier or changed the way household goods were obtained and used. Frances might have experienced these changes in her home life.

5. Philanthropic or Social Interests:

- Awareness and Action: As a woman of higher social standing, Frances might have been involved in philanthropic efforts or social causes related to the impacts of industrialization, such as improving working conditions or supporting social reform initiatives. The societal changes brought about by the Industrial Revolution might have influenced her social interests and activities.

In summary, while Frances's direct involvement in the Industrial Revolution would have been limited by her social position, she would have been impacted by the broader social and economic changes it brought. Her reaction would likely reflect both curiosity and adaptation to the evolving world around her, with changes affecting her household, community, and social status.

When Frances Higginson was 45 years old and gave birth to her only child, Samuel Allen, on February 14, 1780, the following reactions and impacts on her life would have been likely:

Reaction:

1. Joy and Fulfillment:

- Emotional Impact: At 45, having a child might have brought significant joy and fulfillment to Frances, especially if she had longed for a child or had faced previous challenges in conceiving. The birth of her only child could have been a deeply cherished event, enhancing her sense of purpose and connection within her family.

2. Health Concerns:

- Health Risks: Given her age, Frances would have been acutely aware of the increased health risks associated with childbirth. The birth of her child at an older age might have been a challenging experience, both physically and emotionally. She would likely have been cautious and attentive to both her own health and the health of her newborn.

Impact:

1. Family Dynamics:

- New Responsibilities: As a new mother in her mid-40s, Frances would have had to adjust her daily life to accommodate the needs of her infant. This would include changes to her routine, increased responsibilities, and potentially greater reliance on household help.

2. Social Perception:

- Social Reactions: In the 18th century, having a child at a later age might have been uncommon and could have drawn attention or comments within her social circle. Despite this, her position as an Esquire's wife might have afforded her support and understanding from her peers.

3. Inheritance and Legacy:

- Focus on Heir: The birth of Samuel Allen, her only child, would have placed significant importance on ensuring his well-being and future. Frances might have been particularly concerned with securing his inheritance and preparing him to carry on the family legacy.

4. Impact on Marriage:

- Marital Bond: The birth of a child could have strengthened her relationship with her husband, Samuel Allen, Esq. It might have also added a new dimension to their marriage, as they focused on raising and providing for their son.

5. Personal Reflection:

- Life Changes: At 45, Frances might have experienced a period of personal reflection and adjustment as she embraced motherhood later in life. Her perspective on family, life, and her own role would likely have evolved with the arrival of her son.

In summary, Frances's reaction to the birth of Samuel Allen at age 45 would have been a mix of joy, fulfillment, and concern due to the health risks associated with late childbirth. The arrival of her son would have significantly impacted her family dynamics, social standing, and personal life, marking a notable and transformative chapter in her life.

When Frances Higginson was 49 years old and the first successful flight of a hot air balloon occurred in 1784, her reaction and the impact on her life would likely have been as follows:

Reaction:

1. Curiosity and Fascination:

- Interest in Innovation: Frances would likely have been intrigued by the advancement of hot air ballooning, given its novelty and the scientific progress it represented. As someone living in the late 18th century, she might have found the idea of human flight both exciting and impressive.

2. Social Awareness:

- Conversation Topic: The successful flight of the hot air balloon would have been a significant event, likely discussed widely in newspapers and among social circles. Frances, being part of a well-to-do family, would have had access to information about such advancements and might have engaged in conversations about the implications of this new technology.

Impact:

1. Perspective on Technology:

- Admiration for Progress: The development of hot air ballooning would contribute to Frances's admiration for technological and scientific progress. It might have reinforced her awareness of the rapid changes occurring in the world and the possibilities they brought.

2. Influence on Social Standing:

- Prestige: Being aware of and possibly discussing new technological advancements like hot air ballooning could reflect positively on Frances's social standing. It would demonstrate her engagement with contemporary developments and her interest in the broader world beyond her immediate surroundings.

3. Personal Reflection:

- Reflection on Change: At 49, Frances might have reflected on the changes and progress she had witnessed throughout her life. The hot air balloon's success could have symbolized the broader shift towards innovation and modernity, prompting her to consider her place within this evolving landscape.

4. Legacy and Inspiration:

- Legacy Thoughts: Although the impact of the hot air balloon on her daily life would have been indirect, it might have inspired thoughts about her own legacy and the future for her son, Samuel Allen. It could have contributed to her sense of the importance of progress and innovation for future generations.

In summary, Frances Higginson's reaction to the successful flight of the hot air balloon in 1784 would likely have been one of curiosity and admiration, reflecting the broader societal excitement for new technologies. The event would have influenced her perspective on progress and innovation, contributing to her awareness of the transformative changes occurring in her time.

When Frances Higginson was 63 years old during the Irish Rebellion of 1798, her reaction and the impact on her life would likely have been shaped by several factors:

Reaction:

1. Concern and Distress:

- Awareness of Unrest: Frances, being from a prominent family and having likely been well-informed about political and social issues, would have been concerned about the upheaval and violence associated with the rebellion. The rebellion involved significant conflict and social unrest, which would have been alarming for her.

2. Emotional Response:

- Sympathy or Distress: Depending on her political views and her connection to the affected regions, she might have felt sympathy for the suffering of those involved or distress at the instability and violence. As someone of her status, she might have also been anxious about the potential impact on her family and property.

3. Social Impact:

- Discussion Topic: The rebellion would have been a major topic of discussion within social circles. Frances would likely have participated in or been privy to conversations about the causes and consequences of the rebellion, reflecting the broader concerns of her time.

Impact:

1. Personal Safety and Security:

- Increased Precautions: The rebellion might have led Frances to take extra precautions to ensure the safety and security of her family and property. This could include increased vigilance or adjustments to her daily routines to mitigate the risks posed by the unrest.

2. Social and Political Perspectives:

- Shift in Views: The events of the rebellion might have influenced Frances's views on political and social issues. She could have gained new insights into the causes of social unrest and the challenges faced by different groups in Ireland.

3. Emotional Impact:

- Sense of Vulnerability: The rebellion could have made Frances feel more vulnerable, reflecting on the fragility of social order and the impact of political conflict on everyday life. This emotional response might have influenced her outlook on stability and governance.

4. Legacy Considerations:

- Concerns for Family: As a mother, Frances would have been concerned about the future of her son, Samuel Allen, and any potential impact the rebellion might have on his prospects and safety. She might have focused on securing his well-being and ensuring that he was prepared to navigate the uncertain times.

In summary, Frances Higginson's reaction to the Irish Rebellion of 1798 would likely have been one of concern and distress, influenced by the social and political upheaval of the time. The impact on her life would have included increased vigilance for her safety and property, a shift in her perspectives on political and social issues, and emotional stress due to the instability and violence of the rebellion.

When Frances Higginson was 65 years old in 1800, and William Young designed his shoes for the left and right foot, her reaction and the impact on her life would likely have been influenced by several factors:

Reaction:

1. Interest in Innovation:

- Curiosity: Frances, being a person of her time, might have been curious about new inventions and innovations. The design of shoes specifically for the left and right foot would have been seen as a significant improvement in comfort and practicality, which could have intrigued her.

2. Appreciation for Practical Solutions:

- Positive Reaction: Given her age and experience, Frances would likely have appreciated practical solutions that improved everyday life. The idea of shoes designed for each foot would have been a welcome advancement over the more rudimentary footwear of earlier times.

3. Social Awareness:

- Discussion and Networking: As a person of social standing, Frances might have discussed the new shoe design within her social circles. Innovations like this often become topics of conversation among the upper classes, particularly when they promise improved quality of life.

Impact:

1. Improved Comfort:

- Personal Use: If Frances adopted these new shoes, she would have experienced the increased comfort and better fit that came with them. This improvement would have been particularly beneficial given her age, as comfort in footwear becomes increasingly important over time.

2. Influence on Lifestyle:

- Adoption of New Trends: The availability of more comfortable and practical footwear could have influenced Frances's lifestyle choices. She might have been more inclined to embrace new trends that offered better quality of life.

3. Legacy and Status:

- Affluence and Fashion: As an esquire's wife, Frances's choice to adopt or advocate for new, innovative products could have reflected positively on her status. Being seen as someone who embraces progress and innovation might have enhanced her social standing.

In summary, Frances Higginson's reaction to William Young's shoe design in 1800 would likely have been one of interest and appreciation, given the practical benefits of the innovation. The impact on her life would have included improved comfort, a positive influence on her lifestyle, and potentially an enhancement of her social status through the adoption of new trends.

When Frances Higginson was 72 years old in 1807, and Robert Fulton built the first commercially successful steamship, her reaction and the effect on her life would likely have been shaped by several factors:

Reaction:

1. Amazement and Curiosity:

- Fascination: Frances would likely have been amazed by the technological advancement represented by the steamship. Given her age and the dramatic changes she would have witnessed throughout her life, she might have been particularly intrigued by this new mode of transportation.

2. Interest in Progress:

- Engagement with Innovation: Frances, as a person of social standing, might have taken an active interest in technological progress. She could have followed the developments surrounding the steamship, appreciating its potential to revolutionize travel and commerce.

Impact:

1. Broader Impact on Society:

- Awareness of Change: While Frances might not have personally used the steamship due to her age and the geographical constraints of her life, she would have been aware of its impact on society. The steamship would have started to change trade routes, commerce, and travel patterns, which would be significant topics of discussion.

2. Cultural and Social Influence:

- Social Conversations: As an esquire's wife, Frances would have likely engaged in conversations about the steamship within her social circles. The innovation would have been a prominent topic among the upper classes, reflecting changes in societal progress and technological advancements.

3. Indirect Benefits:

- Economic Impact: Although Frances might not have directly benefited from steamship travel, the economic growth stimulated by such innovations could have indirectly improved her quality of life. Increased trade and improved transportation networks could contribute to overall prosperity, affecting everything from market availability to social events.

4. Legacy and Modernization:

- Perspective on Progress: Frances would have been a witness to the modernization of the world. Her awareness of such innovations would reflect her lifetime of experiencing significant changes, from earlier technological advancements to the steamship era.

In summary, Frances Higginson's reaction to Robert Fulton's steamship in 1807 would likely have been one of amazement and curiosity. While she might not have directly interacted with the new technology, the broader societal changes it represented and its impact on commerce and travel would have influenced her understanding of the modernizing world.

At 80 years old, Frances Higginson would have experienced the defeat and exile of Napoleon in 1815 as a significant historical event, with various potential reactions and effects:

Reaction:

1. Historical Context:

- Awareness of Importance: Frances, having lived through much of the 18th and early 19th centuries, would likely have understood the importance of Napoleon's defeat. As someone with a sophisticated background, she might have followed the political and military developments closely.

2. Emotional Response:

- Relief or Concern: Depending on her personal or familial connections to the ongoing European conflicts, she could have felt relief at the end of a turbulent period or concern about the potential aftermath and stability of Europe.

3. Discussion and Reflection:

- Social Conversations: As a member of the upper class, Frances would have discussed the event with her peers. It would have been a topic of significant conversation in her social circles, reflecting on how the shift in European power dynamics might affect global politics and trade.

Effect:

1. Political Impact:

- Influence on European Politics: While Frances might not have been directly affected by the political shifts in Europe, the stability or instability resulting from Napoleon's defeat could influence international relations and trade, which would, in turn, impact her social and economic environment.

2. Economic Implications:

- Indirect Effects: The outcome of the Napoleonic Wars would affect global trade routes and economic stability. As a member of the upper class, Frances might experience indirect effects through changes in commerce, investment opportunities, and social dynamics.

3. Cultural and Social Influence:

- Reflection on Modernity: The defeat of Napoleon marked the end of an era of intense military conflict in Europe. Frances would reflect on the changes she had witnessed throughout her lifetime, including the rise and fall of significant historical figures and the broader implications for societal progress.

4. Legacy and Historical Perspective:

- Understanding Historical Impact: At her advanced age, Frances would likely consider how the end of Napoleon's reign fit into the broader historical narrative she had lived through. This perspective could shape her view on the evolution of European and global history.

In summary, Frances Higginson, at 80 years old, would have reacted to Napoleon's defeat with a mix of historical awareness and personal reflection. While the direct impact on her life might have been minimal, the broader political and economic changes resulting from Napoleon's exile would have influenced her understanding of global events and the era she had witnessed.

At 82 years old, Frances Higginson would have had a range of reactions to the invention of the bicycle in 1817:

Reaction:

1. Curiosity and Interest:
- New Innovation: Frances might have been intrigued by the bicycle as a new technological innovation. Given her background and experience with significant technological advancements in her lifetime, she would likely have been curious about this new form of transportation.

2. Practical Consideration:
- Utility and Feasibility: At her advanced age, Frances might have considered the bicycle's practicality for daily life. While she may not have used it herself, she would likely have appreciated its potential benefits for younger generations.

3. Social and Cultural Implications:
- Impact on Society: Frances might have discussed the bicycle with her family and peers, reflecting on how it could change transportation, travel, and social dynamics. She might have seen it as part of the broader progress in technology and its potential to influence everyday life.

Effect:

1. Perspective on Progress:
- Historical Context: Frances would have viewed the bicycle within the context of the technological progress she had seen throughout her lifetime. It would be another example of how innovation continues to shape society and improve daily life.

2. Legacy and Modernization:
- Witnessing Change: Frances's experience with technological advancements like the steamship and industrial innovations would make her appreciate the bicycle as part of ongoing modernization. She would likely reflect on how each new invention contributes to the evolution of transportation and lifestyle.

3. Influence on Family:
- Legacy Impact: If her family members were interested in or used bicycles, Frances might have seen their enthusiasm as a sign of

continuing progress. Her grandchildren or younger relatives might have adopted the bicycle, and she would observe its role in their lives.

Overall, at 82 years old, Frances Higginson would have reacted with a mix of curiosity, reflection on technological progress, and practical considerations. The bicycle, while perhaps not directly impacting her daily life, would be seen as part of the broader wave of innovation transforming the world around her.

At 85 years old, Frances Higginson would have been deeply affected by the death of her husband, Samuel Allen, Esq., on May 4, 1820. Here's how his death might have impacted her:

Emotional Impact:

1. Deep Grief:

- Loss of a Life Partner: The death of Samuel, her husband of many years, would have been a profound emotional blow. Having shared a long life together, Frances would likely experience significant grief and sadness at his passing.

2. Reflection on Life:

- Memories and Legacy: Frances might spend time reflecting on their life together, their shared experiences, and their accomplishments. Samuel's death would likely prompt her to think about their life's work and their family legacy.

Practical and Social Impact:

1. Adjustment to Loss:

- Daily Life: At her advanced age, Frances would need to adjust to life without Samuel's support and companionship. This could involve changes in her daily routine and responsibilities, particularly if Samuel had been involved in managing their estate or household affairs.

2. Family Dynamics:

- Support System: Frances might rely more on her family for support and companionship. The dynamics within the family would likely shift, and she would need to adapt to her new role within the family structure.

Health and Well-being:

1. Health Concerns:

- Physical and Emotional Strain: The stress and emotional strain of losing her husband could potentially impact Frances's health. At her age, coping with such a significant loss might lead to physical and emotional challenges.

2. Dependence on Others:

- Increased Vulnerability: With the death of her husband, Frances might become more dependent on her family or caregivers for physical and emotional support, especially if Samuel had been actively involved in her care or daily life.

Legacy and Remembrance:

1. End of an Era:

- Final Years: Frances would likely consider her remaining years in the context of Samuel's legacy and their shared life. She might focus on preserving his memory and continuing to manage or distribute their estate.

2. Family Continuity:

- Ensuring Legacy: Frances might take steps to ensure that Samuel's legacy, including their property and family interests, is preserved and properly managed by their descendants.

Overall, Frances's reaction to Samuel's death would encompass a mixture of deep personal sorrow, practical adjustments, and reflections on their shared life. The impact on her would be both emotional and practical, as she navigated the loss of her lifelong partner in her later years.

At 85 years old, Frances Higginson would have been deeply affected by the death of her husband, Samuel Allen, Esq., on May 4, 1820. Here's how his death might have impacted her:

Emotional Impact:

1. Deep Grief:
- Loss of a Life Partner: The death of Samuel, her husband of many years, would have been a profound emotional blow. Having shared a long life together, Frances would likely experience significant grief and sadness at his passing.

2. Reflection on Life:
- Memories and Legacy: Frances might spend time reflecting on their life together, their shared experiences, and their accomplishments. Samuel's death would likely prompt her to think about their life's work and their family legacy.

Practical and Social Impact:

1. Adjustment to Loss:
- Daily Life: At her advanced age, Frances would need to adjust to life without Samuel's support and companionship. This could involve changes in her daily routine and responsibilities, particularly if Samuel had been involved in managing their estate or household affairs.

2. Family Dynamics:
- Support System: Frances might rely more on her family for support and companionship. The dynamics within the family would likely shift, and she would need to adapt to her new role within the family structure.

Health and Well-being:

1. Health Concerns:
- Physical and Emotional Strain: The stress and emotional strain of losing her husband could potentially impact Frances's health. At her age, coping with such a significant loss might lead to physical and emotional challenges.

2. Dependence on Others:
- Increased Vulnerability: With the death of her husband, Frances might become more dependent on her family or caregivers

for physical and emotional support, especially if Samuel had been actively involved in her care or daily life.

Legacy and Remembrance:

1. End of an Era:

- Final Years: Frances would likely consider her remaining years in the context of Samuel's legacy and their shared life. She might focus on preserving his memory and continuing to manage or distribute their estate.

2. Family Continuity:

- Ensuring Legacy: Frances might take steps to ensure that Samuel's legacy, including their property and family interests, is preserved and properly managed by their descendants.

Overall, Frances's reaction to Samuel's death would encompass a mixture of deep

personal sorrow, practical adjustments, and reflections on their shared life. The impact on her would be both emotional and practical, as she navigated the loss of her lifelong partner in her later years.

DR. SAMUEL ALLEN M.D.[9]

WHEN SAMUEL ALLEN WAS born in 1778 in Larne, County Antrim, he would have entered a world marked by both social privilege and significant historical changes. Here's a glimpse of what life was likely like at the time of his birth:

Family and Social Status:

1. Wealth and Status:

- Esquire's Household: Samuel's father, Samuel Allen, was an Esquire, a title denoting a man of social standing, typically a landowner or someone involved in local governance. This status would have placed the family in a privileged position, ensuring financial stability and a certain level of influence within their community.

- Comfortable Upbringing: As the only child of an Esquire, Samuel would have likely been raised in a comfortable home, with access to education, proper nutrition, and care. The family may have employed servants or staff to manage household duties, ensuring a relatively comfortable lifestyle.

2. Parental Expectations:

- High Expectations: Being the only child, Samuel would have been the sole heir to his family's estate, which came with expectations to uphold the family name, manage the estate, and potentially pursue a career in law, politics, or land management.

- Education: Samuel likely received a well-rounded education, focusing on subjects like the classics, literature, mathematics, and possibly law or governance, to prepare him for his future responsibilities.

Historical and Political Context:

1. American Revolutionary War (1775–1783):

- Global Impact: At the time of Samuel's birth, the American Revolutionary War was underway. While this conflict took place across the Atlantic, it would have had an impact on Ireland and Britain, as it sparked debates about governance, colonialism, and individual rights. However, Samuel's family, being in a position of privilege, might have been insulated from the more immediate effects of the conflict.

2. Irish Society in the 18th Century:

- Protestant Ascendancy: Samuel's family likely belonged to the Protestant Ascendancy, a small group of wealthy and influential Protestant landowners who dominated Irish politics, society, and land ownership during this period. This would have provided the family with social and political advantages.

- Tensions in Ireland: During this time, Ireland was experiencing significant political and social tensions between the Protestant ruling class and the Catholic majority, who faced discrimination and economic hardship. While Samuel's family may not have been directly involved in these tensions, they would have been aware of them.

Local Environment:

1. Larne, County Antrim:

- Seaside Town: Larne, being a coastal town, was a place of trade and communication with Scotland, given its proximity to the Scottish coast. Samuel would have grown up in a setting influenced by maritime activity, with the presence of ships, merchants, and trade playing a role in the town's economy.

- Rural Life: Outside of the town, the surrounding areas were likely rural, with agriculture playing a dominant role. Samuel would have been familiar with the agricultural lifestyle, possibly overseeing land or estates as part of his father's responsibilities.

2. Cultural Life:

- Irish Traditions and British Influence: While Samuel's family would have been more aligned with British customs due to their status, they still lived within Irish cultural traditions, and the landscape around them would have been shaped by both Irish and British influences. Music, folklore, and language would have been part of the everyday fabric of life.

Technological and Scientific Developments:

1. Scientific Curiosity:

- Enlightenment Ideas: Samuel was born during the tail end of the Enlightenment, a period of intellectual growth and scientific discovery. Concepts related to science, reason, and individual rights were shaping thinking across Europe. As a member of the upper class, Samuel's family might have been aware of or engaged in discussions on new ideas and inventions.

- Pre-Industrial Revolution: Though Samuel was born just before the Industrial Revolution began, the foundations of mechanization and technological progress were already being laid, which would have significant implications for the economy and society as he grew older.

Religious Context:

1. Religious Influence:

- Protestant Influence: Given that Samuel's family was part of the Ascendancy, it is likely that they were Protestants, possibly Anglicans, given their status. Religion would have played a central role in daily life, with church attendance and religious observances forming a key part of the family's routine.

Conclusion:

When Samuel Allen was born in 1778, his life would have been one of privilege, with the comforts of wealth and status that came from being part of the Protestant Ascendancy in Ireland. He was born into a world of political and social change, where tensions in Ireland simmered alongside global events like the American Revolution and the rise of Enlightenment thinking. While the effects of these broader movements might have been distant from his early childhood, they would have shaped the world he grew up in, eventually influencing the trajectory of his life.

While there are no specific descriptions of Samuel Allen, Esq., we can make some educated guesses about his appearance based on his social status, the time period, and location in which he lived.

Physical Appearance:

1. Build and Height:

- Average to Tall: Men of his class and era were typically of average to above-average height, and Samuel, as a well-to-do gentleman, likely had access to good nutrition throughout his life. He may have been relatively tall, around 5'7" to 6'0", which was respectable for the time.

- Healthy Build: As the son of an Esquire, Samuel probably had a robust or well-fed appearance. Given the family's wealth and social position, he likely had a sturdy or lean build rather than the frail or malnourished appearance common among the lower classes.

2. Facial Features:

- Symmetrical and Refined Features: As a man of privilege, Samuel may have had what were considered refined features—likely symmetrical, with a straight nose and well-defined cheekbones. Men of his social status were often described as having a dignified or noble bearing.

- Complexion: Growing up in Ireland, Samuel likely had a fair to rosy complexion, though spending time outdoors overseeing estates or other land may have given him a slightly weathered or sun-kissed appearance.

- Hair: Samuel likely had light-colored hair, common in Northern Ireland. His hair would have been neatly styled in accordance with the fashion of the time—either tied back or powdered, especially in his earlier years, given his social rank. It's possible he had light brown or blond hair, and in his later years, it may have turned white or gray.

3. Eyes:

- Light Eyes: Blue or light gray eyes would have been common in County Antrim. These features were often noted in the population of Ulster. His eyes might have had a sharp, intelligent gaze, reflective of his position as an Esquire and someone likely involved in local governance or business.

Clothing and Presentation:

1. Fashion of the Time:

- Wigs and Hats: As was customary for gentlemen in his era, Samuel likely wore wigs in his younger days, particularly in formal or professional settings. By the time he was older, the style of wearing wigs had declined, but he might have retained a shorter, neatly groomed style of his natural hair. Hats, such as tricorns or later top hats, were part of the attire for an Esquire.

- Fine Clothing: Samuel would have worn high-quality fabrics such as wool, silk, and linen. His clothes would have been tailored, reflecting the wealth and status of an Esquire. He might have worn waistcoats, breeches, and long coats, possibly adorned with embroidery or other decorations that were in line with his social status.

- Colors: Wealthier individuals like Samuel often wore darker colors—navy, black, burgundy—paired with crisp white shirts and cravats. His clothing would have distinguished him from the working classes, who tended to wear simpler, earth-toned garments.

Overall Impression:

As an Esquire, Samuel likely had an air of dignity, respectability, and refinement. His appearance would have conveyed both his wealth and his position in society. He would have taken great care in maintaining his look, presenting himself as a man of means and influence in both his community and the broader region.

When the American Revolution ended in 1783, Samuel Allen, Esq.'s son, Samuel, was just 5 years old. At this young age, his direct understanding of the war and its consequences would have been minimal. However, being part of an affluent family, he would have likely heard discussions about the conflict within his household or local community.

Possible Reaction and Understanding at 5 Years Old:

1. Limited Awareness:

At 5 years old, Samuel would have had a limited understanding of global politics. However, he would have been aware of the adults around him discussing the war, particularly because it involved the British Empire, of which Ireland was a part. His parents, Samuel Allen, Esq. and Frances, would have likely discussed the impact of the revolution, as it challenged British power and authority.

2. Influence of Family and Community:

Growing up in a relatively well-off family, young Samuel might have overheard his father or other relatives talking about how the loss of the American colonies could affect trade, politics, and the British Empire. As an Esquire, Samuel's father would likely have been invested in the political and economic ramifications of the American Revolution.

Samuel's early life in the late 18th century would have been marked by British colonial interests, and the American Revolution signaled a new era where colonies could potentially seek independence. His family may have been concerned about how this shift would influence British power and stability.

Long-term Effects:

1. Perceptions of Colonialism and Rebellion:

Although Samuel was too young to grasp the full significance of the American Revolution, he would have grown up in its aftermath. His father and other adults in his life might have had differing opinions about the rebellion. As Samuel grew older, he may have developed an understanding of how the American Revolution set a precedent for questioning authority and colonial rule, perhaps influencing his views on the relationship between Ireland and the British crown.

2. Economic Impacts:

While the immediate effects of the revolution may not have directly impacted Samuel at 5 years old, the long-term economic consequences could have influenced his family's estate and fortunes. The British Empire's loss of the American colonies altered global trade, and Ireland, being part of the empire, would have felt some of the ripple effects, especially in trade routes and economic structures.

3. Shifting Attitudes Toward Authority:

Samuel, as he matured, may have been influenced by the broader context of the time. The success of the American Revolution could have stirred ideas of liberty and self-determination within Ireland. Even though Samuel was from a privileged background, these shifting sentiments may have subtly affected his views on governance, the British crown, and Ireland's place in the empire.

Overall Impact:

At 5 years old, Samuel would not have been directly affected by the end of the American Revolution, but growing up in a family of status, he would have been exposed to discussions about it. The revolution would have contributed to shaping his awareness of the British Empire's power and the potential for colonial unrest, with the potential to influence his views on authority and governance as he grew older.

At 6 years old, Samuel Allen would likely have been filled with wonder and excitement upon hearing about the success of the first hot air balloon flight in 1784. Being born into a relatively privileged family, with his father holding the title of Esquire, Samuel may have had more access to news and stories of such remarkable events compared to children from lower social classes.

Possible Reaction at Age 6:

1. A Child's Fascination with Flight:

At that age, Samuel's reaction would probably have been one of amazement. The idea of human flight was novel and groundbreaking, and it might have sparked his imagination. He might have envisioned what it would be like to soar through the sky, which could have seemed almost magical to him and others at the time.

2. Excitement within the Household:

Samuel's father, being an Esquire, likely kept abreast of major innovations and news from around the world. The hot air balloon's success might have been discussed within the household, and Samuel would have been able to sense the excitement and importance of the event, even if he didn't fully understand the mechanics or significance.

3. Curiosity and Inspiration:

The concept of a balloon carrying people into the air might have sparked curiosity in Samuel, leading him to ask questions about how it worked. This could have also inspired a greater interest in science or technology, even at a young age. Given his privileged upbringing, he might have had access to books or educational materials that would later encourage his learning in areas related to innovation and discovery.

Long-term Impact on His Life:

1. Impact on Perception of Technology:

Although Samuel was very young, growing up in a time of great technological advancements, including the industrial revolution and innovations like the hot air balloon, may have shaped his perception of progress. This event could have contributed to an early belief in the possibilities of human ingenuity and the potential for technological breakthroughs.

2. Family Conversations:

Samuel's father and other educated adults in his life might have discussed the hot air balloon flight with excitement or even skepticism. These conversations could have given young Samuel a sense of how revolutionary the idea of flight was and possibly influenced his later views on innovation and progress.

3. Cultural Awareness:

Living in Ireland, Samuel might not have seen a balloon firsthand, but the success of the hot air balloon would have made its way into newspapers or word-of-mouth in his community. It would have been an event that symbolized the expanding horizons of human achievement during a time when science was pushing boundaries, which could have encouraged a sense of awe in Samuel as he grew up.

Overall Impact:

At 6 years old, Samuel's reaction to the success of the first hot air balloon flight would likely have been one of childlike fascination and awe. While he wouldn't have fully understood the implications, the event would have contributed to his growing awareness of the broader world and the remarkable innovations happening during his lifetime. It might have been one of the many technological milestones that shaped his curiosity and appreciation for human achievement.

At 20 years old, Samuel Allen, born into a prominent family with his father holding the title of Esquire, would have experienced the Irish Rebellion of 1798 with a mixture of concern, tension, and potential fear. His reaction and the rebellion's effect on his life would have been shaped by his social status, his geographic location in County Antrim, and his family's political and social allegiances.

Likely Reaction to the Rebellion:

1. Concern for Stability:

As the son of an Esquire, Samuel would have likely been invested in maintaining the social and political order. The rebellion, which aimed to challenge British rule and establish an independent Irish republic, would have been seen as a direct threat to the status quo. His family, possibly loyal to the British crown due to their standing, might have been deeply concerned about the rebellion's potential to disrupt life in Ireland, especially in County Antrim, where some fighting occurred.

2. Tension and Fear:

The rebellion was violent, with widespread uprisings and brutal retaliations by British forces. Even if Samuel was not directly involved in the fighting, he likely lived in a state of tension and uncertainty, worrying about the safety of his family and property. As part of a landowning or prominent family, he would have been acutely aware of the dangers posed by the upheaval, including attacks on estates, families, and loyalists.

3. Political Awareness and Engagement:

At 20, Samuel would have been old enough to understand the political causes of the rebellion, which was fueled by resentment toward British rule, religious tensions between Catholics and Protestants, and economic grievances. He might have been more politically engaged, discussing the uprising with peers, reading about it in newspapers, or even attending meetings that addressed local concerns about the rebellion. His family, likely aligned with the Protestant and Unionist factions, would have viewed the rebellion as a serious threat to their way of life and authority.

Effect on His Life:

1. Increased Awareness of Social and Political Issues:

The Irish Rebellion of 1798 would have heightened Samuel's awareness of the deep divisions within Irish society, particularly the tensions between the Protestant ruling class and the largely Catholic population seeking independence or greater rights. This awareness might have influenced his future political leanings and how he interacted with others, especially if his family had to take sides publicly during the conflict.

2. Impact on Social Class:

As an Esquire, Samuel was part of the Anglo-Irish elite, and the rebellion would have underscored the precariousness of this position. The rebellion likely reinforced his family's loyalty to the British crown and may have increased their involvement in local or national politics to protect their status and landholdings. It could have also deepened his connection to the Protestant Ascendancy, which was the dominant social class in Ireland at the time.

3. Heightened Security Measures:

Samuel and his family may have had to take practical steps to protect themselves during the rebellion. This could have included hiring guards, fortifying their estate, or seeking refuge in safer areas if the violence became too close. These experiences would have left a lasting impression on Samuel, making him more cautious and possibly more conservative in his political views as he witnessed the potential for violent uprisings.

4. Community Relations:

The rebellion might have strained relationships between the Protestant and Catholic communities in his area. Samuel's family, as part of the landowning class, may have had to navigate these tensions carefully to maintain peace on their estate and in their community. The aftermath of the rebellion could have led to a greater mistrust between the classes, which may have affected Samuel's dealings with tenants or neighbors of different religious or political backgrounds.

Overall Impact:

The Irish Rebellion of 1798 would have been a significant and formative event in Samuel Allen's life. As a young man from a prominent family, he likely viewed the rebellion as a dangerous challenge to the established order and a direct threat to his way of life. The violence and political upheaval would have reinforced his family's loyalty to the British crown and deepened his understanding of the volatile political landscape in Ireland. The rebellion would have shaped his political and social outlook, making him more cautious, conservative, and protective of his family's interests in the years to come.

When Samuel Allen was 22 years old in 1800, William Young's invention of shoes specifically designed for the left and right foot would have been seen as an intriguing and possibly luxurious innovation, especially for someone of Samuel's social standing.

Likely Reaction:

1. Curiosity and Interest:

As an educated young man from a wealthy family, Samuel would have been accustomed to fashion and trends, and this new design in footwear would have caught his attention. The idea of shoes tailored for the specific anatomy of each foot was a significant improvement from the previous practice of wearing undifferentiated shoes. Samuel may have been interested in the potential comfort and practicality of these shoes, given his status and access to higher-quality goods.

2. Adoption of the Innovation:

Given that Samuel was likely part of the upper class, he would have had the means to purchase these new shoes, which were likely expensive at first. His family, being of high social standing, might have prided themselves on keeping up with new developments, and Samuel could have been among the early adopters of Young's innovative footwear. Wearing these shoes would have been a status symbol, demonstrating his wealth and access to the latest advancements.

3. Conversations Among the Gentry:

Samuel, being an Esquire, would likely have discussed this innovation with other members of his social circle. Innovations in fashion and practical goods were common topics of interest, especially among the affluent. Samuel's reaction may have reflected a blend of appreciation for the practical benefits and admiration for the ingenuity of the design.

Effect on His Life:

1. Increased Comfort:

If Samuel began wearing these differentiated shoes, the most immediate effect would have been an increase in comfort, especially during long walks or travel. This would have been especially important for someone who frequently moved in social and professional circles that required travel or standing for long periods. Properly fitted shoes would have made daily activities more comfortable.

2. Influence on Lifestyle and Fashion:

Fashion played a significant role in the lives of the upper classes, and Samuel may have been more conscious of how he presented himself in public. Adopting this innovation early could have aligned with a desire to appear fashionable and modern, especially as an Esquire in a community where status and appearance were important.

3. Potential Health Benefits:

Differentiated shoes for the left and right foot were not only more comfortable but also healthier for the feet, helping to prevent foot problems that were common with improperly fitted shoes. Over time, this would have allowed Samuel to avoid foot pain or issues related to poorly fitted footwear, especially as he aged.

Overall Impact:

Samuel's reaction to William Young's invention would have been one of interest and appreciation, likely leading him to adopt the new shoes as part of his wardrobe. For a man of his status, this innovation would have represented both a practical improvement in daily life and an opportunity to stay current with fashionable trends. This small, but significant, advancement would have subtly improved his comfort and health, allowing him to continue his duties and social obligations with greater ease.

At the age of 29, Samuel Allen, a medical doctor, would have viewed Robert Fulton's invention of the first commercial steamship in 1807 as a significant technological advancement. As a professional with a scientific background, he would likely have had an appreciation for the ingenuity behind such an invention and its potential impact on society.

Likely Reaction:

1. Fascination with Innovation:

Given his medical training and scientific mindset, Samuel would have been intellectually curious about the mechanics and technology behind the steamship. He may have been intrigued by the engineering and the ability of the steam engine to power a vessel across water in a way that had never been possible before. The steamship represented a breakthrough in technology, much like advancements in medicine that Samuel may have been studying.

2. Optimism About Progress:

Samuel, being part of a generation experiencing the Industrial Revolution, would likely have viewed the steamship as a symbol of the growing potential for human innovation and progress. He may have seen it as a sign of the new industrial age that was transforming many aspects of daily life, including transportation, trade, and communication. His position as a medical professional would have given him an informed perspective on how such advancements could ripple through various sectors, including health and medicine.

Effect on His Life:

1. Easier Access to Medical Knowledge and Supplies:

The commercial steamship would have made it easier for medical professionals like Samuel to access medical supplies, equipment, and perhaps even medical literature from other regions or countries more quickly. Improved transportation would have opened up new opportunities for trade and exchange, which could have benefited Samuel in his medical practice by giving him access to better tools and resources.

2. Facilitation of Travel for Medical Purposes:

As a doctor, Samuel may have traveled to treat patients or to learn from other medical professionals. The advent of the commercial steamship would have made long-distance travel, especially to coastal cities or foreign lands, more efficient. Samuel may have been able to travel to medical conferences, lectures, or workshops more easily or receive patients who had traveled from distant locations to seek his medical expertise.

3. Social Impact and Professional Growth:

The steamship revolutionized the way people and goods moved, which would have also affected the communities Samuel served. As transportation networks grew, people became more connected, leading to the spread of ideas and innovations, including those in medicine. Samuel could have used this newfound connectivity to expand his medical knowledge and practice, staying at the forefront of medical advancements by networking with other doctors or accessing medical journals from other regions.

4. Future Impact on His Career:

As a medical doctor, Samuel may have begun to think about the broader implications of technological advancements like the steamship on public health. With faster transportation, diseases could spread more quickly between regions, creating new challenges for doctors. However, it also meant that medical aid and supplies could reach affected areas more quickly, presenting opportunities for improving healthcare delivery.

Overall Impact:

The invention of the commercial steamship would have likely sparked Samuel's interest in technological progress and opened new doors in terms of professional opportunities. It would have had a positive impact on his life by improving access to medical resources and information and enabling more efficient travel for both personal and professional reasons. As someone who valued innovation, Samuel would have embraced this development as part of the ongoing march toward a more connected and advanced world.

Samuel Allen's marriage to Millicent Mary Benning, the daughter of an archdeacon, would have been a significant event both socially and personally. Given Samuel's status as a medical doctor and his family's prominence—his father being an Esquire—his wedding would likely have been a formal and notable affair, reflecting their social standing.

What Their Wedding Might Have Been Like:

1. Religious Ceremony:

With Millicent's father being an archdeacon, their wedding would have been conducted in a church, likely with a strong religious tone. The ceremony itself would have been formal, with high church attendance. As the daughter of a respected clergyman, Millicent would have come from a family steeped in religious tradition, so the service would likely follow the Church of Ireland's liturgical practices. The presence of an archdeacon, potentially officiating the ceremony, would have elevated the event's significance.

2. Location and Setting:

The wedding would have taken place in a prestigious church, likely one that was associated with her father's position. The venue would be ornately decorated, with the local community, particularly those of higher social standing, attending. In a rural or small-town setting like theirs, the wedding would have been a major social event.

3. Guest List and Attire:

Given the social standing of both families, the guest list would have included local elites—landowners, professionals like lawyers or fellow doctors, and important figures in the religious community. Attire would have been formal, with Samuel likely wearing a dark suit or coat, typical of gentlemen of his time, possibly with some distinctive flourishes like a waistcoat or cravat. Millicent would have been dressed in elegant but modest attire, reflecting the social norms of the time and her religious background.

4. Reception:

The reception would have likely been a grand affair, with plenty of food and drink for the guests. In keeping with the traditions of the time, there would be music, dancing, and speeches, likely focused on Samuel's accomplishments as a doctor and Millicent's father's status in the Church. The union of two respected families would have drawn significant attention and cemented their social positions.

Effect on Samuel:

1. Social Prestige:

Marrying the daughter of an archdeacon would have greatly increased Samuel's social standing. This connection to the Church would have given him access to new circles of influence, including the clergy and other well-respected families. As a medical doctor, this could have expanded his network, helping him attract more prominent patients or gain access to better opportunities for career advancement.

2. Stability and Respectability:

Marrying Millicent would have reinforced Samuel's image as a respectable and stable figure in the community. The combination of his profession and his wife's background would have solidified his position as part of the local elite, with both secular and religious ties. This would have made Samuel's household one of influence, ensuring his future children would grow up in a respected environment.

3. Religious Influence:

Given that Millicent was the daughter of an archdeacon, religion would have likely played a more prominent role in Samuel's personal life after marriage. His connection to the Church of Ireland through his wife's family could have deepened his involvement in religious and charitable activities, potentially influencing how he approached his work as a doctor. For instance, Samuel may have been encouraged to provide medical services to the poor or sick in his community as an extension of his Christian duty.

4. Financial and Social Security:

The marriage would have provided Samuel with additional financial and social security. As the son-in-law of an archdeacon, he may have gained more access to affluent circles, which could help him establish a more stable and well-connected medical practice. It's also possible that Millicent brought a dowry or inherited wealth, further ensuring Samuel's financial security and allowing them to maintain a comfortable lifestyle.

5. Personal Fulfillment:

On a personal level, Samuel likely felt a deep sense of fulfillment from marrying someone of such high standing and character. Millicent's religious upbringing and likely moral grounding would have complemented Samuel's intellectual and professional pursuits. Together, they could have formed a strong and respected partnership in both personal and social spheres.

Overall Impact on Samuel:

The marriage to Millicent Mary Benning would have had a profound impact on Samuel's life. It would have elevated his status, strengthened his community ties, and potentially deepened his spiritual and moral commitments. Socially, the marriage linked him to the Church and brought him into contact with higher societal ranks, while personally, it would have offered him stability and partnership in both public and private life.

The birth of Samuel Allen's son, Henry Ellis Allen, on February 25, 1808, when Samuel was 30 years old, would have had a profound and multi-faceted impact on his life.

Emotional and Personal Impact:

- Joy and Fulfillment: Samuel, being 30 years old, would have likely experienced immense joy and fulfillment upon the birth of his first child, especially since he himself had been an only child. The birth of a son would have been seen as a continuation of his family line, which was important for someone in his social and professional position. The arrival of Henry would have brought great happiness to Samuel and Millicent, especially after the responsibilities and pressures they had faced as a family of status.

- Parental Pride: As a medical doctor, Samuel would have taken pride in ensuring that Millicent had the best possible care during her pregnancy and delivery. His professional knowledge would have made him particularly attentive to the health and wellbeing of both his wife and his newborn son. Henry's birth would have been a source of pride for Samuel, not just as a father, but as a professional capable of guiding the process with care.

- Increased Responsibility: The birth of Henry would have made Samuel feel a heightened sense of responsibility. As a father, he would have been focused on providing for his family, ensuring Henry's future security, and possibly already thinking about his son's education and the values he wanted to instill in him. As a man of status and a doctor, Samuel would have been determined to pass on his legacy, preparing his son for a life that matched their family's social standing.

Professional Impact:

- Motivation to Succeed: The birth of Henry would have likely motivated Samuel to work even harder in his career as a doctor. Knowing that he had a family to support and a son to provide for would have given him a renewed drive to ensure financial stability and professional success. This would have been especially important, as Samuel would have wanted to provide his son with a privileged upbringing, including access to education and social connections.

- Influence on Career: Samuel may have also thought about how his son could one day follow in his footsteps. The prospect of raising a son who could potentially become a doctor or take on a respected profession of his own would have influenced how Samuel approached his work, perhaps pushing him to continue excelling to set a strong example for Henry.

Social and Family Impact:

- Strengthening of the Family Unit: With the arrival of Henry, Samuel and Millicent's family would have been complete. The birth of a son would have solidified their union and given them a stronger sense of purpose as parents. Millicent, coming from a religious family, would have likely encouraged Samuel to ensure that Henry was raised with strong moral and spiritual values, which would have shaped the family's daily life.

- Increased Social Standing: The birth of a son would have increased Samuel's social standing as well. In early 19th-century society, having an heir was often seen as a symbol of success and continuity. Samuel, with his background as an Esquire's son and a respected doctor, would have felt secure knowing that his lineage would continue through Henry. This would have further enhanced his reputation and ensured his family's legacy would be preserved in the community.

Future Aspirations for Henry:

- Education and Upbringing: Samuel, being a highly educated man, would have begun considering the best education for Henry from an early age. He may have envisioned sending Henry to the best schools available to secure his intellectual development and prepare him for a professional career. Samuel would have wanted Henry to have access to the same or even greater opportunities that he had, which would have made his approach to parenting highly focused on nurturing Henry's potential.

- Connection to Medicine: Given Samuel's profession as a doctor, it's possible that he would have hoped for Henry to follow a similar path. He may have already started thinking about exposing his son to the medical profession, hoping that Henry would take an interest in science and medicine as he grew older. Samuel likely saw his own profession as one that provided social respect and stability, and he would have wanted the same for his son.

Challenges and Worries:

- Health Concerns: Despite the joy of Henry's birth, Samuel would have also been acutely aware of the health risks facing infants in the early 19th century. As a doctor, he would have understood the vulnerability of children in an era without modern medicine, which may have caused him anxiety about Henry's health and survival during infancy.

- Uncertain Times: The early 1800s were a time of political and social change, particularly with the Napoleonic Wars ending around the time of Henry's birth. Samuel may have worried about how these global changes would affect the future of his family, especially regarding economic stability and societal shifts.

Overall Impact:

In summary, the birth of Henry Ellis Allen would have been a momentous occasion for Samuel, both personally and professionally. It would have brought joy, pride, and a renewed sense of purpose to his life, while also increasing his responsibilities as a father. Samuel would have been deeply invested in providing Henry with a stable, educated, and morally guided upbringing, securing both the family's legacy and his son's future.

At 37 years old, Samuel Allen would have likely reacted to the defeat and exile of Napoleon Bonaparte with a mix of relief, interest, and strategic contemplation, given the historical and geopolitical context of the time.

Reaction and Emotional Impact:

- Relief and Satisfaction: As a resident of Britain and a medical professional, Samuel would have likely felt a sense of relief and satisfaction. Napoleon's defeat in 1815 marked the end of the Napoleonic Wars, which had caused widespread disruption across Europe, including economic and social impacts. The resolution of these conflicts would have been a significant relief, both personally and for the broader society.

- Interest in Political Changes: Samuel, being a well-educated man and part of the gentry, would have taken a keen interest in the political and social ramifications of Napoleon's defeat. He would have been aware that the end of Napoleon's rule meant the reorganization of European political boundaries and alliances, which could influence British policies and international relations.

Effects on His Life:

- Economic and Social Stability: With the end of the Napoleonic Wars, Europe, including Britain, would begin to experience a period of economic stabilization. For Samuel, this stability could mean a more secure financial environment, positively impacting his medical practice and personal finances. A more stable economic environment might have led to increased prosperity and fewer disruptions in his professional and personal life.

- Professional and Social Opportunities: The post-war period often brings about changes in social and professional opportunities. Samuel might have found new avenues for his practice or social standing, given the shifting political and economic landscape. The stabilization of Europe could have provided a more predictable environment for his work and personal life.

- Increased National Pride: The defeat of Napoleon would have likely fostered a sense of national pride and patriotism. Samuel, as a British citizen, would have shared in this sentiment, contributing to a sense of unity and optimism in his community. This national pride could have influenced his social interactions and public engagements.

- Impact on Personal and Family Life: The end of the wars and the return to peacetime conditions might have allowed Samuel more time to focus on his family and personal interests. The stability brought by the end of the conflict would have been beneficial for his family life, offering a more secure environment for his wife, Millicent, and their son, Henry.

- Historical Reflection: As someone living through a significant historical period, Samuel might have also reflected on the broader implications of Napoleon's defeat. The changes in European politics and the eventual establishment of the Congress of Vienna would have been of interest to him, influencing his views on governance, diplomacy, and international relations.

Overall Impact:

In summary, at 37 years old, Samuel Allen would have likely reacted to Napoleon's defeat with a combination of relief, interest, and strategic reflection. The end of the Napoleonic Wars would have positively impacted his economic stability and professional opportunities, while also allowing him to focus more on his family and personal interests. The historical significance of the event would have influenced his perspective on the changing political and social landscape of Europe.

At 39 years old, Samuel Allen would have likely had a curious and practical reaction to the invention of the bicycle in 1817, considering both his professional background as a medical doctor and the societal context of the time.

Reaction and Emotional Impact:

- Curiosity and Interest: As a well-educated and progressive individual, Samuel would have likely been intrigued by the invention of the bicycle. The concept of a new mode of personal transportation would have caught his interest, especially given the innovative nature of the invention and its potential for improving mobility.

- Appreciation for Innovation: Samuel, being part of the gentry and with a professional background, would likely have had an appreciation for technological advancements. The bicycle, being an early form of mechanized personal transport, would have been seen as a significant step forward in innovation, possibly sparking discussions among his peers.

Effects on His Life:

- Practical Use: While bicycles were still relatively primitive at this time, Samuel might have considered their practical applications. As a doctor, he might have seen potential benefits in terms of transportation for patients and for his own practice. If the bicycle became more accessible, it could have provided a new, efficient way to travel short distances.

- Social and Recreational Impact: Samuel's reaction to the bicycle might have also been influenced by its social and recreational aspects. The invention of the bicycle could have offered new recreational activities and social interactions, potentially influencing how he and his family engaged in leisure activities.

- Professional Insight: Samuel might have observed or considered the potential health benefits associated with regular cycling, such as improved cardiovascular health and physical fitness. This could have influenced his views on physical activity and its role in maintaining health.

- Economic Considerations: The bicycle's invention could have had an indirect impact on Samuel's economic considerations. If the invention gained popularity, it might have influenced local economies, transportation infrastructure, and social trends, which could indirectly affect his professional and personal environment.

Overall Impact:

In summary, at 39 years old, Samuel Allen would likely have reacted to the invention of the bicycle with curiosity and interest. While the bicycle was still in its early stages and not widely used, Samuel's appreciation for innovation and practical applications might have led him to consider its potential benefits. The bicycle could have influenced his views on transportation and physical activity, and its eventual development might have had a broader impact on societal trends and daily life.

At 42 years old, Samuel Allen would likely have experienced a profound and multifaceted impact from the death of his father, Samuel Allen, Esq., on May 4, 1820. Here's how this event might have affected him:

Emotional Impact:

- Grief and Loss: The death of his father, especially given that Samuel Allen, Esq. was a prominent figure and his only parent, would have been a significant emotional blow. Samuel might have experienced deep grief and a sense of loss, mourning not only his father's passing but also the end of an important family chapter.

- Reflection and Mourning: As an adult and professional, Samuel would likely take time to reflect on his father's legacy and their relationship. This period might involve mourning rituals, such as attending the funeral, organizing memorial services, and coming to terms with the loss in personal and public ways.

Practical and Professional Impact:

- Inheritance and Estate Matters: Samuel might have had to deal with legal and financial responsibilities related to his father's estate. This could include handling the inheritance, settling any debts or legal matters, and possibly making decisions about the family's properties or assets.

- Shift in Family Dynamics: With the passing of his father, Samuel would likely assume a more central role in managing family affairs. If his father had been involved in any business or social activities, Samuel might have had to step into these roles or make significant decisions about the family's future.

Personal and Social Impact:

- Change in Social Status: The death of an esteemed family member might have influenced Samuel's social standing or public perception. As an Esquire's son, Samuel might have inherited or continued certain social responsibilities or roles within the community.

- Impact on Family Relationships: Samuel's relationships with other family members might also be affected by his father's death. The responsibility of maintaining family unity and supporting any remaining relatives could fall more heavily on him.

Overall Impact:

In summary, Samuel Allen would have been deeply affected by his father's death at age 42. The emotional toll, coupled with practical responsibilities related to inheritance and family matters, would have influenced his personal and professional life significantly. This period would likely mark a time of adjustment and reflection as he navigated the changes brought about by his father's passing.

At 45 years old in 1823, Samuel Allen would have encountered rugby football during its early development. Here's how he might have reacted and how it could have affected him:

Reaction:

- Curiosity and Interest: Samuel, as a well-educated and socially aware individual, would likely have been curious about this new sport. Rugby, being an innovative form of football with distinct rules and gameplay, might have piqued his interest as a modern development in recreational activities.

- Skepticism or Acceptance: Depending on his personal inclinations, Samuel could have either been skeptical about the new sport's popularity and future or open to accepting it as a legitimate and enjoyable form of exercise and entertainment.

Effect on His Life:

- Social Influence: As a person of status, Samuel's reaction to new trends might influence his social circle. If he expressed interest in rugby, it could have affected his social interactions, particularly in circles where sports and social activities were discussed. His endorsement could have helped popularize the sport among his peers.

- Personal Impact: The invention of rugby itself might not have had a direct impact on his daily life or professional responsibilities. However, if he chose to participate or support the sport, it could have provided him with a new avenue for social engagement or leisure, contributing to his well-being and social activities.

- Family and Community: Samuel's reaction could also influence his family or community's interest in rugby. If he had children or young family members, his attitude toward the sport could affect their engagement with it. His support or criticism might shape the sport's reception within his local community.

Overall Impact:

While rugby's invention in 1823 might not have had a significant direct impact on Samuel Allen's professional life, it could have influenced his social interactions and personal interests. As a new and emerging sport, rugby represented a change in leisure activities, and Samuel's response to it would reflect his openness to contemporary developments and trends.

When Samuel Allen was 47 years old and his daughter Frances was born around 1827, several factors would have influenced his reaction and the impact on his life:

Emotional Impact:

- Joy and Fulfillment: The birth of a child at an older age often brings great joy and a sense of fulfillment. Samuel, having had significant life experiences and possibly facing the challenges of middle age, might have felt renewed happiness and purpose with the arrival of his daughter.

- Reflection on Legacy: At 47, Samuel might have been particularly focused on his legacy and what he would leave behind. The birth of Frances could have reinforced his desire to build a strong family legacy and ensure that his daughter had opportunities for a good life.

Practical and Social Impact:

- Involvement in Childrearing: Being older, Samuel might have been less physically active than he was in his younger years. This could have influenced how actively he was involved in the day-to-day care of Frances, though he would still be deeply invested in her upbringing and education.

- Family Dynamics: The birth of a daughter at this stage in his life could have shifted family dynamics. Samuel's older age might have meant he had more resources and stability to provide for his new child, but it might also have meant he needed to adjust his plans for the future to accommodate her needs.

Personal Impact:

- Health Considerations: As an older father, Samuel might have had to consider his own health and longevity more carefully, thinking about how he could provide for Frances in the future. This could have led him to make plans for her financial and educational needs.

- Perspective on Parenthood: Samuel's experience as a parent in his late 40s could have been shaped by a broader perspective on life, offering him a more measured and perhaps more thoughtful approach to parenting compared to younger fathers.

Overall, the birth of his daughter Frances would have been a significant and impactful event in Samuel Allen's life. It would have brought joy and a renewed sense of purpose, while also requiring adjustments to his plans and consideration of his role as an older parent.

When Samuel Allen passed away on October 9, 1835, at the age of 57, his life would have been shaped by various personal and historical factors. Here's a summary of what his life might have been like:

Personal Life:

- Family: Samuel would have been deeply affected by the recent losses of his parents, Frances (died in 1823) and Samuel Allen, Esq. (died in 1820). The death of his mother, in particular, would have been a significant emotional blow. He would have been managing his responsibilities as a father to his younger children, including Frances, born in 1827, and his older son, Henry Ellis Allen.

- Professional Life: As a medical doctor, Samuel would have been actively involved in his practice. By 1835, he would have had years of experience in medicine and would be recognized in his community for his expertise. The medical field during this period was evolving, and Samuel would have witnessed advancements in medical knowledge and practices.

Historical Context:

- Technological and Social Changes: The early 19th century was a time of significant change. Samuel would have seen the effects of the Industrial Revolution, including advancements in technology and changes in societal structures. The invention of matches, the first commercial steamboats, and other technological innovations would have influenced daily life and commerce.

- Political Climate: The political climate of the early 19th century was marked by various changes and developments, including the aftermath of the Napoleonic Wars and the ongoing impacts of the Industrial Revolution. In Ireland, there were significant social and political shifts, including the impact of the 1798 Rebellion and its aftermath.

- Personal Impact of Historical Events: Samuel's life would have been influenced by these broader historical events. The technological advancements, such as the introduction of matches, would have affected daily living, while the social and political changes could have impacted his professional and personal life.

In summary, Samuel Allen's life in 1835 would have been a blend of personal and professional responsibilities, shaped by both the advancements of the time and the personal losses he experienced. His work as a doctor and his role within his family would have been central aspects of his life as he navigated a period of significant change.

MILLICENT MARY (BENNING) ALLEN[10]

IN 1777, CARRICKFERGUS, County Antrim, was a small but significant town in Ireland, located near Belfast. The area was experiencing a period of relative stability in the midst of the broader political and economic changes of the time. Here's a look at what life might have been like for Millicent Mary Benning and her family:

- Social Status: As the daughter of Ven. Conway Benning LL.D., an archdeacon and a learned clergyman, Millicent would have been part of the gentry or upper social class. Her family's status would have afforded her a comfortable lifestyle, access to education, and social connections within the church and local community.

- Education and Upbringing: Millicent would likely have received a good education, possibly including instruction in languages, literature, and other subjects appropriate for a young woman of her social standing. Her upbringing would have been influenced by the values and expectations of the Anglican church, given her father's position.

- Cultural Context: The late 18th century was a period of significant change and development in Ireland and Britain, including economic shifts due to the Industrial Revolution and political tensions leading up to the Act of Union in 1801. The local gentry, such as her family, would have been somewhat insulated from these upheavals but still affected by the broader changes.

Appearance

While there are no specific records of her appearance, we can infer some general characteristics based on the era and her social class:

- Clothing: In 1777, Millicent would likely have worn clothing typical of upper-class women of the time, such as a gown with a fitted bodice and a full skirt. Fabrics would have included silk, muslin, or fine wool, with elaborate decorations and trims. Accessories like lace, ribbons, and possibly a bonnet or hat would have been common.

- Physical Appearance: As a young woman in the late 18th century, Millicent's physical appearance would have been influenced by the beauty standards of the time, which favored a pale complexion, a small waist (often achieved with a corset), and a natural-looking, understated hairstyle. She might have had her hair styled in the popular fashion of the time, which often involved curls or waves and could be adorned with accessories.

Family Background

- Ven. Conway Benning LL.D.: As an archdeacon, her father would have been a prominent and respected figure in the Anglican church, with a scholarly background.

- Ann (née Ellis): Her mother's background would also contribute to Millicent's social standing, as family connections and lineage were important in 18th-century society.

In summary, Millicent Mary Benning's life in 1777 would have been marked by the privileges and responsibilities of her upper-class status, with a focus on education and social manners. Her appearance would reflect the fashion and beauty standards of the late 18th century, and her family background would have provided her with a comfortable and influential upbringing.

Given that Millicent Mary Benning was born in 1777 and Samuel Allen was born in 1780, here's how her early years and the potential connection between their families might have been influenced:

Impact on Millicent

- Early Childhood: At the age of 2, Millicent would have been too young to have any direct awareness or impact from Samuel's birth. Her own early childhood would have been shaped by her family's status and the societal expectations of the time, rather than by the birth of a child in a different family.

Potential Family Connection

- Social Circles: Both families, being part of the local gentry in Carrickfergus and its surrounding areas, might have been acquainted with each other. Given that Millicent's father, Ven. Conway Benning, was an archdeacon, and Samuel Allen's father, as an Esquire, would also have been of significant social standing, it's possible that their families moved in similar social circles.

- Community Ties: In smaller communities, especially those with a close-knit social structure like Carrickfergus, families of similar social status often knew each other, attended the same events, and participated in similar social activities. This could have facilitated an early acquaintance or awareness between the two families.

- Future Connection: While Millicent and Samuel would not have been personally aware of each other's existence at the time of Samuel's birth, it's feasible that their families might have been in contact or had mutual acquaintances who could have introduced them later.

In summary, although Millicent would not have been directly affected by Samuel's birth at the age of 2, it is likely that their families, due to their social status and community ties, could have known each other or at least been aware of each other's presence in the same social milieu.

At 6 years old in 1784, when the first successful hot air balloon flight took place, Millicent Mary Benning would have likely experienced the event as a significant and exciting development, though her understanding would have been limited by her age. Here's a closer look at how she might have reacted and the potential impact on her:

Reaction

- Curiosity and Wonder: As a child, Millicent would likely have been fascinated by the idea of flying and the novelty of the hot air balloon. The concept of flight was a groundbreaking and awe-inspiring development at the time, and such an event would have captured the imagination of people of all ages.

- Influence of Family: Given her father's position as an archdeacon, her family might have discussed significant events and innovations. Millicent's reaction could have been influenced by the excitement or interest shown by her family and the wider community.

Impact

- Inspiration and Imagination: While a 6-year-old might not fully grasp the scientific implications, the event could have sparked a sense of wonder and imagination in Millicent. It might have contributed to her overall sense of curiosity about the world and the possibilities of human achievement.

- Cultural Context: Such events were often discussed and celebrated in local communities, so Millicent might have been aware of the ballooning adventure through local news, social gatherings, or family conversations.

- Future Perspectives: Although the direct impact might be minimal at her young age, the hot air balloon's success could have contributed to a broader cultural appreciation for scientific progress and exploration, potentially influencing her later views on innovation and discovery.

In summary, while Millicent's direct reaction as a 6-year-old to the hot air balloon flight would have been one of curiosity and wonder, the event might have subtly contributed to her cultural context and sense of excitement about human achievements.

At 20 years old in 1798, when the Irish Rebellion occurred, Millicent Mary Benning would likely have been deeply affected by the events surrounding the uprising. Here's an overview of how she might have reacted and the potential impact on her life:

Reaction

- Emotional Impact: As a young adult, Millicent would have experienced the rebellion with a mixture of fear, concern, and perhaps confusion. The rebellion was a significant and turbulent event that involved violence, political strife, and widespread unrest.

- Family and Social Circle: Given her background as the daughter of an archdeacon, she might have been influenced by her family's and social circle's perspectives on the rebellion. The impact on her could be moderated by her family's position, which might have influenced how the rebellion was discussed and perceived within her community.

Impact

- Personal Safety and Security: The rebellion's violence and the political instability it caused would likely have made her feel anxious about her personal safety and the safety of her loved ones. The rebellion led to significant disruption in Ireland, which could have affected daily life and created an atmosphere of uncertainty.

- Political Awareness: The rebellion could have heightened her awareness of political issues and the struggles faced by different groups in Ireland. It might have influenced her views on governance, justice, and social issues.

- Social and Economic Effects: The aftermath of the rebellion included increased repression and changes in the political landscape, which could have impacted her family's social standing and economic situation. Changes in landownership, social structures, or local governance could have affected her directly or indirectly.

- Cultural and Historical Context: Experiencing a significant historical event like the rebellion might have shaped her understanding of Irish history and politics. It could have influenced her perspectives on national identity and the complexities of Irish-English relations.

In summary, at 20 years old, Millicent Mary Benning would likely have been deeply affected by the Irish Rebellion, experiencing emotional distress, increased political awareness, and possible changes in her social and economic environment. The rebellion would have left a lasting impression on her life and worldview.

At 21 years old in 1798, when the Battle of Antrim took place, Millicent Mary Benning would have experienced this event through the lens of her social status and location:

Reaction

- Concern and Anxiety: The Battle of Antrim was part of the Irish Rebellion of 1798, which involved widespread unrest and conflict. As a young woman living in Ireland, Millicent would likely have felt a sense of concern and anxiety about the upheaval and violence occurring in her country.

- Local Impact: If she lived in or near Antrim, she might have experienced the immediate impacts of the rebellion more acutely, including disruptions to daily life, increased security, or even direct effects if the conflict reached her area.

- Political Awareness: The rebellion would have heightened her awareness of political tensions and the struggle for Irish independence. As the daughter of an archdeacon, she might have been more attuned to the political and social dynamics influencing the region.

Impact

- Emotional and Social Impact: The turmoil and violence of the rebellion could have caused emotional distress and uncertainty. The conflict would have affected local communities, potentially leading to shifts in social and familial dynamics.

- Economic and Social Disruption: The rebellion might have disrupted local economies and social structures, leading to short-term hardships. If her family was involved in trade or agriculture, they might have faced economic challenges during and after the unrest.

- Influence on Worldview: Experiencing or witnessing the aftermath of such significant events would have likely influenced her worldview, shaping her perspectives on political and social issues. It might have also impacted her views on the future stability and direction of Ireland.

Overall, Millicent Mary Benning's reaction to the Battle of Antrim would have been marked by concern and awareness of the broader implications of the rebellion, affecting her emotionally and potentially influencing her views on the political landscape of Ireland.

At 22 years old in 1800, when William Young designed shoes for the left and right foot, Millicent Mary Benning would likely have had a range of reactions and experiences:

Reaction

- Curiosity and Interest: As a young adult with a likely interest in innovations and improvements, Millicent might have been intrigued by the idea of shoes specifically designed for each foot. This innovation represented a practical advancement in everyday life.

- Social and Practical Perspective: If she was aware of the benefits of this development, she would have appreciated the improved comfort and fit of shoes. The idea of having shoes tailored to each foot would have been a notable improvement over the previous standard of uniform footwear.

Impact

- Improved Comfort and Health: The introduction of shoes designed for the left and right foot would have improved her comfort and health. Properly fitting shoes could reduce foot problems and enhance overall well-being, making her daily life more comfortable.

- Social Status and Awareness: Being part of a social class that valued practical innovations, Millicent might have seen this development as a symbol of progress and refinement. It could have influenced her perception of modernity and advancements in consumer goods.

- Influence on Fashion and Practicality: This innovation would have been a step forward in fashion and practicality. If she was in the social circles where such innovations were discussed, it might have influenced her opinions on contemporary fashion and consumer products.

Overall, Millicent Mary Benning would likely have been positively affected by the introduction of shoes designed for each foot, finding them both practical and innovative. The improvement in footwear comfort and fit would have had a beneficial impact on her daily life.

When Millicent Mary Benning was 31 years old and gave birth to her first child, Henry Ellis Allen, on February 25, 1808, the experience would have had several impacts on her:

Immediate Effects

- Joy and Fulfillment: The birth of her first child would have brought great joy and fulfillment, marking a significant milestone in her personal life and family life.

- Physical and Emotional Changes: The process of childbirth and the early months of caring for a newborn would have involved significant physical and emotional changes. She would have had to adjust to the demands of motherhood, which might have been exhausting but also deeply rewarding.

Impact on Her Life

- Social Expectations: As the wife of a medical doctor and the daughter of an archdeacon, Millicent would have been expected to fulfill her role as a mother and manage her household. The birth of her son would have solidified her role in her family and social circles, potentially influencing her social standing and responsibilities.

- Family Dynamics: Henry's birth would have strengthened the bond between Millicent and her husband, Samuel Allen, as they shared the responsibilities and joys of parenthood. It would have also introduced new dynamics into their family life, including adjustments in their household routines and priorities.

- Health and Well-being: The health and well-being of both mother and child would have been a significant concern. In the early 19th century, childbirth carried risks, so Millicent's experience would have been closely monitored by family and medical professionals.

- Impact on Social Life: Millicent's role as a mother might have affected her social activities and engagements. She would have likely focused more on her family and home life, adjusting her social interactions to accommodate her new responsibilities.

Overall, the birth of Henry Ellis Allen would have been a transformative experience for Millicent, deeply affecting her personal life and responsibilities, while also marking a joyful and significant addition to her family.

When Millicent Mary Benning was 37 years old and Napoleon Bonaparte was defeated and exiled in 1815, the event would have had several impacts on her:

Immediate Reaction

- Relief and Optimism: As the defeat of Napoleon marked the end of the Napoleonic Wars, Millicent likely felt relief and optimism. The wars had caused significant upheaval across Europe, so peace would have been welcomed by many, including her.

- Interest in Political Affairs: Given her background and her husband's profession, Millicent might have had an interest in political and international events. The end of such a major conflict would have been of particular significance to her, both personally and socially.

Impact on Her Life

- Societal Stability: The end of the Napoleonic Wars would have contributed to a period of relative stability in Europe. This stability could have had a positive effect on her family's economic situation and social standing. A more stable political climate often leads to economic recovery and growth, which could benefit her household.

- Increased Focus on Family Life: With the end of the wars, Millicent might have been able to focus more on her family and domestic life without the concerns of conflict and uncertainty overshadowing daily life. This could have included increased involvement in charitable activities or community affairs.

- Cultural and Social Influences: The end of the wars would have influenced cultural and social trends, leading to changes in fashion, art, and social norms. Millicent, being part of a prominent family, might have been affected by or involved in these shifts, adapting to new societal trends and expectations.

- Political and Social Engagement: The aftermath of Napoleon's defeat might have seen shifts in political power and social structures across Europe. Millicent could have observed or participated in these changes, influencing her views and interactions within her social circle.

Overall, Millicent's reaction to Napoleon's defeat and exile would likely have been one of relief and hope, with the event contributing to a period of personal and societal adjustment that impacted her family life and social environment positively.

When Millicent Mary Benning was 42 years old and her mother, Ann Ellis, passed away on September 5, 1819, it would have had a profound emotional and practical effect on her life.

Emotional Impact

- Grief and Loss: Losing a mother at any age can be devastating. As Millicent was in her early 40s, she may have experienced deep sorrow. Ann would have been a significant figure in her life, providing guidance, support, and companionship, and her death could have left a noticeable void.

- Reflection on Family Ties: Millicent might have reflected on the bond she had with her mother, especially as she herself was a mother by that time, with her son Henry Ellis Allen having been born in 1808. The loss may have strengthened her desire to maintain close connections with her own children, cherishing family ties even more after her mother's passing.

Practical and Social Consequences

- Role as the Matriarch: With the death of Ann, Millicent may have stepped into a more central role within her family. She would likely have taken on greater responsibility as the senior woman, both in her immediate family and perhaps in her extended family as well. This would have added to her emotional burdens, as she would need to manage family affairs, maintain traditions, and be a source of support for others in the family.

- Changes in Household Dynamics: If Ann had been living nearby or had an active role in Millicent's life or household, her absence might have led to adjustments. There may have been a shift in how daily matters were managed, particularly if Ann had contributed to caring for grandchildren or managing family affairs.

- Faith and Coping: Given her religious background as the daughter of an archdeacon, Millicent might have turned to her faith to cope with the loss. She may have sought solace through prayer, spiritual reflection, or even through her church community, relying on them for emotional support during her time of grief.

In summary, Ann Ellis's death would have deeply affected Millicent both emotionally and practically. As she dealt with the personal loss of her mother, she would also have had to navigate her new role as a more senior figure in her family, all while finding ways to cope and continue with the responsibilities of her own household and life.

When Millicent Mary Benning was 43 years old and her father-in-law, Samuel Allen, Esq., passed away on May 4, 1820, it would have likely had several impacts on her life, both emotionally and practically.

Emotional Impact

- Sense of Loss: While the relationship between Millicent and Samuel Allen, Esq. is not known in detail, the death of a father-in-law is often felt as a significant loss. Depending on how close they were, she may have mourned him deeply, especially considering how he was the father of her husband and grandfather to her children.

- Support for Her Husband: Millicent's husband, Samuel Allen (the son), would have been 42 years old when his father passed. The death of a parent, even in adulthood, can be difficult, and Millicent would likely have been a source of emotional support for her husband during this time. She may have helped him process his grief, especially as he dealt with the death of a man who likely had a profound influence on his life and career.

Practical and Social Impact

- Family Responsibility: As a member of the Allen family, Millicent may have had new responsibilities following the death of her father-in-law. Samuel Allen, Esq., being an "Esq." and presumably a man of some standing, might have left behind estates, family responsibilities, or legal matters that required attention. Millicent, as the wife of Samuel's only son, may have had to help manage or oversee family affairs, particularly if there were any shifts in property, wealth, or status after his death.

When Millicent Mary Benning was 46 years old and her father, Ven. Conway Benning LL.D., passed away on March 30, 1823, in Rathmoylan, County Waterford, the event would have likely had a profound emotional and practical impact on her life.

Emotional Impact

- Grief and Loss: Losing a parent is deeply emotional, regardless of age, and Millicent would have been heavily affected by the death of her father. Given that her mother, Ann Ellis, had passed away just a few years earlier in 1819, Millicent was now dealing with the loss of both her parents in quick succession. The grief of losing her father might have triggered a reflection on her family upbringing, childhood, and her parents' influence on her life.

- A Close Connection to Her Father: Millicent's father, Ven. Conway Benning, was an archdeacon, which would have likely meant he played an important role not only in the church but also in their family life. If she had a close relationship with him, his passing would have left a significant emotional void. His influence as a religious and moral figure would have been considerable, and his death might have left her feeling as though a guiding figure in her life was gone.

Spiritual and Religious Impact

- Religious Reflection: Given that her father was a high-ranking clergyman in the Church of Ireland, his death might have also caused Millicent to reflect on her own faith, religious beliefs, and connection to the Church. The passing of a religious figure can often deepen a person's spiritual journey, and she may have turned to her faith as a source of comfort during her time of mourning.

- Connection to the Church: As the daughter of an archdeacon, Millicent was likely well-connected to the Church of Ireland's hierarchy. The death of her father might have prompted her to take on more active involvement in church affairs, or conversely, she may have distanced herself for a time while processing her grief. It's also possible that her family's position within the Church would have brought her into contact with other clergy, who might have offered support during this difficult time.

Practical and Familial Impact

- Family Leadership: With the passing of both parents, Millicent may have felt the weight of becoming a senior figure within her family. As the eldest daughter, she could have taken on more responsibility in caring for or supporting her siblings, if she had any, and managing family affairs, especially any inheritance or property matters left behind by her father.

- Inheritance and Estate Matters: Given her father's position as an archdeacon, there may have been estates, church roles, or financial responsibilities that needed attending after his death. Millicent and her husband, Samuel, as an established medical doctor and the son of an Esq., would have likely helped manage these matters, ensuring that her father's legacy was preserved.

Coping with Loss

- Burden of Multiple Losses: Millicent had experienced a series of significant losses within just a few years—her mother in 1819, her father-in-law in 1820, and now her own father in 1823. These consecutive losses could have weighed heavily on her, emotionally and mentally, and she may have struggled with feelings of isolation or sadness. Supporting her children and her husband while also processing her own grief would have been a challenge.

- Support from Her Husband and Family: During this time of personal loss, Millicent would have likely relied on her husband, Samuel Allen, and her children for emotional support. Given her husband's position as a doctor, he may have been able to offer her some stability, while her children, including her son Henry and later her daughter Frances, would have been a source of comfort.

In conclusion, the death of Millicent's father, Ven. Conway Benning, in 1823 would have deeply affected her, both emotionally and practically. She was dealing with the loss of her parents in a relatively short time, likely leading to a period of intense grief, reflection, and adjustment to her new role as the senior member of her family. Balancing these emotions while maintaining her duties as a wife and mother would have been challenging, but her connection to her family and faith may have offered her some solace.

Millicent Mary Benning would have been significantly affected by the death of her mother-in-law, Frances Allen, on May 17, 1823, just two months after losing her own father. The impact of these losses would have been felt on multiple levels: emotionally, socially, and practically.

Emotional Impact

- Grief from Consecutive Losses: Having just lost her father in March of 1823, the death of her mother-in-law so soon after would have compounded her grief. Millicent was already dealing with the emotional weight of losing a parent, and now with Frances' passing, she was confronted with another close familial death. This period in her life would have been marked by deep mourning, and she likely would have felt a heavy burden of sadness.

- Close Relationship with Frances: If Millicent had a close relationship with Frances, the loss of her mother-in-law would have had an even more profound emotional effect. Frances, being a respected matriarch of the family and the wife of Samuel Allen Esq., would likely have been a source of wisdom, guidance, and emotional support for Millicent throughout her marriage. Losing someone who had a significant role in family life would have left a noticeable absence.

- Support to Her Husband: Millicent's husband, Samuel Allen, would have been grieving the loss of his mother. Millicent would have had to provide emotional support to her husband while managing her own grief from both her father's and mother-in-law's passing. Balancing these roles—being a source of comfort to her husband and managing her own emotions—would have been a significant challenge during this time.

Social and Familial Impact

- Increased Responsibilities: With the passing of both Frances and her own father within the same year, Millicent may have had to assume more responsibilities within the family. Frances would have played an important role in the social and familial structure, particularly in maintaining family ties and traditions. After Frances' death, Millicent may have taken on the role of overseeing family gatherings, supporting her husband's emotional needs, and ensuring the stability of the household.

- Role in Family Affairs: With the passing of two key figures within the family, Millicent and her husband would have likely become the senior generation in the family. As the wife of Samuel Allen, and with her own strong background as the daughter of an archdeacon, Millicent would have been expected to step into a more prominent role in managing family affairs and perhaps even caring for extended family members.

Impact on Her Children

- The Grandmother's Death: The death of Frances would have impacted not just Millicent and Samuel, but also their children. Frances would have been their grandmother, and her passing could have been an emotionally difficult time for the family. Millicent would have had to support her children through the loss of their grandmother, offering them emotional stability while grieving herself.

- Generational Shifts: With the passing of Frances, Millicent's family would now have been part of a generational shift. As her children were growing older and reaching adulthood, the death of a grandparent could signify to Millicent the passage of time and the reality of her own aging. This could have been a period of reflection for her as she came to terms with both her own and her husband's changing roles within the family.

Practical Impact

- Inheritance and Family Wealth: Frances' death might have also had practical implications regarding inheritance, property, or financial matters within the Allen family. As the wife of Samuel Allen, Millicent would likely have been involved in discussions about how family wealth or estates were to be managed after Frances' passing. These practical matters would have added to the emotional strain she was already experiencing.

Societal Role as a Widow's Daughter-in-Law

- Social Expectations: In 19th-century society, family structures and social roles were quite rigid, and the death of a matriarch like Frances Allen could shift expectations within the community. Millicent, as the daughter-in-law, would likely have been expected to take on more public-facing responsibilities in maintaining the family's reputation and continuing the Allen family's societal obligations.

Coping Mechanisms

- Faith and Religion: Given her background as the daughter of an archdeacon, it is likely that Millicent turned to her faith for comfort during this time. Both the death of her father and mother-in-law within a short period could have prompted her to lean more heavily on her religious beliefs, finding solace in prayer and church activities.

- Support from Extended Family: Millicent may also have found comfort and strength from her extended family. The Benning and Allen families were both likely to have been well-connected, and Millicent might have relied on the support of siblings, cousins, or friends during this difficult time.

Overall Impact

In conclusion, the death of Millicent's mother-in-law, Frances Allen, would have deeply affected her, especially since it occurred just two months after her own father's passing. She would have been emotionally strained by the compounded grief and would have faced increased responsibilities within the family, both in supporting her husband and maintaining the family's social role. Her faith, family connections, and resilience would have been crucial in helping her cope with this period of loss.

Millicent Mary Benning, being 48 years old when matches were invented in 1826, likely would have been intrigued and appreciative of this new convenience. As a practical innovation, the invention of friction matches would have had a noticeable impact on her daily life, particularly in household management.

Reaction to the Invention

- Curiosity and Interest: Millicent, like many others at the time, would likely have been curious about how matches worked and how they could be used. Matches represented a major improvement over traditional fire-starting methods, which required more effort and skill, such as flint and steel or using tinderboxes. Millicent, being well-educated as the daughter of an archdeacon, may have been aware of the scientific progress behind this invention and appreciated the simplicity and efficiency it offered.

- Embracing the Practicality: Given her role in overseeing the household, Millicent would have welcomed any new invention that made managing her home more efficient. Matches would have been particularly useful for lighting fires in the home, whether for cooking, heating, or lighting candles and lamps. The ease with which a match could strike and instantly produce a flame would have reduced the time and effort required to maintain these daily routines.

Effect on Daily Life

- Increased Efficiency in the Household: Matches would have made it easier and quicker for Millicent or her household staff to start fires in the kitchen for cooking, heat rooms, or light candles. This would have freed up time and energy for other tasks, making the household run more smoothly. For someone in her position, with a family to manage and a social role to fulfill, the invention would have been a welcome improvement.

- Greater Independence: The convenience of matches allowed people to be less reliant on more cumbersome or difficult fire-starting methods. Millicent may have appreciated that even her children or less skilled household members could now safely and easily light a fire, which gave more flexibility to everyone in the household.

- Social Discussions: As a member of a socially prominent family, Millicent may have engaged in conversations about this new invention with her peers. Matches were likely a topic of fascination and discussion among the educated and upper classes, who appreciated the blend of practicality and scientific advancement they represented.

Long-Term Impact

- Impact on Health and Comfort: Matches likely contributed to an overall improvement in comfort within the household. The ease of lighting fires would have ensured more consistent warmth during colder months, and lighting candles or lamps would have been more manageable, enhancing the overall ambiance of the home in the evenings.

- Economic Impact: Matches were a relatively affordable innovation compared to other methods of fire-starting. Though Millicent's family was likely well-off and not concerned about minor household expenses, the cost-effectiveness of matches would have made them a convenient and economical option for the long term.

In summary, Millicent likely would have reacted positively to the invention of matches, appreciating their practicality and the convenience they brought to everyday life. This invention would have contributed to making household management more efficient, allowing for greater ease and comfort within her home.

Millicent Mary Benning, at the age of 58, would have been profoundly affected by the death of her husband, Samuel Allen, on October 8, 1835. His passing likely marked a significant emotional, social, and practical turning point in her life.

Emotional Impact:

- Grief and Loss: Losing her husband of many years would have been deeply painful. After building a life together, raising children, and managing their household, Samuel's death would have left her with a sense of deep sorrow and grief. Millicent likely experienced a profound sense of loss, as Samuel had been a central figure in her life.

- Loneliness: After decades of marriage, Millicent may have felt isolated or lonely without her husband by her side. Their shared experiences, responsibilities, and the bond they had built over time would have been difficult to move on from, especially at an age where she might have relied more on his companionship.

Practical and Social Impact:

- Change in Role: As a widow, Millicent's social and household responsibilities would have shifted. She would have taken on the role of head of the household in the absence of her husband, which may have brought additional pressures, especially in terms of managing finances, property, and any remaining responsibilities that Samuel might have overseen. She would have had to navigate these changes, possibly with the support of her children or extended family.

- Family Dynamics: Millicent's relationship with her children would likely have been impacted. They would have had to come together to support each other in their collective grief. Her son, Henry, born in 1808, would have been 27 years old and could have been a source of support for his mother, helping her cope with the responsibilities that arose after Samuel's death.

Social and Economic Impact:

- Social Position as a Widow: As the widow of a prominent man, Millicent would still have maintained a respectable social position, though widows during this time often faced a change in how they were viewed socially. She might have been invited to fewer social events, and her focus would have shifted to her role as a matriarch in the family rather than as a wife.

- Economic Concerns: Depending on the financial state Samuel left behind, Millicent may have had to consider her own financial security. If the family had a well-maintained estate and financial resources, she might not have struggled, but if there were outstanding debts or issues, managing finances could have been a new challenge for her.

Emotional Resilience:

Despite the grief and loneliness, Millicent may have also displayed emotional resilience. At 58, she had lived through significant events, including the deaths of both her parents and possibly other hardships, which may have equipped her with inner strength to cope with Samuel's death. Her faith, upbringing as the daughter of an archdeacon, and community connections likely helped her find solace and navigate this difficult period.

In summary, the death of Samuel Allen in 1835 would have deeply affected Millicent emotionally, socially, and practically. She would have faced the challenges of widowhood, the shift in her role within the family and society, and the personal grief of losing her life partner.

At 61 years old, Millicent Mary Benning would likely have experienced significant concern and possibly fear during the Irish Hurricane of 1839, also known as "The Night of the Big Wind" (Oíche na Gaoithe Móire). This was one of the most powerful storms in Irish history, causing widespread devastation across the country. It would have deeply affected her both emotionally and practically.

Emotional Reaction:

- Fear and Anxiety: Given the ferocity of the storm, which left buildings destroyed, trees uprooted, and many people displaced, Millicent would likely have felt a great deal of fear. The storm was sudden and violent, catching most people off guard. As a widow in her sixties, she might have felt especially vulnerable, worried about her safety and the well-being of her family and community.

- Memories of Loss: Having lost her husband just a few years earlier, Millicent might have felt the weight of these disasters more heavily, as they could stir up feelings of uncertainty and helplessness. The storm could have also reminded her of previous personal losses, deepening her emotional response.

Practical Impact:

- Damage to Property: Depending on where Millicent was living at the time, her home and property may have been damaged. The storm caused destruction across the country, particularly to homes with thatched roofs, which were torn off, and other structures that were not well fortified. If her home or estate was affected, she would have faced the practical challenge of dealing with repairs and possibly relocating temporarily.

- Disruption to Daily Life: The storm disrupted transportation, communication, and daily activities across Ireland. For Millicent, this would have meant difficulty in accessing supplies, getting in touch with extended family members, or ensuring the safety of her home. The aftermath of the hurricane would likely have caused disruptions to her routines and required her to rely more on her children or community for support.

Social and Community Response:

- Concern for Others: As a widow and matriarch, Millicent would have likely been concerned not only for herself but also for her children, extended family, and community members. She may have taken an active role in providing comfort or support to those around her, especially younger or more vulnerable family members.

- Relief and Resilience: Despite the destruction, Millicent may have also shown resilience. Having lived through significant events and personal hardships, including the deaths of her parents and husband, she may have leaned on her experience and faith to cope with the storm's aftermath. Her ability to endure adversity may have been a source of strength for those around her.

Effect on Her Later Years:

The hurricane could have had a lasting impact on Millicent's later years. The destruction caused by the storm was widespread, and many communities took a long time to recover. If her family's property was affected, she might have had to deal with the financial and emotional burden of rebuilding or assisting others. Alternatively, if her family was spared significant damage, she may have been more involved in helping her neighbors or community recover.

In summary, Millicent Mary Benning would likely have reacted with fear, concern, and possibly a renewed sense of vulnerability during the Irish Hurricane of 1839. The storm's impact on her home, family, and community would have required her to summon emotional resilience, lean on her support network, and navigate practical challenges in the aftermath of one of Ireland's worst natural disasters.

At 61 years old, Millicent Mary Benning would have likely been both intrigued and perhaps a little skeptical when photography became publicly available in 1839. The invention of the daguerreotype, an early form of photography created by Louis Daguerre, would have been a groundbreaking development during her lifetime.

Emotional Reaction:

- Curiosity and Fascination: As a woman who had witnessed several major technological advancements in her lifetime, from the steam engine to the bicycle, Millicent would have likely been curious about this new form of capturing reality. Photography was an entirely new medium for recording images and memories, which would have fascinated someone accustomed to traditional portraits and paintings.

- Awe and Skepticism: The ability to capture lifelike images with such detail would have been awe-inspiring for Millicent. At the same time, given her age and the novelty of photography, she might have been somewhat skeptical of its accuracy or purpose.

She might have wondered how it worked and whether such an invention was practical or merely a novelty.

Practical Impact:

- Opportunity for Family Keepsakes: Photography would have provided Millicent with a new way to preserve family memories. As someone who had lost her husband and parents, the idea of having a lasting image of loved ones, especially her children and grandchildren, would have been emotionally significant. She may have considered having a portrait taken, seeing it as a way to leave behind a visual legacy for future generations.

- Impact on Social Status: As the daughter of an archdeacon and the widow of an Esq., Millicent belonged to a relatively high social class. Photography, in its early years, was expensive and not accessible to everyone. Having a family portrait taken could have been a marker of status and wealth, allowing her family to display their affluence and importance. As a widow, this could have been a way to solidify her family's legacy visually.

- Impact on Memory and Legacy: The invention of photography would have altered Millicent's perception of memory and legacy. In a time when portraits were traditionally painted, having a photograph that could capture true likenesses would have been a powerful tool in preserving family history. It might have deepened her sense of family continuity, especially given the personal losses she had endured.

Effect on Her Later Years:

- Preserving History: If Millicent was forward-thinking, she might have seen photography as a way to preserve not only personal memories but also historical moments. She had lived through significant events like the Irish Rebellion and the defeat of Napoleon, and photography could have offered her a way to document these times for future generations.

- Interest in Progress: Photography was a symbol of technological progress, and Millicent, who had already witnessed so many advances in her lifetime, may have seen it as part of the continuous march toward modernity. Even if she didn't fully embrace it, she would likely have understood its potential importance in shaping the future.

In summary, Millicent Mary Benning would likely have reacted to the invention of photography with curiosity and a mix of awe and skepticism. It would have impacted her by offering a new way to preserve her family's legacy, marking her status in society, and perhaps prompting her to reflect on the rapid technological changes she had seen throughout her life.

At 67 years old during the start of the Irish Potato Famine (1845-1852), Millicent Mary Benning would have witnessed one of the most devastating periods in Irish history. The famine had a profound impact on all levels of society, especially on rural communities and the lower classes, but even the landed gentry and clergy were affected by the social and economic upheaval.

Emotional Reaction:

- Shock and Sorrow: The famine would likely have shocked Millicent, as it led to widespread suffering, starvation, and death. Although she came from a well-off family, the sight of her fellow Irish people enduring such hardship would have deeply saddened her. Being from County Antrim, she may have seen firsthand the effects of the crop failures, with people becoming destitute and starving, and would have heard the stories of families torn apart by death and emigration.

- Empathy and Charity: As the daughter of an archdeacon and the wife of a well-respected man, Millicent likely had a strong Christian background that emphasized charity. She might have felt a personal or religious obligation to help those in need, perhaps donating to relief efforts or encouraging her local community and church to provide assistance. Religious institutions played a major role in providing aid during the famine, and she would likely have been involved in those efforts, especially given her family's ties to the Church of Ireland.

Social Impact:

- Strain on Local Communities: The famine had a devastating impact on rural Ireland, where many tenant farmers depended on the potato as a staple food. Although Millicent's family would have been more insulated from the immediate effects of starvation, she would have been aware of how it impacted tenants on estates like hers and the overall economy. The social structure of Ireland was deeply affected as many tenants could no longer afford rent, leading to evictions, migrations, and a general breakdown of the old ways of life.

- Impact on Estate and Tenants: If Millicent's family owned land or was involved with tenant farmers, she would have faced difficult decisions. Many landlords, faced with failing crops and tenants unable to pay rent, evicted tenants or saw them leave in search of better opportunities abroad. Millicent may have been involved in managing the estate's response, perhaps encouraging leniency or assisting with relief measures for struggling families.

Impact on Family and Legacy:

- Worry for the Future: As a mother and grandmother, Millicent would likely have been concerned about how the famine might affect her family's future. The famine caused significant economic disruption, and even families of higher social standing saw their resources strained. The political and social instability that followed would also have been worrying for Millicent, who had already seen Ireland experience significant turmoil earlier in her life, such as the Irish Rebellion of 1798.

- Emigration of Friends and Family: The famine forced many Irish people to emigrate to places like the United States, Canada, and Australia. Even though Millicent's family likely had the means to avoid such drastic measures, she would have witnessed friends, neighbors, or distant relatives leaving Ireland, perhaps never to return. This loss of people and culture would have weighed heavily on her as she saw the country around her emptying out.

Religious and Moral Reflection:

- Religious Reflection: Given her religious background, Millicent may have turned to her faith for answers or solace during the famine. She might have seen the disaster as a test of faith, a punishment, or an opportunity to show Christian charity. As the daughter of an archdeacon, she was likely involved in the church community and would have encouraged prayer, reflection, and support for those suffering.

- Calls for Reform: The famine exposed the deep inequalities in Irish society, and Millicent might have been moved to advocate for social and political reform, especially if she had seen firsthand the suffering of the poor. The famine led to a growing awareness of the injustices faced by the Irish population, and she may have joined those calling for better treatment of tenants and more government intervention to prevent future disasters.

Overall Effect:

The Irish Potato Famine would have been an emotionally and socially impactful event for Millicent Mary Benning. While her own family may not have faced starvation, the widespread suffering around her, the disruption of society, and the challenges facing Ireland's future would have deeply affected her. She would have likely reacted with sorrow, compassion, and perhaps a sense of duty to help those around her, while also worrying about the long-term consequences of the famine for Ireland and her family's legacy.

Concern for the Country's Future:

- Economic Decline: The famine caused a significant decline in the Irish economy, especially in rural areas, and Millicent would have witnessed the shrinking of communities and businesses. This may have led her to worry about the future of Ireland's agricultural industry and the overall prosperity of the country. She may have been concerned about how the economic collapse would affect her family's estate or holdings, and whether their way of life would ever fully recover.

- Loss of Population: With the mass emigration and deaths caused by the famine, Millicent might have noticed the population around her decreasing rapidly. The exodus from Ireland, particularly of younger people, would have left a lasting emotional and societal impact, leading to a sense of loss and mourning for the country's dwindling population. This depopulation would have also affected her estate if workers or tenants left in large numbers, creating practical difficulties in maintaining her family's property.

Personal Grief and Reflection:

- Reflecting on Loss: By the time of the famine, Millicent had already experienced personal losses, including the deaths of her parents and her husband. The grief and devastation caused by the famine might have brought back these feelings of loss and made her reflect on her own mortality, as well as the changes she had seen in her lifetime. At 67, Millicent may have been thinking about her own legacy and the future of her children and grandchildren in an Ireland marked by such suffering.

- Involvement in Charitable Work: Given her background and position, Millicent may have taken on an active role in charitable efforts during the famine. Churches, including the Church of Ireland, often played key roles in organizing aid and relief for the starving population. As a member of a prominent family, she may have contributed financially or helped organize local efforts to distribute food, clothing, or other necessities to those affected by the famine.

Family Relationships and Impact on the Next Generation:

- Protecting the Family's Future: Millicent likely focused on ensuring the stability and security of her children and grandchildren during this time of uncertainty. She may have encouraged her family to diversify their income sources, perhaps urging them to pursue careers outside of agriculture or Ireland itself if the situation continued to deteriorate. Given the famine's impact on land ownership and the rural economy, Millicent would have been aware that the future might demand adaptation and resilience.

- Passing Down Lessons: As someone who had lived through the Irish Rebellion of 1798, the Napoleonic Wars, and now the famine, Millicent would have accumulated a wealth of life experience that she could pass down to her children. The famine might have strengthened her belief in the importance of preparedness, resilience, and charity, values she would want to instill in her family as they faced the challenges of an evolving world.

Long-Term View of Irish Identity:

- Shaping Irish Identity: The famine had a significant influence on Irish identity, and for someone of Millicent's generation, it would have marked a turning point in how she viewed her homeland. While she might have been raised with a sense of connection to both Irish and British heritage, the suffering of the Irish people during the famine likely deepened her awareness of the social divisions and inequalities that existed in the country. The events of the famine might have made her more sympathetic to the growing calls for Irish self-determination or reform.

Final Years:

By the time of her death, Millicent would have lived through an era of profound change, and the Great Irish Famine would have left an indelible mark on her later years. While her family's status may have shielded them from the worst of the famine's direct effects, the broader social and economic upheaval would have had a lasting impact on Millicent and those around her.

Final Reflections:

- Sense of Resilience: Having lived through significant historical events like the Irish Rebellion of 1798, the Napoleonic Wars, and now the Great Famine, Millicent would likely have developed a strong sense of resilience and adaptability. She might have viewed these events as tests of her strength and faith, seeing her survival as a testament to her endurance and the importance of maintaining family and faith through adversity.

- Concern for the Nation's Future: As she neared the end of her life, Millicent may have been deeply concerned about the future of Ireland. The famine exposed the deep-rooted inequalities and failures in governance that many believed needed to be addressed. Although Millicent came from a relatively privileged background, the mass suffering around her would have likely made her reflect on the need for societal reform, both in Ireland and across the British Empire.

Impact on Family Legacy:

- Emigration and Future Generations: As so many Irish people emigrated during the famine, Millicent would have seen families and communities broken apart. If any members of her extended family or acquaintances left for America or other destinations, this would have been a personal reminder of the toll the famine had taken. She might have encouraged her own descendants to seek opportunities beyond Ireland, as many Irish families with means did during this time, to secure a more stable future.

- Loss and Legacy: By the time of her death, Millicent may have felt a deep sense of loss, not only for her family members who had passed but also for the Ireland she once knew. The country was changing rapidly, and the famine had accelerated the decline of rural communities and the tenant-farming system. While she might have taken comfort in her faith and family, the overall sense of loss would have been profound, knowing that the famine would leave a scar on Ireland for generations.

Summary of the Impact on Millicent:

- Emotional Reaction: Likely profound sadness and empathy for the suffering around her, with an emphasis on charitable actions due to her religious and social background.

- Social Impact: Witnessing the collapse of rural life, the mass exodus of people, and the challenges facing Irish society, Millicent may have felt a growing concern for the future of Ireland and the stability of her family's estate.

- Family Legacy: Her focus likely shifted to ensuring the well-being of her descendants, passing on lessons of resilience, faith, and adaptability in the face of challenges.

- Religious and Moral Reflection: The famine would have reinforced her Christian values of charity and compassion, leading her to reflect deeply on the moral responsibilities of those in positions of privilege.

The Irish Potato Famine would have left a lasting impact on Millicent Mary Benning in her later years, as she witnessed the suffering and transformation of her homeland during one of the darkest periods in Irish history.

VEN. CONWAY BENNING LL.D.[11]

Ven. Conway Benning LL.D., born in 1737 in Lisbon, County Antrim, Northern Ireland, would have likely possessed the physical traits common among men of his time and class. While there are no known portraits of him, we can infer some aspects of his appearance based on general characteristics of 18th-century Irish men of his social standing.

Probable Physical Appearance:

1. Build:

Conway Benning would likely have had an average build for the period, perhaps slightly more robust if he led a relatively comfortable life, as was typical for a clergyman and academic. Men of the clergy and academic world at that time weren't known for heavy physical labor, so his body might have been less muscular than someone from a working-class background.

2. Facial Features:

- Hair: Given the fashion of the time, he likely wore a wig or powdered his natural hair as was common for gentlemen. His natural hair color, if visible, could have been a shade of brown or grey as he aged.

- Complexion: His complexion would likely have been fair or ruddy, typical of people from Northern Ireland.

- Facial Hair: Beards were uncommon in the 18th century for men of his class, so Conway Benning was likely clean-shaven.

- Eyes: Blue or hazel eyes were common among people of Irish descent, though darker colors could also be present.

3. Clothing and Grooming:

- As a man of the clergy and an educated figure, Conway would have been well-groomed and dressed in the formal clerical attire of the Anglican Church, which likely included a cassock, clerical bands (white bands worn around the neck), and perhaps a frock coat and waistcoat for formal occasions. His clothing would have been made of high-quality fabrics such as wool or linen, reflecting his social status.

- His overall appearance would have conveyed dignity, education, and authority, in keeping with his position as an archdeacon and academic.

4. Health and Longevity:

People in the 18th century often lived under harsher conditions compared to modern standards, with limited access to healthcare and sanitation. However, clergy typically had access to better living conditions, so it's possible Conway Benning lived a relatively healthy life for his time, especially since he held the title of LL.D. (Doctor of Laws), indicating his intellectual focus and likely stability.

Conclusion:

While specific details of Conway Benning's appearance remain unknown, he likely had a dignified and well-groomed appearance typical of an 18th-century Anglican cleric and academic. Clean-shaven with powdered hair (or wearing a wig), wearing formal clerical attire, and possessing an average or slightly robust build, he would have projected an air of authority and respectability that was expected from someone of his rank and position in society.

Conway Benning, born in 1737 in Lisbon, County Antrim, Northern Ireland, grew up during a time of social, political, and religious change in Ireland. As the son of a family that would eventually lead him to the clerical profession and to become a learned man with the title of LL.D. (Doctor of Laws), his early life would have been influenced by his social standing and the broader context of 18th-century Ireland.

Social and Religious Environment:

1. Religious Landscape:

- Northern Ireland in the 18th century was predominantly Protestant, specifically Anglican, especially in regions like County Antrim, which was heavily influenced by the Ulster Plantation. This made the Church of Ireland (Anglican) the established church, and Conway Benning, as part of this religious hierarchy, would have grown up in a community where the Church of Ireland was the dominant religious force.

- The Protestant ascendancy held political and economic power, which would have affected the opportunities available to him. As a future cleric in the Church of Ireland, he would have been part of this elite, benefiting from privileges that were denied to the Catholic majority and nonconformist Protestant denominations such as Presbyterians.

2. Education and Intellectual Life:

- As someone who later attained an LL.D., Conway would have received a formal education, likely at one of Ireland's few but prestigious educational institutions, such as Trinity College in Dublin, where many clergy were trained.

- His education would have focused on theology, law, and classical languages, such as Latin and Greek. The curriculum at the time emphasized moral philosophy, the classics, and religious studies, equipping him for a career in the Church of Ireland and academic roles.

- The intellectual life in Ireland was centered around debates on Enlightenment ideas, religion, and politics, and Conway would have been exposed to these discussions as part of his studies and later in his clerical work. His title of LL.D. indicates that he may have been involved in legal and ecclesiastical matters within the church, possibly dealing with church law, property rights, or moral questions of the time.

Political and Economic Conditions:

1. Political Climate:

- Conway's early years coincided with a relatively stable period in Ireland, though tensions between Catholics and Protestants, and among various Protestant sects, simmered beneath the surface. The Penal Laws, which placed severe restrictions on Catholics and some Protestant nonconformists, were in full force, giving the Protestant Anglican population significant advantages.

- As part of the Anglican clergy, Conway would have aligned with the political and social elite of the Protestant Ascendancy, benefiting from these laws and the privileges afforded to his class.

- However, by the end of the 18th century, political upheavals such as the American Revolution (1775–1783) and the French Revolution (1789) inspired calls for reform in Ireland, leading to increased unrest, particularly among Catholics and Presbyterians. This tension would eventually contribute to the Irish Rebellion of 1798.

2. Economic Conditions:

- The economy of Northern Ireland was mixed, with both rural agriculture and the beginnings of industry, particularly in the linen trade, which was vital to County Antrim. As a member of the clergy and a learned man, Conway Benning's family would likely have been well-off compared to the average population, enjoying relative stability.

- His upbringing in County Antrim, an important agricultural region, would have likely meant that his family had connections to both the landowning class and the urban centers involved in trade and industry.

Daily Life:

1. Family and Social Class:

- Conway Benning would have grown up in a household that emphasized education, religion, and social responsibility. His family, connected to the Anglican Church, would likely have been well-regarded within their community, enjoying a stable and relatively comfortable life.

- His daily life would have been structured around church activities, family obligations, and education. As a young boy, he likely attended a local parish school, which would have prepared him for further studies.

2. Clerical Life and Career:

- From a young age, Conway would have been groomed for a career in the church, learning about religious doctrine, studying the Bible, and attending church services. By the time he reached adulthood, he would have undergone theological training, probably at Trinity College, Dublin, before being ordained into the Church of Ireland.

- As a clergyman, his duties would have included preaching, administering sacraments, performing baptisms, marriages, and funerals, and attending to the spiritual needs of his parishioners. His later achievements, including the LL.D. degree, suggest he also had legal and academic responsibilities, possibly within the broader church hierarchy.

Significant Events During His Lifetime:

- The Jacobite Rebellion (1745): Conway would have been a child during the last major attempt by the Jacobites to restore the Stuart monarchy to the throne of Great Britain and Ireland. While this event occurred mainly in Scotland, its repercussions were felt throughout Ireland, particularly among the Protestant population, who feared the return of Catholic dominance.

- American Revolution (1775–1783): This major event influenced the political landscape of Ireland as many Irish people, especially Presbyterians, sympathized with the American cause. The revolution also spurred calls for reform within Ireland, with a growing movement for greater autonomy from Britain.

- The French Revolution (1789) and its Aftermath: The French Revolution had a profound impact on Irish politics, inspiring radical ideas about liberty, equality, and fraternity. By the 1790s, these ideas had spread to Ireland, contributing to the rise of the United Irishmen and the 1798 Rebellion.

Conclusion:

Conway Benning's life in 18th-century County Antrim would have been shaped by his position within the Anglican Church and the Protestant Ascendancy. He would have experienced a relatively privileged upbringing, centered around religious duty, education, and intellectual pursuits. His later career as a clergyman and scholar would have positioned him as an important figure within both the church and local society, navigating the complex political and social changes of 18th-century Ireland.

When Conway Benning was 2 years old, the Methodist movement was founded by John Wesley in 1739. Though he would have been too young to understand the significance of this religious development at the time, the Methodist movement, which emphasized personal faith, social responsibility, and a departure from the more rigid structures of the Anglican Church, would have a profound effect on the religious landscape of Ireland and Britain as he grew older.

Impact on Conway's Life and Career:

1. Religious Context:

- The Methodist movement was initially a reform within the Church of England, seeking to invigorate personal piety and spiritual practice. As a member of an Anglican family and later a clergyman himself, Conway would have grown up aware of these changes and possibly involved in discussions about them.

  - Since the Bennings were part of the Anglican establishment, they may have viewed Methodism with a mix of curiosity and skepticism. The Methodist call for more emotional and personal religious experiences sometimes conflicted with the more formal Anglican practices Conway would have been raised with.

  2. Clerical Response:

  - As a young man entering the Anglican clergy, Conway would have encountered the growing influence of Methodism. The movement, while initially a part of the Church of England, began to draw people away from Anglicanism, creating tension within the church. Conway's education and ordination likely included discussions about how to respond to Methodism's rise, whether through embracing certain reforms or resisting its more radical ideas.

  - Given that Methodism spread rapidly among the lower classes and was particularly active in Ireland, Conway would likely have been faced with the challenge of addressing social and religious changes within his own parish as an Anglican minister.

  3. Personal Impact:

  - By the time Conway became a clergyman, Methodism would have been well-established and would have shaped the religious atmosphere in which he worked. As a result, he may have had to compete with Methodist preachers for parishioners or engage with them on theological issues.

  - If his family or community were strongly Anglican, they might have been resistant to the Methodist movement, viewing it as a challenge to traditional authority. On the other hand, some

Anglicans embraced elements of Methodism, such as its emphasis on personal holiness and social justice.

4. Social and Religious Division:

- The rise of Methodism contributed to the religious diversity and division in Ireland, where Anglicanism was the established religion. Conway's role as a cleric may have involved addressing the concerns of his Anglican congregation regarding Methodist influence while also attempting to bridge the growing divide between different Protestant groups.

- Conway may also have witnessed the Methodist movement's outreach to the poor and marginalized, which could have influenced his own approach to pastoral care and ministry, particularly if he served in areas affected by poverty and social upheaval.

Conclusion:

While Conway Benning was only a child when the Methodist movement began, its growth throughout his lifetime would have affected the religious and social environment in which he lived and worked. As a clergyman in the established Church of Ireland, he likely navigated the tensions between Anglican tradition and the rising influence of Methodism, shaping his ministry and religious views.

When Conway Benning was 15 years old in 1752, Benjamin Franklin famously conducted his kite experiment, demonstrating that lightning was a form of electricity. This groundbreaking discovery would have had a significant impact on the scientific and intellectual communities of the time, even reaching beyond those directly involved in science.

Conway's Likely Reaction:

1. Fascination with Science:

- As a well-educated young man from a respected family, Conway would likely have heard about Franklin's experiment through scholarly or social circles. The idea that lightning, something previously seen as a mysterious and divine force, could be explained scientifically, would have been revolutionary.

- He might have been intellectually curious about the implications of this discovery. Even though Conway pursued a career in the church, educated individuals at the time often had a broad interest in scientific developments. Franklin's work might have sparked discussions within academic or theological circles about the intersection of science and faith.

2. Theological Reflection:

- As a future Anglican clergyman, Conway may have viewed Franklin's discovery through a theological lens. In the 18th century, many people still saw natural phenomena like lightning as signs of divine power or wrath. Franklin's work challenged this view, offering a rational explanation for a previously supernatural occurrence.

- Conway might have been intrigued by how this discovery fit into religious thought. Many religious leaders began to reconcile new scientific findings with their beliefs, seeing science as a way to better understand God's creation. Conway's reflections could have included a deeper appreciation for the order and laws of nature as expressions of divine will.

3. Impact on Daily Life:

- The discovery that lightning was electric eventually led to practical applications, such as the invention of the lightning rod. Franklin's lightning rod, designed to protect buildings from lightning strikes, became widely adopted. Though this development was still in its early stages, by the time Conway was a young adult, these ideas might have been gaining traction in his community.

- Conway may have seen this as an example of how scientific progress could improve society, particularly in protecting churches, homes, and other buildings from damage. This might have influenced how he viewed technology and innovation in general.

Effect on His Life:

1. Intellectual Environment:

- Conway would have grown up in an era of Enlightenment thought, where reason, science, and the pursuit of knowledge were highly valued. Franklin's experiments contributed to this intellectual climate. The discovery that lightning was a form of electricity would have further fueled debates about the role of science and reason in understanding the world, something Conway would have encountered in his education and possibly in his sermons later in life.

2. Potential Discussions in Clerical Circles:

- As someone preparing for a life in the church, Conway might have engaged in discussions with other clergy and scholars about the relationship between science and religion. Franklin's discovery could have been part of broader debates about how new scientific knowledge fit with established religious doctrine, particularly regarding the understanding of natural phenomena as acts of God.

- This period saw a shift in how people viewed natural disasters and phenomena like lightning. Instead of interpreting them solely as divine punishments, some began to see them as part of the natural world's laws. Conway would have likely participated in or been influenced by these evolving ideas.

3. Broader Worldview:

- Franklin's discovery contributed to a growing sense of the power of human reason and experimentation to unlock nature's secrets. Even if Conway wasn't directly involved in scientific work, living during this time of rapid discovery and change would have shaped his worldview, making him more aware of humanity's expanding knowledge and potential to harness the forces of nature.

- As an Anglican clergyman, he may have used such examples to illustrate the wonders of God's creation, blending scientific understanding with religious teachings to help his congregation appreciate the natural world.

Conclusion:

Conway Benning, at 15 years old, would have been intellectually stimulated by the news of Benjamin Franklin's discovery that lightning was electric. While he likely wouldn't have been directly involved in scientific experiments, the implications of this breakthrough would have affected his education, his intellectual environment, and his views on the relationship between science and religion. It would have opened up new ways of thinking about natural phenomena and the power of human understanding.

When Conway Benning entered Trinity College Dublin on September 3, 1755, at the age of 18, this would have been a monumental moment in his life. Trinity College Dublin, one of the leading universities of the time, offered an environment rich in intellectual and cultural opportunities, providing Conway with an education that would shape his future as a scholar and clergyman. Here's how he likely reacted and how this experience would have affected him:

Conway's Likely Reaction:

1. Excitement and Pride:

- At 18, Conway likely felt a sense of pride and excitement about attending such a prestigious institution. Being accepted into Trinity College Dublin was a significant achievement, reflecting his academic abilities and the efforts of his tutor, Mr. McArthur, who had prepared him for higher education.

- This sense of accomplishment would have instilled confidence in Conway as he embarked on his academic journey.

2. Intellectual Curiosity:

- Trinity College Dublin was a hub of Enlightenment thought, where students were exposed to various fields of study, including philosophy, theology, the classics, and emerging scientific ideas. Conway, who had already shown academic promise, would likely have felt intellectually stimulated and eager to engage with the new ideas and knowledge presented to him.

- His early years in college would have been filled with curiosity about the world, both academically and spiritually. Being surrounded by other bright students and professors would have sparked discussions about religion, science, and politics.

3. Challenge and Adjustment:

- Entering college would have been a significant adjustment for Conway. The rigorous academic environment and the expectations placed on students would have required discipline and dedication. While he may have been well-prepared by his tutor, adjusting to the university's demands and the new social setting of living among fellow students would have posed challenges.

- Conway may have felt a sense of pressure to perform well and live up to the high standards of the college, particularly since his education would have been a pathway to his future career in the church.

4. Social and Religious Impact:

- Trinity College Dublin was an Anglican institution, and students like Conway would have been steeped in religious education. Given that he came from a family with a strong religious background, Conway likely embraced the religious aspect of his education, viewing it as preparation for his future role in the Anglican Church.

- However, as Ireland was religiously and politically complex, Conway might have encountered diverse views on religion and politics during his time at Trinity. This exposure could have broadened his understanding of the tensions in Ireland between

Catholics and Protestants, which would shape his worldview as a clergyman.

Effect on His Life:

1. Academic and Theological Growth:

- Trinity College Dublin offered a classical education focused on the liberal arts, theology, and philosophy, which would have profoundly shaped Conway's intellectual development. His studies in theology would have deepened his understanding of religious doctrine, preparing him for his future role as a clergyman and scholar.

- This academic foundation likely made him a well-rounded intellectual, able to engage in theological debates and provide spiritual guidance to his future parishioners.

2. Preparation for the Clergy:

- Conway's time at Trinity was not just about gaining knowledge but about preparing for his calling in the church. The religious training he received would have strengthened his commitment to the Anglican faith and his future role as a leader in the Church of Ireland.

- The education and connections he made at Trinity College would have been crucial in securing his later positions within the church, such as becoming an archdeacon.

3. Social and Political Awareness:

- Trinity College was not only an academic institution but also a place where students would have been exposed to the political and social issues of the day. During the mid-18th century, Ireland was marked by religious conflict and political unrest, especially between the Protestant ruling class and the Catholic majority.

- Conway's education would have given him insight into these tensions, and his time at Trinity may have shaped his views on governance, religion, and society in Ireland. This awareness could have influenced how he later conducted his duties as a clergyman, particularly in navigating the challenges of ministering in a divided society.

4. Network and Connections:

- Attending Trinity College Dublin would have allowed Conway to build valuable connections with fellow students, professors, and members of the Anglican Church hierarchy. These connections would have been instrumental in shaping his career trajectory.

- Trinity's alumni network would have provided Conway with opportunities for mentorship and advancement, which helped him later secure prominent positions in the church, including his role as archdeacon.

Conclusion:

Conway Benning's entry into Trinity College Dublin at the age of 18 was a pivotal moment in his life. It marked the beginning of a rigorous academic and theological education that would shape his career in the Anglican Church. The intellectual stimulation, exposure to Enlightenment ideas, and religious training he received would have had a profound impact on his personal and professional development. Additionally, the social connections and political awareness he gained at Trinity would have influenced his approach to his future clerical duties in Ireland's complex religious landscape.

When Conway Benning was 23 years old in 1760, the same year he received his LL.B., the Industrial Revolution was just beginning. While the revolution's full impact wouldn't be felt for a few more decades, he would have likely started to notice early signs of societal and economic changes. Here's how Conway might have reacted and been affected by the onset of the Industrial Revolution:

Initial Reactions:

1. Curiosity and Intellectual Interest:

- As an educated man with a background in both theology and law, Conway would have likely been intellectually curious about the technological innovations and economic changes occurring during the early stages of the Industrial Revolution. Innovations like the steam engine and mechanized textile production were beginning to take shape, which may have intrigued someone of his intellectual stature.

- Theological debates about the ethics of progress and change may have sparked Conway's interest. As a churchman, he may have engaged in discussions about how these changes would affect traditional ways of life and the moral implications of industrialization.

2. Cautious Skepticism:

- Like many in his time, especially in rural and ecclesiastical circles, Conway may have viewed these early signs of industrialization with caution. The church often represented continuity and tradition, while the Industrial Revolution was associated with disruptive changes. He might have been skeptical of how these technological advancements could alter the social fabric of communities.

- His religious training might have led him to view rapid industrial growth as a potential threat to the moral and spiritual welfare of society. He could have been concerned about how industrialization would affect the rural way of life, the erosion of traditional livelihoods, and the growing emphasis on material wealth and productivity.

3. Concern for the Poor:

- As someone likely involved in pastoral care, Conway would have been sensitive to the needs of his parishioners. The early Industrial Revolution led to changes in labor patterns, migration from rural areas to cities, and the growth of factory work. These shifts often brought with them increased poverty, harsh working conditions, and economic disparity.

- Conway may have been concerned about the social and economic upheavals that industrialization could bring, particularly for the poor and working classes. As a clergyman, he would have felt a duty to ensure the well-being of those in his community, possibly advocating for fair treatment and the moral responsibility of industrialists.

Effects on His Life:

1. Rural Life and Pastoral Responsibilities:

- During Conway's early years, the Industrial Revolution's impact would have been more pronounced in urban centers and in industries like textiles, mining, and transportation. If Conway spent much of his life in rural parts of Ireland, the immediate effects of industrialization might have been minimal in his own community. However, he would have been aware of the broader societal changes taking place.

- His role as a church leader likely placed him in a position where he had to balance tradition with the growing awareness of industrial progress. He may have been involved in providing moral guidance to his parishioners, helping them navigate the changing world, especially if they were faced with decisions like moving to cities for work or adapting to new agricultural technologies.

2. Economic and Social Shifts:

- While the Industrial Revolution is often associated with increased economic growth, the early stages of industrialization were marked by significant inequalities. Conway would have likely witnessed the widening gap between the wealthy industrialists and the working class, which could have influenced his sermons or pastoral work.

- He might have become more engaged in social justice issues, advocating for the rights and well-being of the less fortunate, especially if he saw the adverse effects of industrialization on his parishioners.

3. Influence on the Church:

- The church itself faced challenges during the Industrial Revolution, as urbanization and the rise of new social classes led to a decline in traditional religious practices among some communities. As a leader in the Church of Ireland, Conway may have had to address declining attendance, especially in urban areas, and find ways to make the church relevant to a rapidly changing society.

- He might have been part of discussions within the church about how to respond to the ethical and moral dilemmas posed by industrialization, including issues like child labor, poor working conditions, and the impact of mechanization on people's livelihoods.

4. Legal Implications:

- As someone with a legal education, Conway may have found his expertise increasingly relevant in the face of industrialization. The growing complexity of industrial society brought about new legal challenges, such as property disputes, patent laws, and labor rights. While he was primarily focused on ecclesiastical law, his knowledge might have been useful in navigating the legal questions that arose from industrial progress.

5. Personal Adaptation:

- Though Conway was rooted in traditional values, he may have had to personally adapt to some of the changes brought about by industrialization, particularly as new technologies like the steam engine began transforming transportation and communication. By the later years of his life, industrialization would have touched more aspects of everyday life, from how goods were produced to how people traveled and communicated.

- As someone involved in leadership, Conway would have needed to engage with these changes, at least in a practical sense, to ensure that his parish and community were not left behind by the growing wave of industrial progress.

Conclusion:

At 23, Conway Benning likely approached the Industrial Revolution with a mixture of intellectual curiosity, cautious skepticism, and concern for its social impact. Over time, as industrialization became more pervasive, it would have influenced his role as a clergyman, requiring him to navigate the challenges posed by economic inequality, social upheaval, and the changing role of the church in an industrial society. While the revolution's early stages may not have drastically altered his rural life initially, its ripple effects would have gradually influenced both his community and his responsibilities as a spiritual and community leader.

When Conway Benning received his Bachelor of Arts degree in 1760 and was admitted as Dean at Belfast by William, Bishop of Down on June 7, 1760, these events would have marked significant milestones in his life. Here's how he might have reacted and the likely effects on him:

Conway's Likely Reaction:

1. Sense of Accomplishment:

- Receiving his B.A. degree from Trinity College Dublin would have been a proud moment for Conway. It was the culmination of years of hard work, discipline, and dedication to his studies. Earning a degree from such a prestigious institution would have been a personal triumph, reinforcing his confidence in his academic and intellectual abilities.

- Being admitted as Dean at Belfast on the same day he received his degree would have felt like the ultimate reward for his efforts. Achieving such a position so early in his career would have likely filled him with a sense of accomplishment and validation of his calling in the church.

2. Religious and Spiritual Fulfillment:

- Conway was deeply committed to his faith, and becoming a dean would have felt like a significant spiritual calling. The role of dean came with the responsibility of overseeing the spiritual care and administration of a parish, which would have deeply resonated with Conway's religious aspirations.

- He likely felt that his education, his personal devotion, and the guidance of mentors had led him to this point, where he could now fulfill his mission of serving God and guiding his congregation.

3. Sense of Responsibility:

- Along with pride and excitement, Conway would likely have felt the weight of responsibility that came with his new role as dean. He now had the task of providing spiritual leadership to the parishioners of Belfast, overseeing church activities, and possibly managing clergy under his care. This position required administrative skills, theological knowledge, and the ability to engage with both the common people and the ruling class.

- Conway likely understood that this was the beginning of a larger clerical career and that how he performed as dean would shape his future within the church.

4. Gratitude and Humility:

- Being appointed dean by the Bishop of Down, William, would have been a high honor for Conway. He would likely have felt a sense of gratitude for the bishop's confidence in him and for the support of those who had helped him reach this point in his career.

- As a man of faith, Conway may have seen this as a divinely guided moment, where God was placing him in a position to do

His work. This sense of divine purpose may have kept him humble in the face of such a high office.

Effect on His Life:

1. Career Advancement:

- Being admitted as dean at Belfast was a major step in Conway's clerical career. The position would have provided him with both experience and visibility within the Anglican Church, which would be crucial for further advancement.

- It established him as a trusted and capable leader within the church, opening the door for future roles, such as when he later became an archdeacon. His role as dean would also allow him to form important relationships with other church leaders and prominent figures in the community.

2. Increased Social Standing:

- In 18th-century Ireland, holding a prominent church position like dean would have elevated Conway's social status. The Church of Ireland was closely tied to the ruling class, and clergy in high-ranking positions often interacted with nobility and local gentry.

- Conway's position as dean would have provided him with greater social visibility and influence, as well as the respect of both his congregation and his peers within the church. His family's standing would also have been enhanced by his new role.

3. Administrative and Leadership Skills:

- Becoming dean would have required Conway to develop and refine his leadership and administrative skills. He would have been responsible for overseeing the day-to-day operations of the church, managing finances, and ensuring that church services were conducted properly.

- These responsibilities would have helped him grow as a leader, preparing him for future roles where even greater leadership and organizational skills would be required.

4. Personal Growth and Faith:
- Serving as dean would have deepened Conway's faith and understanding of his religious duties. The role would have allowed him to put into practice the theological knowledge he gained during his education at Trinity College. Preaching, teaching, and offering spiritual guidance to his congregation would have strengthened his connection to his faith and his sense of purpose.

- His new role would have tested his resilience, patience, and empathy as he navigated the spiritual needs of his parishioners. This experience likely had a profound impact on his spiritual maturity.

5. Community Influence:
- As dean, Conway would have been an important figure in the local community. His role was not just spiritual but also involved civic responsibilities. He would have had influence over local matters, and people from all walks of life would have come to him for guidance, spiritual support, and advice.

- This position of influence allowed Conway to impact the moral and social fabric of his community, strengthening his role as a moral leader.

Conclusion:

Conway Benning's appointment as Dean of Belfast at the age of 23, just after receiving his B.A. from Trinity College, would have been both a proud and pivotal moment in his life. It marked the beginning of a significant clerical career, shaped by his faith, academic achievements, and sense of responsibility. This early success set the tone for his future leadership in the Church of Ireland and had a profound effect on his social standing, personal growth, and religious commitment. His time as dean prepared him for greater challenges and opportunities within the church and likely strengthened his faith and leadership skills.

Receiving his LL.B. (Bachelor of Laws) in 1760 at the age of 23 would have been a significant achievement for Conway Benning, affecting both his personal and professional life. Here's how he might have been affected:

Likely Reactions:

1. Sense of Accomplishment:

- Completing an advanced degree in law at such a young age would have brought a strong sense of personal achievement. For Conway, this milestone would have been a validation of his intellectual abilities and academic dedication.

- The LL.B. was a prestigious degree, indicating his high level of education and establishing him as a learned man among his peers and in society.

2. Broader Career Prospects:

- While Conway was on a path to a career in the Church, holding a law degree would have opened up broader opportunities for him, both within ecclesiastical law and in administrative roles within the Church of Ireland.

- He would have been well-prepared for leadership roles that required legal knowledge, such as managing church estates, dealing with legal disputes within the church, or acting as an advisor in legal matters concerning the diocese or local parish governance.

3. Increased Social Standing:

- Having an advanced degree in law would have elevated his social standing considerably. It would have set him apart as not only a religious figure but also an educated and capable individual in legal matters.

- This achievement would have earned him the respect of his peers, both within the clergy and among the gentry, and could have brought him closer to influential circles in society.

4. Enhanced Reputation in the Church:

- The LL.B. degree would have been particularly useful in the context of ecclesiastical law, a critical aspect of church governance. This specialized legal knowledge would have made him a valuable asset to the Church of Ireland.

- His education likely positioned him for rapid promotion within the Church hierarchy, as legal expertise would have been highly regarded in church administration. This would have contributed to his appointment as Dean and eventual ordination as a priest.

Effect on His Life:

1. Preparation for Leadership:

- The LL.B. would have prepared Conway for roles that required not just spiritual leadership, but administrative and legal oversight as well. His education would have helped him navigate complex legal issues related to church property, inheritance, and governance.

- As he later became a priest and held various positions within the church, his legal background would have given him the skills to handle the administrative and financial duties associated with those roles.

2. Increased Responsibilities:

- With his legal degree, Conway likely found himself taking on more responsibilities within the church's administrative structure. His understanding of law would have made him a trusted figure for handling important documents, contracts, and legal affairs involving church lands and estates.

- This new expertise would have required him to balance both his spiritual and legal duties, which could have been demanding but also fulfilling.

3. Improved Financial Stability:

- With his legal education, Conway could have taken on roles that were not only prestigious but also well-compensated within the Church of Ireland. Positions that required legal expertise typically came with higher salaries, which would have contributed to his financial stability and security.

- This may have also allowed him to provide more comfortably for his family in the future, especially as he continued to advance in his career.

4. Respect and Authority:

- Conway's degree would have increased his authority not only within the church but also in the wider community. As someone trained in both theology and law, he would have been seen as a wise and capable leader.

- His legal knowledge would have given him authority on matters where religion and law intersected, such as disputes over church tithes, moral and legal guidance to parishioners, and ecclesiastical court proceedings.

5. Personal Fulfillment:

- On a personal level, the achievement of an LL.B. would have been deeply fulfilling for Conway. It signaled the culmination of years of study and effort, and it likely reinforced his confidence in his abilities and his role within the church and society.

Conclusion:

Receiving his LL.B. in 1760 would have been a defining moment in Conway Benning's life. It marked him as an educated and capable individual, prepared for leadership roles both within the church and in legal matters. This achievement would have opened up new career opportunities, enhanced his reputation, and contributed to his growing influence within the Church of Ireland. It also provided him with the skills and knowledge to handle complex administrative and legal responsibilities, making him an invaluable figure in church governance.

Conway Benning's ordination as a priest in 1761, shortly after being appointed Dean at Belfast, would have been a profound moment in his life, marking the culmination of his spiritual preparation and the start of his full pastoral duties. Here's how he might have reacted and the effects it had on him:

Likely Reaction:

1. Deep Sense of Reverence:

- Conway would have approached his ordination with great reverence and humility. The ceremony would have been a sacred and solemn occasion, filled with spiritual significance. As someone deeply committed to his faith, being ordained would have felt like a fulfillment of his divine calling.

- He likely saw this moment as a covenant with God, where he was fully dedicating his life to serving the Church and its people.

2. Spiritual Responsibility:

- With ordination, Conway would now have the full authority to perform the sacraments, preach, and guide his congregation. This newfound authority would have weighed on him as both a blessing and a responsibility.

- His role as a spiritual leader became official, meaning he now had to uphold the faith and morals of the Church of Ireland, ensuring he led by example.

3. Pride and Achievement:

- Achieving ordination at such a young age—only 24 years old—would have brought a sense of personal accomplishment. Not only had he completed his academic training, but now he was officially recognized as a priest.

- He might have felt a sense of pride not only for himself but also for his family and mentors who had guided him. This would have been a significant moment of joy for them as well, knowing their efforts had borne fruit in his success.

4. Humble Gratitude:

- Ordination wasn't just a career milestone; it was a spiritual milestone. Conway likely felt humbled by the trust placed in him by the Church and God. This humility would have been accompanied by deep gratitude for the opportunity to serve in this capacity.

- He might have reflected on the many blessings that had come his way, including his education and his new position as dean.

Effect on His Life:

1. Greater Spiritual and Community Influence:

- As an ordained priest, Conway would have gained greater influence both within the Church and in his local community. The priesthood carried a certain level of moral authority, and people would now look to him not just as a religious figure but also as a guide in their everyday lives.

- His responsibilities would include offering spiritual counsel, officiating weddings, baptisms, and funerals, and leading religious ceremonies, which would make him central to both the spiritual and social lives of his parishioners.

2. Increased Responsibility:

- Ordination brought with it increased pastoral duties. He would now be the person people relied on for spiritual guidance and moral leadership, which would require him to be constantly attuned to the needs of his congregation.

- This new level of responsibility would have required him to balance both his administrative duties as dean and his pastoral duties as a priest, which would challenge his organizational skills and commitment to his faith.

3. Strengthening of His Faith:

- With ordination, Conway's personal relationship with his faith would have deepened. He was now responsible for shepherding others on their spiritual journeys, which would require him to maintain and grow in his own spiritual practices.

- Preaching regularly and conducting sacraments would have forced him to reflect deeply on his beliefs, which likely would have made him even more devoted and pious.

4. Long-Term Career Impact:
- Conway's ordination marked the beginning of his clerical career in its fullest sense. This achievement would open doors for future appointments and higher offices within the Church. In time, he would be elevated to positions like archdeacon and gain further respect and authority within the Church of Ireland.
- His ordination would be a crucial step in solidifying his standing as a trusted and capable member of the clergy, setting him on a path to greater influence.

5. Enhanced Social Status:
- Ordained clergy were held in high esteem, and Conway's ordination would have further elevated his social standing. As a priest and dean, he would have been a prominent figure in local society, which also meant his family's standing would rise.
- This social elevation could have also brought new opportunities for connections, both within the church hierarchy and among the gentry or local influential families.

6. Stronger Ties to the Church:
- Ordination would have strengthened Conway's ties to the institutional Church of Ireland. He was no longer just a student or a young cleric, but a fully vested priest with responsibilities to both the Church and his parishioners.
- This would also mean an even greater commitment to upholding the doctrines, traditions, and expectations of the Church, which would shape his worldview and actions moving forward.

Conclusion:
Conway Benning's ordination in 1761 would have been a pivotal event in his life, marking the official start of his role as

a priest. It would have filled him with a deep sense of spiritual purpose, responsibility, and pride. His new role would have brought him closer to his community, strengthened his faith, and positioned him for future career advancement within the Church of Ireland. This moment not only solidified his spiritual calling but also impacted his social standing and the trajectory of his life, setting him on the path toward greater roles of leadership within the church.

AT 33 YEARS OLD, WHEN Conway Benning was instituted to the Vicarage of Glenavy, Camolin, and Tullyrush in the Diocese of Connor under the patronage of the Marquis of Hertford, this would have been a significant moment in his life and career. Here's how he might have reacted and how it would have affected him:

Immediate Reactions:

1. Sense of Achievement:

- Receiving such a prestigious appointment at 33 would have been a mark of accomplishment. Being placed in charge of multiple parishes under the patronage of an influential noble like the Marquis of Hertford would have been a sign of the trust placed in him by both the Church of Ireland hierarchy and the Marquis himself. Conway would likely have felt a great sense of pride and validation for his hard work and education.

2. Responsibility and Duty:

- Along with the honor of being named vicar came significant responsibility. Glenavy, Camolin, and Tullyrush were rural parishes, but each would have had its own needs and challenges. Conway would have had to balance pastoral duties, overseeing church administration, and providing moral and spiritual guidance to the parishioners in multiple locations. The scale of the role likely weighed on him, requiring careful planning and management.

3. Spiritual Fulfillment:

- As a committed churchman, Conway would likely have viewed this appointment as an opportunity to further his spiritual mission and provide meaningful guidance to his parishioners. Serving the Church of Ireland as a vicar in this capacity would have allowed him to deepen his connection with the community and put into practice his theological knowledge and pastoral training.

Effect on His Life:

1. Professional Growth:

- Being placed in charge of three parishes gave Conway significant administrative experience. His role would have involved not just preaching and pastoral care, but also managing the resources of the church, organizing services, and possibly overseeing the construction or upkeep of church buildings. This administrative experience would have prepared him for later roles of greater responsibility within the Church.

- It would have also expanded his influence within the broader Church of Ireland community, helping him make connections with other clergymen and prominent figures like the Marquis of Hertford, which could have opened up future opportunities.

2. Social and Political Connections:

- Serving under the patronage of the Marquis of Hertford would have enhanced Conway's social standing. The Marquis was a wealthy and influential figure, and Conway's association with him could have helped him forge connections with other prominent members of Irish society, both within and beyond the Church. This would have allowed Conway to participate in the social and political discussions of the day, possibly even influencing local matters or decisions in the diocese.

3. Intellectual and Spiritual Challenge:

- Managing multiple parishes, each with its own congregation and challenges, would have required Conway to be intellectually and spiritually resourceful. He would have needed to craft sermons that resonated with different audiences, address pastoral issues ranging from poverty to morality, and guide his parishioners through times of spiritual or personal crisis.

- Given that this period followed the religious tensions of the 17th century, Conway likely encountered ongoing complexities regarding the relationship between the Church of Ireland and the largely Catholic population. Navigating these tensions, while maintaining the Church's influence, would have been a significant part of his role.

4. Family and Personal Life:

- This phase of his career likely brought stability for Conway's family, including his wife and young children. As the vicar of multiple parishes, he would have enjoyed a respectable social position with a steady income, which provided financial security. His family would have benefited from the stability this appointment brought, as well as the social status that came with being the vicar of parishes connected to a noble patron.

- Glenavy, in particular, was a relatively small but historically significant parish. Living and working in such a place would have offered Conway a peaceful environment to raise his family, away from the urban centers of political strife.

Challenges He May Have Faced:

1. Balancing Multiple Parishes:

- Serving as vicar of three parishes simultaneously would have posed logistical challenges. Conway likely had to travel between these locations frequently, possibly using horseback or other means of transport, to ensure that all his parishioners were receiving proper spiritual care.

- Balancing the time and resources needed to administer all three parishes effectively would have required excellent organizational skills and possibly delegating some responsibilities to curates or assistants.

2. Religious and Political Climate:

- Ireland in the 1760s was marked by religious divisions, with tensions between the Protestant Church of Ireland and the predominantly Catholic population. Although the Church of Ireland was the established church, it did not represent the majority of the population. Conway's role as a clergyman in this environment might have required him to be sensitive to local tensions while maintaining the Church's teachings and influence.

- He may have also been called upon to act as a mediator or counselor in disputes, given the authority that his position granted him in the community.

3. Evolving Theological and Social Ideas:

- As an intellectual and spiritual leader, Conway would have been aware of the Enlightenment ideas circulating in Europe. Although the Industrial Revolution was just beginning, the intellectual shift toward reason, science, and new social theories would have been part of the broader discourse of the time. He would have had to reconcile these ideas with his traditional religious beliefs and teachings, possibly encountering parishioners who were curious or skeptical about the role of religion in a changing world.

Conclusion:

Conway Benning's appointment to the vicarage of Glenavy, Camolin, and Tullyrush was likely a moment of both pride and responsibility. It marked his rise within the Church of Ireland and would have expanded his social, political, and spiritual influence. While he would have welcomed the opportunity to shepherd his flock and engage with the theological challenges of the time, he also faced the practical difficulties of managing multiple parishes and navigating a religiously divided society. The experience would have helped shape him into a seasoned church leader, preparing him for further ecclesiastical and academic responsibilities later in life.

Conway Benning's marriage to Ann Ellis on January 26, 1770, would likely have been a significant event in their social circles, especially given that Conway was already a respected clergyman and Ann Ellis came from a prominent family in Carrickfergus, County Antrim. Here's what their wedding might have been like, along with a description of what Conway would have worn:

Setting and Ceremony:

1. Location:

- The wedding probably took place in a Church of Ireland parish church, possibly at a local church in or near Carrickfergus, where Ann's family was based, or a nearby town where Conway had ecclesiastical ties.

- The ceremony would have been formal, following the Church of Ireland's rites, with strong religious overtones. Being an Anglican clergyman himself, Conway would have ensured the service adhered strictly to the traditional liturgical practices of the time, likely including prayers, scripture readings, and vows in accordance with the Book of Common Prayer.

2. Guests:

- Guests would likely have included members of both families, particularly Ann's relatives from Carrickfergus and Conway's clerical colleagues. Given Conway's connection to the Marquis of Hertford, some of the more influential figures in their social circle might also have attended.

- Weddings in the 18th century, especially among families of stature, were community events. It's likely that the local gentry and clergy, along with close friends and family, would have gathered to witness the ceremony and celebrate the union.

3. Reception:

- The wedding reception, if held, would likely have been a modest but dignified affair, possibly at the Ellis family estate in Prospect, Carrickfergus. The gathering would have included a formal meal, possibly with toasts and speeches in honor of the newlyweds.

- While weddings at the time were not as elaborate as they became in later centuries, it's likely that some form of entertainment, such as music or dancing, would have taken place.

Conway Benning's Attire:

As a clergyman in the Church of Ireland and a man of some social standing, Conway Benning's wedding attire would have been formal and dignified, reflecting the customs and fashion of the time.

1. Clergyman's Gown and Cassock:

- Conway, being a churchman, might have opted to wear formal clerical robes for at least part of the wedding ceremony, particularly the cassock and gown. The cassock, typically black or dark-colored, was a long, buttoned robe worn by Anglican clergymen. Over this, he may have worn a simple black preaching gown, which would have lent a solemn and dignified air to the proceedings.

2. Wedding Coat and Breeches:

- For the reception or more festive parts of the day, Conway might have changed into fashionable formal wear for a gentleman of his status. This would likely have included a knee-length coat made of fine wool, silk, or velvet in darker, subdued colors like black, dark blue, or brown, which were popular among clergy and other professionals.

- Breeches, tight-fitting trousers that reached just below the knee, would have been paired with white or off-white stockings, and black, buckled shoes, following the fashion of the time.

3. Cravat or Stock:

- Around his neck, Conway likely wore a white cravat or stock, which was a long piece of fabric tied at the neck in a simple but elegant knot. This would have been an essential part of his formal attire, completing the dignified look expected of a man in his position.

4. Waistcoat:

- Beneath the coat, he would have worn a waistcoat (vest), which at that time was usually made of a luxurious material like silk or brocade, often in a contrasting but complementary color to the coat. Waistcoats during the late 18th century were starting to shorten and become more fitted, as fashion shifted toward simpler, more elegant lines.

5. Wig:

- It is likely that Conway would have worn a wig, as was customary for men of status in the 18th century. By the 1770s, wigs were becoming less voluminous than earlier in the century, and a simple, shorter clerical wig, perhaps lightly powdered, would have been appropriate for the occasion.

6. Accessories:

- Conway might have worn a pocket watch with a chain, a common accessory for men of the period, signaling his status and the practicality valued by a clergyman.

- Additionally, white gloves might have been worn, as they were considered an essential part of formal attire at weddings and other ceremonies during this time.

Ann Ellis' Attire:

Ann Ellis would likely have worn a wedding gown reflecting the fashions of the time. This would have been a dress made of silk or satin, in a light color (possibly white, though pastel colors were also popular), with a fitted bodice and full skirt, worn with stays or corsetry underneath to shape the silhouette.

Effect on Their Lives:

1. Family Alliances:

- Marrying into the Ellis family, a notable family from Carrickfergus, would have likely increased Conway's social connections, strengthening ties between prominent families in County Antrim. The union may have also brought Conway a dowry or other forms of financial and social support, which would have benefited him in his clerical career and personal life.

2. Stability and Status:

- The marriage would have provided Conway with a stable family life, which was important for his standing as a clergyman. Being married, particularly to someone from a reputable family, would have enhanced his status and respectability within both the Church of Ireland and the broader community.

3. Personal Fulfillment:

- On a personal level, marriage to Ann Ellis may have provided Conway with a companion to share his life and duties. Having a supportive spouse was often crucial for clergymen who needed someone to manage the household while they focused on their religious duties. Together, Conway and Ann likely fostered a stable and supportive environment, both for themselves and any children they would have.

In conclusion, their wedding would have been a formal yet joyful occasion, marked by both religious solemnity and social celebration. For Conway, it would have solidified his social standing and provided him with a strong foundation for both his clerical duties and personal life.

When Conway Benning was 33 years old and his son, also named Conway, was born later that year, it would have had a profound impact on him, both personally and professionally.

Personal Impact:

1. Pride and Legacy:

- The birth of a son would have been a moment of great pride for Conway Benning. In 18th-century Ireland, especially within more established or professional families, the birth of a son was often seen as the continuation of the family name and legacy. The fact that he named his son after himself could suggest a desire to pass on not only his name but also his values, status, and possibly his vocation in the church.

2. Increased Responsibility:

- The arrival of a child would have increased his sense of responsibility, not only for providing materially but also for guiding his son's education, upbringing, and future prospects. As a clergyman and a man of learning, Conway would have likely envisioned a life of education and professional development for his son, perhaps even hoping that his son would follow in his footsteps into the clergy.

3. Emotional Fulfillment:

- On a personal level, having a child can bring immense emotional fulfillment, and Conway may have felt a deep sense of joy and contentment in starting a family with his wife, Ann Ellis. Children were seen as a blessing, and as a religious man, he would have viewed his son's birth as a gift from God, further solidifying his faith and commitment to family life.

4. Support from Extended Family:

- Conway and Ann would likely have received support from their extended families in raising their son. Ann's family, the Ellis family of Prospect, Carrickfergus, might have been actively involved in their grandson's upbringing, which would have strengthened the ties between the two families and provided Conway with a solid family network.

Professional Impact:

1. Career Focus and Motivation:

- The birth of a son may have provided Conway with new motivation to advance his career within the Church of Ireland. The desire to provide for his family would likely have made him more focused on his duties as a vicar and priest, and it might have influenced his decisions regarding future postings or promotions within the church.

2. Community Expectations:
- As a clergyman, Conway would have been held to high moral standards by his community. Having a family, particularly a son, would have solidified his image as a respectable, established figure within the church. It may have helped him build stronger relationships within his parish and community, as parishioners might have seen him as a model of family values and stability.

3. Educational Aspirations:
- Given his own educational background, Conway would have likely been deeply invested in his son's education. He may have already begun thinking about how to prepare young Conway for future studies, whether in the clergy or another respectable profession. As a father, he might have taken an active role in teaching his son, instilling values of faith, discipline, and learning from an early age.

Long-Term Influence:
The birth of his son may have led Conway to think more deeply about the future, both in terms of his personal legacy and his career. He would likely have been more motivated to ensure that he left behind a stable and respected family for his son to inherit, and this could have influenced his decisions in both his professional and personal life.

In summary, the birth of his son would have been a pivotal moment in Conway Benning's life, strengthening his commitment to family and faith while also motivating him to continue his professional work in the church with renewed purpose. The joy and responsibility of fatherhood would have shaped both his private life and his role within the community.

WHEN CONWAY BENNING was collated to the Rectory of Donaghcloney, the Rectory of Magherally, and the Archdeaconry of Dromore on May 5, 1770, at the age of 33, it would have been a significant moment in both his ecclesiastical career and personal life.

How He Might Have Reacted:

1. Sense of Achievement and Gratitude:

- Being collated to these important positions would have likely instilled in Conway a deep sense of pride and achievement. The Archdeaconry of Dromore was a notable ecclesiastical post, and managing multiple rectories at Donaghcloney and Magherally was no small feat. This advancement would have been seen as a mark of recognition for his dedication and capability in the Church of Ireland. As a religious man, Conway may have expressed his gratitude through prayer, viewing this achievement as a blessing from God.

2. Increased Responsibility:

- Conway likely recognized that with these new roles came greater responsibility, both in terms of administrative duties and spiritual guidance. As the Archdeacon, he would have been responsible for overseeing the clergy within the diocese, assisting the bishop, and ensuring that church doctrine and discipline were upheld. Managing two rectories meant overseeing the spiritual well-being of two parishes, as well as handling the financial and practical affairs of both. Conway may have felt both the weight of these responsibilities and a renewed sense of purpose in his service to the church.

3. Personal Satisfaction and Family Pride:

- On a personal level, this promotion would have been a source of great pride not only for Conway but also for his family. His wife, Ann Ellis, and their newborn son, Conway Jr., were likely viewed as part of this new chapter of his life. It would have given the family an elevated social standing within their community, and this success would have been celebrated by both his family and his in-laws, particularly the Ellis family of Prospect, Carrickfergus. The appointment would have provided a sense of security and stability for his growing family.

4. Ambition and Future Prospects:

- This recognition might have also sparked further ambitions for Conway. Achieving a position like Archdeacon at 33 was impressive, and it may have made him think about future opportunities within the church, such as potentially becoming a bishop one day. He would have been aware that success in his current roles could open doors for greater ecclesiastical authority and influence.

The Effects on His Life:

1. Professional Growth:

- Taking on the Archdeaconry of Dromore and managing two rectories would have enhanced Conway's professional reputation. These roles required strong leadership, administrative skills, and a deep commitment to the spiritual and pastoral needs of his parishioners. Successfully handling these responsibilities would have solidified his standing as a respected clergyman within the Diocese of Dromore and beyond. It likely contributed to his ongoing career trajectory in the church.

2. Greater Influence in the Church:

- As an Archdeacon, Conway would have been one of the senior clerics in the diocese, responsible for inspecting churches, advising the bishop, and ensuring that the clergy under his care adhered to church rules. This would have given him a broader influence within the church and the ability to shape religious life in the parishes he oversaw. His opinions and decisions would have carried more weight, and he would have played a crucial role in maintaining church order and discipline.

3. Increased Workload and Stress:

- While this promotion was undoubtedly a positive development, it also would have come with increased demands. Managing two parishes and serving as Archdeacon required balancing the spiritual care of his parishioners with the administrative and bureaucratic aspects of church leadership. This might have led to more travel between parishes and the diocesan center, as well as increased responsibilities in overseeing church property, finances, and clergy. These duties could have added stress and required careful time management, but his prior experience and education would have helped him adapt.

4. Improved Social Standing:

- Holding multiple ecclesiastical positions would have elevated Conway's social status. He would have been seen as a man of authority and respect within both the church and wider society. This promotion likely enhanced his influence within the local gentry and clergy, making him a figure of importance in local matters. The increased income from holding multiple benefices would have also allowed him to provide more comfortably for his family, improving their lifestyle and social connections.

5. Spiritual Leadership:

- Conway would have recognized the significant spiritual leadership entrusted to him. His role in guiding the faith of his parishioners at both Donaghcloney and Magherally would have given him the opportunity to make a meaningful impact on the spiritual lives of many people. His sermons, pastoral care, and religious decisions would have affected the daily lives and faith of his parishioners, making him a central figure in their religious experience.

Overall Impact:

This collated appointment marked a high point in Conway's early career and personal life. It allowed him to secure a stable and prestigious position for his family while expanding his influence in the Church of Ireland. His life at this point would have been defined by both his growing family and his increasing ecclesiastical responsibilities. The balance of these two major areas of his life would have required thoughtful attention, dedication, and adaptability.

In summary, Conway Benning's promotion to the Archdeaconry and multiple rectories at the age of 33 would have been a significant milestone in his life, shaping his professional future and strengthening his standing both in the church and society. He would have felt pride, responsibility, and a sense of purpose as he navigated the demands of his expanding roles.

When Conway Benning was welcomed as a member of the Amicable Annuity Company of Newry, County Down on August 1, 1770, this would have been a notable event in his life, both socially and financially.

How He Might Have Reacted:

1. Pride in Being Part of an Esteemed Group:

- Joining the Amicable Annuity Company, which was likely a prestigious and influential society, would have filled Conway with a sense of pride. The organization was probably composed of well-established professionals and clergymen, and being accepted into such a group would have been seen as recognition of his status and success. Conway would have viewed this membership as a validation of his social standing, educational background, and reputation.

2. Financial Security:

- Annuity companies were early forms of life insurance and financial security for their members. Conway might have been pleased with the foresight of ensuring long-term financial stability for himself and his family. Joining the company meant that he would have a form of income in his later years, ensuring that his wife, Ann, and any children would be provided for, even if something happened to him. He would have felt relief knowing that he was taking steps to protect his family.

3. Social Networking and Influence:

- Being a member of the Amicable Annuity Company likely expanded Conway's social network. Membership in such organizations often provided opportunities to meet other influential figures, both from the clergy and the gentry. Conway would have likely seen this as a chance to form alliances, make friends, and gain influence within the circles that mattered in 18th-century Ireland. These connections could open doors to further opportunities, both within the Church of Ireland and in other societal roles.

4. Sense of Responsibility:

- As a member of the company, Conway would have felt a responsibility to contribute to the financial well-being of the group and participate in its meetings and decisions. The organization likely operated on principles of mutual aid and solidarity, so he would have been expected to engage with the group's objectives. This might have added to his sense of duty, especially since he was already a clergyman with obligations to his parish and the church.

The Effects on His Life:

1. Increased Financial Stability:

- Joining the Amicable Annuity Company would have added a layer of financial stability to Conway's life. This likely gave him a greater sense of security, allowing him to focus on his ecclesiastical duties without worrying as much about the financial future of his family. It also could have provided him with peace of mind, knowing that he had taken a prudent step to protect his wife and children in case of illness, death, or other unexpected financial burdens.

2. Enhanced Social Status:
- Membership in this type of organization would have raised his social profile. Conway would have been seen as a man of foresight and responsibility, qualities admired by both his peers and the broader community. Being part of an annuity company could have also reinforced his role as a respected community leader, showing that he was invested in the well-being of both his family and his social circle.

3. Professional Advantages:
- Networking with other professionals in the Amicable Annuity Company might have led to opportunities within both the church and other civic or charitable organizations. These types of affiliations often gave members advantages in terms of career progression, business dealings, and opportunities to influence local or regional policies. For Conway, this could have helped further his career in the church or other ventures tied to the land and the social structures of the time.

4. Personal Satisfaction:
- On a personal level, Conway likely experienced satisfaction in knowing that he was taking responsible and practical steps for his family. This move would have solidified his reputation as a provider and protector, especially at a time when financial security could be unpredictable due to health or political changes. His membership would have been a point of personal and family pride, enhancing his image as a man of wisdom and foresight.

Overall Impact:
Conway's membership in the Amicable Annuity Company in 1770 would have had a lasting effect on his personal and

professional life. It offered him financial security, increased social standing, and enhanced connections within influential circles. His decision to join the company demonstrated his commitment to ensuring a stable future for his family and his awareness of the importance of networking and community standing in 18th-century Ireland.

In summary, being welcomed into the Amicable Annuity Company would have been a point of pride for Conway, positively affecting his social, financial, and professional life, while reinforcing his role as a responsible and forward-thinking family man and clergyman.

When Conway Benning's daughter, Eleanor Jones Benning, was born in 1775 in the Diocese of Meath, Conway, at 38 years old, would have experienced a range of emotional and practical effects, both as a father and as a clergyman.

Emotional Impact:

1. Joy and Family Expansion:

- The birth of a daughter would have brought Conway joy, adding to his growing family and balancing the dynamics within the household. Having both sons and daughters was seen as a blessing, and Eleanor's arrival would have further cemented his family's legacy. As a devoted family man, Conway would have cherished the role of father to both a son (Conway) and a daughter (Eleanor), providing emotional fulfillment.

2. Protective Fatherly Love:

- Fathers in the 18th century often felt a strong sense of protection and care for their daughters, especially given the societal expectations for women at the time. Conway would likely have felt a deep responsibility to ensure Eleanor's upbringing in a stable, religious, and respectable environment. He might have been concerned about her future prospects, particularly in terms of marriage and her role within society, given his position as a clergyman.

3. Spiritual Significance:

- As a deeply religious man, Conway might have seen Eleanor's birth as a divine gift. In his role as a priest, he would have believed that children were blessings from God. He may have dedicated her birth to divine providence, reflecting on his own responsibilities to raise her in the faith and ensure she was well-versed in the Church's teachings and values.

Practical Impact:

1. Responsibility for Eleanor's Future:

- The birth of a daughter in the 18th century often led fathers to consider her future, particularly in terms of education, upbringing, and eventual marriage. Conway, being well-educated and well-connected within the Church, would likely have wanted to ensure that Eleanor received the best possible upbringing, even though formal education for girls was not as common as for boys. He may have sought to provide her with some level of education, possibly involving tutors or governesses, especially in the realms of religious and domestic skills.

2. Social Considerations:

- As a prominent clergyman and a member of the Amicable Annuity Company, Conway's social status would have been elevated by the birth of his children. However, with a daughter, he may have begun thinking about social alliances through marriage. Daughters often represented potential connections to other families of standing, so Conway might have started considering the prospects of Eleanor marrying into another respected or influential family in the future.

3. Emphasis on Religious and Moral Upbringing:

- Given Conway's role in the Church, he would likely have emphasized a strict moral and religious upbringing for Eleanor. He would have wanted her to embody the virtues of a pious and moral woman, both for her own spiritual well-being and as a reflection of the Benning family's standing in the community. Her education in religious matters would have been paramount, and Conway would have taken personal interest in ensuring she grew up in a devout and proper environment.

Impact on Conway's Role as a Father and Clergyman:

1. Father-Daughter Relationship:

- Fathers in the 18th century were often deeply attached to their daughters, especially because daughters represented purity, family loyalty, and future homemakers. Eleanor's birth may have softened Conway, leading him to develop a tender, protective relationship with her. Given his religious position, he would have likely been a guiding figure in her spiritual development, ensuring that she adhered to the Christian values he upheld.

2. Increased Focus on Providing for His Family:

- With a growing family, Conway may have felt increased pressure to ensure financial stability and social standing. His role as a father to both a son and a daughter would have given him a renewed focus on maintaining his clerical positions and working hard within the Church. The need to secure his children's futures, including Eleanor's dowry and prospects for marriage, would have weighed on his mind. This could have influenced his decisions regarding career advancements or maintaining influential connections.

3. Impact on His Spiritual Outlook:

- The birth of Eleanor would likely have reinforced Conway's sense of duty as both a father and a religious leader. He may have seen her birth as a reminder of the importance of family in faith, inspiring him to incorporate teachings about the sanctity of family, marriage, and parenthood into his sermons. The joys and challenges of raising children in the Christian faith would have become a lived experience for him, deepening his connection to the spiritual and moral lessons he preached to his congregation.

Overall Impact:

The birth of Eleanor Jones Benning in 1775 would have been a pivotal moment for Conway Benning. Emotionally, he would have experienced the joy of welcoming a daughter and the increased responsibility that came with raising her in a morally and spiritually sound environment. Practically, her birth would have prompted thoughts of her future, including her education, religious upbringing, and eventual marriage. As a clergyman, Conway's experiences as a father would have deepened his sense of purpose and responsibility, both within his family and his community, reinforcing his commitment to his spiritual duties and the well-being of his family.

When Conway Benning received his Doctor of Laws (LL.D.) degree in 1776, it would have had significant effects on both his personal and professional life. Here's how it likely affected him:

Professional Impact:

1. Elevated Status in the Clergy:

- Receiving an LL.D. would have significantly elevated Conway Benning's status within the Church and among his peers. The degree indicated a high level of expertise in both canon law (church law) and civil law, making him a valuable resource for legal matters within the ecclesiastical community. This would have likely opened doors for greater responsibility within the church hierarchy, increasing his influence and prestige.

2. Increased Opportunities for Leadership:

- Holding an LL.D. would have made Conway eligible for higher positions within the Church, such as becoming a bishop or taking on other administrative and legal roles within the diocese. This academic achievement would have strengthened his candidacy for promotions, leading to greater responsibilities and authority in his clerical duties. His legal knowledge would have made him a key figure in ecclesiastical courts and councils, where complex legal disputes needed resolution.

3. Recognition and Respect:

- In 18th-century Ireland, advanced degrees like an LL.D. commanded significant respect. Conway would have been regarded as a scholar and a legal expert, enhancing his reputation not only within the Church but also in society at large. This newfound recognition might have led to increased involvement in community affairs, as well as invitations to contribute to legal and theological discussions.

4. Influence in the Community:

- The combination of his clerical role and legal education would have positioned Conway as a person of authority in legal matters, both within the church and the wider community. Local leaders, parishioners, and even nobility might have sought his counsel on legal and moral issues. This increased his influence in the social and political fabric of the time, potentially aligning him with important figures or even local governance.

Personal Impact:

1. Sense of Accomplishment:

- On a personal level, achieving an LL.D. would have given Conway a great sense of pride and accomplishment. It marked the culmination of years of academic study and dedication to his intellectual pursuits. In a time when advanced education was reserved for a small percentage of the population, earning such a degree would have been a major personal milestone.

2. Increased Confidence:

- The LL.D. degree would have instilled in him greater confidence in handling legal matters, both in his personal life and in his role as a clergyman. He would have felt more capable of addressing complex legal and moral questions, enhancing his decision-making and leadership abilities within the church.

3. Family Legacy and Future Prospects:

- Conway's achievement would have had implications for his family as well. The degree would have strengthened his ability to provide for and elevate the status of his family, particularly his children. Conway, being a well-educated and accomplished man, would likely have felt the pressure to ensure that his children, such as his son Conway and daughter Eleanor, followed in his footsteps and received a strong education. He would have also viewed this degree as a way to create a lasting family legacy.

Historical Context:

1. Time of Enlightenment:

- The mid-18th century was a period of intellectual and scientific development, with the Enlightenment influencing many aspects of society. Conway's legal education and advanced degree would have placed him in alignment with the intellectual movements of the time. He may have felt more equipped to engage with Enlightenment ideas, especially those concerning law, governance, and morality.

2. American Revolution:

- Given that Conway received his LL.D. in 1776, during the early stages of the American Revolution, he may have been affected by the political and legal implications of the revolution. As someone well-versed in law, he would likely have reflected on the broader questions of governance, civil liberties, and legal authority that were at the forefront of revolutionary thought. This could have influenced his own legal and theological beliefs, particularly regarding the relationship between church and state.

Overall Effect:

Receiving his LL.D. in 1776 would have been a transformative moment in Conway Benning's life, enhancing his professional stature and personal pride. It positioned him as a leader in both legal and religious spheres, providing him with opportunities for career advancement and increasing his influence in the community. It also would have cemented his reputation as a learned man, likely affecting how he viewed his role in society and within the church. This degree would have had lasting effects on his personal legacy and his family's future, setting a strong foundation for his continued career success.

When Conway Benning resigned from his position as Archdeacon of Dromore in 1777 at the age of 40, it would have had significant effects on both his personal and professional life. Here's how this decision, along with his travels across the continent that same year, may have affected him:

Professional Impact:

1. Resignation from the Archdeaconry:

- Resigning from such a high-ranking ecclesiastical position like the archdeaconry was a major step, likely taken for personal, professional, or health-related reasons. It might have represented a moment of transition or even dissatisfaction with the administrative responsibilities of church leadership. By stepping down, Conway would have distanced himself from the weight of managing church affairs and may have sought a different kind of fulfillment, whether spiritual, intellectual, or personal.

- He could have viewed this decision as a way to refocus on his intellectual pursuits, given his legal background (LL.D.) and broad education. It may also have allowed him to explore new theological ideas and deepen his faith in ways that were not tied to the strict structures of church administration.

2. Freedom to Pursue Other Interests:

- By resigning from such a prominent position, Conway may have gained more freedom to pursue other intellectual, spiritual, or personal endeavors. He was highly educated and likely had diverse interests, so resigning could have opened doors to activities outside the clergy, such as writing, traveling, or furthering his theological studies.

3. Impact on His Clerical Career:

- While resigning from the archdeaconry might have been seen as a step back in his clerical career, it's possible that Conway viewed it as a necessary break or redirection. His resignation could have been prompted by a desire for personal growth or even the opportunity to take on different roles within the church or community. His career likely remained respected, given his achievements, and stepping down might have been interpreted as a strategic retreat rather than a failure or loss.

Personal Impact:

1. Exploration and Reflection During His Travels:

- Traveling the continent in 1777 likely had a profound personal impact on Conway. Europe during this period was undergoing significant social, political, and intellectual changes, and his exposure to different cultures and ideas could have broadened his worldview. Travel was considered a way to expand one's knowledge, especially for educated individuals like Conway, and it likely allowed him to reflect on his career, faith, and personal goals.

- He may have visited major cultural, religious, and intellectual centers in Europe—such as Paris, Rome, or Vienna—where Enlightenment ideas and religious reform movements were thriving. This exposure to new philosophies and theologies could have influenced his own beliefs, perhaps leading him to reassess his role in the church and the direction of his spiritual journey.

2. Potential for Spiritual Renewal:

- Resigning from a high-ranking church position and traveling could have been a form of spiritual renewal for Conway. The pressures of church leadership might have weighed heavily on him, and the opportunity to step back and travel may have provided the break he needed to refocus on his personal faith. He could have sought out spiritual inspiration in the places he visited, perhaps engaging in theological discussions with fellow clergy and scholars across the continent.

3. Family and Personal Life:

- At this point in his life, Conway was a husband and father, with several young children, including Conway Jr., James, and Eleanor. Traveling might have temporarily separated him from his family, which could have been emotionally challenging for him. On the other hand, the time away may have allowed him to return with new insights and a renewed sense of purpose, which could have benefited his family life.

4. Reflection on his Role as a Leader:

- As a clergyman and father, traveling across the continent might have allowed Conway to reflect on his responsibilities to his family and his community. He may have considered how best to balance his personal life with his professional duties, particularly as someone who had held a high-ranking position in the Church of Ireland. The experience of meeting new people and encountering different ways of thinking could have informed his leadership style going forward.

Historical Context and Broader Impact:

1. The Grand Tour:

- During the 18th century, it was common for wealthy and educated individuals to embark on a "Grand Tour" of Europe, which was considered an essential part of education for young aristocrats and scholars. While Conway was already a mature man, this tradition of travel would have been seen as an opportunity for intellectual and cultural enrichment. He may have engaged in discussions with prominent European intellectuals, theologians, and clerics, further expanding his understanding of the world and his place in it.

2. Exposure to Enlightenment Thought:

- The Enlightenment was in full swing by the 1770s, and Conway would have encountered the ideas of thinkers like Voltaire, Rousseau, and Diderot during his travels. While he was a member of the clergy, the Enlightenment's emphasis on reason, science, and human rights would have offered new perspectives that could have influenced his theological and legal thinking. He might have grappled with how to reconcile his faith with these emerging philosophies, especially regarding questions of governance, ethics, and morality.

3. Changing Religious Landscape:

- The religious landscape of Europe was evolving in the 1770s, with movements such as Methodism gaining ground. Conway, as a well-educated clergyman, would have been aware of these developments. His travels could have introduced him to different forms of worship and religious practices, perhaps leading him to reflect on the future of the Church of Ireland and his role within it.

Overall Effect:

Resigning from the Archdeaconry of Dromore and traveling the continent in 1777 would have provided Conway Benning with an opportunity for personal and professional reflection, spiritual renewal, and intellectual growth. While stepping down from such a high-ranking position might have seemed like a major life change, it likely allowed him to explore new opportunities and perspectives. His travels would have broadened his worldview, allowing him to return with fresh insights and possibly a renewed sense of purpose. This period of transition might have set the stage for the next phase of his life, shaping his decisions in both his clerical duties and personal life moving forward.

When Conway Benning was 40 years old, his daughter Millicent Mary was born in 1777 in Carrickfergus. This event likely had a significant emotional and personal impact on him, given the context of his life at that time.

Emotional and Personal Impact:

1. Joy of Fatherhood:

- The birth of Millicent Mary would have brought Conway great joy, as the arrival of a new child often does. By this point, Conway already had other children, but the birth of a daughter would have added a new dynamic to his family. He would have felt a strong sense of responsibility as a father to protect, nurture, and provide for his growing family.

2. Strengthening of Family Bonds:

- Family life would have been central to Conway at this stage, especially since he had just resigned from the Archdeaconry of Dromore and was likely focusing more on personal aspects of life, such as family. The birth of a daughter might have brought his family closer together, reinforcing his commitment to his wife, Ann Ellis, and their other children, as they welcomed Millicent into the world.

Impact on His Role as a Father:

1. Responsibility as a Father of a Daughter:

- In the late 18th century, fathers, especially clergy and educated men like Conway, took great pride in the upbringing of their children. The birth of a daughter, particularly in a society where women's roles were evolving, may have prompted him to consider her education and future prospects. Conway, being a well-educated man, might have placed emphasis on ensuring Millicent Mary would receive the best possible upbringing and moral guidance.

2. Preparing for Her Future:

- As a father during this time, Conway would have also thought about Millicent's future in terms of marriage and social standing. He likely considered how to provide for her dowry and establish advantageous social connections to secure her well-being, especially since daughters were often seen as an extension of their family's honor and status.

Impact on His Life Amid Transition:

1. Life After Resignation:

- Having resigned from the Archdeaconry and traveled the continent earlier in the same year, the birth of Millicent Mary may have come at a time of personal transition for Conway. It's possible that her birth brought a renewed sense of stability and purpose. With the responsibilities of a growing family, Conway may have found comfort in focusing on his role as a husband and father, as he navigated the changes in his professional and personal life.

2. Focus on Home Life:

- After spending time traveling and reflecting on his clerical career, Conway might have been ready to settle into a more stable routine. The birth of Millicent Mary may have reinforced his decision to focus more on his domestic life and his family's well-being, especially as he continued to serve as a clergyman in other capacities.

Social and Economic Considerations:

1. Economic Responsibility:

- The birth of another child would have added to Conway's financial responsibilities. While he was still serving in various clerical roles, the cost of raising a larger family, ensuring their education, and providing for their futures would have been a consideration. He would have needed to balance his professional income with the demands of raising children in a respectable manner.

2. Clerical Responsibilities and Family Life:

- As a member of the clergy, Conway would have been deeply committed to his community and his faith. Balancing his duties as a priest with his growing family responsibilities might have required him to make adjustments to his daily life and schedule. However, having a large family would also have been a source of pride and support for him, providing emotional sustenance amid his clerical work.

Conclusion:

The birth of Millicent Mary when Conway Benning was 40 years old in 1777 would have had a profound emotional and practical effect on him. It likely deepened his commitment to his family and provided a source of joy during a time of personal transition. As an educated man and clergyman, he would have considered the responsibilities of fatherhood with seriousness, especially in ensuring a good future for his daughter. This period of his life was marked by significant changes, but the birth of Millicent Mary would have been a cherished event, contributing to his legacy and family life.

When Conway Benning was 47 years old in 1783, the first successful flight of a hot air balloon took place. This remarkable technological advancement would have been a significant event in the context of the time, and Conway, as an educated and well-connected man, would likely have been aware of it.

How He Would Have Reacted:

1. Fascination and Curiosity:

- Conway, being a man of letters and an educated member of society, would have been naturally curious about this new invention. The success of the Montgolfier brothers' hot air balloon in France was widely publicized across Europe, and it would have sparked interest among intellectuals, clergy, and professionals. As a clergyman with a strong academic background (he held degrees in law), he might have been fascinated by the implications of such an achievement for science, technology, and human progress.

2. Religious and Philosophical Reflection:

- As a member of the clergy, Conway might also have reflected on the spiritual and philosophical implications of humans rising into the air. The ability to soar above the earth would have been awe-inspiring, perhaps even provoking theological questions about mankind's place in creation and the limits of human ingenuity. He might have discussed these ideas with colleagues or during sermons, framing the invention within the context of human achievement and divine inspiration.

3. Excitement for Technological Progress:

- Conway lived during a time of rapid advancement, with the Industrial Revolution already in motion. The success of the hot air balloon would have been seen as a triumph of human ingenuity. As someone who was likely interested in the intellectual movements of the time, he may have viewed this as further proof that society was advancing and evolving in profound ways. This might have excited him, knowing that the world was entering a new era of technological progress.

4. Interest in Science and Education:

- Given his background in education and the fact that he was part of a scholarly tradition, Conway may have followed developments in natural philosophy (what we now call science). The hot air balloon flight would have been discussed in academic circles, and as a man connected to Trinity College Dublin, he may have engaged in conversations about the physics behind flight and its potential future applications.

How It Might Have Affected Him:

1. Broadened Intellectual Horizons:

- The invention would have likely stimulated Conway's interest in the scientific progress of his time. This event might have encouraged him to stay updated on technological and scientific advancements, as it was a clear sign that the world was evolving in unprecedented ways. He may have begun to see the potential for human innovation to shape the future more dramatically than ever before.

2. Implications for Travel and Communication:

- Although the hot air balloon was still in its infancy and not yet a practical means of transportation, the idea of humans being able to travel through the air would have sparked the imagination of many. Conway might have speculated about what this could mean for the future of travel and communication across nations, even though it was still many years before such dreams were realized.

3. Discussions in Social Circles:

- As a prominent figure in the church and community, Conway would likely have engaged in discussions about the event with his peers and parishioners. The balloon flight would have been a topic of great interest and conversation, and he might have shared his thoughts on its implications for society, science, and perhaps even theology.

4. Increased Interest in Human Achievement:

- The hot air balloon flight would have reinforced the optimism of the time regarding the possibilities of human achievement. Conway, like many in his position, would have seen this as a further indication that the world was on the cusp of incredible change, and he might have viewed the event as a sign of more innovations to come, making the future exciting and unpredictable.

Conclusion:

Conway Benning's reaction to the first successful hot air balloon flight in 1783 would have been one of intellectual curiosity, fascination, and possibly theological reflection. As a man with a strong academic background and a connection to broader intellectual movements, he likely saw the event as a marker of humanity's growing capacity to understand and manipulate the natural world, and it may have sparked conversations and thoughts about the future of technology and society.

Conway Benning Sr.'s daughter Eleanor's marriage to Noah Webb Dalway of Ballyill on May 22, 1795, would have been a significant event for the Benning and Dalway families. Given the families' social standing and the customs of late 18th-century Ireland, the wedding would likely have been a formal and carefully planned occasion.

What the Wedding Might Have Been Like:

1. Venue:
- The wedding would likely have taken place in a church, potentially at a well-known local parish in the Diocese of Meath, where Conway Sr. held his ecclesiastical duties. Given Noah Dalway's status, the event would have attracted attention from prominent local families. Churches were central to communities during this time, and weddings were a public declaration of family alliances.

2. Attendees:
- The wedding would have had a large number of guests, primarily family, friends, and local gentry. Given the connection to the Anglican Church, there might have been members of the clergy, including other high-ranking ecclesiastical figures. The Dalway family, being of notable status, would have had their own set of esteemed attendees. Social events like weddings often served to strengthen ties between influential families.

3. Ceremony:
- The ceremony itself would likely have been traditional, following the rites of the Church of Ireland (Anglican). A priest would have conducted the service, and there may have been some

form of choir or musicians to accompany the event. The vows and rituals would have been solemn and reflective of the high religious status of the families involved.

- After the service, a wedding feast or reception would have been held, possibly at the Dalway estate in Ballyill or another prestigious location. The feast would have featured traditional Irish fare, but with more elaborate and luxurious elements due to the social standing of both families.

4. Social Significance:

- Weddings in 18th-century Ireland were often about family alliances and the continuation of family lines. Given the Dalways' status and Noah's position, this marriage would have been a key social event, solidifying the bond between two respected families. The event would have been seen as prestigious and important within their community.

What Conway Benning Sr. Might Have Worn:

1. Formal Clerical Attire:

- As a senior clergyman, Conway Sr. likely would have worn his formal clerical robes for the wedding, especially during the church ceremony. The traditional Anglican clergy robe in the late 18th century would have included:

- A black cassock (a long robe reaching to the ankles) worn under a surplice (a wide-sleeved white gown).

- He may have worn a gown or mantle over this, possibly trimmed with elements signifying his status as a Doctor of Laws (LL.D.).

- A white neckband or collar (bands) was typical for clergy, often worn beneath the surplice.

2. Accessories and Grooming:

- As a man of distinction, Conway Sr. would have likely paid attention to the finer details. He may have worn:

- A black tricorn hat, the fashionable headwear for men of the period.
 - Shoes with buckles, made from fine leather and polished to reflect his status.
 - A well-groomed wig, as was customary for gentlemen in the 18th century. His wig would have likely been powdered, in keeping with the formal fashion of the day.

3. Post-Ceremony Dress:
 - For the reception or post-ceremony events, Conway Sr. might have changed into more formal civilian dress appropriate for his status. This could have included:
 - A fine woolen or silk coat, typically long and tailored, often in dark or muted colors like black, brown, or navy.
 - Breeches (knee-length trousers) made from silk or velvet.
 - A waistcoat with intricate embroidery or detailing, often made from rich fabrics like satin.
 - Stockings and well-polished shoes with silver buckles.

The Atmosphere:

The atmosphere at the wedding would have been one of elegance and formality, mixed with the warmth of family and community. The occasion would have been a reflection of the Benning family's standing, combining religious reverence with social importance. As the father of the bride, Conway Sr. would have played a central role in the day's events, overseeing the joining of two prominent families.

The music, the church bells, and the gathering of influential families would have made the day memorable not only for Eleanor and Noah but also for everyone present.

How It Might Have Affected Conway Benning Sr.:

1. Emotional Impact:
 - As a father, Conway Sr. would likely have been emotional at seeing his daughter married. Weddings were not just ceremonial

but symbolic of a family's growth and future. Given his close relationship with his children, this marriage would have been a proud moment for him.

2. Strengthening Family Ties:

- Marriages were often strategic in upper-class families, serving to strengthen alliances. The Dalways were a prominent family, and this marriage would have ensured a connection between them, further solidifying the Benning family's position in society.

3. Spiritual Reflection:

- As a clergyman, Conway Sr. might have also reflected on the spiritual significance of the occasion. He likely took great pride in the fact that his daughter's marriage adhered to the values and traditions of the Church of Ireland. It would have reaffirmed his religious beliefs and sense of responsibility toward his family and parishioners.

Conclusion:

Conway Benning Sr. would have played a central role in his daughter Eleanor's wedding, both as her father and as a respected clergyman. The event would have been a grand and formal affair, blending social and religious traditions of the time. Conway Sr. would have worn his finest clerical robes, and his emotions would have been a mix of pride, responsibility, and spiritual fulfillment as his family's legacy continued through this important marriage.

When Conway Benning Sr. was 58 years old in 1795, his son, Conway Benning Jr., entered the Royal Artillery in Ireland as a Lieutenant. This event would have been significant for him, both as a father and as a respected member of society. Here's how he might have reacted and the effect it could have had on him:

How He Might Have Reacted:

1. Pride in His Son's Accomplishment:

- Conway Sr. would have likely felt a great deal of pride in his son's achievement. The Royal Artillery was a prestigious branch of the British military, and for his son to enter as a Lieutenant was a reflection of both family status and personal merit. Conway Sr., having lived through major political and military events, would have understood the significance of such a position.

2. Concern for His Son's Safety:

- Despite his pride, Conway Sr. might also have felt concern for his son's safety. The late 18th century was a tumultuous time, particularly with the ongoing French Revolutionary Wars (1792-1802) and the rising tensions in Ireland. As a father, Conway Sr. may have worried about the dangers his son would face as a young officer in the British military.

3. Patriotic Support:

- As a clergyman, Conway Sr. would likely have had a sense of duty and loyalty to the British Crown. His son's enlistment in the Royal Artillery could have reinforced his own patriotic feelings and connection to the establishment. The military was an essential institution in maintaining British control and stability, particularly in Ireland, so he might have seen his son's role as part of a broader defense of the empire.

4. Familial Legacy and Social Expectations:

- Conway Sr. would likely have viewed his son's entry into the military as a continuation of the family legacy and their place within society. In this period, families like the Bennings often aimed to place their sons in respected professions such as the church, law, or the military. Seeing his son rise to a position of responsibility would have aligned with the social expectations of their class.

The Effect It Would Have Had on Him:

1. Increased Status and Reputation:

- Conway Sr.'s son becoming a Lieutenant in the Royal Artillery would have enhanced the family's reputation. This achievement would likely have been a topic of conversation in their social circles and may have increased the family's standing, both in Ireland and among their peers.

2. Tension Due to Political and Military Climate:

- The political and military situation in Ireland in the 1790s was fraught with tension. The United Irishmen Rebellion would take place in 1798, just a few years after his son's commission. Conway Sr. may have experienced increased tension and anxiety about the political instability and the potential role his son might play in any conflicts. This would likely have been a heavy emotional burden, given the growing unrest in the country.

3. Sense of Duty and Responsibility:

- Conway Sr. may have felt a renewed sense of duty and responsibility as a father and clergyman. Knowing that his son was serving in the military might have influenced his sermons, prayers, and interactions with parishioners, as he sought to provide guidance and comfort in a time of war and uncertainty. It could also have solidified his belief in the role of the British military and government in maintaining peace and order.

4. Personal Fulfillment:

- As someone who had achieved academic and religious success, Conway Sr. may have felt a deep sense of personal fulfillment seeing his son step into a role of leadership. Watching his child grow into a responsible and respected individual would have been a source of satisfaction and pride, contributing to his own sense of accomplishment as a parent.

Conclusion:

Conway Benning Sr. would have likely reacted with a mixture of pride, concern, and patriotism upon his son's entry into the Royal Artillery. This event would have affected him deeply, enhancing the family's social standing while also bringing an element of worry due to the volatile political climate of Ireland in the 1790s. Ultimately, his son's success in the military would have been seen as a continuation of the family's tradition of service and dedication.

The Battle of Antrim, which took place on June 7, 1798, was part of the larger Irish Rebellion of 1798, during which Irish nationalists, inspired by the American and French revolutions, sought to overthrow British rule and establish an independent Irish republic. Given that Conway Benning Sr. was 61 years old at the time and a respected clergyman, his reaction to the battle and the rebellion would have been shaped by his position in society, his religious beliefs, and his social standing.

How He Might Have Reacted:

1. Concern for Stability:

- As a member of the clergy and a prominent figure in the community, Conway would likely have been concerned with maintaining social and political stability. The rebellion posed a threat not only to British rule but also to the established social order, which included the Church of Ireland. As a clergyman in the Anglican tradition, which was closely tied to the British government, he might have viewed the uprising as a dangerous disruption to peace and order in the country.

2. Loyalty to the Crown:

- Given that Conway was a clergyman of the Church of Ireland, which was the state church and strongly associated with British rule, he would have likely been loyal to the Crown. Many in his position would have viewed the rebellion as a threat to both the Church and the established political system. The Anglican clergy were often seen as part of the Protestant Ascendancy, and rebellion by the largely Catholic Irish population would have been seen as a direct challenge to this social hierarchy.

3. Fear for His Family and Community:

- The physical danger posed by the rebellion would also have been a concern. The Battle of Antrim occurred in County Antrim, relatively close to Carrickfergus, where Conway and his family lived. Given the proximity of the violence, he would have likely been worried for the safety of his family, friends, and parishioners. The uprising led to widespread unrest, and many civilians were caught up in the violence. He might have taken steps to protect his home and church from potential attacks or looting by the rebels or government forces.

4. Moral and Religious Reflection:

- As a clergyman, Conway would likely have experienced a deep sense of moral and spiritual conflict. The rebellion, which involved significant bloodshed, would have forced him to reflect on his duties as a religious leader. He may have felt a responsibility to provide spiritual guidance to his parishioners during a time of great fear and uncertainty, perhaps emphasizing messages of peace and reconciliation, even while supporting the Crown.

5. Sympathy for the Rebel Cause:

- While his position as an Anglican clergyman would have made him more likely to support British rule, it is possible that Conway, like some other Protestant clergy of the time, could have felt a degree of sympathy for the causes of the rebels. The rebellion sought to address issues like religious inequality and economic hardship, which might have resonated with him on a personal level. However, his loyalty to the Crown and his vested interest in maintaining the status quo would likely have outweighed any public expressions of support for the rebels.

How It Might Have Affected Him:

1. Impact on His Role as a Clergyman:

- The rebellion and the ensuing violence would have likely reinforced his role as a spiritual leader during a time of crisis. He might have had to offer solace and guidance to those who were affected by the fighting, including families of soldiers or civilians caught in the crossfire. The uncertainty of the times would have increased the demand for religious leaders to provide stability and reassurance.

2. Increased Political Awareness:

- The events of the 1798 rebellion would have forced Conway to become more politically aware. While he was already a member of the higher social and religious hierarchy, the rebellion might have made him more conscious of the growing political tensions in Ireland. He may have felt a need to align himself more strongly with the British authorities or even assist in rallying support for the government.

3. Personal and Family Safety:

- The rebellion would have heightened concerns for the safety of his family and property. Many clergy, especially in areas close to the fighting, faced direct threats or saw their homes and churches attacked. Conway may have taken measures to safeguard his estate at Kilroot and ensure his family was safe from potential violence, especially given that he had several children, including his son, Conway Benning Jr., who was serving in the military.

4. Strengthened Connection to the Anglican Community:

- The rebellion would likely have strengthened Conway's ties to the broader Anglican and loyalist community. Clergy of the Church of Ireland often found themselves rallying around one another in the face of political instability. This could have deepened his sense of duty and responsibility within the Church and the Crown, potentially leading to stronger solidarity with fellow clergy members and loyalists.

5. Impact on His Legacy:

- The rebellion and its aftermath might have made Conway more determined to cement his legacy within the Church and his community. He may have sought to preserve his family's reputation as loyal to the Crown and the Church of Ireland. His later actions could have been influenced by the desire to be remembered as a figure who maintained stability during one of the most turbulent times in Irish history.

Conclusion:

The Battle of Antrim and the 1798 rebellion would have had a profound impact on Conway Benning Sr. As a 61-year-old clergyman with deep ties to the British Crown and the Church of Ireland, he would likely have reacted with concern for social stability and loyalty to the Crown. The rebellion would have tested his role as a spiritual leader, placing him in a position where he had to offer comfort to his community while navigating the dangers and uncertainties of a violent uprising.

At 61 years old, Conway Benning would have likely been deeply involved in his daughter Millicent's wedding to Dr. Samuel Allen, M.D., as this would have been a significant family and social event. Millicent's marriage to the son of Samuel Allen, Esq., would have been seen as a match of considerable prestige, given the Allen family's social standing and Dr. Allen's status as a medical doctor. Here's how the wedding might have affected him and what he would have likely worn:

How It Would Have Affected Him:

1. Pride and Joy:

- As a father, Conway would have experienced great pride in seeing his daughter marry into another respected family. Given his social status and position as a clergyman, Millicent's marriage to Dr. Samuel Allen would have likely been viewed as a favorable match, enhancing the social standing of both families. The event would have been an important personal and family milestone.

2. Emotional Significance:

- While pride would certainly have been a major emotion, the wedding would have also been a poignant moment for Conway. As a father, he would have been reflecting on Millicent's growth and the passage of time. At 61, he was entering a later stage of life, and this marriage would have represented a significant transition in both his daughter's life and his own role as her father.

3. Social and Familial Expectations:

- Millicent's marriage would have had social implications, as weddings at this time were not just personal events but also occasions that involved significant social connections. The union of the Benning and Allen families would have reinforced Conway's social network, ensuring his family's status in the region remained strong. He would have likely invested time and resources into ensuring the wedding was a success, fulfilling social expectations while reinforcing bonds between families of similar standing.

4. Public Role:

- As a clergyman, Conway's public role during the wedding might have been amplified. He may have been involved in officiating, giving speeches, or publicly blessing the union, especially given his standing in both religious and social circles. His participation in the ceremony would have been significant not only for the couple but also for the community, reflecting the connection between the Church and prominent families.

5. Financial Considerations:

- Weddings were often expensive affairs, especially for families of higher social standing. Conway would likely have had to consider the financial implications of hosting or contributing to the event. At his age and with his established position, he would likely have been able to provide a comfortable and fitting celebration, perhaps reflecting his sense of responsibility and duty as both a father and a man of status.

What He Might Have Worn:

1. Formal Clerical Attire:

- Given Conway's position as a member of the Anglican clergy, it is possible that he might have worn formal clerical attire at the wedding, especially if he played an official role in the ceremony.

This would have consisted of a long, black cassock (the traditional garment worn by clergymen), possibly with a white surplice or a stole for more ceremonial purposes.

2. 18th-Century Formal Dress:

- If Conway did not wear clerical garments, he would have been dressed in formal attire appropriate for a gentleman of his standing in the late 18th century. This would likely have included:

- A Tailcoat: A long, dark-colored coat (likely black, navy, or dark brown) with tails, which was standard for formal occasions.

- A Waistcoat: Underneath the coat, he would have worn a waistcoat, typically made of silk or fine wool. Waistcoats of the time were often elaborately embroidered or in lighter colors like cream, gold, or soft blue to contrast with the dark tailcoat.

- Breeches and Stockings: Conway would have worn breeches, which ended at the knee, paired with silk or woolen stockings. These would have been a common choice for formal occasions in the late 18th century.

- Cravat or Neck Stock: Around his neck, Conway would have worn a cravat, which was a long piece of linen or silk that was wrapped around the neck and tied in various styles, or a simpler neck stock, which was more common for older men and clergy.

- Shoes with Buckles: Formal shoes during this period typically featured silver or gold buckles and would have been made from polished leather.

- A Wig or Hair Tied Back: Depending on his preference and how fashionable he was, Conway may have worn a powdered wig or kept his natural hair tied back in a queue (ponytail), which was still common at the time.

3. Accessories:

- For formal events like his daughter's wedding, Conway would likely have worn accessories such as gloves and perhaps a walking stick, which was a common accessory for gentlemen of his age and status. A hat, possibly a tricorn or bicorn hat, would have completed his ensemble, though he would have removed it during the indoor ceremony.

Conclusion:

Conway Benning Sr. would have felt a deep sense of pride, joy, and responsibility at his daughter Millicent's marriage to Dr. Samuel Allen. The event would have reinforced his family's social standing and been a significant emotional milestone for him. His attire would have reflected his dual role as both a father and a clergyman, emphasizing the formality and importance of the occasion. Whether dressed in clerical garments or the fashionable attire of a gentleman, Conway would have been a dignified and proud figure at his daughter's wedding.

At 63 years old, Conway Benning would have been well-established in his clerical and social roles. The introduction of custom-designed shoes by William Young would likely have been a notable event for him, both in terms of practicality and social standing. Here's how he might have reacted and the effect it may have had on him:

Reaction:

1. Interest in Craftsmanship:

- As a man of considerable education and status, Conway would likely have appreciated the craftsmanship and attention to detail that went into custom shoes designed by William Young. In the late 18th century, the idea of having shoes designed specifically for him would have been a sign of refinement, reflecting his appreciation for quality and tradition.

2. Comfort and Practicality:

- At 63, comfort would have been an important factor for Conway. Shoes designed specifically for him would likely have offered a level of comfort not found in mass-produced footwear. Given his responsibilities, both religious and social, he may have walked long distances between parishioners or spent considerable time on his feet during services. Custom shoes would have been a welcome addition to his wardrobe, improving his overall comfort.

3. Status and Prestige:

- Fashion and personal appearance played significant roles in social standing during the period. Custom-made shoes were a luxury, and the fact that William Young, a known shoemaker, designed shoes specifically for Conway would have enhanced his reputation. He might have viewed the shoes as not just practical items, but symbols of his wealth, status, and connection to skilled artisans.

4. Gratitude and Appreciation:

- Conway likely would have expressed gratitude toward William Young for the high-quality footwear. It may have reinforced his appreciation for personalized goods, reflecting his standing in society, where bespoke items were associated with success and prestige. He would likely have worn them proudly, appreciating both their aesthetic appeal and practical function.

Effect on Conway Benning:

1. Enhancement of Personal Comfort:

- The custom shoes would have had a practical effect on Conway's daily life. Tailored to his feet, the shoes would have provided greater comfort compared to off-the-shelf alternatives. This would have been especially important for an older man, who might have begun to experience joint or foot issues common with age.

2. Reinforcement of Social Status:

- Wearing custom-made shoes would have reinforced Conway's image as a man of distinction. In his social circles, owning custom items was a marker of wealth and refinement. The shoes would have added to his outward appearance as someone of authority, especially when performing his clerical duties or attending important social functions.

3. Symbol of Longevity and Achievement:

- At this stage in his life, Conway had achieved significant personal and professional milestones. Custom-designed shoes may have represented a reward or recognition of his successful career and long life. They would have symbolized his continued engagement with society and a reflection of his sustained importance within his community.

Conclusion:

For Conway Benning, the shoes designed by William Young would have been more than just a practical item. They would have been a symbol of his social standing, his appreciation for quality craftsmanship, and a source of personal comfort. At 63, the custom footwear would have likely enhanced both his daily experience and the image he projected to those around him, further solidifying his place as a respected figure in his community.

At 63 years old, when his daughter Jane married Thomas Higginbotham of Dublin in September 1800, Conway Benning would have likely worn formal attire appropriate to his status as a clergyman and gentleman of the time. Weddings, particularly for someone of his social standing, would have been significant events that called for careful attention to dress.

What Conway Might Have Worn:

1. Clerical Gown and Bands:

- As a member of the clergy, Conway may have chosen to wear his clerical gown, especially if he officiated or played a prominent role in the wedding ceremony. His black robe would have been long and flowing, a symbol of his religious office. Underneath, he would have worn a black waistcoat and a white shirt with high, starched collars.

- Bands (a pair of rectangular pieces of cloth hanging from the collar) were typically worn by clergymen, signifying his role within the church.

2. Frock Coat:

- If he opted not to wear his clerical robe for the wedding, Conway may have worn a dark-colored frock coat, which was a formal and fashionable item of men's clothing at the time. Frock coats were typically tailored from high-quality wool or silk and buttoned up the front. Dark colors, such as black, navy, or dark brown, would have been suitable for formal occasions like a wedding.

3. Waistcoat and Cravat:

- Beneath his coat, he would likely have worn a waistcoat, a key piece of 18th- and early 19th-century men's fashion. The waistcoat would have been more decorative, perhaps in silk or wool, with intricate embroidery or patterns in lighter colors like cream, gold, or burgundy, though still in keeping with the dignity of his position.

- Conway would have completed his outfit with a cravat—a neckcloth that was wrapped and tied around the neck, a precursor to modern neckties. Cravats were often made of white linen or silk and were elaborately tied.

4. Breeches and Stockings:

- Men during this period typically wore breeches, which were knee-length trousers fastened just below the knee. These would likely have been made of a high-quality fabric like silk, wool, or velvet, depending on the season and occasion.

- Below the breeches, he would have worn stockings, most likely of silk, in a light color such as white or cream. These stockings would have been secured with garters and covered the lower leg up to the knee.

5. Buckled Shoes:

- Conway would have worn shoes with silver or brass buckles, typical of formal men's footwear at the time. The shoes would have been made of polished leather, usually black, and paired with silk stockings for a polished and formal appearance.

6. Tricorn Hat:

- For formal occasions like his daughter's wedding, Conway might have worn a tricorn hat, a fashionable choice for men during the late 18th century. These hats, with their distinctive three-cornered shape, were worn at an angle and would have been a mark of elegance and status.

7. Accessories:

- As a man of status, Conway may have accessorized with a pocket watch with a gold or silver chain, carried in his waistcoat pocket.

- Additionally, a walking cane with a silver or carved handle was often used by gentlemen of his age and status, both as a practical item and a symbol of dignity.

Conclusion:

Conway Benning would have been dressed in formal, dignified attire for his daughter Jane's wedding. Whether in his clerical gown or a formal frock coat, he would have been mindful of both his religious role and social standing. His clothing would have been made of fine materials and tailored to reflect his position as a respected figure within his community. The occasion would have called for a balance between his clerical duties and his role as a father, celebrating a significant family event in his daughter's life.

Given that the wedding of Conway Benning's son, James, and Charlotte Berry took place at St. Peter's Church in Dublin in 1801, the setting would have been a formal and significant occasion. St. Peter's was a prominent Church of Ireland parish at the time, which added prestige to the event.

The Wedding Atmosphere:

- St. Peter's Church in Dublin, known for its importance and historical significance, would have been a grand and solemn venue. The ceremony would have followed traditional Anglican rites, conducted with a sense of reverence and formality.

- The church's architectural design, with its high ceilings, tall windows, and formal décor, would have created a solemn, elegant environment, befitting a wedding of a well-regarded family like the Bennings.

Conway Benning's Role:

As the father of the groom and a member of the clergy, Conway might have played a special role during the ceremony. Given his religious background, he could have assisted in officiating, offering blessings or prayers for his son and daughter-in-law. His presence at such a notable church would have likely brought him a sense of pride and fulfillment, not only as a father but also as a man of faith.

His Clothing at St. Peter's Church Wedding:

At a wedding in such a significant location, Conway would have dressed in formal attire appropriate for a member of the clergy and the father of the groom:

1. Clerical Gown or Frock Coat:

- As previously mentioned, if Conway had a religious role in the ceremony, he might have worn a clerical gown. St. Peter's would have required high formality, so a long, black clerical cassock would have been appropriate.

- If not in his clerical role, he might have chosen a formal frock coat in dark colors, still befitting the serious tone of the occasion.

2. Waistcoat: Beneath the frock coat, Conway would have worn a silk or velvet waistcoat, perhaps with an embroidered pattern, adding a touch of luxury to his attire.

3. Cravat: A white cravat tied in an elaborate knot or bow would have been a necessary accessory for such a formal event.

4. Breeches and Stockings: Conway likely wore breeches with white silk stockings, typical of formal attire in this era, though trousers were becoming more popular by 1801.

5. Shoes: He would have worn black leather shoes with silver buckles, which were the norm for formal wear during this period.

6. Hat: If outdoors at any point, Conway might have worn a bicorne hat, the fashionable replacement for the tricorn hat in the early 19th century.

7. Gloves and Cane: Formal gloves, likely in white or cream, and a walking cane would have completed his dignified look.

Emotional Impact on Conway:

- As a 64-year-old father watching his son marry in such a notable location, Conway likely felt a mixture of pride, joy, and nostalgia. The family's establishment in high society, connections to notable families like the Berrys, and the grand setting would have given the day a sense of accomplishment for him.

- The event would have further solidified Conway's role as a patriarch in his family and community, influencing his sense of legacy and his pride in his son James's successful match and promising future.

This wedding at St. Peter's would have been a significant moment in Conway's later life, a formal, joyous occasion set against the backdrop of early 19th-century Dublin society.

When Conway Benning was 70 years old, in 1807, Robert Fulton built the first commercial steamship, the Clermont, which revolutionized travel and commerce. This achievement would have been both intriguing and potentially transformative for someone like Conway, who was a well-educated and religious man with a keen interest in the events of his time.

His Likely Reaction:

- Astonishment and Curiosity: Like many intellectuals of the era, Conway would likely have been astonished by the development of a machine capable of traversing waterways without relying on wind or manpower. The steam engine was already making waves in the Industrial Revolution, and Fulton's success in applying it to a commercial ship would have piqued Conway's curiosity. As someone likely involved in thoughtful discussions on innovation and progress, he might have found this technological advance to be symbolic of the broader changes taking place in society.

- Interest in Scientific Advancements: Given Conway's academic background, particularly as a recipient of a Doctor of Laws (LL.D.), he would have appreciated the engineering and mechanical ingenuity behind Fulton's steamship. He may have read about it in newspapers or intellectual publications, discussing its implications with colleagues and friends.

Impact on His Life:

- Improved Travel and Communication: Even though Conway resided in Ireland, the development of steam-powered vessels had profound implications for travel and commerce globally, including between Britain, Ireland, and the United States. While it might not have directly affected his everyday life initially, the introduction of steamships could have sparked discussions about faster, more reliable transportation between countries. This would have opened up new possibilities for trade, communication, and movement of people.

- Expansion of Knowledge and Trade: As a religious and academic figure, Conway might have seen the invention as an example of human progress, fulfilling the Enlightenment ideals of reason and scientific advancement. The steamship would have made it easier for ideas, goods, and even missionaries to travel farther and faster, which could have resonated with his intellectual and spiritual interests.

- Potential Religious Reflection: With his religious background, Conway may have reflected on the moral and philosophical implications of such a transformative invention. Some clergy of the time viewed technological advances as signs of human potential or even divine providence, while others feared that rapid changes could disrupt traditional ways of life. Conway, as a forward-thinking individual, might have been cautiously optimistic, recognizing the potential for good while reflecting on the responsibility that came with such power.

Broader Societal Implications:

- Impact on Irish Economy: Over time, steamships would have contributed to increased trade and economic growth, even in Ireland. As these technologies became more widely available, they would have influenced Ireland's ability to trade with other countries and connect more easily with global markets.

- Conversations with His Family: Conway's children, now adults themselves, would have likely shared his amazement at such innovations. The family could have discussed how steam-powered ships might change the way they traveled, particularly between Ireland and Britain, and how it would influence the future.

In summary, Conway Benning would likely have reacted to Robert Fulton's steamship with curiosity, admiration, and intellectual interest, recognizing its potential to reshape the world. While it might not have immediately impacted his daily life, it would have signaled the beginning of a new era of transportation and commerce that would eventually affect Ireland and his own family in profound ways.

The death of his son, Captain Conway Benning Jr., at the Battle of Albuera on May 16, 1811, would have had a profound and devastating impact on Conway Benning Sr., who was 74 years old at the time.

Emotional Impact:

- Grief and Devastation: Losing a child is a deep and painful experience for any parent, and for Conway Benning Sr., the grief would have been especially acute. His son had served with distinction in the British military, and the news of his death in such a brutal and significant battle during the Peninsular War would have been a terrible shock. The fact that his son was killed in action, possibly dying far from home, would have added to the emotional toll.

- Pride and Sorrow: As a father, Conway would have felt pride in his son's service and sacrifice for his country. However, this pride would have been mingled with sorrow and perhaps anger, as he might have questioned the cost of war and the tragic loss of life it demanded. The death of a soldier son would have also been seen as a significant blow to the family, especially during an era when the continuation of the family line and legacy through sons was deeply valued.

Reflection on Mortality and Faith:

- Faith as a Comfort: Conway Benning Sr. was a religious man, and his faith likely played a crucial role in how he processed the loss. As a clergyman, he would have turned to his Christian beliefs for comfort, possibly seeing his son's death as part of a divine plan, even though it would have been incredibly painful. He may have sought solace in the hope of eternal life and reunion with his son in the afterlife, finding strength in the teachings of the church.

- Deep Reflection on Life: At 74 years old, Conway Sr. was already in the later years of his life. The loss of a child so tragically and violently might have led him to reflect deeply on his own life, his family's legacy, and the impermanence of life. The war, which had taken his son, would have seemed closer and more personal than ever before. He might have spent time contemplating the sacrifices made by families like his across Britain and Ireland during the Napoleonic Wars.

Family Impact:

- Impact on His Health: The grief and stress of losing a son at his advanced age could have had physical repercussions for Conway Benning Sr. It's possible that the emotional toll would have affected his health, contributing to a decline in his well-being in the years that followed. While there is no direct record of this, it's common for elderly parents to experience significant health effects after the loss of a child.

- Support from Family and Community: Conway would have likely relied on the support of his wife, Ann, and his surviving children during this time of grief. The community around him, including members of his church, might have also offered comfort and consolation, understanding the magnitude of such a loss. Public mourning for fallen soldiers was common, and his son's death in battle would have been seen as a noble, though tragic, sacrifice.

Legacy and Memory of His Son:

- Preserving His Son's Legacy: As a father, Conway Sr. would have wanted to preserve the memory of his son and his military service. He may have ensured that his son was remembered in family records, church memorials, or local history as a hero who died for his country. This desire to honor Conway Jr.'s legacy would have been important not only for his family but also for the wider community.

- Connection to National Events: The Battle of Albuera was a significant event during the Peninsular War, and it was widely reported across Britain and Ireland. Conway Sr. would have been deeply affected by the fact that his son was part of such a major battle, adding to the personal and national mourning. His son's involvement in this critical moment in history would have marked the Benning family's connection to the wider geopolitical struggles of the time.

In conclusion, the death of his son, Captain Conway Benning Jr., in battle would have been a heartbreaking and life-altering event for Conway Benning Sr. at the age of 74. While his faith and the support of his family may have helped him endure the grief, the emotional toll of such a loss would have left a lasting impact on his remaining years.

At 80 years old, Conway Benning Sr. would have experienced the invention of the bicycle, which occurred in the early 19th century, with a mix of curiosity and possible skepticism. The invention of the bicycle, particularly the "Dandy Horse" or "Laufmaschine" by Karl von Drais in 1817, marked a significant step in transportation technology.

Reaction to the Bicycle:

- Curiosity and Interest: As someone who had witnessed many technological advancements throughout his life, Conway would likely have been intrigued by the bicycle. The concept of a human-powered vehicle that could provide faster mobility than walking would have been a novel and fascinating development for him.

- Skepticism: Given his age and the limited exposure to new technology, Conway might have been skeptical about the practical utility and safety of bicycles. Early bicycles were quite different from modern ones and were known for their instability and difficulty in use. Conway may have questioned whether such a device would gain widespread acceptance or practical use.

- Appreciation for Innovation: Conway had lived through significant technological changes and advancements, such as the Industrial Revolution and the advent of steam power. He may have appreciated the bicycle as part of the ongoing progress in transportation and technology, viewing it as another example of human ingenuity and improvement.

- Reflection on Change: At 80, Conway would have seen many changes in his lifetime and might have reflected on how the bicycle fit into the broader trend of technological evolution. He might have considered how such innovations were reshaping society and affecting people's daily lives.

Effects on His Life:

- Limited Practical Impact: Given Conway's advanced age, the bicycle would likely have had minimal direct impact on his own life. He might have seen it as an interesting development but would not have experienced its benefits firsthand, especially since early bicycles were not widely used or practical for older individuals.

- Influence on Society: While the bicycle may not have affected him personally, Conway would have been aware of its potential to transform transportation and mobility for others. He might have seen it as a symbol of progress and a reflection of the changing times.

In summary, Conway Benning Sr. would have likely reacted to the invention of the bicycle with a mixture of curiosity and skepticism, appreciating its innovation while questioning its practical application. The invention would have been one of many advancements he observed in his long life, contributing to his broader understanding of technological progress.

At 83 years old, Conway Benning Sr. would have experienced the death of Samuel Allen Esq with a mix of personal and professional emotions. Here's how he might have been affected:

Personal Impact:

- Sense of Loss: Given that Samuel Allen Esq was a prominent figure and the father of his son-in-law, Conway would have likely felt a profound sense of loss. This would have been especially significant if he had a close relationship with Samuel or if he respected him for his role in the community.

- Reflection on Mortality: At his advanced age, Conway might have been particularly reflective on the theme of mortality. The death of someone he knew, especially a figure of importance, would serve as a reminder of his own aging and the limited time remaining in his own life.

Professional and Familial Impact:

- Impact on Family Dynamics: Samuel's death would have had a direct impact on Conway's family, particularly on his daughter, Millicent Mary, and her family. Conway might have been involved in supporting his daughter and her family during this period of grief, which could have affected him emotionally and practically.

- Changes in Social Standing: Samuel Allen Esq's death might have led to changes in social and familial dynamics, possibly affecting Conway's status or interactions within his community. If Samuel held any positions of influence or had substantial assets, Conway might have had to navigate these changes or deal with any resultant issues in family matters.

- Estate Matters: If Samuel's estate required any legal or administrative attention, Conway, given his own background and experience, might have been involved in or affected by these processes, adding another layer to his experience of the loss.

In summary, at 83 years old, Conway Benning Sr. would have been deeply affected by the death of Samuel Allen Esq. The impact would be both personal, as he processed the loss and its emotional consequences, and practical, as he dealt with any changes or responsibilities arising from the death within his family and social circle.

At 86 years old in 1823, Conway Benning Sr.'s life would have been marked by several key aspects:

Health and Living Conditions:

- Health: At his advanced age, Conway would likely have experienced the typical health challenges of elderly individuals during the early 19th century. This might have included ailments such as arthritis, diminished vision, and overall frailty. Medical care at the time was limited, so his health issues would have been managed with home remedies and the occasional intervention from a local physician.

- Living Conditions: He would likely have been living in a home adapted for his old age, possibly with the assistance of family members or servants. Given his status and previous roles, he might have lived in a comfortable setting, although it would not have had the modern conveniences of later times.

Family and Social Life:

- Family: At this stage in life, Conway would have been surrounded by his children, grandchildren, and possibly even great-grandchildren. His family would have been a central aspect of his life, providing support and companionship. He might have been involved in family affairs and possibly took on a role as a patriarch within his extended family.

- Community Involvement: Conway's long service as a clergyman and his various roles in his community would have made him a respected figure. Even in his old age, he might have been consulted for his wisdom and experience, though his physical capacity to engage in active duties would have been limited.

Personal Reflections and Legacy:

- Reflection: At 86, Conway would have had ample time to reflect on his long life, including his career, family, and experiences. He might have spent his time reminiscing about his achievements, the changes he witnessed, and the legacy he hoped to leave.

- Legacy: His legacy would likely have been well-established, with a lasting impact on his family and community. His contributions as a clergyman and his role in various institutions would be remembered, and he would have been honored by his family and community for his long service and dedication.

Death and Burial:

- Death: By 1823, Conway's passing would have been a significant event for his family and community. His death would have been mourned by those who knew and respected him.

- Burial: Being buried in Rahmolyon would have been a fitting end, as it was the parish he served. His burial there would have allowed him to remain close to the community he had served for many years, providing a sense of closure and continuity for his family and parishioners.

Overall, at the time of his death, Conway Benning Sr.'s life would have been characterized by his advanced age, reflections on his past, and the impact he had made on his family and community. His final years would have been spent in a mix of familial devotion, health challenges, and the legacy of his long career and personal contributions.

ANN (ELLIS) BENNING[12]

Ann Ellis, born in 1743 in County Antrim, might have had the following characteristics and appearance, given the period and her social standing:

Physical Appearance:

1. Facial Features: Ann would likely have had a delicate and refined appearance, common among women of her social class. Her facial features might have included a graceful nose and chin, with a gentle expression reflecting the elegance of the 18th century.

2. Hair: Her hair would have been styled according to the fashion of the time. In the mid-18th century, women's hairstyles were often elaborate, involving curls or ringlets, sometimes piled high and decorated with ribbons or feathers. By the late 18th century, simpler styles like the "pouf" or "coiffure" became popular, with hair arranged in soft, voluminous waves.

3. Complexion: She might have had a fair complexion, as pale skin was highly prized among the upper classes during this period.

Clothing:

1. Dress: Ann's clothing would have reflected the fashion of the 18th century. Early in her life, she might have worn gowns with a fitted bodice, low neckline, and full skirts supported by panniers or crinolines. Fabrics would have been luxurious, such as silk or brocade, with elaborate trims or embroidery.

2. Accessories: She would likely have accessorized with items like lace shawls, gloves, and possibly a small bonnet or hat

decorated with feathers or ribbons. Jewelry, such as pearls or delicate gold pieces, would have been common.

3. Colors and Fabrics: Popular colors for women's clothing during her time included pastels and soft hues. Fabrics would have been chosen for their quality and appearance, with silk, satin, and fine wool being typical choices.

Overall Impression:

Ann Ellis would have projected an image of elegance and refinement, suitable for a woman of her social standing. Her appearance would reflect the fashions of her time, blending grace with the luxury expected of someone in her social position.

In 1743, life in County Antrim, Ireland, would have been shaped by several key factors:

Social and Economic Context:

1. Agricultural Society: The local economy was predominantly agricultural. Most people lived in rural areas and worked on farms. Life revolved around the seasons and agricultural cycles, with community events and festivals marking key points in the year.

2. Land Ownership: Land ownership was a major factor in social status. Many large estates were owned by the Anglo-Irish gentry, including families of higher social standing. The local society was stratified, with a clear distinction between landowners and tenants.

3. Religion: Religion played a significant role in daily life. The Church of Ireland (Anglican) was the established church, and many in the upper classes adhered to it. However, the population was also diverse, including Presbyterians and Catholics, with religious tensions sometimes impacting social relations.

Lifestyle and Culture:

1. Housing: Wealthier families, such as those Ann Ellis's family might have belonged to, lived in well-built homes with stone or brick walls, often with multiple rooms and comfortable

furnishings. Those of more modest means lived in simpler, thatched-roof cottages.

2. Education: Education for the upper classes included instruction in classical languages, literature, and manners. For those in the gentry, private tutors were common. Formal education for children of lower classes was limited.

3. Fashion and Society: The mid-18th century was characterized by elaborate fashions. Wealthy women wore intricate dresses, often with wide skirts supported by crinolines, and their attire was adorned with lace, ribbons, and embroidery.

4. Transportation and Travel: Travel was slow and often difficult. Roads were poor, and most people traveled by horseback or carriage. Major travel was typically limited to journeys between estates or trips to urban centers.

5. Political Climate: The political climate in Ireland was marked by tensions between the Anglo-Irish ruling class and the native Irish population. There were also broader geopolitical concerns, including relations with Britain.

At 9 years old, Ann Ellis would have likely been a child in a society where scientific discoveries were beginning to influence everyday life, albeit slowly. Here's how she might have reacted to Benjamin Franklin's discovery and how it might have affected her:

Reaction:

1. Curiosity and Awe: As a child, Ann might have been intrigued or fascinated by the stories of Franklin's experiments with lightning. If she was exposed to news or discussions about scientific discoveries, she might have heard about Franklin's work and found it exciting or mysterious.

2. Limited Direct Impact: At her age and in rural County Antrim, the direct impact of Franklin's discoveries might have been limited. The practical applications of his work, such as improved

lightning rods, would not have been immediately apparent in her daily life.

Effects:

1. Educational Influence: Franklin's work contributed to the broader scientific understanding of electricity, which eventually influenced educational curricula. As she grew up, she might have encountered scientific principles that were based on or inspired by Franklin's discoveries.

2. Cultural Context: The awareness of scientific advancements, even if indirect, could have contributed to a broader cultural appreciation for science and learning. It might have influenced the intellectual environment of her upbringing, potentially encouraging curiosity and education.

3. Indirect Impact: While the immediate effects on her daily life might have been minimal, the general progress in science and technology would have gradually impacted society. Over time, improvements in technology and infrastructure influenced by such discoveries would become more apparent.

Overall, while Ann Ellis might not have been directly affected by Franklin's discovery at such a young age, the general excitement and progress in science of the period would have shaped her worldview and the intellectual environment she grew up in.

In 1770, Ann Ellis would have worn a wedding outfit typical of the late 18th century. Here's a description of what she might have worn:

Wedding Attire for Ann Ellis:

1. Gown: Ann's gown would likely have been made from luxurious fabrics such as silk, satin, or brocade. Popular styles of the time included the "robe à la française" or "robe à l'anglaise." The "robe à la française" had a full, pleated back with a wide, low neckline, while the "robe à l'anglaise" was more fitted and had a higher waistline.

2. Color: Wedding gowns in the 18th century were often made in colors like white, cream, or pastel shades. White was becoming increasingly popular as a symbol of purity, though it was not yet the exclusively traditional choice it would later become.

3. Undergarments: Ann would wear a petticoat, which was a type of underskirt worn over a supportive hoop or pannier to give the gown its wide, structured shape. She would also wear a chemise, a linen shift worn directly against the skin.

4. Headwear: For headwear, Ann might have worn a lace or silk bonnet, which was fashionable at the time. Alternatively, she could have had a hairstyle adorned with ribbons, flowers, or a small decorative hat.

5. Accessories: Her accessories might include a lace shawl or stole, gloves, and perhaps a small fan. Jewelry such as a pearl necklace or simple gold or silver pieces would be appropriate for the occasion.

6. Footwear: She would likely wear soft leather shoes or slippers, often decorated with bows or buckles, which were the fashion at the time.

7. Overall Look: The overall look would be elegant and understated, reflecting the fashion of the period with an emphasis on delicate fabrics and refined details.

Ann's wedding attire would be a reflection of her social standing and the current fashion trends, combining formality with personal elegance.

When Ann Ellis was 27 years old and her son Conway was born in Carrickfergus in 1770, several factors would have influenced her life:

Emotional Impact:

1. Joy and Fulfillment: The birth of her son Conway would have brought Ann significant joy and fulfillment. As a new mother, she would have experienced a deep emotional bond with her child.

2. Family Role: As a mother, Ann's role in the family would have become central, focusing on the upbringing and care of her son. This would have marked a significant shift in her daily life and priorities.

Social and Practical Aspects:

1. Support Systems: Ann would likely have relied on family support during and after childbirth. In a close-knit community like Carrickfergus, extended family members and local women might have provided practical help and advice.

2. Local Community: Being in Carrickfergus, Ann would have been part of a community with strong social ties. The community's support and involvement in child-rearing practices would have influenced her experience as a mother.

3. Health and Well-being: The health and well-being of both Ann and her newborn would have been a major concern. In the 18th century, childbirth was risky, and Ann would have needed to ensure proper care for both herself and her baby.

Lifestyle Changes:

1. Domestic Life: Ann's daily routine would have changed significantly with the arrival of a child. Her responsibilities would now include caring for Conway, managing household tasks, and ensuring a suitable environment for his upbringing.

2. Social Expectations: In 18th-century Ireland, there were strong social expectations surrounding motherhood and family life. Ann would have been expected to fulfill these roles diligently, which could impact her social status and reputation.

Long-Term Impact:

1. Legacy: Ann's focus on her son's upbringing would have been central to her legacy. As Conway grew up, her role as his mother would influence his future and, by extension, her own place in the family's history.

2. Family Dynamics: The birth of Conway would have also affected the family dynamics, potentially bringing Ann closer to Conway's father and integrating her more deeply into the Benning family's social and economic circles.

Overall, Ann's experience as a mother to Conway would have been a pivotal moment in her life, reshaping her daily routines, emotional landscape, and social interactions within the community of Carrickfergus.

When Ann Ellis's husband, Conway Benning, was collated to the rectory of Donaghcloney, the rectory of Magherally, and the Archdeaconry of Dromore on May 5, 1770, it would have had several implications for her and their family:

Reaction and Emotional Impact:

1. Pride and Support: Ann would likely have felt pride and support for her husband's new ecclesiastical positions. Such appointments were significant achievements, and she would have been pleased with Conway's advancement in his career.

2. Adjustment: She might also have felt a mix of anticipation and apprehension about the changes that would come with the new responsibilities and expectations. This could have involved emotional adjustments to the increased demands on Conway's time and attention.

Impact on Daily Life:

1. Relocation and Residence: Although Conway was non-resident and kept a curate at Donaghcloney, Ann would have had to adapt to the implications of this role. If they moved to a new residence or had to spend considerable time away from Carrickfergus, it would have affected her daily routine and family life.

2. Increased Social Standing: The new positions would elevate their social standing. Ann would have enjoyed increased social prominence and possibly greater influence in the local community,

both through her husband's roles and her own position as the wife of a prominent clergyman.

3. Household Management: Managing a larger household or estate associated with these roles would have been a significant responsibility. Ann would have had to oversee domestic affairs, ensuring that everything ran smoothly in their absence.

Social and Community Life:

1. Community Involvement: Ann's role would involve more prominent participation in social and community events related to her husband's ecclesiastical duties. She might have hosted gatherings or been involved in charitable activities linked to the church.

2. Networking: The new positions would expand Ann's social network, introducing her to new people and possibly enhancing her family's influence and connections in the region.

Personal Adjustments:

1. Support for Conway: Ann would have played a supportive role in Conway's career, helping him balance his new responsibilities with family life. Her understanding and support would have been crucial for his success and their family's well-being.

2. Adaptation to Changes: The transition would have required Ann to adapt to the changing dynamics of their lives, including potentially managing additional responsibilities and adjusting to different social and professional circles.

Overall, Conway's appointment to these significant positions would have marked a major shift in Ann's life, bringing both opportunities and challenges as she navigated her role in a more prominent social and ecclesiastical context.

When Ann Ellis was 30 years old and gave birth to her son James in Carrickfergus in 1773, several aspects of her life would have been affected:

Emotional Impact:

1. Joy and Fulfillment: The birth of her son would have been a source of immense joy and personal fulfillment. Having a child was a significant event in her life, reflecting her growing family and enhancing her role as a mother.

2. Increased Responsibility: Ann would have felt a deeper sense of responsibility with the arrival of James. Balancing her duties as a wife and managing the household would become more complex with the addition of a new child.

Family Life:

1. Domestic Role: Ann's role as a mother would have increased her involvement in daily child-rearing tasks. She would have devoted time to caring for James, including his upbringing, education, and well-being.

2. Support from Conway: Conway's position might have provided some stability, but Ann would still bear a significant portion of the childcare and household management responsibilities. Her support network, including possibly hiring help or relying on extended family, would have been important.

Social and Community Impact:

1. Social Expectations: In the 18th century, motherhood was highly valued, and Ann's new role as a mother would have reinforced her status in the community. Her involvement in social and religious activities would also be influenced by her role as a mother.

2. Family Growth: The birth of James would further solidify her family unit. As a mother of multiple children, Ann would likely have gained additional respect and support from her community.

Personal Adjustments:

1. Health and Well-being: Ann's health and well-being would be impacted by childbirth and the demands of caring for a

newborn. She would need to adjust her routines and manage the physical and emotional challenges of new motherhood.

2. Balancing Duties: The arrival of James would require Ann to balance her roles more effectively, integrating the care of her children with her other responsibilities, including those related to her husband's ecclesiastical positions.

Overall, the birth of James would have been a transformative event in Ann's life, marking a period of increased familial responsibility and emotional fulfillment while also introducing new challenges and adjustments to her daily routine.

At 32 years old, when Ann Ellis gave birth to her daughter in the diocese of Meath in 1775, the event would have had several impacts on her life:

Emotional Impact:

1. Joy and Pride: Ann would likely have experienced deep joy and pride at the birth of her daughter, celebrating the expansion of her family and the addition of a female child.

2. Increased Parental Commitment: With a daughter, Ann's sense of responsibility would grow as she prepared to guide and nurture another child, which would enhance her role and identity as a mother.

Family Dynamics:

1. Balancing Roles: Managing the needs of a newborn daughter along with her existing responsibilities for her other children, including Conway, would have required careful balancing. Ann would have to manage both her new infant's needs and the demands of her growing family.

2. Support Network: The presence of her husband Conway and possibly other family members or domestic help would have been crucial in supporting her through this period, ensuring that both her and her children's needs were met.

Social and Community Impact:

1. Social Status: In 18th-century society, having a daughter was viewed positively, and Ann's role as a mother of both a son and a daughter would have strengthened her status within her community. She would be seen as a successful matriarch.

2. Community Involvement: Ann's involvement in community and religious activities might be influenced by her role as a mother of multiple children. Her participation in local life would be complemented by her family responsibilities.

Personal Adjustments:

1. Health and Recovery: Ann's health would be a primary concern following childbirth, especially managing the physical recovery and adapting to the demands of caring for a newborn daughter.

2. Family Routine: Ann would need to adapt her daily routines to accommodate the new member of the family. This includes adjustments to household management and ensuring the well-being of both her new daughter and her existing children.

Overall, the birth of her daughter in 1775 would be a significant event for Ann Ellis, bringing both joy and additional responsibilities. It would have required adjustments in her daily life and roles within her family and community.

At 33 years old, Ann Ellis would have experienced several effects when her husband, Conway Benning, received his LL.D. in 1776:

Personal Impact:

1. Pride and Satisfaction: Ann would likely have felt immense pride and satisfaction in her husband's academic achievement. His LL.D. (Doctor of Laws) would be seen as a significant honor and a testament to his professional and intellectual capabilities.

2. Enhanced Social Status: The attainment of such a prestigious degree would elevate the family's social standing. Ann might have

experienced increased respect and recognition in their social circles due to Conway's accomplishments.

Family Dynamics:

1. Support and Celebration: The achievement would be a source of family pride, and Ann would likely have been involved in celebrating Conway's success. This might have involved social gatherings or public acknowledgment of his achievement.

2. Increased Expectations: With Conway's new title and prestige, there might have been increased expectations and pressures on both him and Ann to maintain or enhance their social and professional standing.

Social and Community Impact:

1. Enhanced Reputation: The recognition of Conway's LL.D. would enhance their family reputation within the community. Ann would benefit from this elevated status, possibly leading to new opportunities for social connections and influence.

2. Community Involvement: As Conway's prominence grew, Ann might have been more involved in local and social events, often accompanying him to functions or being involved in charitable or community activities associated with his new role.

Personal Adjustments:

1. Adapting to New Status: Ann might have had to adjust to her husband's new professional status, which could involve changes in their social life, interactions with others, and expectations placed on their family.

2. Emotional Support: Ann's role as a supportive spouse would be crucial, providing emotional and practical support as Conway navigated the implications of his new title and responsibilities.

Overall, Conway Benning's attainment of an LL.D. in 1776 would bring a mix of personal pride, social elevation, and new expectations for Ann Ellis, affecting both her personal life and their family's standing in the community.

During the American Revolution (1775-1783), when Ann Ellis was between 33 and 40 years old, she would have experienced various impacts:

Reactions and Personal Impact:

1. Awareness and Concern: Ann would have likely been aware of the American Revolution through news and correspondence, especially as it could have impacted trade and politics in Europe. Her reaction might have been one of concern for the stability of British interests and its implications for her own and her family's well-being.

2. Sympathy and Political Opinions: Depending on her personal views and those of her social circle, she might have had sympathies toward either the British or the American cause. However, as a British subject and a member of a prominent family, her public stance would likely align with the British government.

Effects on Her Life:

1. Social and Economic Impact: The war could have had indirect effects on her life through disruptions in trade, economic uncertainty, and increased taxes. This might have led to economic pressures or adjustments in their lifestyle and finances.

2. Political and Social Discussions: The revolution would have been a frequent topic in social and political discussions. Ann might have engaged in conversations about the conflict, and it might have influenced her social interactions and relationships with others who held differing views.

3. Impact on Family Connections: If her husband, Conway Benning, was involved in any political or clerical discussions related to the revolution, Ann would have been impacted by these professional and social discussions. Her family's status and connections might have been affected by the shifting political landscape.

4. Emotional Impact: Ann could have experienced emotional stress due to the uncertainty and changes brought about by the revolution. The conflict would have been a source of anxiety regarding its outcomes and the broader implications for the British Empire and her own family's position within it.

5. Adaptation and Resilience: Ann's ability to adapt to these changes, support her family, and navigate the social and economic impacts of the revolution would have been crucial. Her resilience and practical adjustments would have been key in managing the effects of the conflict on her personal and family life.

Overall, Ann Ellis would have experienced a combination of concern, adaptation, and social adjustment due to the American Revolution, reflecting the broader impact of this significant historical event on individuals and families in Britain.

When Ann Ellis was 34 years old in 1777, and her husband Conway began traveling the continent, she would have been significantly affected in several ways:

Emotional and Social Impact:

1. Separation and Loneliness: Ann would have faced emotional strain due to her husband's absence. The separation might have caused feelings of loneliness and anxiety, especially as travel was lengthy and communication was slow.

2. Increased Responsibilities: With Conway away, Ann would have needed to manage their household and family affairs, including the care of their children and any other domestic responsibilities. This would have required considerable effort and adjustment on her part.

Practical and Social Effects:

1. Household Management: Ann would have taken on the responsibility of managing the household and any property they owned. This would have included financial management,

overseeing servants or staff, and handling any issues that arose in Conway's absence.

2. Social Status and Support: Depending on her social standing and the support network available to her, Ann might have relied on family, friends, or local social circles for support and companionship. Her social interactions and status might have been affected by her husband's absence.

Personal Adaptation:

1. Adaptation to Change: Ann would have needed to adapt to the changes in her life due to her husband's absence. This might have included adjusting to new routines and finding ways to manage without his presence and support.

2. Emotional Resilience: Coping with her husband's travels and managing household affairs would have required emotional resilience and practical skills. Ann's ability to handle these challenges would have been a testament to her strength and adaptability.

In summary, Ann Ellis would have experienced emotional strain, increased responsibilities, and necessary adaptations due to her husband Conway's travels. Her resilience and ability to manage the household and support her family during his absence would have been crucial in maintaining stability and coping with the changes brought about by his extended travels.

When Ann Ellis was 34 years old and gave birth to her daughter Millicent Mary in Carrickfergus in 1777, the birth would have had several effects on her:

Emotional Impact:

1. Joy and Fulfillment: The birth of a new child, especially a daughter, would likely have brought Ann joy and a sense of fulfillment. Children often strengthen family bonds and bring emotional enrichment.

2. Increased Responsibility: With a new baby, Ann would have faced the demands of caring for an infant, which includes physical and emotional challenges. This would have added to her existing responsibilities, particularly as Conway was away traveling.

Practical and Social Impact:

1. Household Dynamics: The arrival of Millicent Mary would have changed the dynamics within the household. Ann would need to adjust her daily routines to accommodate the needs of a newborn, which might have included altering her household management and possibly the roles of any servants or staff.

2. Social and Community Roles: Ann's role in her local community might have been influenced by her new status as a mother of a young child. The birth of a child could also strengthen her social connections within the community, as families often interact and support each other during significant life events.

Personal Adaptation:

1. Health and Well-being: Ann's physical health would have been a concern following childbirth. She would need time to recover from the birth, manage her own well-being while caring for her newborn, and balance this with her other responsibilities.

2. Emotional Adjustment: Balancing the demands of motherhood with managing her household and coping with Conway's absence would require emotional resilience. Ann would need to adapt to the new challenges and responsibilities that come with raising a child.

In summary, Ann Ellis's life would have been significantly impacted by the birth of her daughter Millicent Mary. The arrival of a new child would bring joy and fulfillment but also introduce additional responsibilities and challenges, particularly in the context of managing a household and coping with her husband's extended travels.

When Ann Ellis was 35 years old and her husband, Conway Benning, was instituted to the Vicarage of Rathmolyon, diocese of Meath on March 7, 1778, several aspects of her life would have been affected:

Relocation and Lifestyle Changes:

1. Relocation: Although Conway was appointed to the Vicarage of Rathmolyon, the family continued to live at Kilroot. This arrangement meant that Ann would have experienced a significant shift in her domestic life. The need to manage two residences—Kilroot and the vicarage—would have required careful coordination.

2. Adjustments to Kilroot: Living at Kilroot while Conway was based in Rathmolyon would involve adjustments to her daily routine and responsibilities. Ann would need to manage the household affairs in Kilroot, ensuring that it was maintained in a way befitting her husband's position and their social status.

Social and Professional Impact:

1. Increased Social Role: As the wife of a vicar, Ann's social role would have been elevated. Even though they lived at Kilroot, she would still be expected to engage with the local community associated with Rathmolyon. This might include attending events, hosting gatherings, and participating in church-related activities.

2. Support for Conway: Ann's support would be crucial for Conway in his new role. While Conway's work involved duties at Rathmolyon, Ann's role at Kilroot would involve supporting him in managing his new responsibilities, whether through correspondence or assisting with matters related to his parish.

Personal and Emotional Impact:

1. Emotional Adjustment: The new responsibilities and lifestyle changes would require Ann to adjust emotionally. Managing two residences and fulfilling her role as a vicar's wife

while maintaining the household at Kilroot would involve balancing numerous demands.

2. Focus on Family: With a young family to care for, including Millicent Mary, Ann would need to balance her domestic responsibilities with her husband's new role. This could lead to a sense of additional pressure but also a feeling of fulfillment from supporting Conway's career.

Community Impact:

1. Involvement in Church Life: Even though they were primarily based at Kilroot, Ann's role as the vicar's wife in the diocese of Meath would likely involve some level of engagement with the local church community. This could influence her social interactions and community involvement.

In summary, the appointment of her husband to the Vicarage of Rathmolyon would have brought about significant changes in Ann Ellis's life, requiring her to manage household responsibilities at Kilroot while supporting Conway's role. The adjustments would involve balancing her domestic duties with her new social and community expectations, impacting her daily life and emotional well-being.

When Ann Ellis was 36 years old and her daughter, Jane, was born at Carrickfergus in 1779, it likely had a profound impact on her both personally and emotionally:

Personal and Emotional Impact:

1. Joy of Motherhood: The birth of another child would have brought joy to Ann, especially since she was already an experienced mother. However, having a new baby would have added new responsibilities to her daily life, particularly with managing the needs of her other children, such as Millicent Mary and James.

2. Physical and Emotional Demands: At 36, childbirth could have been more physically demanding than earlier pregnancies. The emotional and physical recovery, combined with caring for a

newborn, would have required Ann to focus much of her energy on her household and children. This may have also resulted in temporary shifts in her social responsibilities, allowing her to focus on her family.

3. Increased Family Responsibilities: With four children now in the family, Ann's role as a mother would have expanded. Balancing the needs of her older children while caring for an infant like Jane would have required more attention and organization.

Impact on Daily Life:

1. Managing a Larger Household: The birth of Jane likely meant that Ann would need additional help in the household, possibly employing more servants or seeking support from extended family members. As her children grew, education and their upbringing would become an increasing focus.

2. Adaptation to Conway's Responsibilities: Given Conway's busy career and his non-resident role as vicar of Rathmolyon, Ann may have shouldered more responsibilities at home. While Conway likely provided guidance and support, his career demands may have left Ann to take a primary role in raising their children during this time.

Social and Community Impact:

1. Community Perception: As the wife of a prominent figure like Conway Benning, having a growing family could have increased her status in the community. Families were often seen as a reflection of their social and moral values, so the addition of another child could have reinforced her reputation as a nurturing and respectable woman.

2. Participation in Local Society: Depending on her recovery and well-being, Ann's involvement in social circles may have slowed temporarily, allowing her to focus on her family. However, she likely remained a figure of importance within her community, especially given her role as the wife of a vicar.

In summary, the birth of Jane at Carrickfergus in 1779 would have been a time of both joy and responsibility for Ann. She would have experienced the physical and emotional demands of motherhood while balancing the needs of her growing family and supporting her husband's career. This period in her life was likely marked by a mix of fulfillment and the challenges of managing a large household.

When Ann Ellis was 41 years old and the first successful hot air balloon flight occurred in 1783, it would have been an event that sparked wonder and curiosity. The Montgolfier brothers' invention was a groundbreaking moment in human history, representing the first time humans achieved flight. Here's how it might have affected her:

Reaction:

1. Fascination and Curiosity: Ann likely would have been fascinated by the news of the hot air balloon's success. It was a moment of scientific and technological marvel, and even though she may not have been directly involved in scientific circles, this achievement would have piqued the curiosity of educated individuals and the general public alike.

2. Discussions in Social Circles: As a member of a prominent family, Ann would have likely encountered discussions about the hot air balloon in her social circles. Intellectuals and the upper class were typically the first to hear about scientific advancements, and the event could have been a topic of conversation at gatherings and in letters exchanged with friends and relatives.

3. A Sense of Awe: Given the era, flight would have been seen as something almost magical. For someone like Ann, who lived in a time when transportation was limited to horse-drawn carriages and ships, the idea of humans being able to fly in the air would have seemed astonishing. The hot air balloon might have been seen as a symbol of human progress and ingenuity.

Effect on Her Life:

1. Expanding Worldview: News of the hot air balloon could have made Ann more aware of the rapidly changing world. The Industrial Revolution was already in progress, and new inventions were transforming society. The balloon's success may have made her think about how technology was advancing and how it could potentially affect her children's futures.

2. Education and Family: Ann may have discussed this achievement with her husband and children, using it as a way to inspire curiosity about science and exploration. For her sons and daughters, hearing about such groundbreaking technology might have encouraged them to take an interest in education, invention, or broader scientific endeavors.

3. Interest in Travel and Exploration: Though the hot air balloon wasn't yet a practical mode of transport, it symbolized new possibilities in travel and exploration. Ann might have considered how these advancements could one day make long-distance travel more accessible, even if such ideas still seemed like distant dreams at the time.

Overall, Ann's reaction to the first hot air balloon flight would have been one of wonder and amazement, like many others in her era. While the event may not have directly impacted her daily life, it likely expanded her sense of what was possible in the world and sparked discussions within her social and family circles.

When Ann Ellis was 52 years old at her daughter Eleanor's wedding to Noah Webb Dalway on May 22, 1795, she would have likely worn a gown reflecting the fashions of the late 18th century, specifically within the Georgian period. Here's what she might have worn:

Dress Style:

1. Robe à l'Anglaise or Empire-style Gown: By 1795, the transition from the more structured, elaborate Rococo styles of

earlier decades to the simpler, high-waisted Empire style had begun. Ann might have worn a robe à l'Anglaise—a fitted bodice with a full skirt—or even an early Empire-style gown, which featured a higher waistline under the bust and a more flowing silhouette. Both styles emphasized a more natural figure compared to earlier tightly corseted fashions.

2. Fabrics: The gown would likely have been made of fine fabrics such as silk, taffeta, or muslin, which were popular at the time. For a wedding, the color would have been elegant but not necessarily white, as the trend of white wedding gowns didn't fully emerge until the 19th century. She might have worn pastel shades like lavender, soft blue, or pale pink or more subdued colors like cream or dove grey.

3. Trimmings and Embroidery: Her dress could have had subtle embroidery or lace detailing, particularly around the neckline, sleeves, and hem. Delicate floral patterns or intricate lacework would have been in keeping with the style of the time.

Accessories:

1. Shawl or Mantle: Given that May could still have cool weather in Ireland, Ann might have draped a shawl or mantle over her shoulders. These would be made of wool, silk, or even cashmere, and would complement the gown, perhaps embroidered or with fringe.

2. Bonnet or Hat: It was customary for women to wear a bonnet or hat to formal occasions like a wedding. Ann might have worn a fashionable wide-brimmed hat adorned with ribbons, feathers, or flowers, or a more modest bonnet with lace detailing.

3. Gloves: As gloves were a standard accessory for formal occasions, Ann likely would have worn a pair of elbow-length silk gloves in a pale color to match her gown.

4. Shoes: Ann's shoes would likely have been made of silk or satin, with a low heel, and possibly decorated with bows or small

buckles. The color would have coordinated with her gown, in pastel shades or light tones.

5. Jewelry: She would have worn tasteful jewelry, such as a string of pearls or a delicate gold necklace. Earrings and a brooch might also have been part of her ensemble, adding a touch of elegance without being too ostentatious.

Hairstyle:

1. Natural and Elegant: By 1795, women were moving away from the highly elaborate powdered wigs of previous decades and opting for more natural hair. Ann may have worn her hair curled or pinned up with some soft waves framing her face. A few fashionable accessories like ribbons or combs might have been added to her hairstyle.

Overall, Ann would have chosen an elegant, refined outfit appropriate for a woman of her status attending her daughter's wedding. The emphasis would be on grace and simplicity, reflecting the changing trends of the time toward more natural and less extravagant styles.

When Ann Ellis was 52 years old and her son, Conway Benning Jr., entered the Royal Artillery in 1795 as a lieutenant, it likely had a significant impact on her both emotionally and practically. Here's how she might have been affected:

Pride and Concern:

1. Pride in Her Son's Accomplishment: Ann would likely have felt a deep sense of pride that her son was joining the prestigious Royal Artillery, a branch of the military known for its discipline and expertise in artillery and engineering. This would have been seen as a notable achievement, reflecting well on her family and on Conway Jr.'s capabilities.

2. Concern for His Safety: As a mother, she likely felt a strong concern for his safety. The military at the time was frequently involved in conflicts, especially with the ongoing French

Revolutionary Wars (which later evolved into the Napoleonic Wars). She would have known that a military career, particularly in the artillery, was dangerous and fraught with the risks of injury or death.

Emotional Impact:

3. Fear of War: With Europe embroiled in wars during the 1790s, Ann might have felt anxiety about the prospect of her son being sent into battle. Mothers of the time often had to cope with the constant fear of losing their sons in military service. Even though military service was a source of pride, the looming threat of war would have weighed heavily on her.

4. Distance from Her Son: Depending on where Conway was stationed, Ann might have had to cope with his absence from home. Military service often required long periods of separation, which could have been emotionally difficult for her as a mother. Letters and communication were slow, which would have added to her sense of worry and longing for news of his well-being.

Social Status:

5. Prestige of a Military Family: Having a son in the Royal Artillery would likely have elevated the family's social standing to some degree. Military service was respected, especially in a time when patriotism and loyalty to the crown were highly valued. Ann might have taken comfort in knowing that Conway Jr.'s position would bring honor to the family.

Maternal Worry and Support:

6. Role as a Supportive Mother: Despite any fears or concerns she had, Ann would likely have been supportive of her son's career, understanding that military service was a common path for young men seeking honor and advancement. She may have offered him words of encouragement and expressed her hopes for his success and safety.

In summary, Ann was likely a mix of pride and anxiety when her son entered the Royal Artillery. While she would have recognized the prestige and honor of his position, the risks and dangers inherent in military service during a turbulent period in history would have weighed heavily

on her as a mother.

When Ann Ellis was 55 years old in 1798, the Irish Rebellion and the Battle of Antrim would have been significant and deeply distressing events for her, especially as someone living in Ireland during this time. Here's how she might have reacted and been affected:

Fear for Her Family's Safety:

1. Heightened Anxiety: The Irish Rebellion of 1798 was marked by widespread unrest and violence, with clashes between Irish rebels seeking independence from British rule and government forces. Living in Carrickfergus or Kilroot, Ann would have likely felt intense anxiety for the safety of her family, including her husband and children. The Battle of Antrim, part of the wider rebellion, was not far from her home, and she would have been acutely aware of the danger.

2. Worry for Her Son in the Military: Her son, Conway Jr., had entered the Royal Artillery a few years earlier in 1795, and the conflict could have made her more fearful for his safety. Since British military forces were actively involved in suppressing the rebellion, she might have been deeply concerned that Conway could be called to fight or be put in harm's way.

Political Tensions:

3. Divided Loyalties: As the wife of a Church of Ireland rector, Ann and her family were likely seen as part of the Protestant Anglo-Irish establishment, which was generally aligned with the British government. The rebellion, led by the United Irishmen, was primarily composed of Irish Catholics and dissenters who sought

to overthrow British rule. This division could have created tension or fear of reprisal against her family, especially in rural or smaller communities where loyalties were sharply divided.

4. Fear of Local Violence: Given the unrest across Ireland, including areas like Antrim, Ann might have feared that violence could spill over into her own community. Reports of attacks, property destruction, and brutal reprisals by both the rebels and British forces would have spread fear across the country, particularly for families like hers, who were more closely aligned with the government.

Personal and Social Impact:

5. Social Unrest: The rebellion was not just a military conflict; it represented deep social and political unrest in Ireland. Ann would have witnessed or heard about neighbors and communities being divided, possibly even encountering people she knew taking opposing sides. This could have caused a sense of isolation or unease, particularly if the rebellion led to distrust within her social circle.

6. Religious Concerns: As the wife of a rector, Ann would likely have had a strong attachment to the Church of Ireland, which was closely tied to British governance. The rebellion had significant religious overtones, with Catholic and Protestant tensions rising. Ann may have feared for the future of the Protestant minority in Ireland and the stability of the Church of Ireland's influence in society.

Emotional Strain:

7. Emotional Turmoil: The combined fears for her family's safety, concerns over her son's military involvement, and the general uncertainty of the time would have caused significant emotional strain. It's likely that she would have experienced a mix of fear, grief for the country's unrest, and worry about the future of Ireland under British rule.

8. Sympathy for Both Sides: Depending on her political and personal leanings, she may have had conflicting feelings about the rebellion. While loyal to the British government, she might have had some sympathy for the grievances that led to the uprising, especially regarding the harsh conditions many Irish people faced under British rule. However, this would be tempered by her immediate concern for her family's safety and well-being.

In conclusion, Ann Ellis would have likely reacted to the Battle of Antrim and the Irish Rebellion of 1798 with a combination of fear, anxiety, and concern for her family's safety, especially her son in the military. The rebellion would have affected her on both a personal and social level, causing emotional strain as she navigated the dangers and uncertainties of living in a country torn by conflict.

When Ann Ellis was 57 years old, her daughter Millicent Mary married Dr. Samuel Allen M.D. on November 14, 1798. Here's how the event might have affected her, and what she likely would have worn for the occasion:

Emotional Impact:

1. Pride and Joy: The marriage of Millicent to a respected medical doctor would likely have brought Ann immense pride. Marriages were important milestones, not just for the individuals but for the family's social status. Dr. Samuel Allen was likely a well-established figure, which would have secured Millicent's future and brought respect to the family.

2. Relief and Satisfaction: As the mother of the bride, Ann would have felt relief knowing that her daughter was making a good match, ensuring stability and security. In that era, marriage was central to a woman's status and well-being, so a union with a prominent physician like Dr. Allen would have eased any concerns about Millicent's future.

3. Nostalgia and Reflection: By this point in her life, Ann had seen many of her children grow up, and Millicent's wedding

may have stirred feelings of nostalgia. She may have reflected on her own marriage to Conway Benning and the life they had built together, which could have been bittersweet as their family continued to grow and evolve.

4. A Blend of Joy and Anxiety: While the wedding would have been a happy occasion, Ann was still living during a period of political unrest in Ireland following the Irish Rebellion earlier that year. The ongoing conflict and instability in the country might have tempered the celebration, adding a layer of anxiety for the future.

What Ann Would Have Worn:

For her daughter's wedding, Ann would have worn something formal and appropriate for a woman of her age and social standing in late 18th-century Ireland. The fashion of the late 1790s reflected the transition from the elaborate styles of the Georgian era to the simpler, more classical styles inspired by French Revolution fashion.

1. Silk Gown: Ann would likely have worn a silk or satin gown in a soft, elegant color such as pale blue, lavender, or light grey, colors that were fashionable at the time. The gown would have featured a high waistline (influenced by the emerging Empire style) and a fitted bodice. The skirt would have been long and flowing, reaching the floor, with minimal embellishments compared to earlier Georgian styles.

2. Accessories:

- Shawl or Spencer Jacket: Given the cooler November weather, Ann might have worn a shawl or a Spencer jacket, which was a short, fitted jacket popular at the time. The shawl could have been made of a fine wool or cashmere, adding warmth and modesty to her outfit.

- Bonnet or Cap: Ann would have worn a bonnet or a lace cap. By 1798, large hats had given way to more delicate, understated bonnets, often adorned with ribbons or lace. Indoors, she may have worn a simple lace cap to match the formality of the occasion.

- Gloves: Gloves were an essential accessory for formal occasions. Ann would have worn kid leather gloves, likely in a light color to match her gown.

3. Jewelry: As the mother of the bride, Ann would have worn understated yet elegant jewelry. Pearl earrings, a simple necklace, and perhaps a brooch were common accessories for a woman of her age and standing. Her jewelry would have complemented her gown without drawing too much attention.

4. Footwear: Ann would have worn flat or low-heeled shoes made of silk or leather, probably in a light color to match her dress. Shoes during this time were simple but refined, often with ribbon ties or small buckles.

Conclusion:

Ann Ellis would have been filled with pride and happiness at Millicent Mary's marriage to Dr. Samuel Allen, knowing that her daughter had made a prosperous and respectable match. While the occasion would have been joyful, the ongoing unrest in Ireland would have been in the background of her thoughts. On this important day, Ann would have dressed in the latest fashion of the time, wearing a silk gown with elegant accessories, reflecting her social status as the mother of the bride and a member of a respected family.

When Ann Ellis was 57 years old, in 1798, William Young's shoe designs marked an advancement in footwear craftsmanship. Here's how she might have reacted and been affected by this development:

Reaction to William Young's Shoes:

1. Curiosity and Interest: As someone from a well-established family, Ann would likely have been intrigued by innovations in fashion and craftsmanship. New designs by a skilled shoemaker

like William Young would have piqued her curiosity, especially if they promised better comfort or style. Footwear was an important aspect of women's attire in the late 18th century, and any improvements in the design or quality of shoes would have been welcomed.

2. Practical Considerations: By this point in her life, Ann might have valued practicality and comfort more than pure fashion. If William Young's designs were more comfortable or supportive, they would have appealed to her, especially as she aged. Shoes that offered better support for daily activities would have been attractive for practical reasons, particularly for someone of her social class who might attend formal events and travel between homes.

3. Access to New Fashion: If Young's shoes were fashionable and sought after, Ann might have been pleased to keep up with the latest trends in refined society. As a mother with children marrying into other prominent families, such as the Allens and Dalways, staying fashionable would have been a point of pride for her.

Effect on Her Life:

1. Enhanced Comfort: If she acquired a pair of William Young's newly designed shoes, she would likely have enjoyed greater comfort and style. Shoe design was evolving to focus more on structure and support, which could have made walking and attending social events more pleasant for her.

2. Aesthetic Appeal: Fashion-conscious women like Ann would have appreciated shoes that added elegance to their attire. The new designs might have complemented her gowns and formal wear, making her feel more refined and well-dressed for family gatherings, weddings, and church events.

3. Social Perception: Owning shoes from a well-known designer like William Young could have elevated her social standing or reaffirmed her family's wealth and taste. Fashionable

shoes were often a sign of prestige, so wearing them might have given her a sense of satisfaction, knowing she was presenting herself in the best light possible within her social circles.

Conclusion:

Ann likely would have reacted with interest to William Young's shoe designs, appreciating their practicality, comfort, and potential to enhance her wardrobe. As someone living in a society where appearance and fashion held significant value, she may have enjoyed the boost in comfort and status that came from wearing shoes designed by a reputable shoemaker.

When Ann Ellis was 57 years old and her daughter Jane married Thomas Higginbotham in September 1800, Ann would have likely worn formal attire appropriate for her age, social standing, and the occasion. Fashion at the turn of the 19th century was influenced by the Neoclassical styles of the late 18th century, and women of her status would have dressed elegantly, reflecting the trends of the time.

What Ann Might Have Worn:

1. Gown:

- Empire Waist: The fashionable silhouette of the time featured an empire waist, with the waistline positioned just below the bust. Ann would likely have worn a gown with this high waistline, as it was popular and considered flattering for women of all ages.

- Fabric: The gown would have been made of fine fabrics such as silk, satin, or muslin, depending on the formality of the event. For her daughter's wedding, she might have chosen a silk or satin gown in soft, elegant colors such as ivory, pale blue, lavender, or pastel shades.

- Sleeves: Her gown would likely have had long sleeves, given her age and the formality of the occasion. Sleeves could be slightly puffed at the shoulders or fitted, with delicate detailing like lace or ribbon trim.

- Length: The gown would have been floor-length, with a flowing skirt that might have featured light pleating or gathering for a soft, elegant drape.

2. Shawl or Cape:

- Ann may have worn a shawl, cape, or wrap made of cashmere, silk, or lace to drape over her shoulders. This would have been both a practical and fashionable addition to her outfit, especially if the wedding took place in cooler weather.

3. Accessories:

- Gloves: Gloves were a must for formal occasions. Ann would likely have worn long, white or cream-colored gloves made of kid leather or silk, which would extend up her arms and complement the elegance of her gown.

- Bonnet or Headdress: Women of her age often wore bonnets or headdresses. Ann might have worn a bonnet adorned with lace, ribbons, or even small feathers, in colors that matched her gown. Alternatively, a cap with intricate lace detailing could have been worn indoors.

- Jewelry: Ann's jewelry would have been understated yet refined, likely including pearls, cameos, or simple gold pieces. A necklace with a pendant, drop earrings, and perhaps a delicate bracelet would have completed her look.

4. Footwear:

- She would have worn delicate silk or leather slippers, in a color that matched her gown. Shoes at the time were simple and low-heeled, often with a slight point at the toe.

Color Palette:

Given her age and the formality of the wedding, Ann would have likely chosen soft, muted tones for her gown. Shades of pale blue, lavender, cream, or dove gray were popular choices for women of her standing and age. These colors were considered dignified and elegant, suitable for a mother of the bride.

Conclusion:

Ann's attire at Jane's wedding would have reflected the refined and elegant fashion of the early 19th century. Her gown would likely have been made of luxurious fabric, with an empire waist and flowing skirt, accessorized with gloves, a shawl or cape, and delicate jewelry. The overall look would have been sophisticated and appropriate for her role as the mother of the bride, enhancing her graceful presence at the wedding.

When Ann Ellis was 58 years old and her son James married Charlotte Berry on September 13, 1801, she would have once again worn formal attire, suitable for her age and the significance of the occasion. Her outfit would likely reflect the style of the early 19th century, influenced by the Neoclassical fashion of the Regency era.

What Ann Might Have Worn:

1. Gown:

- Empire Waist: Like at her daughter's wedding the previous year, Ann's gown would have featured the high-waisted, empire silhouette that was still in vogue. The gown would be elegant, perhaps even more understated than what she wore to Jane's wedding.

- Fabric: For her son's wedding, Ann might have chosen luxurious but conservative fabrics such as silk, satin, or even fine muslin. The color could have been light or soft-toned, possibly in shades of lavender, dove gray, or soft blue, as these colors conveyed dignity and refinement.

- Sleeves: Long sleeves were customary for women of Ann's age. These might have been puffed at the shoulder with a fitted lower arm, or perhaps draped more gracefully, with delicate detailing such as lace or ribbon at the cuffs.

- Length and Style: The gown would have been floor-length, with a simple yet elegant skirt. It may have featured some pleating or gathering, though the overall design would have been more subdued compared to the elaborate gowns worn by younger women.

2. Outerwear:

- Spencer Jacket or Shawl: For outdoor or church settings, Ann might have worn a Spencer jacket—a short, tailored jacket that ended just below the bust—or a shawl made from silk, cashmere, or lace. A shawl would have added warmth and complemented the gown's style.

3. Accessories:

- Gloves: As with most formal occasions, Ann would have worn gloves, likely in white or cream. Kid leather or silk gloves would have been appropriate, extending to her elbows or slightly below.

- Headdress: A bonnet or cap would have been appropriate for a woman of her age and status. Ann might have chosen a simple yet elegant bonnet, perhaps adorned with lace, ribbons, or delicate floral decorations, coordinating with her gown. For indoor settings, a lace cap could have been worn.

- Jewelry: Ann would likely have worn understated but refined jewelry. A string of pearls, a cameo brooch, or simple gold earrings would have added a touch of sophistication. She may also have worn a delicate necklace or pendant, though her jewelry would have been modest compared to the younger women at the event.

4. Footwear:

- Slippers: Ann would have worn soft leather or silk slippers, in a color matching her gown. These shoes would have been flat or very low-heeled, in keeping with the fashion of the time and her age.

5. Colors:

- As she was nearing 60, Ann would have likely chosen more subdued, neutral, or pastel colors for the wedding. Soft blues, light grays, lavender, or cream would have been both fashionable and appropriate for her role as the mother of the groom. These colors were dignified and understated, reflecting her status.

Conclusion:

At the wedding of her son James and Charlotte Berry, Ann Ellis would have dressed in the elegant, refined style typical of early 19th-century fashion. Her gown would have been simple but made from luxurious fabric, with long sleeves and an empire waist, accessorized with a shawl or Spencer jacket, gloves, and modest jewelry. The overall look would have been dignified, befitting her age and social standing as the mother of the groom.

When Ann Ellis was 64 years old in 1807, Robert Fulton's successful launch of the first commercial steamship, the Clermont, would have been an extraordinary development. Given that she lived in an era defined by significant technological and societal changes, she would likely have reacted with a mix of curiosity, wonder, and perhaps even a little apprehension.

How She Might Have Reacted:

1. Fascination and Curiosity:

- News of Fulton's steamship would have quickly spread throughout the British Isles, including Ireland, where Ann lived. As someone living in a time when travel was slow and often difficult, the idea of a steam-powered vessel able to travel efficiently against the wind and current would have likely sparked a sense of awe. It might have seemed like an incredible advancement, opening up possibilities for faster travel and commerce.

- Ann might have been particularly interested in how the steamship could impact trade and communication, especially as someone connected to an educated and influential family. With several children who had careers or interests that could benefit from faster transportation, she might have seen the steamship as a breakthrough that would change the future for her family and society.

2. Skepticism or Concern:

- As a woman of her time, Ann might have also been cautious or skeptical about such an innovation. Steam power was new, and any new technology often raised concerns about safety and reliability. She may have wondered if it would truly be a sustainable mode of transportation or simply a passing innovation.

- Additionally, the transition from traditional sailing to steam-powered ships would have been a significant cultural shift, and she may have questioned whether such mechanical power could ever fully replace natural elements like wind and water for travel.

3. Impact on Her Life:

- While Ann herself might not have directly experienced a steamship voyage at the age of 64, the invention would have likely influenced the world around her. It would have impacted trade, communication, and even the movement of people, both within Ireland and across the Atlantic. This might have brought more goods, news, and even people into her world at a faster pace.

- The invention could have sparked discussions within her family and community about the potential for faster and more efficient travel, especially if they were involved in commerce or travel. With some of her children living in different places or involved in military or professional careers, the steamship could have represented new opportunities for travel and connection.

4. Long-term Perspective:

- As someone who had witnessed major technological advancements during her lifetime—the American Revolution, the Industrial Revolution, and now the dawn of steam-powered travel—Ann may have reflected on how rapidly the world was changing. The steamship would have been another sign that progress was moving quickly, affecting not only daily life but also the future of global trade, warfare, and society.

Conclusion:

Ann's reaction to the invention of the first commercial steamship would likely have been a mixture of curiosity, excitement, and cautious skepticism. The impact on her personal life would have been indirect but profound, as it signaled the start of an era where travel and trade would be faster and more efficient. For someone in her position, the steamship represented the continuation of the rapid changes that had defined her lifetime, reshaping the world around her.

At 65 years old in 1808, Ann Ellis would have experienced a mix of emotions and impacts upon the birth of her grandson, Henry Ellis Allen.

Emotional Impact:

1. Joy and Pride:

- The arrival of a grandchild would have been a source of joy and pride. Grandchildren often bring renewed energy and happiness into a grandparent's life, and Henry's birth would have been a significant and celebratory event for Ann and her family.

2. Reflection on Legacy:

- Ann might have reflected on her own life and the legacy she was passing on through her children and grandchildren. Seeing her family grow and knowing that her lineage would continue could have been deeply fulfilling.

Effects on Her Life:

1. Family Dynamics:

- As a grandmother, Ann would likely have taken a keen interest in her grandson's growth and development. She might have become more involved in family events, sharing wisdom and support with her children and their families.

- Her role in the family could have included helping with childcare or providing guidance, especially given her experience and age.

2. Health and Energy:

- At 65, Ann's physical vitality would have been less than in her younger years. However, the joy of a new grandchild might have provided a burst of emotional and mental energy. Interaction with her grandson could have been a refreshing and meaningful aspect of her later years.

3. Social and Community Impact:

- Ann's family would likely have celebrated Henry's birth with social gatherings and announcements, reinforcing her social status and connections within the community. As a respected matriarch, she would have been a central figure in these celebrations.

Conclusion:

The birth of her grandson, Henry Ellis Allen, at the age of 65 would have brought Ann Ellis significant joy and pride. It would have reinforced her sense of family and legacy while adding a new dimension to her life as a grandmother. Despite her advancing age, the arrival of a grandchild would have invigorated her spirit and strengthened her ties to her family and community.

At 68 years old in 1811, the death of her son, Conway Benning Jr., at the Battle of Albuera would have been a profound and deeply distressing experience for Ann Ellis.

Emotional Impact:

1. Overwhelming Grief:

- The loss of a child, regardless of age, is an immense emotional blow. Ann would have been devastated by Conway's death. As a mother, the grief of losing a son, especially one who had achieved a notable position in the Royal Artillery, would be immense.

2. Sense of Loss and Helplessness:

- Conway's death in battle would have left Ann feeling a deep sense of loss and helplessness. She might have struggled with the finality of his death and the impact it had on her family. The fact that he was killed in a distant battle would also have added to her feelings of helplessness, as she could not be there to support him or provide comfort.

3. Emotional and Physical Health:

- Ann's advanced age would have made it harder for her to cope with such a traumatic event. The stress and sorrow could have taken a toll on her physical health, potentially leading to ailments or exacerbating existing conditions.

Effects on Her Life:

1. Family Dynamics:

- Ann's grief would have deeply affected her relationship with her surviving children and family members. The loss of Conway might have brought the family closer together in their shared mourning, or it could have led to strained relationships as they all dealt with their grief in different ways.

2. Social Impact:

- Ann's community would likely have been aware of her loss, and she might have received condolences and support from friends and neighbors. Public expressions of mourning, such as wearing black or holding memorial services, would have been a part of her experience.

3. Legacy and Reflection:

- The death of Conway might have led Ann to reflect on her own life and legacy. She could have been preoccupied with thoughts about her remaining children and how to ensure her family's well-being in the face of such a loss.

Conclusion:

The death of her son Conway at the age of 68 would have been an incredibly painful and life-altering experience for Ann Ellis.

The emotional impact of such a loss would have been profound, affecting her physical and emotional health, her family relationships, and her role in her community. The sorrow from losing her son in battle would have left a lasting mark on her remaining years.

At 72 years old in 1815, Ann Ellis would have witnessed a major historical event with significant implications for Europe. Here's how she might have reacted and how it would have affected her:

Emotional Reaction:

1. Relief and Hope:

- The defeat and exile of Napoleon would have likely been a source of relief for Ann, given the instability and turmoil caused by the Napoleonic Wars. She might have felt a sense of hope that Europe would now experience a period of peace and recovery.

2. Reflection on Family and Loss:

- Given the recent loss of her son Conway, Ann might have reflected on the broader impact of the wars on families and individuals. The end of the conflict could have been bittersweet, reminding her of the personal sacrifices and losses experienced during the war.

Effect on Her Life:

1. Social and Political Impact:

- Ann's life might have been influenced by the broader political and social changes that followed Napoleon's defeat. The restoration of monarchies and the redrawing of political boundaries could have had effects on her community and family dynamics. She might have engaged in discussions or reflected on these changes within her social circle.

2. Sense of Stability:

- With the end of the Napoleonic Wars, there might have been a return to more stable conditions. This stability could have positively affected Ann's daily life, reducing the uncertainties and disruptions that the wars had caused. It might have also influenced her sense of security and well-being in her later years.

3. Impact on Family:

- Ann might have seen this period as an opportunity to focus more on her family, especially in light of the recent loss. She could have been more involved in family matters or supportive of her remaining children and their families.

4. Personal Reflection:

- At her age, Ann would likely be reflecting on her life and the changes she has witnessed. The end of such a significant historical event would have provided a moment for her to consider her own legacy and the future of her family in a newly reshaped world.

Conclusion:

The defeat and exile of Napoleon at 72 would have been a significant historical milestone for Ann Ellis. Her reaction would have likely been one of relief and cautious optimism for the future. The event would have influenced her perspective on stability, her family life, and her reflections on the impact of the wars on her and her community.

At 74 years old in 1819, when the bicycle was invented, Ann Ellis might have had a range of reactions to this new innovation:

Reaction:

1. Curiosity and Intrigue:

- As a woman who had lived through significant historical changes, Ann would likely have been curious about this new mode of transportation. The idea of a machine that could move people efficiently might have intrigued her.

2. Skepticism:

- She might have been skeptical about the practical utility of the bicycle. Given the state of technology in her time, she might have wondered if it would become widely used or remain a novelty.

3. Interest in Innovation:

- Ann may have shown interest in how the bicycle worked and its potential applications. As someone who had witnessed various technological advancements, she might have been open to learning about new inventions.

Effect on Her:

1. Cultural and Social Impact:

- While the bicycle itself might not have had an immediate direct effect on Ann's daily life, the concept of such innovations would have contributed to her awareness of the rapidly changing world around her. She might have discussed it with family and friends or read about it in newspapers.

2. Influence on Family:

- If her children or grandchildren were intrigued by the bicycle, she might have observed their interest or involvement in this new technology. It could have sparked conversations or even influence on their activities and interests.

3. Personal Perspective:

- Ann's reaction to the bicycle could have been a reflection of her broader view on technological progress and its impact on society. It would have added to her understanding of how innovation continues to shape the world.

Conclusion:

At 74, Ann Ellis would likely have been interested and perhaps somewhat skeptical about the bicycle. While it might not have directly impacted her life, the invention would have been part of the broader context of technological progress she was experiencing.

At 76 years old in 1819, Ann Ellis would have been experiencing the closing years of a long and eventful life. Here's a picture of what her life might have been like at that time:

Personal Life:

1. Family:

- By 1819, Ann would likely have been surrounded by a large extended family, including her children, their spouses, and possibly several grandchildren. Her children would be established adults with their own families.

2. Health:

- At 76, Ann's health might have been declining. Common ailments of the elderly during that period included joint pain, mobility issues, and general frailty. The healthcare available at the time was limited, so managing health issues would have been challenging.

3. Home:

- Ann may have lived in a relatively comfortable home, possibly with the support of her family. If she resided in Carrickfergus or nearby, it would have been a place she was familiar with, surrounded by her community.

Socio-Political Context:

1. Political Climate:

- The early 19th century was a period of significant political and social change in Britain and Ireland. The Napoleonic Wars had recently ended, and the region was experiencing the effects of political and economic adjustments post-war.

2. Technological and Social Change:

- The world around Ann was evolving with innovations like the bicycle and early industrial advancements. While these changes might not have directly affected her daily life, they were shaping the society and economy around her.

Emotional and Social Life:

1. Reflection:

- At 76, Ann might have been reflecting on her long life, including her experiences, the growth of her family, and the changes in the world around her. It would have been a time of contemplation and sharing her wisdom with younger generations.

2. Community Involvement:

- She may have continued to be involved in her local community, attending social events, and participating in local affairs, depending on her health and mobility.

Conclusion:

In her final years, Ann Ellis would have been navigating the challenges of aging while reflecting on a lifetime of significant events. Surrounded by family and witnessing ongoing societal changes, she would have been part of a rapidly evolving world as she neared the end of her life.

CONWAY BENNING JR.

While there's no specific documentation about Conway Benning Jr.'s appearance, we can make some educated guesses about what he may have looked like based on the typical physical traits of his time and family background.

General Features:

- Hair Color: Given his family's Irish and Anglo roots, Conway may have had fair skin and light-colored hair, possibly brown, blonde, or even auburn, which were common among people of Irish descent.

- Eye Color: He could have had blue or green eyes, as these are also commonly associated with people of Irish and Anglo ancestry.

- Build: As a male growing up in the late 18th century, he would likely have had a lean and possibly tall build, especially considering that nutrition and physical activity were different during that era, particularly in the military lifestyle that he would later adopt.

- Complexion: His complexion would likely have been fair, which was typical of people in Ireland and Britain during that time.

Clothing and Grooming:

As he was born into a respected family and later served in the Royal Artillery, his appearance would have reflected the standards of the time, with a formal and well-groomed look:

- Hairstyle: Young boys during this period often had their hair tied back in a queue (a ponytail-like style), as it was common for men to wear wigs or powdered their natural hair in formal settings. By the time he was older, short hairstyles had become more fashionable, so he may have adopted this style.

- Clothing: As a child, Conway would have worn traditional boys' clothing of the era, such as frock coats, waistcoats, breeches, and stockings. These were typically made from wool, linen, or cotton, depending on the occasion and season.

While his exact appearance cannot be known, Conway Benning Jr. likely embodied the features and fashion of a well-to-do Irish family during the late 18th century.

In 1771, the world was on the cusp of significant change, with important social, political, and technological developments beginning to take shape. Here's an overview of what life was like during that time:

Political Climate:

1. American Colonies:

- Tensions between the American colonies and Britain were simmering, as colonial dissatisfaction with British taxation and governance increased. The Boston Massacre had occurred the year before (1770), highlighting the growing unrest that would eventually lead to the American Revolution in 1775.

2. Europe:

- In Europe, monarchies were still dominant, but enlightenment ideas about democracy, individual rights, and freedom were spreading, influencing intellectual and political movements. The major powers—Britain, France, and Spain—were all engaged in maintaining their empires, including competing for influence in the Americas and elsewhere.

3. Ireland:

- Ireland was under British control, with the Irish Protestant Ascendancy holding significant power. The Catholic majority in Ireland faced many restrictions, but there were growing demands for reforms. The Penal Laws, which discriminated against Catholics and dissenters, were still in effect.

Social Life:

1. Family and Society:

- In 1771, society was largely hierarchical, with strict divisions between the nobility, middle classes, and lower classes. Wealth and social status determined much of a person's life, including marriage prospects, education, and career opportunities.

2. Daily Life:

- Most people lived in rural areas, working on farms or in small trades. Life was centered around agriculture, with towns and villages being hubs of trade and social activity. For the wealthy and aristocracy, life revolved around landownership, social events, and politics.

3. Religion:

- Religion played a central role in daily life, especially in Ireland. The Anglican Church was the established church, but the majority of the population was Catholic, leading to tensions. Church attendance and religious observance were expected, and religious festivals marked the yearly calendar.

Technological and Scientific Advancements:

1. Industrial Revolution:

- The early stirrings of the Industrial Revolution were beginning to take place in Britain. New inventions in textiles, mining, and steam power were laying the groundwork for the massive societal and economic shifts that would soon follow.

However, in 1771, the majority of production was still done by hand or with the help of simple machinery.

2. Scientific Exploration:

- The Age of Enlightenment was in full swing. Scientists and thinkers like Benjamin Franklin and Isaac Newton had already revolutionized the understanding of natural phenomena. Franklin's experiments with electricity had been conducted a few years earlier, leading to growing interest in science and innovation.

Notable Events in 1771:

- First Edition of the Encyclopædia Britannica: Published in 1771, this reflected the growing thirst for knowledge and rationality that characterized the Enlightenment era.

- James Cook's Voyages: The famous British explorer James Cook was on his first voyage of exploration (1768–1771), which mapped New Zealand and the east coast of Australia. His discoveries were expanding European knowledge of the world.

Fashion and Culture:

1. Clothing:

- Fashion in 1771 was elaborate, especially for the wealthy. Men wore powdered wigs, breeches, waistcoats, and tailcoats, while women's fashion featured wide skirts supported by panniers, corsets, and detailed fabrics. Silk, lace, and embroidery were popular among the upper classes.

2. Arts:

- The arts flourished in the 18th century, with classical music by composers like Mozart and Haydn gaining popularity. Literature, theater, and painting were also thriving, with works reflecting both the grandeur of the age and the growing interest in personal experience and emotion.

Economy:

1. Agriculture:

- Agriculture dominated the economy. Most people worked on farms, growing staple crops like wheat, barley, and oats, as well as raising livestock. In Ireland, tenant farming was common, with many farmers renting land from wealthy landlords.

2. Trade and Industry:

- The early stages of industrialization were underway, but it was still a largely agricultural economy. Trade routes with the Americas and other colonies were well-established, leading to the import of luxury goods like sugar, tea, and tobacco.

Conclusion:

In 1771, when Conway Benning Jr was born, the world was on the verge of revolutionary changes. Ireland was still under British rule, and society was rigidly structured. Yet, Enlightenment ideals were spreading, and early industrialization was beginning to transform economies and ways of life. As Conway grew up, he would witness some of the most significant events of the 18th century, including the American Revolution, the Irish Rebellion, and the Industrial Revolution.

When Conway Benning Jr. was 2 years old and his brother James was born, he would have experienced several changes typical of a young child with a new sibling:

1. Shift in Attention:

- Less Parental Attention: At two years old, Conway Jr. was still in a phase of early childhood where he relied heavily on his parents for attention and care. With the arrival of a new baby, he may have felt a shift in the focus of his parents, particularly his mother, who would need to care for the newborn. This could have led to feelings of jealousy or confusion as he adjusted to the new family dynamic.

- Growing Independence: At the same time, this shift might have encouraged Conway Jr. to become more independent. With his parents occupied with James, he may have had more opportunities to explore and develop his own abilities, possibly leading to early growth in self-reliance.

2. Role as an Older Sibling:

- Introduction to Responsibility: Even at a young age, Conway Jr. may have been introduced to the idea of being an older sibling, though it would be a simple and basic understanding of it. He might have been encouraged to "help" with small tasks, like bringing toys for James or watching over him, fostering a sense of responsibility early on.

- Bonding with His Brother: Although still very young, Conway Jr. would likely have developed a sibling bond with James over time. As they grew, the closeness in age would have allowed them to be playmates and companions, possibly sharing similar experiences and interests in their early years.

3. Emotional Development:

- Mixed Emotions: Conway Jr. may have experienced a mix of emotions with the arrival of his brother. Feelings of excitement, curiosity, and possibly confusion could have surfaced. It's not uncommon for toddlers to show both affection and frustration toward a new sibling, and Conway Jr. may have felt a combination of these emotions.

- Increased Social Interaction: Having a sibling close in age would have contributed to Conway Jr.'s social and emotional development. Growing up with James, Conway Jr. would have learned important social skills such as sharing, empathy, and cooperation.

4. Family Dynamics:

- Strengthening Family Bonds: The birth of James would have likely brought changes to the family dynamic. For Conway Jr., the expanding family would have meant adapting to new routines and sharing the attention and affection of his parents. However, this also would have reinforced a sense of family and connection as he grew older.

- Stability of the Household: Given the likely stable and educated household environment of the Benning family, the arrival of a new child was likely celebrated and managed with care. Conway Jr. would have grown up in a setting where education, faith, and family unity were central, which would have helped him navigate these early changes with support.

Conclusion:

At 2 years old, the arrival of a new sibling, James, would have introduced Conway Jr. to the dynamics of sharing attention and forming bonds with a younger brother. Though he was likely too young to fully grasp the responsibilities of being an older sibling, the experience would have had a lasting impact on his early emotional and social development. The presence of James would have shaped his early childhood experiences, helping him to grow in a household that valued family and structure.

When Conway Benning Jr. was 4 years old and his sister Eleanor was born, it likely had a notable effect on him, as the birth of a sibling often impacts a young child's life. Here's how he might have been affected:

1. Family Dynamics:

- Shifting Attention: As the oldest child, Conway would have been the center of his parents' attention before Eleanor's birth. With the arrival of a new sibling, he may have experienced a shift in focus as his parents devoted more time to caring for the newborn. This change could have led to feelings of jealousy or confusion, as he adjusted to sharing his parents' attention.

- New Role as the Older Brother: Conway may have been encouraged to take on a protective or guiding role as the elder sibling. Even at a young age, families often encourage older children to help with younger ones, fostering a sense of responsibility.

2. Emotional Development:

- Sibling Bonding: Depending on the family's structure and dynamics, Conway could have developed a close bond with Eleanor, forming a lifelong connection. It was common for siblings to be companions in everyday activities, especially in larger households, where children often relied on one another for play and support.

- Empathy and Social Skills: The presence of a sibling likely contributed to Conway's emotional growth. Having a younger sister could have helped him develop empathy and patience, as he learned to navigate the challenges of interacting with a baby.

3. Daily Life Changes:

- Routine Adjustments: The household routine likely changed with the addition of a new baby, affecting meals, sleeping arrangements, and general activity within the home. Conway would have had to adjust to these changes, which could have helped him become more adaptable.

- Cultural and Societal Expectations: At the time, the birth of a new child was a celebrated event, especially in families with social standing. Conway might have been aware of the excitement surrounding his sister's birth, which could have influenced his own perception of family and societal roles.

4. His Parents' Influence:

- Influence from Parents: His parents, Conway Sr. and Ann Ellis, would likely have instilled in Conway Jr. a sense of duty toward his younger siblings. Given the family's standing, they may have emphasized the importance of looking after Eleanor, which would have shaped his sense of responsibility early on.

Overall, the birth of Eleanor likely had a profound impact on Conway Jr.'s early years, shaping his personality, sense of responsibility, and his role within the family. He may have felt a mixture of emotions—ranging from excitement at having a new sibling to adjusting to the changes this brought to his daily life.

At 5 years old, Conway Benning Jr. would have been relatively unaware of the full significance of his father, Conway Benning Sr., receiving an LL.D. (Doctor of Laws). However, the event would likely have had some indirect effects on him, primarily due to how it impacted the family's social standing, his father's responsibilities, and their overall lifestyle. Here's how it might have affected him:

1. Elevated Social Status:

- Family Reputation: The achievement of an LL.D. was a prestigious accomplishment, elevating Conway Sr.'s status in both academic and social circles. This could have affected the family's standing within their community, making Conway Jr. more aware of social expectations and perhaps treated with a higher regard due to his father's intellectual achievements.

- Greater Opportunities: A higher social status often led to better opportunities for education and networking for children, meaning Conway Jr. might have received more attention from tutors or been prepared for a similar path of intellectual or military service.

2. Role Model Effect:

- Admiration for His Father: Even at a young age, Conway Jr. may have sensed that his father had accomplished something important. Children often look up to their parents, and this achievement might have planted early seeds of admiration, especially as he grew older and understood the importance of education and social distinction.

- Expectations: As the son of an educated and respected man, there may have been unspoken expectations placed on Conway Jr. to follow in his father's footsteps. While he was still young, these expectations could have influenced how he was raised, with a greater emphasis on his own education or future career.

3. Household Changes:

- Increased Responsibilities for His Father: Receiving an LL.D. could have opened up new professional or societal obligations for Conway Sr., potentially increasing his workload or requiring him to travel more. This might have meant that Conway Jr. saw less of his father, leading to a shift in the family's dynamics.

- Impact on Parenting: With his father taking on more academic or clerical responsibilities, Conway Jr. might have spent more time under the care of his mother, Ann Ellis, or other family members, which could have shaped his early upbringing and attachment patterns.

4. Exposure to Education and Intellect:

- Intellectual Environment: Growing up in a household where his father had achieved a high level of education, Conway Jr. would have been exposed to intellectual discussions and perhaps encouraged to think critically from an early age. This would have shaped his worldview and intellectual development over time.

5. Long-Term Effects:
- Inspiration for Career: While he may not have fully understood the significance at age 5, as Conway Jr. grew older, his father's accomplishment might have inspired him to pursue his own prestigious career, particularly in the military, as he later became an officer in the Royal Artillery.

In summary, although Conway Jr. might not have grasped the full impact of his father's LL.D. at such a young age, the accomplishment likely influenced the family's social standing and household dynamics, and may have subtly shaped the expectations and opportunities for his own future.

When Conway Benning Jr. was 6 years old and his father traveled the continent, it likely had a significant effect on him in several ways:

Emotional Impact:
- Separation from His Father: At 6 years old, Conway would have been old enough to notice and feel the absence of his father. Given the close family structure of the time, his father's extended absence might have been confusing or unsettling. Children at that age often look to their parents for stability, and Conway may have missed the daily presence and guidance of his father.
- Responsibility Shift: With his father away, his mother, Ann Ellis Benning, would have likely taken on additional responsibilities in managing the household. Conway may have had to mature more quickly, especially if he had younger siblings, and may have been asked to help out more around the home.

Curiosity and Imagination:
- Exposure to New Ideas: Conway might have been fascinated by the stories his father told upon his return from the continent. In the 18th century, travel to the continent (likely to places like France, Italy, or Germany) was seen as a grand adventure, exposing people to different cultures, ideas, and knowledge. His father would have likely brought back news of scientific, political, and social developments, sparking Conway's curiosity.

- Anticipation: Children often have a sense of excitement and wonder when a parent travels to faraway places. Conway may have been eager to hear about his father's travels, the people he met, and the things he saw. This could have inspired a sense of adventure in Conway and planted the seeds of curiosity about the world beyond Ireland.

Family Dynamics:

- Bond with His Mother: During his father's absence, Conway's bond with his mother may have strengthened as she became the primary figure in his day-to-day life. The absence of his father could have made Conway more reliant on his mother, fostering a closer relationship.

- Role Model: The experience of watching his father travel might have shaped Conway's understanding of duty and responsibility. His father's trips were likely for professional or intellectual reasons, and Conway may have admired this, feeling proud of his father's accomplishments and learning from his example.

Possible Challenges:

- Instability: Long trips could sometimes create feelings of instability for children, especially when communication was slow and infrequent. Conway might have experienced worry or uncertainty during the long stretches when his father was away, though he would likely have been reassured by his mother and other family members.

Overall, Conway likely experienced a mix of emotions, including pride in his father's travels, curiosity about the wider world, and possibly some feelings of separation or uncertainty during his father's absence.

When Conway Benning Jr. was 6 years old and his sister Millicent Mary was born in 1777, it likely affected him in several ways:

Emotional Impact:

- Excitement of a New Sibling: At 6 years old, Conway may have been excited to welcome a new sibling into the family. Children often have a sense of curiosity and wonder when a baby is born, and Conway might have been eager to meet his new sister, Millicent.
- Feeling Important: Being the oldest sibling, Conway may have felt a sense of responsibility or pride in being the "big brother." His parents may have involved him in simple tasks to help with the baby, which could have made him feel valued and important in the family.

Adjustment to Attention Shift:

- Adjustment to Less Attention: The arrival of a new baby often shifts the focus of the household. Conway may have had to adjust to sharing his parents' attention with Millicent. While this might have made him feel a bit overlooked at times, it's also possible that he was used to this dynamic, as he already had younger siblings, like James.

Developing Family Role:

- Learning Responsibility: With a newborn in the house, Conway may have been asked to take on more responsibility, such as helping care for his younger brother James, or even assisting his mother around the house. This would have encouraged him to become more independent and responsible at a young age.

New Dynamics:

- Strengthened Family Bond: The birth of a new sibling often brings families closer together. Conway may have felt a stronger connection to his family as they celebrated the arrival of Millicent. He may have developed a protective instinct toward her as the older brother, watching out for her as she grew.

Routine Changes:

- Household Changes: The arrival of a new baby often changes the household routine. Conway may have noticed his parents, especially his mother, being more preoccupied with the needs of the baby, which could have affected the usual daily flow in the household.

Overall, Conway's experience when Millicent was born likely involved a mix of excitement, pride in his role as the older sibling, and adjusting to the new family dynamics with the arrival of his baby sister.

It is possible that Conway Benning Jr. and his future brother-in-law, Dr. Samuel Allen, could have known each other, given the geographical proximity and the social circles they likely moved in due to their families' status. Both were born in County Antrim, and Conway's father, Conway Benning Sr., was a rector, a respected position in the Church of Ireland, while Samuel Allen's father was an Esquire, which denotes a person of higher social standing.

Factors Influencing Whether They Knew Each Other:

- Social Circles: Being the son of an Esquire, Samuel Allen would have belonged to a prominent family. Conway, as the son of a rector, also had a respected position in society. It is possible that their families would have attended the same social events, church services, or gatherings of the local elite, which would have increased the likelihood of the two knowing each other from a young age.

- Geographical Proximity: Both Conway and Samuel were born in the same county, County Antrim, with Conway being born in Carrickfergus and Samuel in Larne. Though these towns are about 12 miles apart, in that era, people in neighboring towns often knew each other, especially within higher social classes.

- Family Connections: Over time, as Conway's sister Millicent eventually married Samuel Allen, it is likely that the two families would have known each other well before the marriage. This could mean that Conway and Samuel would have had opportunities to meet at family gatherings or social events as they grew older.

Impact of Samuel's Birth on Conway:

- At the Age of 7: It's unlikely that Samuel's birth would have had a direct or noticeable impact on Conway when he was 7 years old. At that age, Conway would have been focused on his own life, schooling, and family dynamics, with little awareness of a newborn in a nearby town.

- Awareness of Social Standing: However, over time, as both boys grew older, Conway may have become aware of Samuel's family's position and status, potentially interacting with Samuel at social or religious events. They may have even attended similar functions or educational institutions for young boys of their class, which would have built a connection.

- Later Life Connection: By the time Samuel Allen became a doctor and married Conway's sister Millicent, it's likely that their relationship would have deepened. Their shared social background would have fostered mutual respect, and the marriage would have tied their families together formally.

While Samuel's birth may not have affected Conway much directly when he was 7 years old, their shared social status and eventual family ties would have fostered a connection later in life, possibly starting in their early years within the same social circles of County Antrim.

When Conway Benning Jr. was 7 years old, his father, Conway Benning Sr., was instituted to the vicarage of Rathmolyon in the diocese of Meath, while the family primarily lived at Kilroot. This would have likely had a number of effects on young Conway Jr., shaping his upbringing and development in various ways:

Effect on Conway Jr.'s Childhood:

1. Increased Stability and Responsibility:

- As his father took on the vicarage, Conway Jr. would have been introduced to a more structured and stable lifestyle, with his family's status tied to his father's religious duties. This would have brought with it a sense of responsibility and expectation, as children of clergy were often seen as reflections of their parents' values and beliefs.

- He may have been expected to behave in a certain way, given his father's position of moral and spiritual authority in the community, instilling in him discipline and a sense of duty from a young age.

2. Religious Influence:

- Growing up in the household of a vicar, Conway Jr. would have been heavily influenced by religious teachings, church customs, and the importance of faith. He may have attended church services regularly and would have been surrounded by the moral teachings his father emphasized in his role.

- His father's role in the church could have shaped Conway's worldview, making religion a significant part of his identity and values, and potentially influencing his respect for authority and tradition.

3. Sense of Community:

- Living at Kilroot, while his father held the vicarage at Rathmolyon, Conway would have likely felt a connection to both communities. He would have interacted with people from both areas, seeing firsthand how his father's work impacted different congregations. This would have given him a broader understanding of community and leadership from a young age.

- The family's prominence within these communities could have fostered pride in his father's role, but it could also bring expectations on him to maintain a certain reputation, affecting how he interacted with peers.

4. Education:

- Given his father's clerical position, Conway Jr. would have likely had access to a solid education. Children of clergy often received a formal education, and his father's intellectual pursuits, such as earning an LL.D., would have influenced his own academic environment.

- His education may have been more rigorous due to the family's focus on faith and scholarly matters, preparing him for potential roles in the church, military, or other respected professions in the future.

5. Potential Feelings of Isolation or Expectation:

- With his father focused on his duties as a vicar, Conway Jr. might have experienced periods of isolation or absence, especially if his father spent significant time at the vicarage in Rathmolyon while the family lived at Kilroot. This could have led to feelings of being distanced from his father or placed extra pressure on him to meet certain expectations while his father was away.

- Alternatively, his father's influence and presence as a clergyman could have strengthened Conway's sense of purpose and identity, knowing that his family had an important role to play in the religious and social fabric of their communities.

6. Social Status and Networking:

- His father's clerical position would have placed the family in the middle-to-upper echelons of society. Conway Jr. would likely have mixed with other prominent families, giving him an awareness of social hierarchies and connections that would serve him in adulthood, particularly as he entered the military.

- Growing up in such a household may have led to early friendships with other children of clergy or professionals, creating a network that would prove useful in his adult life, especially in later military service.

In Summary:

At 7 years old, Conway Jr. would have been at a formative age when his father took on the vicarage. This event would have reinforced religious, social, and moral structures in his life, instilled a sense of duty, and exposed him to the responsibilities and expectations that came with being the son of a vicar. These influences would shape his character, education, and social interactions, likely preparing him for the life of discipline and service he would experience as he grew older.

When Conway Benning Jr. was 8 years old and his sister Jane was born, this significant family event would have had several potential effects on him:

Impact on Conway Jr.:

1. Increased Family Responsibilities:

- At the age of 8, Conway Jr. would be old enough to understand and possibly take on small responsibilities associated with the arrival of a new sibling. This might include helping his parents with the baby, which could have fostered a sense of responsibility and maturity.

2. Shift in Family Dynamics:

- The birth of Jane would have shifted family dynamics, with Conway Jr. potentially feeling a change in the amount of attention he received from his parents. The arrival of a new sibling often means that older children may have to adapt to new routines and share their parents' attention.

3. Role in the Family:

- As the older brother, Conway Jr. might have felt a new role as a protector and mentor to his younger sister. This could have influenced his sense of duty and family loyalty, shaping his interactions with her as she grew up.

4. Emotional Response:

- Conway Jr.'s reaction to his new sister would largely depend on his personality and the family environment. He may have felt excitement, curiosity, or even a bit of jealousy as he adjusted to the changes in the family structure.

5. Social and Emotional Development:

- The presence of a new sibling can have a positive effect on a child's social and emotional development. Conway Jr. would have had the opportunity to develop empathy, patience, and caretaking skills by interacting with and helping to care for his baby sister.

6. Impact on Family Life:

- The addition of Jane would have brought more focus on the immediate family's daily life and routines. Conway Jr. would have observed and participated in the changes that come with a new baby, contributing to his understanding of family life and dynamics.

7. Potential for Stronger Family Bonds:

- Growing up with a younger sister might have strengthened Conway Jr.'s bonds with his family, creating lasting relationships. The shared experiences and responsibilities related to raising Jane could have fostered a close-knit family environment.

In summary, the birth of his sister Jane when Conway Jr. was 8 years old would have introduced him to new family dynamics and responsibilities. While he might have experienced some adjustment in terms of attention and family roles, this event would also have contributed to his growth in empathy, responsibility, and familial bonds.

At 13 years old, Conway Benning Jr. would have been at an age where he was developing his understanding of the world and keenly observing technological advancements. The successful flight of the first hot air balloon in 1783 would likely have had a notable impact on him in several ways:

Reaction to the Hot Air Balloon:

1. Awe and Curiosity:

- Conway Jr. would likely have been fascinated by the idea of human flight. The hot air balloon, being a groundbreaking invention of its time, would have sparked his imagination and curiosity about technology and science.

2. Interest in Innovation:

- The hot air balloon's success might have inspired Conway Jr. to take an interest in scientific and technological advancements. As a teenager, he may have been motivated to learn more about aeronautics and other innovations of the period.

3. Social and Cultural Impact:

- Witnessing such a revolutionary event could have made Conway Jr. more aware of the broader changes occurring in society and technology. It might have influenced his views on progress and the role of scientific exploration in shaping the future.

Effect on His Life:

1. Educational and Career Aspirations:

- The balloon's success could have inspired Conway Jr. to pursue studies or a career in fields related to science and engineering. It might have encouraged him to seek out education or experiences that aligned with these interests.

2. Impression of Technological Progress:

- Experiencing the excitement of such an innovation would have reinforced the notion that the world was undergoing rapid technological change. This awareness might have shaped his perspective on the importance of adapting to and embracing new technologies.

3. Influence on Personal Interests:

- The event could have influenced Conway Jr.'s hobbies and interests. He might have become more inclined to experiment with mechanical or scientific projects, reflecting his fascination with the balloon and its implications.

4. Impact on Worldview:

- Seeing a hot air balloon successfully fly might have broadened Conway Jr.'s worldview, leading him to appreciate the possibilities of human ingenuity and the potential for future discoveries.

In summary, at the age of 13, Conway Benning Jr. would have likely been both amazed and inspired by the successful flight of the first hot air balloon. This event could have significantly influenced his interests and aspirations, reinforcing the excitement of technological progress and potentially shaping his future educational and career choices.

When Conway Benning Jr. entered the Royal Artillery on June 25, 1795, at the age of 24, it would have been a significant and life-changing event. Here's how he might have reacted and how it could have affected him:

Excitement and Pride:

- Sense of Duty and Honor: Joining the Royal Artillery in 1795, during the Napoleonic Wars, would have been seen as an honorable and prestigious path, particularly for someone of Conway's background. He likely felt a deep sense of duty and pride in serving his country, especially in a technical and highly regarded branch of the military like the artillery.

- Professional Ambition: At 24, he was still relatively young, and entering the military would have offered him the opportunity for personal growth, professional advancement, and social distinction. The artillery was known for requiring skilled and disciplined officers, and Conway might have seen this as a chance to prove his capabilities and rise through the ranks.

Challenges and Adaptation:

- Rigorous Training: Joining the Royal Artillery meant undergoing rigorous training, both physically and mentally. He would have had to master the complex mathematics and physics involved in artillery work, which required precision and discipline.

The intellectual challenge might have been demanding, but also stimulating, for a man with his background.

- Military Lifestyle: Transitioning into the structured and disciplined life of the military would have required adjustment. The life of a soldier was regimented, and he would have had to adapt to a more rigorous daily routine, possibly moving away from the relative comfort of his family's home and civilian life.

Emotional Impact:

- Separation from Family: Entering military service would likely have taken Conway away from his family, including his mother, Ann, and siblings. This could have been emotionally challenging, as he would have been aware of the dangers involved, especially with the Napoleonic Wars ongoing. His family may have worried about his safety, and he might have felt the weight of responsibility to protect and make them proud.

Camaraderie and Military Bonds:

- Building Relationships: The military environment fostered strong camaraderie among soldiers. Conway would have begun to form close bonds with fellow officers and artillerymen, which could have been a source of support and friendship throughout his service.

Long-Term Impact:

- Sense of Identity: Joining the Royal Artillery would have become a defining part of his identity. His career in the military likely shaped much of his later life, including his values, skills, and social standing. Being in the artillery placed him in a highly technical and respected position within the army, which would have elevated his standing within both military and civilian circles.

- Future Prospects: Service in the Royal Artillery could have opened doors for future advancements in both the military and civil sectors, offering him a secure and prestigious career path.

Overall, Conway would have likely felt a mix of excitement, pride, and the pressure of entering such a respected military force at a time of great international conflict. His entry into the Royal Artillery would have significantly shaped his personal and professional life, reinforcing a sense of duty and responsibility while also requiring resilience and adaptability.

As a lieutenant in the Royal Artillery during the Irish Rebellion of 1798, Conway Benning Jr.'s experiences would have been marked by the unique responsibilities and pressures of his rank. Here's how his role and status as a lieutenant might have shaped his reaction and the effects of the rebellion on him:

Military Duties and Leadership:

- Command Responsibilities: As a lieutenant, Conway would have been in a position of leadership, commanding a small unit or battery of artillery. During the rebellion, his primary duty would have been to organize and manage his men, ensuring that they were prepared for action, maintained discipline, and executed their artillery operations effectively.

- Tactical Role: His responsibilities would have included overseeing the positioning and firing of artillery, which was crucial in battles. Artillery played a key role in controlling the battlefield, and as an officer, Conway would have been involved in strategic decisions about where to place cannons, how to support infantry, and how to counter enemy positions.

- Direct Combat Involvement: Although artillery officers were not typically on the front lines, Conway would have been close to the action, directing fire and making quick decisions in the heat of battle. The violence and intensity of the rebellion, especially during the Battle of Antrim, would have exposed him to the harsh realities of war, likely leaving a lasting emotional and psychological impact.

Personal Reaction to the Rebellion:

- Loyalty and Duty: As a career officer, Conway's loyalty to the Crown and his duty to the British Army would have been his primary focus. He would have seen the rebellion as a threat to the stability of Ireland and the authority of the British government. His military training and sense of duty would have compelled him to view his role in suppressing the rebellion as necessary, even if the conflict involved Irish civilians.

- Conflicted Feelings: Given his Irish heritage and background in Carrickfergus, Conway might have experienced internal conflict. While committed to his duties, he might have felt sympathy for the Irish rebels' grievances, particularly if he had connections to the local population. However, as a lieutenant, his focus would have been on carrying out orders and maintaining military discipline, possibly suppressing any personal feelings of ambivalence.

Impact on Career:

- Potential for Advancement: The rebellion may have offered Conway opportunities for professional advancement. Officers who performed well in suppressing the uprising could have been recognized with promotions or commendations. His involvement in such a significant conflict would have been a defining moment in his military career.

- Greater Responsibility: The rebellion likely demanded more from Conway as a lieutenant, testing his leadership, decision-making, and ability to manage the stresses of combat. Successful performance during this period could have solidified his reputation as a capable officer.

Effect on Personal Life:

- Strain on Family and Relationships: The rebellion likely placed a strain on Conway's family life. The instability in Ireland during the uprising could have caused anxiety for his family, particularly if they were living in or near areas of conflict.

Additionally, the demands of his military service would have taken him away from home for extended periods, creating stress in his personal relationships.

- Sense of Duty vs. Personal Risk: Conway would have been aware of the personal risks involved in his military service during the rebellion. As an artillery officer, he would have been involved in dangerous operations, and the possibility of injury or death would have been a constant reality. This may have affected his outlook on life, increasing his sense of responsibility to his family and duty to his country.

Long-Term Impact:

- Shaped Views on Rebellion: Having lived through the Irish Rebellion as a military officer, Conway's views on Irish nationalism and political unrest would have been shaped by his experiences. He may have developed a more hardened stance toward rebellion, viewing it through the lens of military suppression and loyalty to the British Crown.

- Emotional Aftermath: The rebellion likely left Conway with emotional scars. The violence and unrest, coupled with the stress of leadership during a period of conflict, could have taken a toll on his mental health. Officers often carried the weight of responsibility for the lives of their men, and the trauma of the rebellion might have stayed with him long after the fighting ended.

In summary, Conway Benning Jr.'s role as a lieutenant in the Royal Artillery during the Irish Rebellion would have been one of leadership, duty, and personal conflict. The rebellion would have tested his abilities as an officer while also challenging his personal beliefs, leaving a lasting impact on both his career and emotional well-being.

Conway Benning Jr., being a 27-year-old lieutenant in the Royal Artillery, would have likely worn formal attire appropriate to his military status and the occasion when attending his sister

Millicent's wedding to Dr. Samuel Allen in 1798. Here's an idea of what he might have worn:

Military Uniform:

As a military officer, it would have been customary for him to wear his dress uniform to such an important event. His Royal Artillery uniform would have reflected his rank and standing:

1. Coat: He would have worn a dark blue (navy) coat, which was the standard for artillery officers at the time, with red facings (cuffs and collar) that were typical of British Army uniforms.

2. Gold or Silver Epaulettes: Epaulettes on his shoulders would have indicated his rank as a lieutenant. They would have been decorated in gold or silver thread depending on the specific regulations of the Royal Artillery.

3. White Breeches: White or cream-colored breeches were often worn as part of the formal military dress, paired with knee-high black leather boots.

4. Waistcoat: Underneath his coat, he would likely have worn a white or buff waistcoat, which was typical for formal military attire at the time.

5. Cravat or Stock: A white cravat or neck stock, tied neatly around his neck, would have added to the formality of his outfit.

6. Sword: As an officer, he would have carried a ceremonial sword, likely a small sword or sabre, which was an important part of his uniform, symbolizing his status and readiness for duty even at formal events.

7. Decorations and Insignia: If he had received any decorations or military honors by that time, he would have worn them on his coat to signify his achievements.

Civillian Attire (Possible Alternative):

If for any reason he opted for civilian clothing instead of his military uniform, his attire would have reflected the fashions of the late 18th century for a man of his status:

1. Tailcoat: A well-tailored tailcoat in dark colors (such as navy, black, or dark green) would have been appropriate. The coat would have had wide lapels and a fitted waist, following the style of the late 1790s.

2. Breeches and Stockings: Knee-length breeches, worn with silk stockings, were still common for formal occasions, though full-length trousers were becoming more popular.

3. Linen Shirt and Cravat: A crisp white linen shirt with a high collar, paired with a cravat or neckcloth, would have been worn underneath his coat.

4. Waistcoat: A silk or brocade waistcoat, possibly in a lighter color such as ivory or gold, would have added a touch of elegance to the outfit.

5. Shoes: Black leather shoes with buckles would have completed his look.

In either case, Conway's outfit would have reflected both his status as a military officer and his family's standing in society, showing respect for his sister's wedding while maintaining the formal standards of the time.

At the age of 29, Conway Benning Jr. would likely have been intrigued by William Young's innovative shoe designs, though the level of impact it had on him would depend on his lifestyle and interests at the time. Here's a more detailed look at how he might have reacted:

Reaction:

1. Curiosity and Practicality: As a lieutenant in the Royal Artillery, Conway was likely accustomed to military boots designed for function and durability rather than comfort or fashion. Young's designs, which focused on improving the fit, comfort, and practicality of shoes, would likely have sparked curiosity, especially if they were widely discussed or marketed as

innovative. He may have seen them as a practical improvement, especially if they were adapted for military use or civilian life.

2. Interest in Fashion: Given the importance of appearance and presentation for officers of the time, Conway may also have been interested in how these new shoes might enhance his formal or civilian attire. If Young's shoes were seen as fashionable, Conway could have considered them for special occasions, such as social gatherings or family events.

Effect:

1. Enhanced Comfort: If Conway ever adopted Young's shoes, he likely would have appreciated the increased comfort they provided, particularly when transitioning from his military duties to civilian life. For an officer who spent time in both formal settings and on the move, more comfortable and well-fitting shoes would have been a welcome improvement.

2. Social Influence: Depending on his level of exposure to social circles where fashion innovations were discussed, wearing Young's shoes might have signaled that Conway was up-to-date with the latest trends. Shoes designed by Young could have become a status symbol among the upper class or military officers, affecting his perception among peers.

3. Influence on Military Gear: While Young's shoes were primarily civilian-focused, there may have been some discussion among military personnel about whether these innovations could be adapted for military use. If so, Conway might have been part of conversations about improving soldier footwear, which would have directly influenced his military experience.

Overall, Conway's reaction to William Young's shoe designs would have been a mixture of curiosity, appreciation for innovation, and possible adoption of more comfortable footwear for both civilian and military life. The designs would not have drastically altered his life, but they could have had a subtle influence on his daily comfort and social interactions.

When Conway Benning Jr. attended his sister Jane's wedding in September 1800, as a military officer and a member of a respectable family, his attire would likely have reflected his social standing and the fashion of the late Georgian era. Here's what he likely would have worn:

Military Uniform (If in Attendance in an Official Capacity):

1. Royal Artillery Uniform: As a lieutenant in the Royal Artillery, if he chose to wear his military uniform, Conway would have likely been dressed in his formal officer's attire. This would have included:
   - Dark blue coat with red facings (collar and cuffs) typical of the Royal Artillery.
   - Brass buttons and white crossbelts to hold his sword and other military accessories.
   - White breeches and high black leather boots.
   - A bicorn hat with a cockade and possibly a plume or feather, which was standard for officers in formal settings.

Civilian Attire (If Not in Uniform):

1. Tailcoat: Conway would have worn a well-tailored coat, likely in dark colors such as navy blue, black, or deep green, with high lapels and a fitted waist. Tailcoats were popular at the time, and for a formal occasion like a wedding, it would have been made from fine wool or silk.

2. Waistcoat: Beneath the tailcoat, he would have worn a waistcoat in a contrasting color or pattern. Light-colored silk waistcoats with intricate embroidery or brocade designs were fashionable for formal occasions.

3. Shirt and Cravat: A white linen shirt with a high, stiff collar would have been standard, accompanied by a cravat or stock, which was a large piece of fabric tied neatly around the neck. The cravat

would likely have been white or cream, and carefully tied in a fashionable manner.

4. Breeches or Pantaloons: Conway would have worn knee-length breeches, likely made of silk or fine wool, and paired with white stockings and buckled shoes. Alternatively, as fashion shifted, he might have worn the longer, slim-fitting pantaloons that were becoming more popular by 1800.

5. Shoes: If he wore civilian shoes, they would have been black leather, likely with silver or brass buckles. Highly polished and elegant shoes were a must for formal events.

6. Accessories:

- Gloves: White or light-colored gloves, possibly made of kid leather, would have been appropriate for a formal event like a wedding.

- Watch and Fob: A pocket watch with a decorative fob (chain) would have been a common accessory for men of his standing, tucked into his waistcoat.

- Top Hat: For formal occasions, a black silk top hat would have completed the ensemble, though he might have removed it during the ceremony.

Conway's attire for his sister Jane's wedding would have been refined, reflecting both his military status and the fashion of the early 19th century, blending formality and elegance.

When Conway Benning Jr. was stationed at Dundalk on January 1, 1800, at the age of 30, it would have been a significant time in his military career and personal life. Here's how he might have reacted and been affected by this stationing:

Reaction and Experience:

1. Professional Duty: As a lieutenant in the Royal Artillery, Conway likely approached his new posting with a sense of duty and commitment. Dundalk, located in County Louth, Ireland, was a strategic location, especially considering the turbulent political

climate of Ireland following the Irish Rebellion of 1798. He would have been focused on his military responsibilities, likely overseeing artillery operations, training soldiers, and managing the logistical aspects of his unit.

2. Tensions in Ireland: Given the lingering effects of the Irish Rebellion and the ongoing unrest, Conway's role in Dundalk would have been both challenging and potentially dangerous. The stationing would have involved maintaining order and readiness for any potential uprisings or conflicts. As an officer, he would have needed to navigate the complex political and social landscape of the time, balancing military duties with the local tensions.

3. Personal Sacrifices: Being stationed away from his family in Dundalk might have brought personal challenges. With his family living primarily in Kilroot and his siblings, such as Millicent and Jane, getting married around this time, Conway may have felt a sense of distance from his loved ones. His military obligations would have required him to be away from family events and milestones, which could have led to feelings of isolation or homesickness.

4. Professional Ambition: Despite the challenges, Conway likely saw this posting as an opportunity to further his career. Dundalk, being an important military location, might have offered him the chance to prove himself as a capable officer, potentially opening doors for promotions or future opportunities within the Royal Artillery.

Effect on His Life:

1. Military Advancement: His time stationed at Dundalk would have contributed to his experience and growth as a military officer. Successfully managing his responsibilities there could have bolstered his reputation within the Royal Artillery, increasing his chances for promotion and recognition.

2. Exposure to Political Unrest: Stationed in Ireland during a time of political unrest, Conway would have gained firsthand experience dealing with conflicts that were both military and political in nature. This would have sharpened his leadership skills and possibly affected his views on the political situation in Ireland and Britain at the time.

3. Connection to Local Communities: Being stationed in Dundalk would have also connected him to the local Irish communities, potentially influencing his views on Irish society and the complex relationship between Ireland and Britain. It may have given him a deeper understanding of the tensions and the impact of British military presence in Ireland.

4. Personal Growth: The stationing would have tested Conway's resilience and adaptability, key traits for any military officer. As a 30-year-old man with significant responsibilities, this experience would have shaped his character, making him more seasoned and experienced both in life and in his profession.

Overall, being stationed in Dundalk would have been a formative period in Conway's life, blending military duty with personal challenges during a pivotal time in Irish history.

Conway Benning Jr.'s transfer to the infantry after his time in the Royal Artillery would have marked a significant shift in his military career. Here's how he might have reacted and how this transfer would have affected him:

Reaction to the Transfer:

1. Career Opportunity:

Being transferred from the Royal Artillery to the infantry could have been seen as either a challenge or an opportunity. If the transfer was a result of his superiors' decision, Conway may have initially felt uncertain, given the difference in the nature of duties between the two military branches. However, such a transfer would also likely be viewed as a chance to gain new experience and further his career within the British Army.

2. Adaptability:

Conway would have needed to adapt to a new branch of the military, one that focused more on ground combat and foot soldier maneuvers than on artillery strategy and management. This could have been both a practical and mental shift, requiring him to learn new tactics, formations, and the daily routines of infantry life. His officer status would have meant overseeing troops, ensuring their discipline, and leading them in potentially dangerous situations.

3. Increased Responsibility:

Serving in the infantry often involved more direct engagement in battles, especially during this turbulent period in Irish and British history. Conway may have felt the increased responsibility of being on the front lines with his men, where leadership skills were critical in maintaining morale and effectiveness in combat.

Effect on His Life:

1. Exposure to Different Military Experiences:

The infantry would have exposed Conway to a more hands-on, combat-focused aspect of military life. As artillery dealt more with long-range attacks and logistics, infantry work involved direct engagement with enemy forces. This would have increased his understanding of warfare and the harsh realities of ground combat.

2. Physical and Mental Strain:

The infantry often faced tougher physical demands than artillery units. Marching long distances, enduring harsh weather, and engaging in close combat would have required both physical and mental resilience. Conway would have needed to adapt to this more rigorous lifestyle, which could have been challenging but also rewarding as he gained new skills.

3. Opportunities for Leadership:

As an officer in the infantry, Conway would have had the opportunity to directly lead men in battle. This would have offered him the chance to develop strong leadership skills, essential for commanding troops under pressure. The experience could have been invaluable for his professional growth, positioning him as a versatile officer capable of succeeding in different branches of the military.

4. Impact of Political and Military Context:

During this period, with the Napoleonic Wars and the ongoing tensions in Ireland, being in the infantry might have placed Conway in more immediate conflict zones. This exposure could have deepened his understanding of the political and military complexities of the time, influencing his views on British military policies and their effects on regions like Ireland.

5. Social and Personal Life:

The demands of infantry life might have kept Conway away from home and family for extended periods, potentially straining personal relationships. However, as an experienced officer, he would likely have adapted to the military lifestyle, balancing duty with personal obligations as best as possible.

Summary:

Conway's transfer to the infantry would have broadened his military experience, giving him firsthand exposure to ground combat and expanding his leadership skills. While the physical demands and direct involvement in battle could have posed challenges, the experience would likely have made him a more seasoned and capable officer. The shift in duties and the heightened responsibilities of infantry service would have tested his adaptability but also offered new opportunities for advancement and personal growth.

In 1801, Conway Benning Jr., at 30 years old, would have likely worn formal attire suitable for a wedding, particularly one in a prestigious location like St. Peter's Church in Dublin. Given his military background, his clothing could have reflected his status, potentially incorporating both civilian fashion and elements of military influence. Here's a detailed look at what he might have worn:

Formal Civilian Attire:

1. Tailcoat:

Conway would have worn a well-fitted tailcoat, which was a key part of men's formal attire in the early 19th century. Tailcoats were typically cut away in the front and had long tails in the back. These coats were often dark in color, such as black, navy, or dark green, and made from fine wool or broadcloth. For a wedding, it's likely he would choose a more somber or neutral color like black, reflecting the formal nature of the occasion.

2. Waistcoat (Vest):

Underneath the tailcoat, he would have worn a waistcoat. Waistcoats were typically more colorful and could include patterns, such as stripes or florals. For a wedding, a man of status might choose a waistcoat in cream, white, or a pale pastel color, possibly with embroidery or brocade to add an elegant touch.

3. Shirt and Cravat:

The shirt would have been white and made from linen or cotton, featuring a high, stiff collar. Around his neck, he would have worn a cravat, which was a long strip of fabric tied in a bow or intricate knot. The cravat was often white or off-white for formal occasions. Conway's cravat might have been neatly arranged and made from silk for a more refined look.

4. Breeches or Trousers:

At the turn of the 19th century, breeches were still worn, though trousers were becoming more common. Breeches, which ended just below the knee, were worn with stockings and were often paired with formal shoes. Alternatively, Conway may have opted for the more modern high-waisted trousers, which were long and fitted, reflecting the transition in men's fashion at the time. Breeches would be more formal, but trousers were gaining acceptance for events like weddings.

5. Stockings and Shoes:

If Conway wore breeches, he would have paired them with silk or wool stockings. For footwear, he would have worn polished leather shoes with a low heel, possibly with a buckle or lace-up fastening.

6. Accessories:

For a wedding, Conway would have likely added accessories such as a fob watch with a chain, and perhaps gloves for a more formal and polished appearance. Gloves were an essential accessory for formal occasions, made from fine leather or silk. He may have also carried a top hat, which was a fashionable accessory for men attending formal events.

Military Influence:

Given Conway's position in the Royal Artillery, it's possible that he incorporated elements of his military status into his attire. He may have opted for military-style decorations, such as a medal or sash, or even chosen to wear his dress uniform if the wedding had a particularly formal or ceremonial aspect.

Military officers often wore their uniforms to formal events, especially if they wanted to signify their rank and achievements. In this case, his uniform would likely have been adorned with gold braiding, epaulettes, and other distinguishing features.

Summary:

Conway would have attended the wedding in formal attire, likely choosing a tailored tailcoat, waistcoat, and either breeches or trousers. His outfit would have been polished and elegant, befitting a man of his social and military standing. Depending on the level of formality, he might have added military decorations or even attended in his full dress uniform, highlighting his status as an officer in the Royal Artillery.

At 40 years old, Conway Benning Jr.'s death at the Battle of Albuera on May 16, 1811, would have had significant emotional and practical impacts:

Impact on Family:

1. Deep Grief and Loss:

Conway's death would have caused profound grief and sorrow among his family, particularly his parents, siblings, and any spouse or children he might have had. Losing a family member, especially someone serving in a prominent military role, would have been a heavy emotional blow.

2. Impact on Family Dynamics:

The family would likely have experienced shifts in their dynamics. His death might have led to changes in responsibilities among family members, with some potentially stepping up to fill Conway's role or to support his surviving family members.

3. Legacy and Memory:

Conway's death in battle would have impacted how he was remembered. The family might have honored his service and sacrifice, which could have involved public memorials or private family tributes. His bravery and contributions would have been a source of pride but also a reminder of the personal cost of war.

Impact on His Career and Reputation:

1. Military Recognition:

Conway's death as a captain in the 2nd Battalion, 66th Foot would have been noted within military circles. His sacrifice at the Battle of Albuera, a significant and bloody conflict in the Peninsular War, would have contributed to his military legacy and reputation.

2. Emotional and Psychological Effects:

As a soldier, Conway would have faced the harsh realities of combat. His death at a relatively mature age, after years of service, reflects a life marked by dedication and commitment to his military career. The emotional toll of war, including the stress and trauma experienced, would have been significant.

Impact on His Personal Life:

1. Unfulfilled Plans:

Conway's death might have cut short any personal or professional plans he had for the future. This could include any aspirations for promotion, changes in his personal life, or future contributions to his family or community.

2. Impact on His Loved Ones:

His immediate family and close friends would have been deeply affected by his loss. They would have to cope with the absence of his presence, support, and contributions.

Overall Effects:

- Legacy: Conway Benning Jr.'s death would have been a moment of profound loss for his family and a significant event in the context of the Napoleonic Wars. His service and sacrifice would have been remembered and honored by those who knew him and by those who learned of his contributions.

- Historical Context: In the broader historical context, Conway's death would be part of the larger narrative of the Peninsular War, which was marked by intense battles and significant loss of life. His sacrifice would be a reminder of the personal costs of the conflict and the bravery of those who served.

JAMES BENNING[13]

JAMES BENNING, BORN in 1773, would likely have had the following characteristics based on common traits of the era:

Physical Appearance:

1. Facial Features:

- Face Shape: James might have had a moderately oval or rectangular face, which was typical of the period.

- Eyes: His eye color would have varied, with common colors being blue, green, or brown. Eyebrows were often natural, not heavily groomed.

- Nose and Mouth: He likely had a straight or slightly aquiline nose and a fairly regular mouth, reflecting the common European features of the time.

2. Hair:

- Color and Style: His hair might have been dark brown, light brown, or even black, depending on his genetic background. During the late 18th century, hairstyles for men included short or shoulder-length hair, sometimes tied back or in a simple queue, which was common in the 1770s.

3. Build:

- Body Type: James was probably of average height and build for the period. He might have been slim or slightly muscular, reflecting the physical activity levels typical of the time.

Clothing and Accessories:

1. Infancy and Childhood (1773-1780s):
- Infants and Toddlers: As a child, he would have worn simple, comfortable clothing. Infants and toddlers often wore gowns or dresses in light fabrics.
- Young Boy: As he grew, he would have transitioned to knee-length breeches and jackets with waistcoats. Colors and fabrics would have been practical, reflecting both the fashion and the family's status.

2. Late 18th Century Fashion:
- Teen Years (1780s): As a teenager, James would have worn a tailored suit with breeches, a waistcoat, and a jacket. Fabrics would include wool, linen, or silk, with darker colors and patterns becoming more common.

Overall Impression:

James Benning would have reflected the typical styles and appearances of late 18th-century European children, with clothing and grooming practices typical of the time. His look would have been influenced by both fashion trends and practical considerations of the period.

In 1773, Carrickfergus, located in County Antrim, Northern Ireland, was a bustling market town with a rich history and a strategic location. Here's an overview of what life in Carrickfergus would have been like during that period:

1. Economic and Social Aspects:
- Market Town: Carrickfergus was a key market town in the region, serving as a hub for trade and commerce. The local economy was supported by agriculture, fishing, and a growing trade network.
- Industry: While Carrickfergus was primarily agricultural, it had some local industries, including shipbuilding and textiles. The port played an important role in facilitating trade.

2. Architecture and Infrastructure:

- Carrickfergus Castle: The castle, a prominent feature of the town, was originally built in the 12th century and remained a key landmark. By 1773, it was no longer a military stronghold but still an important symbol of the town's history.

- Buildings: The town's buildings in the 18th century were mostly Georgian in style, with a mixture of stone and brick constructions. Streets were generally narrow and paved with cobblestones.

- Port: The port was active, with ships regularly coming and going. It played a vital role in the town's economy and was a key point for the import and export of goods.

3. Daily Life:

- Community: The population was a mix of local Irish residents and settlers of English and Scottish origin. Social life centered around the market, religious services, and community events.

- Transportation: Transportation was primarily by horse and carriage or on foot. The town was well-connected by sea and had basic road links to other parts of Ireland.

4. Social and Cultural Life:

- Religion: The dominant religion was Protestantism, with several churches serving the community. The local population was involved in regular church activities and community gatherings.

- Education: Formal education was available but limited compared to modern standards. Wealthier families might have had private tutors, while others would attend local schools or receive informal education.

5. Military and Defense:

- Defense: The town's location and the presence of Carrickfergus Castle meant that it was of strategic importance. While there was no immediate military threat in 1773, the castle remained a significant symbol of historical defense.

Overall, Carrickfergus in 1773 was a lively market town with a blend of historical significance and growing economic activity, reflecting the broader developments of 18th-century Ireland.

When James Benning was three years old in 1776, and his father, Conway Benning Sr., received his LL.D. (Doctor of Laws), the impact on James would have been more indirect due to his young age. However, here are a few potential effects and influences this event might have had on him:

1. Family Status and Influence:

- Elevated Status: The attainment of an LL.D. by his father would have elevated the family's social and professional status. This prestige might have led to better opportunities and connections for James in the future, as his father's enhanced reputation could open doors for him as he grew older.

- Pride and Expectations: James would have been raised in an environment where his father's academic and professional achievements were a source of pride. This could foster a sense of pride in his own heritage and potentially lead to high expectations for his own accomplishments.

2. Educational Environment:

- Educational Emphasis: Growing up with a father who had a distinguished academic degree might have encouraged an emphasis on education in the Benning household. James might have been expected to pursue higher education or achieve notable accomplishments himself.

- Access to Resources: The family's improved status might have provided James with access to better educational resources and opportunities, including private tutors or attendance at reputable schools.

3. Social Perception:

- Community Status: The recognition of his father's achievements might have positively influenced how the family was perceived in their community. This enhanced social standing could impact James's own social interactions and opportunities.

4. Family Dynamics:

- Influence of a Role Model: As James grew up, the presence of his father's academic and professional success would likely serve as a role model or benchmark for his own aspirations and achievements.

While the direct impact on a three-year-old would be limited, the long-term effects of his father's LL.D. would influence James's upbringing, opportunities, and expectations throughout his life.

When James Benning was 4 years old, his father's travels across the continent in 1777 would have had several potential effects on him:

1. Family Dynamics:

- Absence of Father: His father's absence might have created a sense of instability or loss of paternal presence in James's early childhood. This could affect his emotional development and his relationship with his father.

- Involvement of Mother: His mother, Ann Ellis Benning, would likely have taken on a greater role in managing the household and caring for the children. This shift might have influenced James's relationship with his mother and the household dynamics.

2. Social and Emotional Impact:

- Feeling of Loss or Change: Young children are often sensitive to changes in their family structure. James might have experienced a sense of loss or confusion due to his father's prolonged absence, impacting his emotional well-being.

- Adaptation: As a young child, James would need to adapt to the absence of his father, potentially forming closer bonds with other family members or caregivers.

3. Economic and Social Influence:

- Financial Stability: The travels might have been linked to professional or economic reasons. If the family's financial situation was stable, James might not have experienced immediate economic hardship. Conversely, if the travels impacted the family's financial stability, this might have affected James's quality of life.

- Social Status: The social status of the family might have been affected by the father's absence. If his travels were seen as prestigious or beneficial, it could positively influence the family's social standing.

4. Educational and Cultural Exposure:

- Influence of Travels: Although James was very young, the travels could have brought new experiences and influences into the family home. His father might have shared stories or items from his travels, which could indirectly impact James's early understanding of the world.

- Cultural Impact: Exposure to different cultures and ideas from his father's travels could eventually influence James's perspectives, even if he was too young to grasp the details at the time.

In summary, while James Benning was too young to directly engage with his father's travels, the absence would have had implications for family dynamics, his emotional development, and potentially his perception of the world as he grew older.

When James Benning was four years old and his sister Millicent Mary was born in 1777, several effects on him can be anticipated:

1. Family Dynamics:

- Shift in Attention: With the arrival of a new sibling, James would likely experience a shift in the family's attention. As a young child, this could mean less focused attention from his parents, particularly his mother, who would be occupied with the newborn.

- Role Adjustment: James might have been encouraged to take on new responsibilities or roles within the family, such as helping with his sister in small ways appropriate for his age. This can contribute to his sense of growing up and his place within the family.

2. Emotional Impact:

- Feelings of Jealousy or Rivalry: Young children often experience feelings of jealousy or rivalry when a new sibling arrives. James might have felt a range of emotions, from excitement and curiosity to jealousy or confusion about the changes in family dynamics.

- Bonding and Attachment: Over time, James would likely develop a bond with Millicent Mary. This sibling relationship could provide him with companionship and emotional support as they grew up together.

3. Social Development:

- Social Skills: Interacting with a sibling can help develop a child's social skills, including sharing, empathy, and cooperation. James's interactions with his sister might contribute to his social development and emotional intelligence.

- Role Model: As he grew older, James might take on a role as a protector or guide for Millicent Mary, fostering a sense of responsibility and leadership.

4. Parental Attention and Care:

- Adjustment for Parents: The birth of Millicent Mary would require James's parents, especially his mother, to adjust their routines and focus. James might see changes in how his parents interact with him and how they manage household tasks.

- Family Dynamics: The addition of a new family member can alter family dynamics and routines. James would need to adapt to these changes, which could affect his daily life and interactions.

In summary, the birth of his sister Millicent Mary would have introduced several changes in James's life, impacting family dynamics, his emotional responses, and his social development.

Over time, he would likely adjust to these changes, developing a sibling relationship that could become an important part of his life.

When James Benning was five years old and his father was instituted to the vicarage of Rathmolyon on March 7, 1778, several effects on him can be anticipated:

1. Change in Residence:

- Shift in Family Base: The family's primary residence moving to Kilroot while his father took on the vicarage role at Rathmolyon would have impacted James's daily life. He would experience a change in his home environment, including potentially new routines and living conditions.

- Separation from Parish: Living primarily at Kilroot while the vicarage was at Rathmolyon might have meant less direct involvement in parish life for James's family. He may have had limited exposure to the local community and church activities associated with Rathmolyon.

2. Adjustment to New Routines:

- Parental Absence: James might have experienced periods where his father was away at Rathmolyon, which could affect the time spent with him and the overall family dynamic. His father's role might have required additional responsibilities and time away from home.

- New Responsibilities: With the shift in the family's base, James might have had to adapt to new routines or responsibilities, such as adjusting to different living arrangements or changes in household management.

3. Impact on Social Life:

- Community Interaction: The family's primary residence at Kilroot could influence James's social interactions and friendships. He might have developed relationships with people in Kilroot and had less frequent contact with the community around Rathmolyon.

- Exposure to New Environments: Depending on the nature of Kilroot and Rathmolyon, James might have experienced different social or cultural environments. This could impact his social development and understanding of the surrounding areas.

4. Family Dynamics:

- Parent-Child Relationships: With his father's new responsibilities and the family living primarily at Kilroot, James might have experienced shifts in family dynamics. The increased focus on his father's ecclesiastical duties could influence the time and attention given to him and his siblings.

- Role of Mother: James's mother would play a crucial role in managing the household and maintaining family routines during this period. Her role would be essential in adjusting to the changes and ensuring a stable environment for the children.

5. Educational and Social Development:

- Schooling and Social Activities: The move and the new family routines might have impacted James's schooling and social activities. He would need to adjust to any changes in his educational environment or social interactions due to the family's primary residence being at Kilroot.

In summary, the shift in residence and the new vicarage role for his father would have influenced James's daily life, social interactions, and family dynamics. The changes would require adaptation to new routines and environments, potentially affecting his overall experience and development during this period.

When James Benning was 6 years old and his sister Jane was born in 1779, this event would have had several potential effects on him:

1. Sense of Responsibility:

- Becoming an Older Brother: At six years old, James would have been old enough to understand the birth of a new sibling.

He may have been encouraged by his parents to help care for his younger sister, fostering a sense of responsibility.

- Shift in Attention: With a newborn in the house, much of his parents' attention would likely have been focused on Jane, which could have made James feel either excited to help or a bit jealous of the new attention given to the baby.

2. Impact on Family Dynamics:

- Adjustment to a Growing Family: The addition of a new sibling would have altered the family dynamics. With multiple young children, the household may have become more lively or chaotic, and James would need to adjust to the presence of a new baby.

- Parental Focus on the Newborn: While his parents tended to Jane, James might have experienced less direct attention from his mother, who would have been focused on caring for the infant. However, this could also have been an opportunity for James to bond more closely with other family members, such as his father or older siblings.

3. Influence on Emotional Development:

- Developing Nurturing Skills: Having a younger sibling could have provided James with early opportunities to develop nurturing and protective instincts. He might have taken pride in being an older brother and helping his mother with simple tasks related to the baby.

- Jealousy or Rivalry: Depending on his personality, James could also have experienced feelings of sibling rivalry or jealousy due to the shift in attention. This is common among young children when a new sibling is born.

4. Impact on Routine:

- Changes in Daily Life: The presence of a new baby likely brought some disruption to the household routine, which might have affected James. There may have been more noise, less sleep for everyone, and a different rhythm to the day-to-day activities in the household.

5. Development of Patience and Empathy:

- Learning Patience: As a growing child, James would need to learn patience and understanding, particularly if Jane's needs, such as feeding and crying, took up a lot of family time. This could help him develop empathy and emotional intelligence early on.

In summary, the birth of his sister Jane when he was 6 years old would have impacted James by encouraging him to take on a more responsible role in the family, adjust to changes in attention from his parents, and develop emotionally through the experience of becoming an older sibling.

When James Benning was 11 years old and the first hot air balloon was successfully launched in 1783, he would likely have been fascinated and intrigued by the news. Here's how he might have reacted and how it could have affected him:

1. Sense of Wonder and Fascination:

- Astonishment: The idea of humans flying for the first time would have seemed magical and extraordinary to an 11-year-old. He likely would have been captivated by the concept of leaving the ground and soaring through the air.

- Curiosity about Invention and Science: The success of the hot air balloon could have sparked James's interest in science and innovation. Children during that time, especially boys, often looked up to inventors and explorers, and this groundbreaking event might have inspired dreams of adventure or a desire to learn more about the natural world.

2. Impact on Imagination:

- Fueling Imaginative Play: The launch of the hot air balloon could have fired his imagination, possibly inspiring pretend play where he envisioned flying in the sky or traveling to distant places. This event may have expanded his understanding of what was possible in the world, opening his mind to the rapid advancements of the time.

3. Conversations and Awareness:

- Family and Social Discussions: News of the balloon launch would have been discussed in his household or among his peers. James might have been part of conversations about this astonishing achievement, hearing adults speak with excitement about what the future might hold for travel and exploration.

4. Interest in Future Technology:

- Fascination with the Future: As a young boy living through the Enlightenment period, James would have been growing up during a time of significant scientific progress and discovery. The balloon flight might have planted the seed for an interest in technology and the possibilities of human innovation.

5. Potential Career Aspirations:

- Dreams of Exploration: The successful flight could have influenced James to dream of careers that involved adventure, travel, or exploration. Seeing the potential for new modes of transportation might have ignited a sense of curiosity about the world beyond his immediate surroundings.

6. Sense of National or Cultural Pride:

- Interest in the Achievements of Other Countries: Since the balloon launch was a French achievement (the Montgolfier brothers), it may have sparked an interest in events happening abroad. James might have felt awe toward this foreign achievement and wanted to learn more about developments in other nations.

In summary, at 11 years old, James would likely have been deeply fascinated and inspired by the first hot air balloon launch. This event could have sparked his curiosity about science, technology, and exploration, fueling his imagination and shaping his sense of what was possible in the world.

When James Benning attended his sister Eleanor's wedding to Noah on May 22, 1795, he would have dressed in the fashionable style of the late 18th century, reflective of his social class and the formal occasion. Here's a likely description of what he might have worn:

1. Coat:

- Tailcoat: James would likely have worn a well-fitted, long-tailed coat made of fine wool or a similar fabric. The coat would have been in a dark, formal color such as navy blue, black, or brown, which were typical for formal events. It would have featured wide lapels and buttons down the front.

2. Waistcoat:

- Vest or Waistcoat: Under the coat, he would have worn a waistcoat, often in a contrasting color, such as cream, light blue, or even a patterned brocade. The waistcoat would be shorter than the coat and feature buttons down the front, giving a layered and refined look.

3. Breeches:

- Knee-Length Breeches: Breeches that fastened just below the knee were typical of the time. James would likely have worn light-colored breeches, such as tan, cream, or grey, paired with white stockings that covered his lower legs.

4. Shirt:

- Linen Shirt: Beneath the waistcoat, he would have worn a crisp white linen shirt with a high, stiff collar. The shirt would have featured a cravat or neckcloth tied around the neck, which was a key element of men's fashion at the time.

5. Cravat:

- Cravat or Neckcloth: A white cravat, delicately tied around his neck, would have added an element of formality to the outfit. Cravats could be elaborately tied in different styles, and James likely would have worn one suitable for a wedding.

6. Stockings and Shoes:

- Silk Stockings: James would have worn white or cream silk stockings, which were standard with breeches.

- Shoes: Buckled shoes made of polished leather, typically black, with silver or brass buckles, would have completed the outfit. These shoes would have been low-heeled and finely crafted for formal wear.

7. Accessories:

- Pocket Watch: As a gentleman, James might have carried a pocket watch with a chain, tucked into the pocket of his waistcoat.

- Gloves: For a formal occasion like a wedding, he may have worn light-colored gloves, likely made of leather or silk.

- Hat: Although he wouldn't wear it indoors during the ceremony, James may have carried a bicorne hat (the two-cornered hat that replaced the tricorn around this time), which was fashionable during the late 18th century.

8. Hair:

- Wig or Styled Hair: By the 1790s, powdered wigs were becoming less common, but he might have worn his natural hair powdered and tied back in a queue (ponytail) with a ribbon. His hair would likely be neatly styled in line with the formal attire.

Conclusion:

James would have worn an elegant, formal ensemble suited to his social standing and the significance of the occasion. His attire would have been fashionable, with attention to detail in the fabric, cut, and accessories, presenting him as a refined gentleman of the late 18th century.

When James Benning's older brother, Conway Benning Jr., joined the Royal Artillery as a lieutenant on July 25, 1795, James, who was 22 years old at the time, would likely have had a mix of emotions and reactions. The significance of this event and how it would have affected him can be understood in several ways:

1. Pride and Admiration:
   - Sense of Family Honor: James likely would have felt proud of his brother for achieving such a prestigious position. The Royal Artillery was an elite branch of the military, and becoming a lieutenant was a notable accomplishment. This would have reflected well on their family's social standing, and James might have admired Conway's skills, discipline, and ambition.
   - Role Model: As the younger brother, James may have looked up to Conway as a role model. Seeing his brother take on such an important role could have inspired James in his own pursuits, whether military or otherwise.

2. Concern for Conway's Safety:
   - Worry About the Dangers of Military Life: On the other hand, James likely would have been concerned about the dangers Conway might face. The late 18th century was a turbulent period, with Britain involved in the French Revolutionary Wars. Being in the military meant that Conway would be exposed to the risks of battle, and James may have worried about his brother's safety, especially given the growing conflicts in Europe.
   - War Anxiety: With military campaigns on the horizon, Conway's entry into the Royal Artillery would have brought the reality of war closer to home for James and the rest of the family. James might have felt anxiety about the broader political and military landscape and how it could impact his family.

3. Changing Family Dynamics:
   - Separation from the Family: With Conway joining the military, James might have felt the impact of his brother's absence from family life. The military life required discipline and duty, which often meant being stationed far from home. James would have had to adjust to Conway not being around as frequently, especially if they had been close.

- Increased Responsibility: Depending on the family structure, James might have taken on more responsibilities at home or within the family as Conway embarked on his military career. Being the second eldest son, he might have felt an increased role in supporting the family or maintaining household affairs.

4. Sense of Duty:

- Influence on Career Choices: Conway's enlistment might have made James consider his own future more seriously. He may have felt a sense of duty to pursue his own career path, whether in the military or another field. Conway's commitment to service could have encouraged James to think about how he could contribute to his family's legacy or the larger community.

- Possible Desire to Join Military: Depending on James' own ambitions, Conway's entry into the Royal Artillery might have sparked thoughts of joining the military himself. Some younger siblings followed in the footsteps of their older brothers, especially in families where military service was valued.

5. Social Standing and Connection:

- Elevated Social Status: Having a brother in the Royal Artillery would have elevated the Benning family's social status. James might have found that this brought more respect or opportunities for himself in social circles. The military was a respected institution, and being associated with a rising officer could have brought him certain social advantages.

- Pride in Family Connections: If James was active in social life or had aspirations in public service or politics, Conway's position might have enhanced his own reputation by association.

6. Impact on Family Relationships:

- Strengthened Bond: The gravity of Conway's military service could have brought the brothers closer together, especially if they exchanged letters or shared thoughts about the wider world. James might have felt a stronger connection with Conway, knowing that his brother was taking on significant duties.

- Emotional Distance: On the other hand, the practical realities of military life—distance, long deployments, and the unpredictability of war—might have led to a sense of emotional distance over time as their paths diverged.

Conclusion:

James likely would have reacted with a sense of pride mixed with concern when his brother Conway joined the Royal Artillery. The event would have affected him by deepening his awareness of the realities of war and military life, while also shaping his own views on duty, responsibility, and family honor. His admiration for his brother's achievement would be tempered by the natural worries about his brother's safety and the impact it might have on their family dynamics.

When James Benning was 25 years old during the Battle of Antrim and the Irish Rebellion in 1798, these events likely had a profound effect on him both personally and emotionally. As a young man living in Ireland during such a turbulent period, his reactions would have been shaped by the political, social, and familial contexts of the time.

1. Heightened Awareness of Political Instability:

- Increased Awareness of Conflict: The 1798 Irish Rebellion, driven by the Society of United Irishmen, aimed to end British rule in Ireland and establish an independent Irish republic. The Battle of Antrim was one of the pivotal clashes during the rebellion. Living through these events would have heightened James's awareness of the political instability in Ireland, particularly the tensions between the Irish population and British rule.

- Personal Concern for Safety: Given the violence of the rebellion, James likely would have been concerned about his own safety and the safety of his family. The rebellion involved uprisings, violent skirmishes, and government crackdowns, and living in or near such upheaval would have brought a sense of unease and fear.

2. Conflicted Loyalties:

- Torn Between Allegiances: As someone from a family with likely ties to the British establishment, James may have felt conflicted. On one hand, he may have had some loyalty to the British Crown, especially if his family benefited from British rule or had ties to the British military, such as through his brother Conway's service in the Royal Artillery. On the other hand, living in Ireland during this time might have exposed him to the grievances and frustrations of the Irish population, which could have made him sympathize with the rebels' cause.

- Family Dynamics: James's brother Conway was a lieutenant in the Royal Artillery at this time, actively serving in the British military. This might have created a strong sense of duty and loyalty to the British Crown within the family. James could have been influenced by Conway's military service and may have felt pressure to support the British government against the rebels. This could have strained his feelings, particularly if he harbored any sympathies for Irish independence.

3. Emotional Impact of Violence:

- Exposure to Brutality: The Irish Rebellion was marked by brutal violence on both sides. The British forces and loyalists were known for harsh reprisals against suspected rebels, while the rebels themselves engaged in violent acts against British troops and loyalists. Witnessing or hearing about such violence would have left a deep emotional impact on James. He may have felt shock, fear, or anger at the chaos unfolding around him.

- Sense of Vulnerability: The rebellion likely created a pervasive sense of vulnerability. Even if James was not directly involved in the fighting, the proximity of the conflict would have been a source of anxiety, knowing that rebellion could spread unpredictably, and that his own town or village could be affected.

4. Impact on Personal and Social Life:

- Disruption of Daily Life: The rebellion would have disrupted daily life for James and his community. Economic instability, travel restrictions, and martial law in certain areas could have affected trade, access to goods, and general societal functioning. This may have had a practical impact on James's life, especially if his family was engaged in commerce or landholding that relied on stability.

- Social Tensions: The rebellion deepened divisions within Irish society. James would likely have been aware of these tensions, which could have affected his relationships with others, depending on their political allegiances. Conversations, friendships, and business dealings could have become more cautious or fraught due to the polarization of loyalties.

5. Personal Reflection on the Future of Ireland:

- Questions About Ireland's Future: As a young man, James might have found himself questioning the future of Ireland during such a significant upheaval. He may have reflected on the broader social and political changes that were occurring and how they would affect the lives of his generation. This period might have shaped his views on governance, independence, and national identity, particularly as Ireland grappled with its relationship to Britain.

- Impact on Career Choices: If James was considering a career in law, politics, or the military, the rebellion would have given him insight into the complexities of political authority and the challenges of maintaining order in a divided society. It could have influenced his future choices, potentially making him more cautious about political involvement or more committed to supporting stability and order.

6. Influence of Family and Local Community:

- Family Influence: The Benning family's position in society would have influenced James's reaction. If his father and older brother supported the British, James might have felt compelled to align with their views, even if he had personal reservations about British rule. However, if his family had more mixed views, this could have allowed him to form a more nuanced perspective on the rebellion.

- Community Reactions: The views of those in his immediate community would have also shaped James's reaction. If his local community largely supported the British, he might have felt a stronger sense of duty to oppose the rebellion. However, if his community was sympathetic to the rebels, James may have felt conflicted, especially if he saw neighbors or friends become involved in the conflict.

Conclusion:

During the Battle of Antrim and the Irish Rebellion of 1798, James Benning likely experienced a complex range of emotions. He may have felt pride in his brother Conway's military service while grappling with the realities of the violence and political instability surrounding him. His reaction would have been influenced by family dynamics, community pressures, and his own understanding of the rebellion's impact on Ireland. This period likely left him more aware of the fragility of political order and the challenges of navigating loyalties in a time of national crisis.

At the time of his sister Millicent Mary's marriage to Dr. Samuel Allen on November 4, 1798, James Benning, at 25 years old, would have dressed according to the fashion trends of the late 18th century, particularly those influenced by British styles. Weddings in that era were relatively formal, and as the brother of the bride, he would have been expected to wear something that reflected both the occasion and his social standing.

Likely Outfit for the Wedding:

1. Coat:
- James would have worn a tailored frock coat or cutaway coat. These were long and often made from fine wool or silk, depending on the season and the formality of the event.
- The coat would have had a high collar and was likely single- or double-breasted with decorative buttons, a common style of the time.

2. Waistcoat:
- Underneath his coat, he would have worn a waistcoat made of silk, satin, or wool, often in a contrasting color to the coat. Waistcoats during this period were highly decorative, with embroidery or elegant patterns.

3. Shirt and Cravat:
- A white linen shirt with full sleeves and a high, stiffened collar was customary.
- He would have worn a cravat (an early form of a necktie), which was typically a long strip of fabric wrapped around the neck and tied in various fashionable knots or bows.

4. Breeches or Pantaloons:
- By the late 18th century, breeches (knee-length trousers) were still common but pantaloons (tight-fitting, ankle-length trousers) were becoming fashionable, especially for younger men.
- Breeches would have been worn with silk stockings and knee-high boots, while pantaloons were typically paired with low shoes.

5. Footwear:
- If he wore breeches, he would likely have worn silk stockings and buckle shoes or dress boots.
- If he opted for pantaloons, he may have worn low leather shoes or ankle boots.

6. Accessories:

- Gloves: It was typical for men to wear gloves, often made of leather or silk.

- Hat: James may have worn a bicorne hat (a two-cornered hat), which was a popular style for formal occasions.

- Cane: A gentleman might carry a walking cane as a symbol of status, though it was more of a decorative accessory than a functional item.

- Watch: He may have had a pocket watch, attached to his waistcoat with a chain.

Colors and Fabrics:

- Colors: Dark, muted tones like navy, dark green, burgundy, and black were popular for formal attire. The waistcoat, however, could be in a lighter, more decorative color such as cream, light blue, or gold.

- Fabrics: Wool, silk, and velvet were commonly used for outer garments, while shirts were typically made of fine linen.

James would have looked sharp and well-dressed for his sister's wedding, reflecting his status and the formal nature of the occasion. His attire would have balanced elegance with the understated formality expected at a late-18th-century wedding.

At 27 years old, when William Young designed his shoes (around 1800), James Benning would have been living in a world where technological advancements and new innovations were beginning to influence daily life, including fashion. William Young's shoe designs likely introduced more durable, comfortable, and fashionable footwear options, and James, being part of a well-educated and socially conscious family, may have appreciated the significance of such improvements.

Possible Reactions:

1. Interest in Innovation: Given that James was living through a time of change, where inventions and industrial advancements were becoming more frequent, he might have been intrigued by

the innovation in shoe design. The idea of footwear that was both more functional and stylish would have been appealing, especially as social standing was often reflected in one's appearance.

2. Practical Considerations: Shoes during this period were transitioning from being purely utilitarian to being a blend of style and comfort. James, as a gentleman, would likely have appreciated the improvements in design and craftsmanship, especially if the shoes offered more comfort for walking or riding. As someone possibly concerned with maintaining his appearance, good quality shoes were important to him.

3. Fashion and Status: Shoes were also a marker of social class. If Young's designs became fashionable among the upper classes, James might have seen them as an opportunity to display his awareness of current trends. He may have wanted to own a pair to keep up with fashion, enhancing his image in social and professional circles.

Effects on James:

- Enhanced Comfort and Utility: If he adopted Young's shoes, they would have likely improved his daily life in terms of comfort, especially for activities such as walking or attending formal events.

- Social Influence: Wearing shoes designed by someone as notable as William Young could have been a subtle way for James to align himself with the modern, progressive trends of his time, demonstrating his connection to the latest fashions.

In summary, James would have likely been curious about the new designs and seen them as a reflection of both the changing times and his own position in society. Owning such shoes could have elevated his social standing and improved his comfort in daily life.

When James Benning was 27 years old and attending his sister Jane's wedding to Thomas in 1800, he would have dressed in formal attire typical of the late Georgian era, which reflected both elegance and propriety. As a gentleman, his outfit would have been carefully chosen to show his social status and respect for the occasion.

Likely Outfit:

1. Tailcoat: James would have likely worn a well-fitted, dark-colored tailcoat (usually in navy, black, or dark brown), which was common formal wear for men. The coat would have had long tails at the back and a short front, emphasizing the waist.

2. Waistcoat: Underneath the tailcoat, he would have worn a waistcoat. Waistcoats at this time were often made of silk or wool and came in various colors, sometimes with decorative patterns. It added a layer of formality and could include gold or silver buttons.

3. Breeches: Knee-length breeches were still in fashion in 1800. These would have been made of fine fabric like wool or silk and fastened just below the knee, worn with stockings.

4. Stockings and Shoes: He would have worn white or cream-colored silk stockings, and his shoes would have been black leather with small silver or brass buckles, polished for the event.

5. Crisp Linen Shirt: A white linen shirt with a high, stiff collar would have been standard. The shirt might have been adorned with lace or ruffles at the cuffs and neckline, adding a touch of elegance.

6. Cravat: Around his neck, James would have worn a cravat, a long piece of fabric tied around the collar. It was an important fashion element and would likely have been white or off-white to complement the rest of his outfit.

7. Accessories: As part of his formal attire, James may have carried a cane, worn gloves, and perhaps a top hat to complete his ensemble. A watch chain might have hung from his waistcoat as a sign of sophistication.

Overall Effect:

James' outfit would have been both stylish and reflective of his social standing, as weddings were formal occasions where families took great care to dress appropriately. His attire would have demonstrated respect for his sister and the importance of the day while aligning with the fashion trends of the early 19th century.ames would have been conscious of his appearance and the social expectations surrounding a family event like his sister Jane's wedding. In 1800, family weddings were important social gatherings, and everyone, especially the men, would have dressed to reflect their status and respect for the occasion.

- Grooming: James would have been clean-shaven or worn subtle sideburns, as facial hair trends at the time leaned toward a more polished, clean-cut look. His hair, likely cut short, would have been styled neatly, possibly with light powder to give it a fashionable appearance.

- Behavior and Manners: In addition to his appearance, James would have displayed impeccable manners. Weddings were not just family affairs but also public displays of one's upbringing and character. As a 27-year-old gentleman, James would have been expected to engage in polite conversation, show deference to older relatives, and participate in any traditional formalities, such as giving a toast or escorting guests.

- Cultural Context: The year 1800 was marked by significant social and political changes, with the Irish Rebellion of 1798 still fresh in people's minds. Although weddings were a time for celebration, the political climate might have influenced conversations during the event, and James, being an educated gentleman, would have been well aware of these larger societal issues. His conversation with other guests may have touched on current events, but the focus would likely remain on celebrating Jane's marriage.

- Emotional Impact: As James was close to his family, the marriage of his sister would have been an emotional and joyous occasion for him. It would have solidified family ties, and he may have viewed it as part of his own family's progression and legacy. His role as a brother during the ceremony and festivities would have been a source of pride.

In summary, James would have carefully chosen an elegant outfit that reflected the fashion and expectations of the time. He would have been a polished, respectful presence at his sister's wedding, both in his appearance and in his conduct.

When James Benning married Charlotte on September 18, 1801, at St. Peter's, Dublin, his attire would have reflected the fashion of the Regency era, characterized by elegance, simplicity, and a departure from the more extravagant styles of the earlier Georgian period.

Likely Attire for James Benning:

1. Tailcoat:

- James would have worn a dark-colored tailcoat, likely in navy, black, or a dark green. Tailcoats were a staple of formal wear at the time, with a cutaway front and long tails at the back. The lapels were often high and slightly exaggerated.

- The coat would have been fitted to the body, with buttons either decorative or functional down the front.

2. Waistcoat:

- Underneath the tailcoat, he would have worn a waistcoat, likely of a lighter color, such as cream, pale yellow, or even patterned with subtle stripes or embroidery. The waistcoat was a key piece, adding contrast to the darker tailcoat.

- Waistcoats were often made of silk or fine wool and could be single- or double-breasted.

3. Shirt and Cravat:

- The shirt would have been white and made of linen, with a high collar to support the cravat. Cravats were wide strips of fabric wrapped around the neck and tied in elaborate knots at the throat.

- James likely wore a white or cream-colored cravat, tied neatly in a style popular during the Regency era, such as the "stock" or "waterfall" knot.

4. Breeches:
- Breeches were still in fashion for formal occasions in 1801. James would have worn knee-length breeches in a neutral or matching color to his tailcoat, made from fine wool or silk. They were fastened just below the knee with buttons or buckles.
- Breeches would have been worn with stockings that reached up to the knee, usually in white or off-white.

5. Footwear:
- On his feet, James would have worn formal leather shoes, likely black, with a small heel and either buckles or laces. Buckled shoes were still common at the turn of the century, though lace-up shoes were starting to become fashionable as well.

6. Accessories:
- For a formal occasion like his wedding, James may have worn white gloves and carried a top hat, which had become a fashionable accessory for gentlemen by the early 1800s.
- He would have also worn a fob watch, likely attached to his waistcoat by a chain.

7. Hair and Grooming:
- During this period, men's hairstyles were transitioning from the powdered wigs of the 18th century to a more natural look. James might have worn his hair cut short and brushed forward, styled in the fashion of the day. Powdered wigs were becoming less common but were still worn by some, especially for formal occasions.
- He would have been clean-shaven, as facial hair was not in style during the early 19th century.

Overall Look:

James would have presented a formal, refined appearance, appropriate for a man of his standing in Dublin society. His attire would have reflected the elegant yet subdued style of the Regency era, focusing on clean lines, dark colors, and sophisticated accessories.

The listing of "gentleman" as James Benning's occupation on his marriage certificate reflects his social status rather than a specific job or trade. At the time, the term "gentleman" was used to describe a man of means, who did not need to work for a living or was engaged in a professional career such as law, medicine, or military service.

What "Gentleman" Meant in 1801:

- Social Standing: Being a "gentleman" implied that James came from a respectable, well-off family and was considered part of the upper middle or upper classes. His family's connections, land holdings, or investments would likely have supported his status.

- Education: It often indicated that James had received a good education, potentially in classical studies, philosophy, and languages, which were common for someone of his rank.

- Conduct: The title also referred to his expected behavior—he would have been known for good manners, refined behavior, and participation in social obligations, such as charity, church functions, and civic duties.

- Property Ownership: In some cases, being called a gentleman indicated property ownership, though it wasn't required. James may have owned or stood to inherit land or investments that would maintain his standing.

Impact on Marriage:

Being listed as a gentleman on his marriage certificate would have signaled that he was a respectable and suitable match for Charlotte, likely from a family of similar or slightly lower status. His prospects and the social prestige of being a gentleman would have reflected well on both families, contributing to the match's approval.

Profession and Future:

Although "gentleman" indicated that James wasn't engaged in labor-intensive work, he could still have had professional pursuits, particularly in areas like law, business, or military service, common for men of such standing who had both time and financial means.

ELEANOR (BENNING) DALWAY[14]

When Eleanor Jones Benning was born in 1776 in the Diocese of Meath, Ireland, she entered a world shaped by significant historical, social, and political factors. Here's a glimpse of what life was like during that period:

Historical Context:

1. American Revolution (1775-1783): Eleanor was born in the midst of the American Revolutionary War. While this conflict primarily took place across the Atlantic, it had ripple effects in Ireland and the rest of the British Empire. The war put pressure on the British economy and raised questions about governance, taxation, and the role of colonies. Irish politics were also influenced by these events, as some Irish nationalists saw the American struggle as inspiration for their own independence efforts.

2. British Rule in Ireland: Ireland was under British rule, and political power was concentrated in the hands of the Protestant Ascendancy, a privileged class of landowners and clergy who were Anglican (Church of Ireland). Catholics and Presbyterians faced significant restrictions under the Penal Laws, which limited their rights to own property, vote, or hold public office. Eleanor's father, as an archdeacon in the Church of Ireland, would have been part of this elite Protestant establishment.

Religious and Social Landscape:

1. Church of Ireland: The Diocese of Meath, part of the Anglican Church of Ireland, was one of the most important ecclesiastical regions in the country. The Church of Ireland was the established church, supported by tithes from landowners, including many who were not members of the church (mostly Catholics). Eleanor's father, as an archdeacon, held a significant religious position and would have been well-respected in the community.

2. Catholic Majority: While the Church of Ireland was the official state church, the majority of the population in the Diocese of Meath, as in the rest of Ireland, was Roman Catholic. Catholics faced many legal and social restrictions, but they continued to practice their faith, often in secret or under difficult conditions. The Benning family, as part of the Protestant elite, would have lived in a relatively privileged position but within a society divided along religious and class lines.

Social Class and Family Life:

1. Protestant Elite: As the daughter of an archdeacon, Eleanor was born into the Protestant Ascendancy, the upper class in Ireland at the time. This meant she would have had access to a relatively comfortable life, likely growing up in a well-furnished house with servants. Education and religious instruction would have been important in her upbringing, and she may have received formal schooling, especially since the Church of Ireland valued education for its clergy and their families.

2. Rural and Agricultural Setting: The Diocese of Meath was predominantly rural, with agriculture being the main economic activity. Large estates were owned by the Protestant elite, while much of the Catholic majority worked the land as tenant farmers. The rural landscape of the diocese would have been dotted with small villages, churches, and large country estates. Eleanor would

have been familiar with this agricultural economy and the class divisions that came with it.

Political Tensions and Reforms:

1. Calls for Reform: The late 18th century saw increasing demands for political reform in Ireland. The Irish Parliament, while technically independent from Britain, was controlled by the Protestant elite. There were growing movements, both among the Protestant middle class and some Catholics, for greater political representation and economic reforms. These movements would eventually lead to the Irish Rebellion of 1798, but in the 1770s, they were still in their early stages.

2. Volunteers and Nationalism: By the late 1770s, the formation of the Irish Volunteers, a militia composed of Protestants, reflected a growing sense of Irish identity and desire for self-governance. Though initially formed to defend against possible French invasion during the American War, the Volunteers later became a political force advocating for greater autonomy for Ireland. Eleanor would have grown up in an environment where these ideas were discussed, particularly among the Protestant elite.

Life for Women in the 18th Century:

1. Gender Roles: In the 18th century, women's roles were primarily domestic. Eleanor, as the daughter of a clergyman, would have been raised to be well-mannered, educated in household management, and prepared for marriage. Upper-class women like her were often taught skills such as needlework, music, and perhaps reading and writing, but their primary function was to manage the household and raise children.

2. Marriage and Dowries: As she grew older, Eleanor's family would likely have been concerned with finding her a suitable husband. Marriages among the Protestant elite were often arranged to secure alliances and maintain social status. Her dowry would have been an important factor in securing a favorable match.

Cultural and Intellectual Climate:

1. Enlightenment Ideas: The 18th century was the Age of Enlightenment, a period of intellectual and cultural development. Ideas about reason, science, and individual rights were spreading across Europe and influencing educated classes, including the Protestant elite in Ireland. Eleanor's father, as a clergyman, might have been engaged in discussions about these new ideas, particularly as they related to religion and governance.

2. The Arts and Literature: The 1770s were also a time of flourishing arts and literature. Dublin, in particular, had a vibrant cultural scene, with theaters, literature, and music. While living in a rural setting, Eleanor may have had some exposure to this cultural life through her family's connections to the Church of Ireland and the Protestant Ascendancy.

Conclusion:

When Eleanor Jones Benning was born in 1776, she entered a world shaped by political upheaval, religious divisions, and intellectual change. As the daughter of an influential clergyman, she would have grown up in a privileged environment, surrounded by the values and expectations of the Protestant elite. Her life would have been influenced by the political tensions of the time, as well as by the intellectual currents of the Enlightenment, while her family's position in the Church of Ireland would have provided her with security and status in a rapidly changing Ireland.

When Eleanor Jones Benning was just one year old in 1776 and her father, Archdeacon Benning, received his LL.D (Doctor of Laws), the immediate effect on her life would likely have been indirect, given her young age. However, there would have been several key impacts on her upbringing and family environment as a result of her father's academic achievement:

Social Status and Family Reputation:

- Enhanced Family Status: Achieving an LL.D would have significantly boosted her father's social and professional standing. In 18th-century Ireland, advanced academic qualifications, especially in law or theology, were highly respected. This would have elevated the family's status within the Protestant Ascendancy, increasing their social prestige in the Diocese of Meath and beyond. Eleanor would have grown up in a household that commanded more respect and influence, which could have impacted her own future prospects, including marriage and social connections.

- Connections and Influence: As the daughter of a well-educated and distinguished man, Eleanor would have been part of an intellectual and socially connected family. Her father's new credentials would likely have opened doors to higher-ranking circles within the Anglican Church and the elite, bringing more prestigious visitors and interactions into her life as she grew up.

Educational Environment:

- Emphasis on Education: While Eleanor was only an infant at the time, her father's academic achievements likely set a tone in the household that valued education and learning. This emphasis would have trickled down to her as she grew older, possibly giving her access to better educational opportunities, such as private tutors or access to books and intellectual discussions within the family. It was common for the children of clergymen, especially those with prestigious degrees, to be well-educated, even the daughters, who were often groomed to become well-mannered and cultured women.

Financial Stability and Future Prospects:

- Financial Stability: An LL.D would have likely resulted in more lucrative opportunities for her father, including potential higher ecclesiastical appointments, legal consultancies, or other influential positions. This financial stability could have translated into a more comfortable upbringing for Eleanor, with the possibility of living in a well-appointed home, access to finer clothing, and the means to secure advantageous marriage prospects.

- Marriage Prospects: As Eleanor grew older, the prestige of her father's academic qualifications would likely have enhanced her marriage prospects. In the 18th century, a woman's marriage was often influenced by her family's social standing, and being the daughter of a respected clergyman with a doctorate would have made her an attractive prospect for a potential suitor from a similarly prestigious family.

Cultural Influence:

- Intellectual Environment: The attainment of a high-level degree like an LL.D would also likely have brought Eleanor into contact with the intellectual and cultural life of her time. Her father, being an educated man, would have been part of the intellectual conversations and debates of the era, especially regarding religion, law, and governance. This intellectual atmosphere could have subtly influenced Eleanor's worldview and upbringing, giving her a broader perspective on life than many of her contemporaries.

Emotional Impact:

- Family Pride: As Eleanor grew older and became more aware of her father's achievements, she would likely have taken pride in being part of a family with such an esteemed and well-educated patriarch. This could have shaped her self-perception and confidence, knowing that she came from a family of status and influence.

Conclusion:

While Eleanor's young age at the time of her father's receipt of an LL.D in 1776 meant she would not have immediately understood its significance, the achievement would have shaped the environment in which she was raised. Her father's increased social standing and intellectual stature would have provided her with opportunities for a more privileged upbringing, better education, and more advantageous social connections, all of which would have influenced her development and future prospects.

BETWEEN THE AGES OF 1 and 8, Eleanor Jones Benning would have experienced the American Revolution (1775-1783) primarily through the lens of her family and community in Ireland. While she would not have been directly impacted by the conflict, there are several ways the American Revolution could have affected her upbringing during those years.

1. Political Climate and Conversations at Home

- Influence of the Political Atmosphere: The American Revolution was a significant event not only in America but also in Britain and Ireland, as it challenged the authority of the British Crown and raised questions about governance, liberty, and colonialism. As the daughter of a prominent clergyman with an LL.D., Eleanor would likely have been raised in a household where political discussions were common. Her father and other family members might have engaged in conversations about the war, British policies, and the implications for the British Empire. Although she would have been too young to fully grasp the details, the tone of these discussions could have shaped her early understanding of loyalty to the Crown and the tension between colonial independence and British authority.

- Family's Loyalty to the British Crown: Given her father's position as a clergyman in the Anglican Church, it is likely that her family was loyal to the British Crown and supported the British side of the conflict. This would have influenced the household's view of the American Revolution, portraying the American rebels as challengers to the established order. Growing up with this narrative could have shaped Eleanor's sense of British identity and loyalty to the monarchy.

2. Economic Impact

- Economic Repercussions in Ireland: While Ireland was not directly involved in the American Revolution, the war had economic consequences for the British Empire and its territories. Trade disruptions, military expenditures, and changes in global markets could have indirectly affected the Irish economy. If her family was affected by any economic downturns or shifts in trade, Eleanor might have experienced changes in her family's financial situation, such as tightened budgets or fluctuations in the availability of goods. However, given her father's role as an Anglican clergyman with a secure position, any economic impact on her family would likely have been moderate compared to others.

3. Social and Cultural Influence

- Increased Awareness of Rebellion and Change: The American Revolution was a symbol of rebellion against established authority, and this idea of challenging the status quo could have influenced the intellectual and cultural environment in which Eleanor grew up. Even though she was in Ireland, the revolution may have sparked discussions about freedom, governance, and reform. This could have subtly affected the way she understood societal hierarchies, power dynamics, and change as she matured.

- Reflection on Irish Colonial Status: Ireland, like the American colonies, was under British control during the revolution. The American fight for independence may have resonated with some Irish people, particularly those who were dissatisfied with British rule. While Eleanor was likely too young to engage with these political ideas directly, the revolution may have stirred sentiments in her community about Ireland's own relationship with Britain. Over time, these discussions could have influenced her perspective on Ireland's political situation and her own national identity.

4. Family and Community Impact

- Potential for Family Members in the Military: Many Irishmen fought for the British during the American Revolution, either in the British Army or as part of local militias. If Eleanor's extended family or community members were involved in the conflict, it might have created a sense of anxiety or pride depending on their involvement. Stories of the war and those fighting in it could have filtered into Eleanor's early childhood, shaping her understanding of conflict and the role of soldiers in protecting the empire.

- Effect on Social Life and Community Discussions: In a small community like the one Eleanor lived in, news about the war would have spread through church services, town meetings, and social gatherings. The adults around her would have discussed the progress of the war, important battles, and the eventual British defeat. Even if she didn't fully understand these discussions as a child, they would have formed part of the backdrop of her early life, influencing her awareness of the wider world and the political issues of the day.

5. Impact on Religious Identity

- Church's Role During the Conflict: As the daughter of an Anglican clergyman, Eleanor's family would have been aligned with the Church of England, which had strong ties to the British monarchy. The American Revolution had religious as well as political implications, as many of the American colonists were dissenters from the Church of England. The conflict may have been framed in her household as a challenge not just to British authority but also to the Anglican Church's influence. This might have reinforced Eleanor's identification with the church and its role in maintaining order and tradition within the British Empire.

Conclusion:

While Eleanor would not have directly experienced the violence or upheaval of the American Revolution, the political, social, and economic ramifications of the war would have indirectly influenced her early childhood. Growing up in a loyalist, Anglican household, she would have been exposed to conversations and attitudes that emphasized loyalty to the Crown and the established social order. The revolution might also have shaped her awareness of rebellion and change, which could have subtly influenced her worldview as she matured. Overall, her young age during the conflict means its impact would have been felt more through her family's reactions and the broader community's response than through any personal engagement with the war itself.

When Eleanor Jones Benning was 2 years old, her sister, Millicent Mary, was born in 1777. At that young age, the arrival of a new sibling would have had several effects on her:

1. Emotional Impact

- Shift in Attention: At 2 years old, Eleanor would have been used to receiving a significant amount of attention from her parents and caregivers. The birth of a younger sibling would have shifted some of that attention toward Millicent, which could have caused Eleanor to feel a sense of jealousy or displacement. She might have struggled to adjust to sharing her parents' time and affection with her newborn sister.

- New Role as an Older Sibling: Although Eleanor was still very young, she would have gradually been introduced to the concept of being a "big sister." Even at such a young age, children often sense the expectations placed on them, and Eleanor may have been encouraged to help in small ways or to be gentle with her new sibling. This would have been a time of emotional adjustment, learning to interact with and care for her younger sister.

2. Household Dynamics

- Changes in Routine: The birth of a baby often brings changes to the household routine. Eleanor's daily schedule might have shifted to accommodate the needs of the newborn. There may have been more noise, busier days, and new people coming and going from the house, such as midwives or visitors congratulating the family. All of these changes could have impacted how Eleanor experienced her day-to-day life.

- Increased Time with Other Caregivers: With her mother, Ann Ellis Benning, focused on the care of the newborn, Eleanor may have spent more time with other family members, caregivers, or her father, Archdeacon Conway Benning (when he was not traveling). This could have given her more independence or a stronger bond with other relatives.

3. Developmental Effects

- Early Socialization: The presence of a sibling could have enhanced Eleanor's early social development. She would have started to learn how to share, interact, and play with someone else, even if Millicent was still a baby. This experience of having another child in the household may have encouraged Eleanor to develop empathy, patience, and social skills at an earlier age.

- Potential Jealousy: As a 2-year-old, Eleanor might not have fully understood why her mother had to focus so much on the new baby. This could have led to occasional feelings of jealousy or frustration, especially if Eleanor still required a lot of care and attention herself.

4. Emotional Bonding

- Long-Term Bond with Millicent: Although Eleanor was very young when Millicent was born, the arrival of a sibling could have laid the foundation for a strong emotional bond between the two sisters. Over time, as they grew up together, Eleanor might have developed a protective, nurturing relationship with her younger sister. Sharing a home and growing up in the same environment could have brought them close, despite any initial feelings of jealousy or rivalry.

5. Impact of Father's Absence

- Absence of Her Father During Millicent's Birth: Since their father, Archdeacon Conway Benning, was traveling the continent during this period, his absence would have affected both Eleanor and Millicent. Eleanor might have felt her father's absence more acutely with the arrival of a new sibling, as she would have had less of both parents' attention. However, his return from travel might have also been a time of joy and adjustment for the growing family, bringing a sense of stability back to the household.

Conclusion:

Eleanor's sister Millicent's birth would have been a significant event in her early life. At 2 years old, Eleanor might have experienced a mix of emotions, including confusion, jealousy, and curiosity, as her household dynamics changed. Over time, she would have adjusted to her new role as a big sister, and the arrival of Millicent likely helped shape her emotional and social development. Additionally, with their father traveling, Eleanor may have leaned more on her mother and other caregivers during this transitional time.

When Eleanor was three years old in 1778, her father, Conway Benning, was instituted as the vicar of Rathmolyen, and the family lived primarily at Kilroot. This event would have had several impacts on young Eleanor's life, both directly and indirectly:

1. Relocation or New Surroundings

- Moving to Kilroot: If the family had previously been living elsewhere, the institution of her father to the vicarage may have meant a move to Kilroot, a small, rural village. Moving at a young age can be a significant change for children. While Eleanor might not have fully understood the reasons for the move, she would have experienced a new environment, with different scenery, people, and routines.

- Rural Life at Kilroot: Kilroot was a quiet, rural village, which would have provided Eleanor with a peaceful environment to grow up in. Surrounded by the natural landscape of County Antrim, Northern Ireland, she would have been exposed to the rhythms of rural life. This might have included interactions with the local community, farm life, and the church parishioners. These experiences would have shaped her early childhood, providing a stable and nurturing backdrop to her development.

2. Impact of Father's New Role

- Father's Increased Responsibilities: As the vicar of Rathmolyen, Conway Benning would have taken on new responsibilities, which might have required more of his time and attention. His duties in the parish would have included pastoral care, overseeing the spiritual needs of the community, and administering the church. Eleanor may have noticed that her father was busy with church duties and the community, though at her young age, she might not have fully understood the significance of his role.

- Status of the Vicar's Family: Being the daughter of a vicar would have placed Eleanor and her family in a position of respect and prominence within the local community. Although she was still very young, Eleanor would have grown up with a sense of her family's standing within the parish. Her father's role likely instilled values of faith, duty, and service, which would have been central to her upbringing.

3. The Influence of Church Life

- Exposure to Religion: Growing up in a vicarage, Eleanor would have been exposed to church life from an early age. The church would have been a central part of her family's life, and she would have participated in religious services and activities regularly. This early immersion in the church would have influenced her worldview and upbringing, instilling a sense of spirituality and community from a young age.

- Community Involvement: As the daughter of the vicar, Eleanor would likely have been involved in community activities and events connected to the church. She may have accompanied her parents to church gatherings, festivals, and charitable activities, developing an early understanding of social responsibility and community care.

4. Stability of Family Life

- Growing Family: With her sister Millicent born a year earlier, Eleanor was growing up in a household with young siblings. Her father's new position would have provided financial stability and security for the family, giving Eleanor a relatively comfortable upbringing. The family's residence at Kilroot would have offered a stable environment where she could form early relationships with her siblings, parents, and the local community.

- Support from Other Family Members: With her father taking on more responsibilities, Eleanor might have spent more time with her mother, Ann Ellis Benning, and possibly other caregivers. This would have deepened her bond with her mother and influenced her early development in terms of learning social and familial roles.

5. Early Socialization and Education

- Opportunities for Education: As the daughter of a learned man, Eleanor likely had access to a good education, even in her early years. Her father's academic background, especially having received his LL.D., would have placed a strong emphasis on learning and education in the household. Although formal schooling might not have started yet, Eleanor could have been exposed to reading, writing, and religious instruction at home.

- Interactions with Parishioners: Being part of a vicar's family would have meant that Eleanor had regular interactions with the local community. She would have been introduced to people from different walks of life, helping to broaden her social experiences. These interactions would have developed her early social skills and her understanding of the world outside her family.

Conclusion

At three years old, Eleanor's life would have been influenced by her father's new role as the vicar of Rathmolyen and the family's residence at Kilroot. This would have provided her with a stable, religious, and community-oriented upbringing. The experience of living in a rural village, the exposure to church life, and the responsibilities of being part of the vicar's family would have shaped her early social and emotional development, as well as her future outlook on faith, community, and family.

When Eleanor was four years old in 1779, her younger sister, Jane, was born in Carrickfergus. This event would have had several effects on Eleanor, both emotionally and within her family dynamics:

1. New Responsibilities as an Older Sister

- Shift in Attention: As the eldest child, Eleanor may have experienced a shift in her parents' attention with the arrival of a newborn. At four years old, she was old enough to notice changes in family dynamics as her mother and father focused on caring for the new baby. This could have brought some feelings of rivalry or confusion, especially if she was used to being the center of attention.

- Developing a Caregiving Role: Eleanor might have been encouraged to help care for her newborn sister, which could have instilled a sense of responsibility and nurturing. While she was still young herself, many children in this era took on small tasks to help with younger siblings. This experience could have shaped her sense of family duty and attachment to her younger siblings.

2. Emotional Response to a New Sibling

- Excitement or Curiosity: Eleanor may have felt excited or curious about her new baby sister. At four years old, children are often intrigued by babies and enjoy being involved in their care, even in small ways like fetching items or simply observing. The arrival of Jane would have been a significant event in Eleanor's life, and she might have been eager to play a role as the "big sister."

- Jealousy or Insecurity: On the other hand, Eleanor could have experienced some feelings of jealousy, as the arrival of a new sibling sometimes leads to competition for parental attention. This was a common reaction in young children, especially in families where parental time and resources were more focused on the care of infants.

3. Strengthened Family Bonds

- Developing Sisterly Bonds: The birth of Jane marked the beginning of what could have developed into a close sisterly relationship as the two girls grew older. As they shared the same household and upbringing, their early years together would lay the foundation for their bond. Eleanor may have seen herself as a protector or guide to her younger sister as they both navigated their childhood.

- Shared Childhood Experiences: Growing up together in the same family, Eleanor and Jane would have shared many experiences, including education, religious teachings, and social activities. Even though Eleanor was four years older, they would likely have played together, creating memories and learning from each other.

4. Impact of Living in Carrickfergus

- Life in Carrickfergus: Carrickfergus was a historic town with a strong sense of community, and living there in the late 18th century would have been quite structured around family life and local traditions. With the arrival of another sibling, Eleanor's experience of Carrickfergus would have expanded as her family grew. The town's close-knit atmosphere would have meant that the birth of a new child was a significant event, celebrated by neighbors and the wider community.

- Adaptation to a Growing Household: As the family adjusted to the arrival of Jane, Eleanor would have observed how her parents, particularly her mother, managed a growing household. This could have provided her with early lessons in family management and caregiving, traits that would be valuable later in life.

Conclusion

The birth of Eleanor's younger sister, Jane, in 1779 would have had a significant impact on her early childhood. As a four-year-old, Eleanor likely experienced a mix of emotions, from excitement about her new sister to potential feelings of jealousy. Over time, however, the shared experiences of growing up in Carrickfergus and being part of a religious and community-focused family would have shaped Eleanor's sense of responsibility and her bond with Jane.

When Eleanor was 5 years old, in 1783, the first successful hot air balloon flight took place in France, an event that would have captured the imagination of people around the world. Although she was a young child and the event occurred far from her home in Ireland, there are several ways this achievement might have influenced or affected her:

1. Sense of Wonder and Imagination

- Childlike Fascination with Flight: At five years old, Eleanor likely had a vivid imagination. News of a balloon flying through the sky, a previously unthinkable idea, could have sparked her sense of wonder and curiosity. Even though she may not have fully understood the science behind it, the idea of humans taking to the air would have been thrilling, akin to hearing a magical story.

Adults around her might have talked about it with awe, fueling her own excitement.

- Inspiring Play and Stories: Eleanor may have incorporated the idea of flight into her playtime or her imagination, imagining what it would be like to fly in the sky. Stories about flying, whether shared by adults or invented in her own mind, could have become part of her childhood daydreams.

2. Family Conversations and Community Buzz

- Parental Influence: Her father, Archdeacon Conway Benning, was an educated man, and it's likely that he would have heard about the flight and perhaps even discussed it at home. Eleanor may have listened to her parents talk about the wonder of this achievement, picking up on their amazement or intrigue. In an era when such news spread slowly, any major event like this would have been a topic of conversation in educated households and communities.

- Community Conversations: Even if the news took some time to reach Carrickfergus, where she lived, it would eventually have been a popular subject of discussion, especially among those who were interested in science or new inventions. Local talk of "men flying in the air" would have created a sense of marvel in the community, which Eleanor might have absorbed from the adults around her.

3. A Broader Understanding of the World

- Expanding Worldview: Although Eleanor was still very young, hearing about a human achievement as groundbreaking as flying could have expanded her sense of what was possible in the world. This event, combined with the travels of her father, could have helped Eleanor start to understand that amazing things were happening beyond her immediate surroundings in Ireland.

- First Glimpse into Scientific Innovation: Growing up in a time when major scientific breakthroughs were starting to take shape, this event could have been her earliest exposure to the possibilities of human ingenuity. Even though she might not have grasped the significance, the concept of progress and discovery was part of the world she was being raised in. As she grew older, she might reflect on this as one of the first big milestones of her lifetime.

4. Emotional Impact

- Excitement About the Future: For a five-year-old, learning about a hot air balloon flight would have been an awe-inspiring and almost fantastical event. It might have fostered a sense of excitement about the future and an understanding that the world was full of surprising developments.

- Dreams of Adventure: Like many children, Eleanor might have imagined herself participating in such adventures, dreaming of flying through the sky or taking part in other grand explorations. Even if it was just for fun, it could have fostered a sense of adventure and curiosity about the world.

Conclusion

While Eleanor, being only five years old in 1783, might not have fully grasped the technical details of the first hot air balloon flight, the event would still have inspired a sense of wonder and excitement. It may have contributed to her early sense of a broader world full of possibilities, and it would certainly have been a talking point in her community and home. The achievement would have sparked her imagination, perhaps leaving a lasting impression as she grew up during a time of rapid discovery and innovation.

When Eleanor Jones Benning married Noah on May 22, 1795, at 20 years old, her wedding attire would have reflected the fashion trends of the late 18th century. During this period, wedding dresses were typically chosen for their practicality, as they were often worn again for other formal occasions, rather than being a one-time garment. Here's what she may have worn:

Style of Dress

- Empire Waist Gown: By the 1790s, the high-waisted silhouette of the *Empire* style had become fashionable. Eleanor likely wore a gown with a fitted bodice ending just below the bust, and a loose, flowing skirt that reached to the floor. This was an elegant but comfortable style, ideal for formal events like a wedding.

- Natural Colors: Unlike the white wedding dresses that became popular later in the 19th century, wedding gowns of the 1790s were often made in soft colors like ivory, pale blue, lavender, or delicate pastels. Eleanor's dress might have been made from silk, satin, or muslin, which were popular fabrics of the time. Ivory or a soft champagne tone would have conveyed both elegance and a sense of occasion.

- Delicate Embellishments: Her dress may have featured light embellishments such as lace trims, embroidery, or small floral details. These were often subtle and refined, adding to the dress's overall delicacy without overwhelming the simplicity of the design.

Accessories

- Bonnet or Veil: Although veils were not yet a widespread wedding tradition, Eleanor might have worn a fashionable bonnet or cap made of fine lace or silk. This would have completed her outfit in keeping with the modesty and elegance of the time.

- Gloves: Gloves were an essential part of formal attire for women in the 18th century. She likely wore light-colored gloves, possibly made of kid leather or silk, to complement her gown and maintain decorum.

- Jewelry: Eleanor may have accessorized with simple, elegant jewelry, such as a string of pearls or a delicate necklace and earrings made of gold or silver. Jewelry at the time was usually understated, meant to enhance rather than overshadow the rest of the attire.

- Shoes: Her shoes would likely have been made of silk or satin, in a color matching her gown. They would have had a slight heel and been decorated with small bows or ribbons. These shoes were often dainty and not meant for long wear, as they were designed for special occasions.

Hairstyle

- Soft, Curled Hair: Hairstyles in the 1790s were starting to become more natural compared to the towering powdered wigs of earlier decades. Eleanor may have worn her hair softly curled and pinned up, with a few tendrils framing her face. If she followed fashion closely, she might have added a small tiara or headpiece to further highlight her bridal look.

Conclusion

Eleanor's wedding attire in 1795 would have been a beautiful blend of practicality and elegance, featuring the soft, flowing lines of the Empire style gown, complemented by refined accessories and understated jewelry. Her look would have been fashionable yet modest, reflecting the sensibilities of the time and her social standing as the daughter of an Archdeacon.

ELIZABETH BOYD[15]

Elizabeth Boyd, the daughter of Archibald Boyd, passed away on July 20, 1716, and was buried in Dervock, Ireland. To imagine what she might have looked like and the context of her life, we can piece together general aspects of her appearance and the environment in Ireland at the time.

What Elizabeth Boyd Might Have Looked Like:

As we don't have specific details about her physical appearance, we can only make assumptions based on common traits and styles of the time:

- Clothing: Elizabeth would have dressed according to her social class. By 1716, women's fashion in Ireland was influenced by broader European styles, especially from England and France. She might have worn long dresses made of wool, linen, or silk depending on her family's wealth, with a fitted bodice and wide skirts, sometimes adorned with lace or ribbons. Modest head coverings such as bonnets or caps were common for women, especially for those from religious or conservative families.

- Hair: Women typically wore their hair pinned up, often in tight curls or styled into buns, sometimes covered with a cap. For formal occasions, the wealthier classes might have added decorative pins or small pieces of lace to their hair.

- Health and Body Shape: Considering the era, life expectancy was relatively low, and diseases or hardships could affect physical appearance. If Elizabeth was in her later years, she might have had a frailer build with wrinkles, possibly worn teeth due to a lack of modern dental care, and signs of wear from daily life. However, women were often expected to appear modest and well-kept in public settings, so her clothing and grooming would reflect the values of her time.

Life in Ireland in 1716:

In 1716, Ireland was in a period of significant political, social, and religious transition. The key events and conditions that would have shaped Elizabeth's life at the time include:

1. Political Climate:

- Post-Williamite Wars: The Williamite Wars, which took place between 1689 and 1691, had a profound impact on Ireland. The Protestant King William III of England defeated the Catholic King James II, securing Protestant control of Ireland. This led to significant social and political changes, with the Protestant Ascendancy consolidating power in the country.

- Penal Laws: By the time of Elizabeth's death, the Penal Laws had been enacted to restrict the rights of Catholics and dissenting Protestants (such as Presbyterians). These laws were meant to ensure the dominance of the Anglican Church of Ireland, and they imposed restrictions on property ownership, education, and religious practice for Catholics and non-Anglican Protestants. If Elizabeth was from a Protestant family, especially an Anglican one, her family might have benefited from the laws. If she was part of the dissenting Protestant community, her family might have faced social and political limitations.

2. Economic Conditions:

- The early 18th century in Ireland was marked by widespread poverty and agrarian unrest. While the ruling Protestant class often controlled large estates and lived relatively comfortably, many tenant farmers, especially Catholics, struggled to make a living. Rents were high, and the agricultural economy was vulnerable to crop failures and harsh winters.

- The linen industry was beginning to grow, especially in Ulster (Northern Ireland), where Dervock is located. If Elizabeth's family had connections to this emerging industry, they might have been involved in the weaving or trading of linen, which would have provided economic stability.

3. Social and Religious Life:

- Religion played a central role in everyday life. The Protestant community, particularly the Anglicans, held a privileged position. However, many Presbyterians and Catholics lived under significant legal and social restrictions due to the Penal Laws. Church attendance, family life, and community events would have revolved around religious institutions.

- If Elizabeth was part of the Protestant Ascendancy, her life would have been relatively secure, and she would have enjoyed certain social privileges. She might have been part of a landowning family or involved in the social circles of the Anglican Church. On the other hand, if her family were Presbyterians, they may have faced more challenges, despite being Protestant, due to the Anglican domination.

4. Local Life in Dervock, County Antrim:

- Dervock, located in County Antrim, was a rural area at the time, largely dominated by farming and small-scale local industries. Families in such areas lived close-knit lives, with communities centered around the church and the land.

- Community Life: Life in rural towns like Dervock would have been community-oriented, with church attendance, farming, and small-scale trades making up daily routines. Social status was often determined by land ownership, religious affiliation, and one's standing within the community.

Conclusion:

By the time of her death in 1716, Elizabeth Boyd likely led a life that was shaped by the political and religious dynamics of post-Williamite Ireland. If she came from a Protestant family, especially one tied to the Anglican Church, she may have enjoyed relative privilege, but also would have witnessed or experienced the tensions between different religious groups. Her appearance and manner of living would have reflected the modesty and formality of the era, with practical clothing and simple, yet dignified, habits fitting for a woman of her standing in rural Ireland.

GEORGE BOYD[16]

In 1609, George Boyd's birth likely took place in a time of significant political, religious, and social changes, particularly in Ireland and the broader context of Britain. Here's an overview of what life may have been like in 1609, especially in Ireland:

1. Ireland in 1609:

- Plantation of Ulster: One of the most significant events occurring in Ireland around 1609 was the *Plantation of Ulster*, which began in earnest that year. Following the Nine Years' War and the Flight of the Earls in 1607, the English Crown initiated a large-scale colonization project. Land in Ulster, previously held by Gaelic Irish chieftains, was confiscated and granted to settlers from Scotland and England. This created deep divisions between the Protestant settlers and the native Catholic Irish population.

- Political Landscape: Ireland in 1609 was largely under English rule, following the subjugation of Gaelic lords. English governance was expanding, particularly in areas like Ulster, where the Crown was attempting to enforce tighter control. Tensions between native Irish Catholics and English Protestants were rising, sowing the seeds for future conflict.

- Religion: The Reformation had led to the establishment of Protestantism as the state religion, but Ireland remained predominantly Catholic. The Catholic majority often faced discrimination and pressure to conform to Protestantism, which created religious strife throughout the country.

2. Social and Economic Life:

- Agrarian Society: Most of the population in Ireland at this time lived in rural areas and worked in agriculture. Life was challenging, with people primarily engaged in subsistence farming, growing crops like barley, oats, and potatoes, and raising livestock.

- Feudal System: The remnants of the Gaelic clan system were still influential, although it was declining under English rule. Local lords and chieftains held significant power, though many had fled or lost their land by 1609, particularly in the northern parts of the country.

- Daily Life: The majority of people lived in simple homes made from local materials like wattle and daub or stone. Families were large, and life expectancy was low, with disease, famine, and conflict regularly taking lives. The average person had few material possessions, and survival depended on cooperation within the family and community.

3. British Isles Context:

- James I of England: James I had become the King of England and Ireland (James VI of Scotland) in 1603. His reign was marked by efforts to unify the crowns of England, Scotland, and Ireland, and to establish peace after the long reign of Elizabeth I. His rule brought some stability, but also religious tension, as he was a Protestant king ruling over predominantly Catholic Ireland.

- Colonization Efforts: James I supported the colonization efforts in Ireland, particularly the *Plantation of Ulster*, which aimed to strengthen English rule and settle loyal Protestant Scots and Englishmen in Irish lands.

- Scientific and Cultural Advances: While rural life in Ireland remained difficult, the early 17th century was also a period of significant cultural and intellectual activity in Europe, known as the Renaissance. Advances in navigation, science, and the arts were occurring, but such developments would have had little immediate impact on rural Ireland, where the focus was on daily survival.

4. Key Events in 1609:

- Colonization of Ulster: As mentioned earlier, 1609 was a critical year in the colonization of Ulster, and it likely had a direct or indirect impact on George Boyd and his family, especially if they were involved in the settlement process or affected by the changes in land ownership.

- Settlement Patterns: Many Scots and English settlers were arriving in Ireland during this period, changing the demographic and cultural makeup of the northern part of the country. If George Boyd's family were among these settlers, they would have been part of this major historical transformation.

Conclusion:

George Boyd's birth in 1609 occurred during a pivotal period in Irish history. The country was undergoing significant social, political, and religious upheaval due to the growing influence of English rule, the plantation system, and tensions between Catholic and Protestant communities. Life would have been challenging, with a strong focus on survival and navigating the turbulent political landscape of the time. If George Boyd's family were involved in the colonization efforts, they would have been part of a major moment in Irish history that would shape the country for centuries.

When George Boyd was 34 years old and serving as a mayor, the invention of the barometer in 1643 by Evangelista Torricelli would have been an intriguing scientific advancement with potential practical implications for someone in his position. Here's how Boyd might have reacted and how the invention of the barometer could have affected him:

Potential Reaction:

1. Interest in Science and Innovation: As a mayor, Boyd would likely have been exposed to a range of intellectual and societal developments. The invention of the barometer would have been a

notable event in the scientific community. If Boyd had any interest in science or natural philosophy, the barometer could have been seen as a fascinating innovation that contributed to the growing body of knowledge about the natural world, especially the study of atmospheric pressure and weather patterns.

2. Practical Application in Governance: Boyd might not have been directly involved in scientific experiments, but as a mayor, he could have seen the potential for the barometer to improve local decision-making, especially concerning agriculture, trade, and maritime activities. In a time when weather predictions were highly valued for planning sea voyages or managing crops, a tool that could measure atmospheric pressure would have been very useful.

3. Advancement in Knowledge: The barometer's invention marked a leap forward in understanding atmospheric phenomena. This could have sparked conversations and curiosity among the educated elite, and Boyd, as a public figure, might have been part of discussions regarding the implications of this new device. As mayor, he would have been keenly aware of how scientific advancements could benefit his community.

Effect on George Boyd:

1. Improved Weather Prediction for Maritime and Agricultural Activities: The barometer was a game-changer in terms of weather forecasting. If Boyd's town was involved in agriculture or trade (especially maritime trade), the ability to predict weather changes more accurately using a barometer could have been a significant asset. It might have helped farmers better prepare for adverse weather conditions and enabled ship captains to avoid storms, improving safety and efficiency in trade.

2. Influence on Public Health and Safety: In his role as mayor, Boyd would have been responsible for the well-being of his town's inhabitants. With the barometer offering a more accurate understanding of weather patterns, it might have been used to

prepare the town for extreme weather, potentially reducing the risks of floods, droughts, or storms that could devastate the local economy and impact public health.

3. Increased Prestige of the Town: If Boyd embraced the use of new technologies like the barometer, it could have enhanced his reputation as a forward-thinking leader. Supporting the adoption of scientific tools for practical purposes (like weather prediction) would have reflected positively on his governance, possibly attracting more commerce or intellectual engagement to the town.

4. Connection to Broader Scientific Movements: The 17th century was a time of scientific discovery, and the invention of the barometer fit within the larger context of the Scientific Revolution. If Boyd was attuned to the intellectual currents of the time, he might have recognized the barometer as part of the broader movement towards empirical observation and experimentation. This could have led to an increased interest in other scientific tools and ideas.

Conclusion:

As a mayor, George Boyd would have likely viewed the invention of the barometer as both a curiosity and a practical tool with potential benefits for his community. Its application in weather prediction could have had a direct impact on agriculture and trade, key economic activities in his town. Additionally, Boyd's embrace of scientific advancements could have enhanced his standing as a progressive and competent leader, particularly if he found ways to apply such innovations for the benefit of the people he governed.

When George Boyd was 47 years old and serving as a mayor, the invention of the first accurate pendulum clock by Christiaan Huygens in 1656 would have been a major technological advancement that could have had various effects on his life and work.

Potential Reaction:

1. Fascination with Precision: The pendulum clock was revolutionary because it greatly improved timekeeping accuracy, reducing the margin of error from 15 minutes to less than 10 seconds per day. As a mayor, Boyd likely recognized the importance of time in governance, trade, and daily life. The ability to have more accurate timekeeping might have intrigued him, especially in an era when punctuality was becoming increasingly important in social and economic activities.

2. Interest in Innovation: The pendulum clock would have been a topic of conversation among intellectuals and the upper class. Boyd, as a public figure, might have taken interest in acquiring one of these clocks or at least understanding its importance. If he was involved in trade or public services, he would have been keenly aware of how the ability to keep time more accurately could affect business and civic operations.

3. Adoption for Public Use: As mayor, Boyd might have considered the public benefits of the pendulum clock. Accurate timekeeping could improve the coordination of civic activities, such as the regulation of markets, religious services, and legal proceedings. This new technology could also symbolize a town's advancement and prestige, perhaps prompting Boyd to consider installing such a clock in a public building or a town square.

Effect on George Boyd:

1. Improved Governance and Civic Operations: Accurate timekeeping would have had a direct impact on the way a town was managed. If Boyd integrated this technology into civic life, it could have improved scheduling for court sessions, council meetings, and other governmental duties. It also would have helped regulate local markets or public gatherings, making them more efficient and organized.

2. Impact on Trade and Commerce: Pendulum clocks made it easier to coordinate trade, especially in ports or markets. For a mayor like Boyd, accurate time could have helped merchants and traders ensure that transactions and deliveries were done punctually. This might have enhanced economic growth and efficiency in his town, especially if it was involved in trade or had a strong mercantile class.

3. Symbol of Prestige: Owning or having access to a pendulum clock in the town hall or another prominent location could have been seen as a status symbol. As a forward-thinking mayor, Boyd might have used the pendulum clock to elevate the town's standing, showing that it was modern and in touch with the latest technological advancements. This could have attracted more visitors or traders, further enhancing the town's reputation.

4. Increased Coordination with Religious Institutions: Churches often played a central role in the lives of people during the 17th century, and more accurate timekeeping would have allowed for more precise scheduling of religious services. This would ensure punctuality and better organization for daily prayers, festivals, and other important community gatherings. Boyd, as a mayor, would have valued this improvement in civic and religious life.

Conclusion:

The invention of the pendulum clock in 1656 would likely have had a significant effect on George Boyd as a mayor. It would have improved the management of both civic duties and trade, helped streamline public activities, and served as a symbol of prestige and modernization. Boyd might have embraced this technological advancement as a tool to enhance governance and demonstrate his town's sophistication and forward-thinking leadership.

When George Boyd was 58 years old and serving as a mayor, the first successful blood transfusion was performed in 1667 by

Jean-Baptiste Denis, a French physician. This groundbreaking medical achievement would have been remarkable news across Europe, and it could have impacted Boyd's worldview as a public figure.

Potential Reaction:

1. Astonishment and Curiosity: Boyd, like many others of his time, would likely have been fascinated by the news of this medical breakthrough. The idea of transferring blood to save lives was revolutionary and would have sparked curiosity and discussions among the educated and influential members of society. As a mayor, Boyd might have viewed this as a monumental step in the field of medicine.

2. Skepticism or Caution: While the idea of a blood transfusion might have piqued his interest, it is possible that Boyd, like many in his time, could have been cautious or even skeptical about the safety and ethics of such a procedure. Medical practices were still evolving, and new innovations often took time to be fully accepted. The idea of transfusing blood between species (since the first successful transfusions were from animals to humans) might have raised concerns about the implications for human health or religious and moral beliefs.

3. Interest in Its Practical Applications: Boyd may have recognized the potential practical implications of blood transfusions for the health and welfare of his community. Given the constant threat of disease and injury in the 17th century, Boyd could have seen this development as a hopeful advancement in saving lives, especially in times of war or illness.

Effect on George Boyd:

1. Enhanced Civic Responsibilities: As mayor, Boyd was likely involved in the health and well-being of his citizens. Hearing about this new medical practice might have encouraged him to support local physicians and medical advancements in his town. He may

have been interested in how this procedure could eventually benefit his community, particularly during outbreaks of illness or medical crises.

2. Public Health Awareness: The news of this medical breakthrough could have increased Boyd's awareness of the importance of health and medical progress. It might have prompted him to engage more closely with physicians or advocate for better medical care and practices within his jurisdiction.

3. Impact on Morale and Perception of Science: The 17th century was a time of great scientific progress. The blood transfusion, along with other medical and scientific advances, may have contributed to a growing sense of optimism regarding human capacity to solve problems and prolong life. Boyd, as an influential figure, could have been supportive of such progress, seeing it as a sign that humanity was moving toward a brighter and more enlightened future.

4. Reputation and Governance: If Boyd's town had any direct connections to medical professionals or scholars, he might have taken pride in being associated with these advancements. Encouraging or hosting medical discussions could have elevated the town's reputation and Boyd's standing as a progressive mayor open to new ideas.

Conclusion:

The first successful blood transfusion in 1667 would have been a significant medical milestone during George Boyd's time as mayor. While his initial reaction might have been a mix of astonishment and caution, he likely would have seen its potential for improving public health and saving lives. This development could have inspired him to support medical innovations and encourage a greater focus on health and well-being in his community, reinforcing his role as a forward-thinking leader.

When George Boyd was 67 years old, in 1676, Danish astronomer Ole Rømer first determined the speed of light. This was a groundbreaking scientific discovery that likely intrigued scholars and intellectuals across Europe, including Boyd if he was exposed to such knowledge during his time as mayor.

Potential Reaction:

1. Fascination and Awe: The concept of measuring something as abstract and seemingly instantaneous as the speed of light would have been awe-inspiring. Boyd, as a public figure and possibly an educated man, might have found this discovery both intriguing and a testament to the growing power of scientific inquiry. Given that this was during the Scientific Revolution, a time of major advancements in science, Boyd may have seen it as a sign of human progress.

2. Skepticism: While the discovery was revolutionary, many people of the time would have been skeptical about such abstract ideas. Boyd could have questioned the practicality of measuring light's speed and its relevance to everyday life. Science was still closely tied to philosophical and religious interpretations of the world, and such a discovery might have been hard for the average person to fully grasp.

3. Intellectual Curiosity: If Boyd had any interest in or exposure to scientific ideas, this discovery could have sparked further curiosity about the natural world. The idea that the speed of light could be measured might have led to discussions among the educated elite about the broader implications for astronomy, physics, and even theology.

Effect on George Boyd:

1. Increased Interest in Astronomy and Science: Rømer's discovery was related to astronomical observations of Jupiter's moons. If Boyd had a passing interest in astronomy, which was a growing field at the time, this discovery could have encouraged

him to explore these topics further or at least follow scientific discussions more closely.

2. Strengthened Belief in Human Progress: The late 17th century was a period of rapid advancements in science, and Boyd may have viewed this discovery as further evidence of the power of human intellect and the natural order. The ability to calculate something as mysterious as the speed of light could have reinforced the idea that humanity was on the verge of understanding the universe in greater depth.

3. Impact on Governance: While the discovery of the speed of light might not have had immediate practical applications for his role as mayor, Boyd could have recognized that such scientific progress would eventually lead to technological and societal advancements. As a leader, being aware of such changes could have influenced his views on education, trade, or even international relations, knowing that scientific achievements were shaping the world.

Conclusion:

The determination of the speed of light in 1676 would have likely amazed and fascinated George Boyd, though it might have also been met with some skepticism due to the abstract nature of the discovery. This significant scientific milestone could have deepened Boyd's appreciation for human progress during the Scientific Revolution and perhaps inspired greater intellectual curiosity. While it may not have directly impacted his day-to-day life as a mayor, it certainly would have shaped the broader intellectual climate of the time, contributing to the sense that humanity was on the cusp of understanding much more about the universe.

At the age of 70, George Boyd, as a mayor, would have been significantly affected by the death of his wife, Jean Gordon, in 1679. Given his advanced age and the cultural context of the time, the impact of her death would have reverberated through both his personal and public life. Here's how it might have affected him:

Emotional and Personal Impact:

- Profound Grief: As a man in his later years, losing a lifelong partner like Jean would have caused deep emotional pain. In 17th-century society, marriage was often seen as a strong partnership, and spouses relied heavily on each other for support, both emotionally and in managing household affairs. Jean's death would have left a significant void in George's life, both personally and in his home.

- Loneliness: At 70, George may have faced the prospect of living the remainder of his life without his closest companion. The companionship and care that Jean provided over the years would have been irreplaceable, and he might have struggled with feelings of isolation, especially if his children were grown and living elsewhere.

- Increased Responsibility at Home: With Jean gone, George would have faced new challenges in managing the household. Even though wealthier families like his likely had servants, Jean would have overseen much of the household management. Without her, George may have had to rely on family members or hire additional help to maintain the household's daily operations.

Impact on His Public Role as Mayor:

- Distraction from Duties: As mayor, George had significant civic responsibilities, but the grief over losing his wife could have affected his ability to perform his public duties. He might have struggled to focus on his role, especially in the immediate aftermath of her death. Grieving in 17th-century Ireland was often a deeply personal and lengthy process, and George may have needed time to step back from his duties to mourn.

- Public Sympathy: Given his position as a mayor, the community would likely have offered sympathy and support during his time of mourning. His status as a civic leader might have led to formal displays of condolence from the townspeople or other leaders. In that era, death was a frequent and visible part of life, and the public would have understood the gravity of losing a spouse, particularly at his age.

- Need for Continuity: Despite his personal grief, George might have been expected to continue fulfilling his duties as mayor, as leadership was crucial in maintaining the stability of the town. His age and emotional state might have made it difficult to balance his personal loss with his public role, but the sense of duty could have driven him to remain active in his position, even during his mourning period.

Religious and Spiritual Considerations:

- Religious Comfort: During the 17th century, religion played a central role in coping with death and loss. As a Christian, George likely turned to his faith for comfort. The belief in an afterlife would have been a source of solace, giving him hope that he would one day be reunited with Jean. The local church would have likely been involved in her funeral, and religious leaders might have provided ongoing spiritual support to help him through his grief.

- Memorialization of Jean: It was common for widowers of George's status to commemorate their wives through memorials, such as headstones or inscriptions. If George was financially well-off, he might have ensured that Jean's burial in Dervock, Ireland, was marked with a significant gravestone or memorial, reflecting both his love for her and their social status.

Impact on His Health:

- Physical Decline: At 70, George was already at an advanced age for the time, and the stress of losing his wife could have taken a toll on his health. The emotional strain of grief might have exacerbated any existing physical ailments, and he could have found himself struggling with both mental and physical challenges in the wake of her death.

- Care Needs: Without Jean, who might have played a role in ensuring his well-being, George may have faced difficulties in managing his own health. In 17th-century Ireland, medical care was limited, and the support system provided by a spouse was often vital in maintaining health, particularly for the elderly.

Family Dynamics:

- Support from Children: If George and Jean had children, they likely would have played an essential role in helping their father through this difficult time. Adult children might have returned home to offer support or taken over some of the responsibilities Jean had shouldered, including providing emotional comfort and practical help with household matters.

- Changes in Household Structure: The household dynamic would have shifted significantly after Jean's death. If there were still younger family members or dependents in the home, George would have had to adjust to running the household without his wife's guiding hand. This could have meant new challenges in maintaining the familial structure or delegating more responsibilities to others.

Long-term Effects:

- Legacy of His Marriage: In the long term, George would have carried the memory of his wife with him for the rest of his life. As a man of his age and position, he might have reflected on their shared life, their children, and the role Jean played in supporting his career and public duties. Her death could have prompted him to consider his own mortality and the legacy he would leave behind, both as a mayor and a family patriarch.

- Public Perception: The death of a prominent figure's spouse often impacted how the community viewed the family. Jean's death might have been a moment of reflection for the town as well, particularly if she had been active in local affairs. George's ability to navigate his public and private life during this time would have been observed by the community, potentially influencing their respect and admiration for him.

In summary, George Boyd's life would have been deeply impacted by Jean's death on multiple levels. While he faced significant emotional loss, he would have also had to balance the responsibilities of his public office, the practical challenges of managing his household, and the support (or potential lack thereof) from his family and community.

By the time George Boyd passed away at 79 years old on January 14, 1688, his life would have been shaped by significant political, social, and scientific changes that defined the 17th century. As a mayor, and likely a man of influence, he would have experienced both personal and public shifts in his later years. Here's an overview of what his life might have been like at the time of his death:

Political Landscape:

1. Post-Restoration England and Ireland: In 1688, the political environment was heavily influenced by the events following the English Civil War, the Restoration of the monarchy under Charles II in 1660, and the reign of James II. Boyd would have witnessed the changing tides of power between monarchy and parliament, with Protestant-Catholic tensions growing under James II's rule.

- The Glorious Revolution: Just months before Boyd's death, tensions were reaching a peak, culminating in what would become the Glorious Revolution of 1688. William of Orange's invasion and the impending deposition of James II were imminent, signaling a dramatic shift in power that Boyd would have been aware of, even if he didn't live to see its full outcome.

- As a public figure, Boyd might have been involved or at least influenced by political discussions of loyalty, religion, and governance during this volatile time.

Religious Context:

1. Protestant-Catholic Tensions: Ireland was particularly affected by religious divides, and Boyd would have been aware of or possibly involved in navigating these tensions, especially as they impacted his role as mayor. If he was Protestant, he may have felt uneasy about James II's Catholic policies, which were unpopular among Protestants in Ireland.

- Public Role: As a mayor, Boyd likely had to carefully manage religious issues in his community, ensuring peace and order amidst growing concerns about James II's policies favoring Catholics.

Social and Intellectual Climate:

1. Scientific Advancements: Boyd had lived through the Scientific Revolution, a period that saw the development of new ideas in astronomy, physics, biology, and chemistry. Discoveries like the speed of light (1676) and the invention of the pendulum clock (1656) would have amazed or intrigued him, though as a mayor, these advancements might not have directly impacted his daily responsibilities.

- Intellectual Curiosity: In his later years, he might have been exposed to new ideas through academic or intellectual circles, discussing the scientific advancements of the time or even witnessing the broader application of technology in society.

2. Urban Life in the 17th Century: Life in the late 17th century in Ireland (or if he was from an English colony) would have involved increasing urbanization. Cities like Dublin were growing, influenced by trade and economic development. Boyd, as a mayor, would have seen the expansion of infrastructure, markets, and possibly the rise of new buildings and public spaces.

- Public Duties: His role as mayor would have placed him at the center of urban governance, responsible for local laws, trade regulation, and perhaps disputes, especially in a time of religious and political instability.

Family and Personal Life:

1. Elderly Concerns: By 79, Boyd was likely experiencing the common ailments of old age in the 17th century. Medical care was still rudimentary, and living to such an advanced age would have been seen as a mark of good fortune or robust health.

- Family Support: If he had children or extended family, they would likely have played a significant role in caring for him during his final years. In his last days, his family would have been by his side, ensuring his affairs were in order.

2. Legacy: Given his role as mayor, Boyd would have been concerned about the legacy he left behind. He might have been reflecting on his public service, his contributions to the community, and the impact he made on the political and social fabric of his time. Ensuring that his family's social standing remained secure might have been a priority.

Death and Burial:

- Religious Observance: Boyd's burial would have followed the religious customs of the time, likely involving a formal church ceremony if he were Protestant. His status as a mayor would have meant his death might have been marked with some public recognition.

- Burial Customs: In 17th-century Ireland, funerals were an important communal event. Depending on his standing and wealth, Boyd could have had a larger, more ceremonious funeral, with family, friends, and community members paying their respects.

Conclusion:

At the time of George Boyd's death in 1688, his life would have been defined by the significant changes of the 17th century, from political upheavals to scientific advancements. As a mayor, he would have experienced the challenges of governance in a rapidly changing world, dealing with political, religious, and societal issues. His personal life would have likely centered around family and health, with reflections on his legacy and contributions to his community. The era's tension, especially with the approaching Glorious Revolution, would have likely colored his final years, as he passed away at a time of great uncertainty in Ireland and beyond.

JEAN (GORDON) BOYD[17]

Jean Gordon, wife of Mayor George Boyd, passed away on October 8, 1679. Her life at the time of her death would have been shaped by the social, political, and economic realities of 17th-century Ireland, particularly as the wife of a prominent figure like a mayor. Here's a closer look at what her life might have been like:

Social Status and Role:

As the wife of a mayor, Jean Gordon would have held a significant social position within her community. Mayors were prominent civic leaders responsible for overseeing local governance, so her family would likely have been well-respected and well-connected within the town or city they lived in.

- Public Role: Jean would have likely participated in social and charitable activities befitting her position as the wife of a mayor. She might have helped organize local events, assisted with church-related duties, and acted as a mediator in community affairs.

- Household Management: In the 17th century, women of her social class often oversaw the household, managing servants and ensuring the home ran smoothly. She would have been responsible for maintaining the family's reputation, especially in a public role. Her daily duties would likely have involved managing the household finances, supervising the running of the home, and possibly participating in social gatherings with her husband's associates.

Political and Religious Context:

Ireland in the late 1600s was marked by political and religious turbulence, particularly between Catholics and Protestants. While Jean's specific religious affiliation isn't mentioned, this context would have influenced her life.

- Religious Tensions: The aftermath of the English Civil War and Cromwell's conquest of Ireland (1649–1653) left deep religious divisions in Ireland. By 1679, Protestant rule was firmly established, and the penal laws against Catholics were either already in place or being reinforced. If Jean and her husband were Protestants, they would have aligned with the ruling class in Ireland. If they were Catholics or Presbyterians, they would have been navigating a society increasingly hostile to their religious rights.

- Local Governance: As the wife of a mayor, Jean likely had an awareness of the political landscape and how it impacted the town or city her husband governed. She would have been familiar with civic duties and the responsibilities of leadership, as well as the pressures her husband faced in maintaining law and order during a time when Ireland was deeply divided.

Life in 1679:

Ireland in the late 17th century was primarily rural, with towns and cities being centers of trade, governance, and religious life. As part of the upper class, Jean likely lived in a well-furnished home and had access to goods imported from England or Europe, especially since Ireland was part of the English colonial economy at the time. Some aspects of her life may have included:

- Daily Life: Jean would have been engaged in overseeing her household, managing servants, and ensuring the well-being of her family. For a woman of her standing, this involved a combination of practical household tasks and social responsibilities. The family's diet would have been relatively rich compared to the peasantry, with access to fresh produce, meat, and dairy products from local farms.

- Health: Health and medicine in 1679 were primitive by today's standards. The average life expectancy was much lower due to disease, poor sanitation, and limited medical knowledge. Jean, at the time of her death, may have been in her 40s or older, a considerable age for someone in that era. The causes of death for women often included infections, childbirth complications, or illnesses like smallpox, tuberculosis, or fevers.

- Social Circle: As the wife of a mayor, she would have had a close-knit social circle, including the wives of other civic leaders, clergy, and local merchants. Jean likely attended social gatherings, church services, and events related to her husband's role as mayor. She may also have been involved in charitable work, such as assisting the poor or helping with local church activities.

Political and Economic Conditions:

- Restoration Era: By 1679, Ireland was under the rule of Charles II, following the Restoration of the monarchy in 1660. This period was one of relative political stability compared to the chaos of earlier decades. The Restoration allowed for some recovery from the previous civil wars and Cromwell's occupation, but tensions between Irish Catholics and English Protestants persisted.

- Economy: The Irish economy in the 1670s was primarily agrarian, with most people involved in farming. As part of the upper classes, Jean's family would likely have had access to land, either through direct ownership or connections to the landowning gentry. The economy also depended on exports of wool, beef, and other agricultural products to England. Jean's family may have been involved in these economic activities if they owned or managed land.

Legacy:

By the time of her death, Jean Gordon would likely have seen her children grown, potentially involved in the civic life of their community or married into other prominent families. Her legacy would have been shaped by her role as a wife and mother in a respected household, and she may have left behind a reputation for being a strong and capable figure in her community.

In summary, Jean Gordon's life in 1679 would have been shaped by her position as the wife of a mayor, managing a household, navigating the social expectations of her class, and living in a politically and religiously complex Ireland. While she may have enjoyed certain privileges due to her family's status, she would have also lived in a time of significant hardship, with the potential for disease, political upheaval, and religious tensions affecting her family and community.

THOMAS BOYD[1]
KATHRIN (PEEBLES) BOYD[2]

---

1. https://www.wikitree.com/wiki/Boyd-23283
2. https://www.wikitree.com/wiki/Peebles-2660

JOSEPH ANDERSON[18]

IN 1732, CARROWREAGH, Ireland, like much of rural Ireland, would have been a small, agrarian community, shaped by the social, economic, and political conditions of the 18th century. Here's an overview of what life might have been like during that year:

Agrarian Economy

Carrowreagh, likely a farming hamlet in County Down or County Londonderry, would have been centered around agriculture. Ireland in the early 18th century was predominantly rural, with small tenant farmers and laborers making up most of the population. The land was often divided into small plots, which tenants rented from Anglo-Irish landlords. Many farmers grew oats, barley, and potatoes, and raised livestock, but most were subsistence farmers, meaning they grew enough to support their families, with little surplus for sale.

The tenant-landlord system dominated rural life, with large estates owned by Anglo-Irish or English landlords, who collected rent from Irish tenant farmers. This system often led to economic hardship for the Irish tenants, who faced high rents and periodic poor harvests.

Political Climate

In 1732, Ireland was part of the Kingdom of Great Britain under English rule, following the Acts of Union of 1707. The Irish Parliament existed, but real power was held by the English monarchy and Parliament. Protestant Ascendancy was firmly established, with the Anglican Church (Church of Ireland) as the official religion. Catholics, who made up the majority of the population, were subjected to the Penal Laws, a series of oppressive laws designed to maintain Protestant control. These laws severely restricted the rights of Catholics, preventing them from owning land, holding political office, or practicing their religion freely.

For the Anderson family, life would have been shaped by their religion. If they were Catholic, they would have faced significant legal and social restrictions. If they were Protestant, particularly part of the Presbyterian or Anglican communities, they would have enjoyed greater rights and privileges, though Presbyterians, while not as restricted as Catholics, also faced some discrimination.

Daily Life

Life in Carrowreagh in 1732 would have been simple and rural. The community would have been tightly knit, with families working together on farms and relying on each other for support. Thatched cottages were typical homes, built from local materials like stone and mud, with thatch made from reeds or straw.

Life was largely dictated by the seasons and the agricultural calendar. People worked long hours on the land, and survival was often a struggle, particularly during harsh winters or poor harvests. Food would have been simple and hearty, consisting mainly of oats, potatoes, and dairy, with meat being a luxury for many. The majority of people were poor, and the gap between the rich (landowners and the Protestant elite) and the poor (tenant farmers) was stark.

Religion and Community

Religion was central to community life. In 1732, church attendance was a vital aspect of social and spiritual life. For Protestants, the Church of Ireland would have played a central role, while Presbyterians (primarily of Scottish descent in Ulster) and Catholics practiced their faith, though Catholics often had to do so discreetly because of the Penal Laws. Religious identity was closely tied to social and political status, and tensions between different religious groups, particularly Protestants and Catholics, were common.

Political and Social Tensions

The Protestant Ascendancy and the enforcement of the Penal Laws created social tensions. Catholics faced discrimination in many aspects of life, from land ownership to education. While these laws were not always enforced with equal severity in all places, they created an atmosphere of inequality and division. By the 18th century, many Irish Catholics, particularly in the north, had emigrated to the American colonies, seeking better opportunities and freedom from the oppressive legal system in Ireland.

Technological and Cultural Context

In 1732, Ireland was still largely pre-industrial, with few technological advancements. However, Europe was beginning to experience early stirrings of the Enlightenment, which brought ideas of reason, science, and progress. These ideas were slowly spreading to Ireland, influencing a small but growing intellectual and political elite. However, for the people of Carrowreagh, life would have been focused more on survival and daily routines than on scientific or political revolutions.

Conclusion

For Joseph Anderson, born in Carrowreagh in 1732, his early life would have been shaped by the agricultural economy, religious divisions, and political realities of rural Ireland. He would have grown up in a close-knit, farming community, with the struggles of tenancy and the Penal Laws likely influencing his family's life. The landscape of his early years was one of both hardship and resilience, deeply connected to the rhythms of the land and the challenges of the time.

Joseph Anderson, born in 1732, would have been 7 years old when the Methodist movement began in the late 1730s, led by John Wesley and Charles Wesley. While it's unlikely that Joseph would have directly engaged with the movement at such a young age, the arrival of Methodism in Ireland in the coming years could have affected his life, especially if he lived in a community influenced by it.

Early Reactions

At age 7, Joseph's immediate understanding of the Methodist movement would have been limited. However, his reaction would have been shaped by the religious environment of his family and community. If his family were Protestant, particularly Anglican or Presbyterian, they may have viewed the early Methodists with skepticism, as Methodism was initially a movement within the Church of England but soon developed into a more evangelical and emotional form of worship. Methodism challenged the more formal, liturgical approach of the Anglican Church and emphasized personal salvation, piety, and charitable works.

If Joseph's family were Presbyterian, they may have noticed some theological similarities with the Methodists, particularly regarding the emphasis on personal faith, but may have still been wary of the movement's methods, such as outdoor preaching and its emotional fervor. On the other hand, if the family was Catholic, they might have been more removed from the immediate impact of the movement, as Methodism mainly targeted Protestant communities initially.

Effects on Joseph's Life

As Joseph grew older, the spread of Methodism could have influenced his religious and social landscape in a few key ways:

1. Increased Religious Activity in Rural Areas:

Methodism spread quickly among the poorer, rural populations of Ireland, including Ulster where Carrowreagh is located. The movement's emphasis on evangelism, preaching outdoors, and the formation of "societies" could have brought new religious energy and activity to Joseph's community. He may have witnessed Methodist preachers traveling through his area, holding revivals, and calling for personal conversion, which could have had a profound effect on local culture.

2. Community Division or Revival:

Methodism had a polarizing effect in many areas, as it was seen as a challenge to established religious norms. Some communities embraced the fervor of Methodist preachers, while others, particularly the Anglican clergy, resisted it. If Methodism reached Carrowreagh during Joseph's lifetime, he could have observed either religious revival or division in his community. Some of his neighbors might have joined Methodist societies, while others might have viewed it as disruptive to traditional church authority.

3. Opportunity for Spiritual Renewal:

If Joseph was drawn to the Methodist movement as he matured, it could have offered him an opportunity for spiritual renewal. Methodism focused on egalitarian ideals and encouraged participation from ordinary people, not just the clergy. This could have empowered him or others in his community, particularly if they felt disconnected from the established church.

4. Impact on Religious Practice:

Methodism's focus on personal piety and moral living could have had a lasting influence on Joseph's religious practices and beliefs. Methodists often emphasized strict moral codes, including abstaining from alcohol, gambling, and other vices. If Joseph or his community were influenced by these ideas, it could have shaped daily life, encouraging more disciplined and devout behaviors.

Conclusion

Although Joseph Anderson might not have been directly involved with the Methodist movement as a child, its spread through Ireland in the following years could have had a lasting impact on his life. The movement would have brought new religious ideas, methods of worship, and possibly social change to the communities of Ireland. Whether he was a participant or an observer, Methodism could have influenced the religious environment in which Joseph grew up, potentially affecting his faith and the religious dynamics of his community.

When Joseph Anderson was 16 years old in 1748, the death of James Moore I, a notable figure, could have had a significant impact on him depending on his family's relationship to the Moore family and their status within the community.

Potential Reaction:

1. Emotional Impact:

If Joseph's family had any personal connection to James Moore I, such as a working or social relationship, the death might have been felt more personally. James Moore I could have been seen as a figure of authority or influence, and his passing might have sparked a sense of loss, uncertainty, or respect within the local community. Joseph, being in his formative years, might have been influenced by the way adults around him reacted to the news, possibly attending the funeral or participating in community mourning rituals.

2. Awareness of Mortality and Status:

At 16, Joseph would have been mature enough to understand the significance of death, especially of an important figure like Moore. The passing of a prominent local figure could have prompted thoughts about social standing, responsibility, and the fragility of life, especially if Joseph aspired to rise in local ranks or was influenced by figures like Moore in terms of land, leadership, or economic opportunity.

Effects on Joseph Anderson:

1. Shift in Local Leadership:

The death of James Moore I would likely have shifted leadership or landownership to James Moore II, Esquire. This could have affected local dynamics if Moore I had been an important landowner, decision-maker, or patron. If Joseph or his family worked for or interacted with the Moore estate, this transition might have caused changes in employment, land usage, or local governance. Joseph might have viewed this change as an opportunity or a time of uncertainty depending on Moore II's leadership style compared to his father's.

2. Economic or Social Opportunities:

If the Moore family was involved in landownership, politics, or trade in the area, Joseph might have been impacted by shifts in local economics. The transition of power to Moore II could have presented new opportunities for trade, employment, or patronage. Alternatively, if Joseph's family was dependent on the favor of the Moore family, the change in leadership could have introduced concerns about security and stability.

3. A Reminder of Social Hierarchies:

The death of a prominent figure like James Moore I could have reinforced social hierarchies in Joseph's mind. In 18th-century Ireland, social class and landownership were key components of power. Joseph's awareness of Moore's death could have highlighted the privileges of the upper class and the responsibilities that came with such positions. As Joseph matured into adulthood, witnessing the change of power might have deepened his understanding of the importance of leadership and influence.

Conclusion:

Joseph Anderson's reaction to the death of James Moore I would have depended on his family's connection to the Moore family and the local community. He might have experienced a combination of respect, reflection on mortality, and a recognition of the shifts in social and economic power that came with the transition from James Moore I to James Moore II. The event likely shaped his view of leadership, status, and the role of influential families in Irish society during the 18th century.

When Joseph Anderson was 20 years old in 1752, Benjamin Franklin's discovery that lightning was electrical would have been a groundbreaking event in the scientific world. However, considering Joseph's location and the era, the impact on his life and his reaction would have been shaped by several factors.

Potential Reaction:

1. Curiosity and Fascination:

If Joseph had access to news about Franklin's experiments, particularly the famous kite experiment, he might have been fascinated by the idea of understanding natural phenomena like lightning. For someone in the 18th century, where scientific knowledge was expanding rapidly, this revelation would have been both surprising and intriguing. It would have sparked curiosity about how such discoveries might change the world.

2. Skepticism or Caution:

In rural Ireland, where traditional beliefs were still strong, Joseph and others around him might have reacted with skepticism or caution. Lightning was often seen as a divine or supernatural force, and the idea that it was simply an electrical phenomenon might have challenged existing beliefs. He could have been hesitant to fully accept the implications of this discovery, especially if he was influenced by religious or folk traditions.

3. Admiration for Franklin's Ingenuity:

Franklin's experiments were widely praised for their ingenuity. Joseph may have viewed Franklin as a figure to admire for his courage in exploring dangerous and mysterious forces like lightning. This admiration could have inspired a greater interest in learning, science, or understanding the natural world.

Effect on Joseph Anderson:

1. Shift in Understanding of Nature:

If Joseph followed news of scientific advancements, Franklin's discovery could have broadened his understanding of the natural world. The realization that lightning was electrical might have prompted Joseph to see nature in a more mechanistic way, where natural events could be explained by science rather than purely by divine intervention.

2. Practical Implications:

Franklin's experiments with electricity eventually led to practical innovations, such as the lightning rod. While this might not have directly impacted Joseph's life immediately, over time, the knowledge that buildings and homes could be protected from lightning strikes using these devices could have had practical value, especially if he lived in areas prone to storms.

3. Intellectual and Cultural Change:

Franklin's discovery was part of a larger movement in the 18th century, often referred to as the Enlightenment, where reason and science increasingly challenged traditional views. Joseph, as a young adult, might have experienced a shift in cultural attitudes toward science, technology, and knowledge. The growing importance of rational thought could have influenced his view of progress and modernity, even in a rural area like Carrowreagh.

Conclusion:

Joseph Anderson's reaction to Benjamin Franklin's discovery about lightning would likely have ranged from curiosity to cautious acceptance, depending on his exposure to new scientific ideas. The long-term effect on his life might have been a gradual shift in understanding the natural world through a more scientific lens, while also reflecting the broader intellectual changes happening during the Enlightenment. However, in rural Ireland, such discoveries might have taken time to reach and fully influence everyday life.

When Joseph Anderson was 28 years old, around 1760, the Industrial Revolution was just beginning, primarily in Britain. While Ireland's economy and society were still largely agrarian at this time, the impact of the Industrial Revolution would gradually make its way to Ireland, including the rural areas like Carrowreagh where Joseph was born.

Possible Reaction:

1. Curiosity and Skepticism:

Being from a rural, likely farming-based community, Joseph might have initially been skeptical or unaware of the early industrial changes occurring in England. News about innovations in manufacturing, such as the development of the steam engine or the mechanization of textile production, would have spread slowly to rural areas like his. If Joseph did hear about these changes, he may have been curious, but also uncertain about how such developments could affect his life.

2. Cultural Resistance:

Rural communities in Ireland tended to be conservative and resistant to sudden changes.

Joseph Anderson, aged 44 to 51 during the American Revolution (1775-1783), would have experienced significant global and local events during this time.

Possible Reactions and Effects:

1. Awareness of Global Events:

As a man in his mid-40s, Joseph would have been aware of the American Revolution, especially if he had access to news through local networks or newspapers. The revolution would have sparked conversations about governance, liberty, and independence, possibly influencing his views on politics and society.

2. Economic and Social Impact:

While the direct impact of the American Revolution on Ireland would be less pronounced compared to Britain, it could have led to heightened awareness of political movements and ideas about independence. This period might have influenced local political and social debates, especially if Joseph engaged with or observed discussions about governance and reform.

3. Community Reactions:

If Joseph was involved in community or business activities, the economic and political disruptions in Britain and the colonies might have had indirect effects on Ireland. This could include shifts in trade or economic conditions that might affect him and his community.

4. Personal Reflection:

Given his age and experience, Joseph might have reflected on the revolutionary ideas of liberty and self-governance, considering how these ideas could relate to or contrast with his own experiences and the conditions in Ireland.

In summary, Joseph Anderson would have been impacted by the broader political shifts and discussions of the time, influencing his perspectives and possibly affecting his community's interactions with global events.

Joseph Anderson, at 51 years old, would likely have been amazed by the launch of the first hot air balloon in 1783. Living in Ireland during the Industrial Revolution and the Age of Enlightenment, he may have been aware of scientific advancements and intrigued by this feat of human ingenuity. The hot air balloon, as the first human-carrying flight, would have been seen as a miraculous and groundbreaking achievement, symbolizing human progress and the potential to master the skies.

This event could have sparked a sense of curiosity and wonder in Joseph, especially given the historical context of increasing interest in scientific discovery. Depending on his personal views and social circles, the hot air balloon might have inspired conversations about the future of travel and technology. While it may not have had a direct, immediate effect on his daily life, it likely added to the general excitement about technological advancements that were transforming society during his time.

At 68 years old, when William Young designed shoes specifically for left and right feet in 1800, Joseph Anderson would have likely seen this as a remarkable innovation in personal comfort. For most of his life, shoes were generally made straight and without distinction between the left and right foot, which could lead to discomfort over time.

His reaction to this advancement might have been one of curiosity and appreciation, especially given his age, where comfort in daily wear would become more important. He may have been excited by the thought of shoes that would mold more naturally to the foot, reducing pain from walking or standing, which would have been increasingly valuable to an older individual.

The introduction of left and right shoes would have had a significant effect on him, making walking and movement more comfortable, particularly if he was active or traveled regularly. This improvement in footwear may have been considered a small but meaningful enhancement to his quality of life in his later years.

AT 75 YEARS OLD, WHEN the first commercial steamship was built by Robert Fulton in 1807, Joseph Anderson would have witnessed a revolutionary moment in transportation and technology. The steamship represented a major shift from traditional wind-powered sailing vessels, and it would have sparked intrigue and possibly amazement in someone of his generation, who had grown up with far more primitive modes of transportation.

Given his age, Joseph may not have personally experienced traveling on a steamship, but the implications of this invention would have been clear. The idea of faster, more reliable, and predictable travel by sea or river would have been a topic of great discussion in communities, as it opened up new possibilities for trade, communication, and exploration. It was a significant leap toward the modernization of the world he had known for so long.

The introduction of the steamship might have also left Joseph reflecting on the many technological advancements he had witnessed throughout his life, from the beginnings of the Industrial Revolution to now the first commercial steam-powered vessels. It would likely have seemed both a marvel of progress and a symbol of the rapidly changing world around him.

At 83 years old, Joseph Anderson would have been aware of the significant global events surrounding Napoleon's defeat and exile in 1814. Napoleon's rise and fall had dramatically shaped the political landscape of Europe, and even in Ireland, the impact of the Napoleonic Wars would have been felt.

As someone who had lived through numerous historical events—including the American Revolution, the Irish Rebellion, and the early stages of the Industrial Revolution—Joseph might have viewed Napoleon's defeat as a monumental moment in history. It signaled the end of a long period of war and turmoil across Europe. For Joseph, the news would have been significant, but likely experienced from a distance, as Ireland was largely on the periphery of the direct conflict.

Given his age, he may have felt a sense of relief or optimism that the wars that had ravaged Europe were finally coming to an end. It would also have been a moment for reflection on how the world had changed in his lifetime, from the rise of empires to their falls, and how these global shifts impacted life even in smaller regions like his own. Napoleon's exile to Elba would have been seen as a turning point in European history, and Joseph, though older, would have been aware of its importance.

At 86 years old, Joseph Anderson would have lived a long and eventful life, witnessing many innovations. The invention of the bicycle in 1817 would have been another remarkable development in a time of rapid technological and social change.

Given his advanced age, Joseph might not have been directly affected by the invention, as bicycles were initially a novelty and not widely accessible for everyday use. However, as a curious observer of the world around him, he likely would have seen it as an interesting and somewhat revolutionary idea. The ability to travel short distances faster than on foot without the need for horses might have fascinated him.

The invention of the bicycle represented a shift toward personal mobility and hinted at further changes in transportation that would come in later decades. For Joseph, who had seen the first commercial steamship built and Napoleon's defeat, the bicycle might have felt like another piece of a rapidly modernizing world, marking a significant change in how people moved through their environments. It was likely one more indicator that the world was continuing to progress, even in his later years.

By the time of Joseph Anderson's death on April 2, 1818, innovations such as the first commercial steamship (1807) and the bicycle (1817) were beginning to reshape society and transportation. While he may not have been directly involved in these advancements, Joseph likely witnessed the early impact of these technologies on trade, communication, and daily life.

Life in Rural Ireland:

At 86, Joseph would have likely been living a quieter life in rural Ireland. The introduction of new farming techniques and early industrial methods might have affected agricultural practices, but traditional ways of life were still dominant in the countryside. Living in Carrowreagh, he would have seen gradual changes in how land was used and farmed, though likely maintaining much of the old ways of managing a rural household.

Political Landscape:

Joseph's life was marked by major political upheavals. Having lived through the American Revolution (1775–1783), the French Revolution (1789), the Irish Rebellion (1798), and the Napoleonic Wars (1803–1815), he would have seen empires rise and fall. The defeat of Napoleon in 1815 would have been a major event during his later years, signaling a shift in European power and the return to a more stable political environment.

Personal Life:

At 86, Joseph likely had an extended family, and may have witnessed his children and grandchildren take on responsibilities in a changing world. As someone who had lived through such turbulent times, he may have shared his wisdom and experiences with younger generations, offering a sense of continuity and stability.

In conclusion, by the time of his death, Joseph Anderson would have witnessed profound social, political, and technological changes, while still maintaining a connection to the traditional, rural life of Ireland. He lived through wars, rebellions, and revolutions, all of which would have left an indelible mark on his perspective of the world.

WILLIAM DUNLOP[19]

Given William Dunlop's time and place of birth and death, here's a general description of what he might have looked like:

Facial Features: As a man from 18th-century Northern Ireland, he likely had features common to people of that region and era. This could include a relatively robust and weathered appearance, with facial characteristics like a strong jawline and prominent cheekbones.

Hair: During the 18th century, men often wore their hair in styles such as powdered wigs, particularly in formal settings. However, many also wore their hair natural, in a shorter cut or tied back. By the late 1700s, shorter natural styles became more common.

Clothing: Dunlop would have worn clothing typical of his time. In the early 18th century, this might include a knee-length coat, waistcoat, and breeches, often in subdued colors. By the latter half of the century, men's fashion moved towards simpler, more tailored suits with less ornate decoration.

General Appearance: He would likely have a sturdy build, reflecting the physical demands of life in that era. His skin might show signs of a life spent working outdoors, given the agrarian lifestyle prevalent in Northern Ireland during that period.

For more precise details, local historical records or portraits, if available, could provide additional insights.

In 1723, Priestland, Northern Ireland, was a rural area in a period marked by significant social and economic changes. Here's an overview of what life might have been like:

1. Agrarian Society: Priestland would have been a primarily agricultural community. Most residents would have been engaged in farming, with small-scale subsistence farming common. The land would have been used for growing crops such as oats, barley, and potatoes, as well as for raising livestock.

2. Economic Conditions: The early 18th century was a time of economic transition. While agriculture was the mainstay, there was gradual growth in trade and local industries. Improvements in farming techniques and tools were slowly being adopted.

3. Social Structure: Society in this period was hierarchical. Landowners and wealthy farmers held significant influence, while the majority of people were laborers or tenant farmers. The local church played a central role in community life and governance.

4. Living Conditions: Homes in rural Ireland were simple, often built with local materials such as stone or timber. They typically had thatched roofs and a single room serving as both living and sleeping space. Heating was provided by a central hearth, and sanitation facilities were rudimentary.

5. Education and Literacy: Education was limited, with few formal schools. Literacy rates were relatively low, and education was often informal, provided by local clergy or through apprenticeships.

6. Political Context: Ireland in the early 18th century was under British rule. The period saw political tensions and religious conflicts, particularly between Catholics and Protestants. This was a time of relative stability following the Williamite War, but tensions simmered beneath the surface.

7. Community Life: Life in Priestland would have been closely knit, with strong community ties. Social events, church services, and local markets were key aspects of daily life.

Overall, life in Priestland in 1723 would have been characterized by hard work, close community ties, and a deep connection to the land.

SARAH (UNKNOWN) BARRY[20]

SARAH BARRY, BORN IN Ireland in 1775, would have entered the world during a time of significant political and social transformation. Here's an overview of what life would have been like that year:

1. Political and Social Climate:

In 1775, Ireland was still under British rule, part of the Kingdom of Great Britain. The penal laws, designed to discriminate against Catholics and ensure Protestant dominance, were still in force, although there were gradual relaxations throughout the latter half of the 18th century. If Sarah was from a Catholic family, her family would have faced legal and social restrictions, including limitations on land ownership, public office, and education. If her family were Protestant, they would have been part of the ruling class in Ireland, benefiting from the established political order.

The American Revolution also began in 1775, and while Ireland wasn't directly involved, the tensions between Britain and its colonies may have been felt, especially as Ireland would later see the ripple effects of revolutionary ideals. This could have sparked some discussion about Ireland's own relationship with Britain.

2. Economic Conditions:

Economically, Ireland was largely agrarian, with a majority of the population living in rural areas and relying on agriculture for their livelihoods. Wealthy landowners, often of English descent, controlled vast estates, while tenant farmers worked the land. Many Irish families lived in poverty, especially in rural areas, and would have been at the mercy of crop failures and fluctuations in grain prices. In contrast, towns and cities like Dublin and Belfast were growing centers of trade and commerce, benefiting from Ireland's position in the British Empire.

If Sarah was from a rural area, she would have grown up in a farming community with limited economic opportunities, but if she were from a wealthier or urban family, she might have experienced a more comfortable life, with access to education and a broader social network.

3. Daily Life and Culture:

Life in Ireland in the late 18th century was still deeply rooted in tradition. People lived in extended family units, with roles and expectations clearly defined by gender and social status. Women like Sarah would have been expected to focus on domestic duties, learning skills such as spinning, weaving, cooking, and managing a household, though the specifics would have varied depending on her family's class and location.

Religion played a central role in daily life, and church attendance was an important social obligation. If Sarah's family was Catholic, their religious practice might have been more covert due to the penal laws, which restricted Catholic worship in public settings. Protestants, especially members of the Anglican Church (Church of Ireland), would have had more freedom and influence in society.

In terms of culture, storytelling, music, and folk traditions remained strong in rural Ireland. People would have gathered for festivals and fairs, and oral traditions kept Irish culture and history alive during this period.

4. Health and Medicine:

Healthcare was rudimentary in 1775. Most medical care was provided by local healers or physicians in urban areas, and disease was common, especially in the poorer, rural areas. High infant mortality rates and the threat of outbreaks like smallpox or tuberculosis were everyday realities. Remedies often involved herbal medicine, but advancements in medical science were still in their early stages.

5. The Irish Language and Education:

By the late 18th century, the Irish language was still spoken widely in rural areas, though English was becoming more dominant, especially in towns and among the upper classes. If Sarah was from a rural community, she might have grown up speaking Irish, though her education would likely have been minimal unless she was from a wealthier Protestant family, in which case she may have been taught English and some of the liberal arts.

6. Influence of Britain:

Culturally and politically, Ireland was heavily influenced by Britain, which maintained control over Irish affairs through the Anglo-Irish Protestant Ascendancy. This elite group, primarily composed of landowners, controlled Ireland's economy and government. The tensions between the largely Catholic Irish population and the Protestant Ascendancy continued to simmer during this period, laying the groundwork for future political unrest, including the Irish Rebellion of 1798.

Conclusion:

In 1775, Ireland was a land of contrasts. The lives of people like Sarah Barry would have been shaped by their social class, religion, and geographic location. For a rural Catholic family, life would have been marked by hardship, religious restrictions, and limited opportunity. For a wealthier, Protestant family, the world would have been more expansive, with access to education, political influence, and the benefits of being part of the ruling class. Regardless, Sarah's early years in Ireland were shaped by a society on the verge of significant political and social change.

Sarah Barry, born in 1775, would have been between 1 and 8 years old during the American Revolution (1775–1783). Although she was living in Ireland, the Revolution would have indirectly affected her and her family, particularly in the following ways:

1. Political Awareness:

- Early Childhood: At such a young age, Sarah herself may not have fully understood the larger political events unfolding in the American colonies, but her family and community would certainly have discussed the revolution. If her family had ties to Britain, they would have followed the news more closely, possibly expressing concern about the rebellion against the British crown. In Ireland, which was under British rule, many people would have had mixed feelings—some sympathized with the American cause, seeing parallels to Ireland's own struggles for autonomy, while others, especially the Anglo-Irish Protestant elite, might have been loyal to the British crown and worried about the implications of such a revolution.

- Later Childhood: By the time Sarah was 8, she might have had some basic understanding of what the American Revolution was, especially if her family was politically active or well-informed. The talk of independence, rebellion, and the fight for rights could have piqued her curiosity and possibly made her more aware of Ireland's political status.

2. Economic Impact:

- The American Revolution disrupted British trade and affected the economy across the British Empire, including Ireland. There could have been shortages of goods or fluctuations in the prices of commodities. If Sarah's family was involved in trade or farming, they might have experienced economic difficulties.

Additionally, British resources were stretched thin because of the war, which may have reduced their ability to control or invest in Ireland, leading to some uncertainty or instability in the country.

- For a rural or middle-class Irish family, these economic impacts might have meant less stability or fewer resources. If Sarah's family was relatively well-off, they might have felt the strain through reduced profits from agriculture or trade. Conversations in the household may have revolved around these concerns, shaping her understanding of how global events could affect local life.

3. Cultural and Intellectual Influence:

- The ideals of the American Revolution, such as liberty, independence, and self-governance, began to circulate more widely throughout Europe, including Ireland. Even though Sarah was quite young, the adults in her life would have been discussing these revolutionary ideas. As she grew older, this atmosphere of political change could have subtly influenced her views on governance, freedom, and Ireland's relationship with Britain.

- Intellectual circles in Ireland, particularly among the educated classes, would have been discussing the philosophy of the Enlightenment, which inspired much of the American Revolution. These discussions might have influenced Sarah's family if they were part of the more educated or elite circles, contributing to a more politically conscious upbringing for her.

4. Potential for Irish Rebellion:

- The success of the American Revolution inspired various independence movements across Europe, including in Ireland. The American victory emboldened groups in Ireland, such as the United Irishmen, who were pushing for Irish independence. This growing sentiment would have permeated Irish society in the years following the American Revolution, and Sarah may have grown up in a period where there was increasing tension and calls for Irish rights and self-governance.

- By the time Sarah was an adult, Ireland would experience the Irish Rebellion of 1798, a direct consequence of the revolutionary spirit that was ignited in part by the American Revolution. Even though she was young during the actual American conflict, the atmosphere of rebellion and the quest for freedom would have been part of the political landscape in her later life.

5. Military Presence and Activity:

- During the American Revolution, the British military was stretched thin, having to fight on multiple fronts. Ireland, being part of the British Empire, would have seen its military presence change during this period. There may have been recruitment efforts for soldiers to fight in the American colonies, and this military activity could have been noticeable in her community. Seeing soldiers come and go or hearing about battles and war efforts could have left an impression on Sarah as a child.

Conclusion:

For Sarah, as a young child, the American Revolution would have been something she likely observed more through her family's discussions and the local effects it had on life in Ireland. The political and economic ripple effects of the war would have shaped her early years, especially as Ireland itself grappled with its relationship to Britain. As she grew older, the revolutionary spirit and ideas of independence would become more significant in her life, potentially influencing her views on Irish politics and freedom.

When Sarah Barry was 8 years old, in 1783, the first hot air balloon was successfully flown by the Montgolfier brothers in France. Although she was living in Ireland, this remarkable achievement would have captured the imagination of many people throughout Europe, including children like Sarah. Here's how she might have reacted and how it could have affected her:

1. Sense of Wonder and Curiosity:
- As an 8-year-old, Sarah would likely have been filled with a sense of wonder upon hearing the news of a balloon rising into the sky, something that had never been done before. The idea of human flight, which was previously only imagined in myths and legends, would have seemed magical and extraordinary. She may have been fascinated by the possibility of soaring through the air, inspiring her imagination and sense of adventure.

2. Influence on Education and Science:
- The hot air balloon flight was part of the broader Enlightenment era, which was marked by scientific discovery and intellectual progress. Even though Sarah was still a child, she may have been exposed to conversations about this event within her community or family, especially if they had an interest in science or education. It could have sparked an early curiosity in scientific ideas, technology, or exploration. It might have encouraged her to look at the world differently, fostering a sense of curiosity about what humans could achieve with knowledge and innovation.

3. Community Discussions and News:
- News of the hot air balloon flight would have likely spread across Europe, and people in Ireland may have gathered to discuss this revolutionary event. If Sarah's family or community were engaged with current events, they might have shared stories about this remarkable achievement. Her parents or other adults could have explained the science behind it, possibly igniting an early interest in learning or a fascination with the technological advances of the time.

4. Inspiring Dreams of Travel and Exploration:
- The idea of flight might have made Sarah dream of seeing distant lands or traveling in ways previously thought impossible. For someone living in Ireland, which was relatively isolated compared to continental Europe, the concept of flying could have

inspired a sense of wonder about what lay beyond the horizon. This fascination with exploration and the unknown might have stayed with her as she grew up, influencing her worldview and making her more open to new ideas and possibilities.

5. Impact on Her View of Progress:

- Being a child during a time when such groundbreaking inventions were taking place could have had a lasting impact on Sarah's view of human progress. Witnessing such advancements at a young age might have given her a sense of optimism about the future and humanity's potential. It may have shaped her belief in innovation and the idea that the world was rapidly changing, with new discoveries making what once seemed impossible a reality.

Conclusion:

For an 8-year-old Sarah Barry, the first successful hot air balloon flight would have been an exciting and awe-inspiring event. While she may not have fully understood the scientific principles behind it, the spectacle of human flight could have sparked her imagination, curiosity, and interest in the world beyond her immediate surroundings. It would have introduced her to the possibilities of innovation and exploration, themes that could have shaped her thinking and worldview as she grew older.

When Sarah Barry was 23 years old in 1798, the Irish Rebellion and the Battle of Antrim were significant and tumultuous events. Here's how she might have reacted and what effects these events may have had on her:

1. Fear and Uncertainty:

- The Irish Rebellion was a violent and chaotic time in Irish history, marked by uprisings and brutal crackdowns. The Battle of Antrim was a key part of this rebellion, where the United Irishmen, inspired by the American and French revolutions, sought to overthrow British rule in Ireland. Sarah likely would have experienced fear and uncertainty as the rebellion spread, especially if her family or community was directly affected by the violence.

- She may have feared for the safety of her family and friends, particularly if they were caught up in the fighting or if the rebellion led to increased military presence or reprisals in her area. News of battles and skirmishes would have been on everyone's lips, and the atmosphere in the country would have been tense.

2. Political Awareness and Discussions:

- At 23 years old, Sarah would have been old enough to engage with the political discussions of the time. The rebellion was driven by a desire for Irish independence, civil rights, and religious equality, particularly for Catholics and Presbyterians, who were disenfranchised by the Protestant Ascendancy. If Sarah was from a family affected by these issues, she might have felt a strong sense of injustice and may have been sympathetic to the cause of the United Irishmen.

- On the other hand, if her family was loyal to the British Crown or benefited from the existing political order, she might have viewed the rebellion as a dangerous threat to stability and order. The rebellion would have forced people to take sides, and Sarah likely would have been exposed to passionate debates about the future of Ireland.

3. Community Impact:

- The rebellion had a widespread impact on communities throughout Ireland, especially in places like Antrim where fighting occurred. Even if Sarah wasn't directly involved, she would have seen the effects in her community — wounded soldiers, the destruction of property, and possibly the loss of life among people she knew. The rebellion may have caused disruptions in daily life, with curfews, shortages of goods, and heightened tensions between neighbors of different political or religious backgrounds.

- In areas affected by the fighting, there may have been reprisals by British forces, causing further fear and hardship. Sarah may have witnessed these events or heard about them, shaping her views on the rebellion and British rule.

4. Shaping Her National Identity:

- The rebellion of 1798 is often seen as a defining moment in Irish history, and for someone like Sarah, it could have played a role in shaping her sense of national identity. If she was sympathetic to the rebels' cause, the events may have deepened her sense of Irish nationalism and a desire for greater freedom from British rule.

- On the other hand, if the rebellion was seen as a failure or led to great suffering for her community, she might have become disillusioned with the idea of rebellion and more accepting of the status quo. Either way, living through such a significant historical event would have influenced her political views and her sense of what it meant to be Irish.

5. Personal and Family Impact:

- Depending on her family's involvement or position during the rebellion, it could have had a direct impact on her personal life. If her family supported the rebels, they might have faced persecution or retaliation. If they were loyalists, they might have been targeted by the rebels. The rebellion may have created divisions within her family or community, leading to lasting tensions or conflicts.

Conclusion:

For Sarah Barry, the Irish Rebellion of 1798 and the Battle of Antrim would have been life-altering events. At 23, she was old enough to understand the political and social turmoil around her, and the rebellion would have left a lasting impression. Whether it instilled fear, hope, or a sense of political disillusionment, it undoubtedly shaped her views on Irish independence, British rule, and her place in the evolving landscape of Ireland.

When Sarah Barry was 25 years old in 1800, William Young's invention of shoes specifically designed for the left and right feet would have been a remarkable development. Here's how she might have reacted and what effect it may have had on her:

1. Fascination with the Innovation:
- Shoes that fit specifically to the left and right foot were a groundbreaking concept in 1800. Before this innovation, shoes were typically made the same for both feet, which often resulted in discomfort. Sarah, like many at the time, may have been intrigued by the idea of such a functional improvement in footwear.
- If she was part of a well-off family, she might have had the means to purchase a pair and would have appreciated the comfort and practicality of the design.

2. Impact on Fashion:
- The late 18th and early 19th centuries were a time of evolving fashion, with attention being given to practicality as well as appearance. Shoes specifically designed for each foot would have been seen as aa luxury, improving not only comfort but also enhancing a person's gait and appearance. Sarah may have found this innovation to be a desirable addition to her wardrobe, complementing her fashion choices as she entered adulthood.
- For women, footwear was often both a functional and fashionable item, so this innovation could have influenced her perspective on how fashion was advancing.

3. Social Status and Accessibility:
- Sarah's reaction to William Young's shoes would have also depended on her social and economic standing. If she came from a wealthier background, the concept of owning such shoes would have been exciting and a mark of status. If she was from a more modest background, the innovation may have been something she observed from afar, potentially influencing future trends in fashion.

- As someone living in Ireland, Sarah's access to these shoes might have depended on the local market or trade connections, and the spread of such innovations may not have been immediate.

4. Comfort and Health:

- From a practical standpoint, wearing shoes designed for left and right feet would have significantly improved comfort. For someone walking long distances or working in less-than-ideal conditions, this innovation would have had a positive impact on foot health, reducing blisters or discomfort that came with ill-fitting shoes.

- This innovation may have contributed to a greater appreciation for more tailored, practical clothing items, reflecting the broader changes of the era towards more thoughtful design in daily life.

Conclusion:

At 25, Sarah Barry would likely have viewed William Young's innovation as a notable advancement in everyday fashion and comfort. Whether or not she immediately benefited from it, the creation of left and right foot-specific shoes would have been an exciting development in an era when comfort and practicality were becoming more important in fashion. The impact of this would have reflected the broader shifts of the time, as society embraced improvements in design and technology.

When Sarah Barry was 40 years old in 1815, the defeat and exile of Napoleon Bonaparte would have had a significant impact on her and the world around her. Here's how she might have reacted and how this event would have affected her life:

1. Relief and Stability:

- Napoleon's defeat at the Battle of Waterloo on June 18, 1815, marked the end of more than a decade of widespread warfare and instability across Europe. For Sarah, living in Ireland, which was part of the British Empire, Napoleon's defeat would have been met with relief, as Britain and its allies had been engaged in constant conflict with France during this period.

- The end of the Napoleonic Wars would have brought a sense of hope for peace and stability in Europe, which had experienced years of disruption due to Napoleon's campaigns.

2. Impact on Irish Life:

- Ireland had been significantly affected by the Napoleonic Wars. Many Irish soldiers fought in the British army, and the war had placed a strain on the economy, with resources directed toward the war effort. With Napoleon's defeat, there may have been hope that the British government would focus more on domestic issues, including the situation in Ireland.

- However, the post-war period didn't necessarily bring immediate benefits to Ireland. Economic problems and political discontent continued, and Sarah might have experienced or witnessed ongoing struggles, particularly if she lived in a region impacted by poverty or political unrest.

3. Nationalism and Political Movements:

- The period following Napoleon's defeat saw a rise in nationalist movements across Europe, and in Ireland, calls for independence and Catholic emancipation were growing. While Sarah was in her 40s, she may have noticed a growing sense of political agitation, particularly among those seeking greater rights for the Irish Catholic population.

- If Sarah came from a family that was politically aware, the defeat of Napoleon might have sparked discussions about Ireland's future, as the British government turned its attention to internal matters after years of focusing on European conflicts.

4. Cultural and Economic Changes:

- Napoleon's defeat also had cultural and economic repercussions across Europe. Trade and travel, which had been heavily restricted during the wars, began to open up again. New ideas, goods, and cultural influences would have started flowing more freely, impacting life in Ireland as well.

- Sarah may have seen changes in the availability of goods or heard more news of continental developments, as Europe adjusted to a post-Napoleonic world.

5. Personal Impact:

- At 40 years old, Sarah may have reflected on how Napoleon's wars had shaped the world she lived in for most of her adult life. From her 20s through her 40s, the Napoleonic Wars had dominated European affairs, and their conclusion would have marked the beginning of a new chapter.

- Depending on her family's social standing, they may have had personal stakes in the war, such as family members serving in the British army. Napoleon's defeat could have brought relief or emotional closure if her family had been directly affected by the conflict.

Conclusion:

At 40 years old, Sarah Barry would likely have felt a sense of relief and hope for the future with Napoleon's defeat and exile. The event signaled the end of a long and tumultuous period of warfare, opening the door to new possibilities for stability in Ireland and across Europe.

When Sarah Barry passed away at the age of 44 on February 13, 1819, her life would have been shaped by the significant historical, social, and political changes happening in Ireland and the broader world during that period. Here's a look at what her life might have been like in the final years leading up to her death:

1. Post-Napoleonic Era:

- Political Climate in Ireland: By 1819, Ireland was still feeling the effects of the Napoleonic Wars, which had ended in 1815. The Irish economy, which had been strained by the war, was slow to recover. Many people faced poverty and hardship, particularly in rural areas. Tensions between Ireland's Catholic majority and the Protestant ruling class were also simmering, especially concerning the fight for Catholic emancipation, which sought to grant Catholics the right to sit in Parliament and hold public office. Sarah, depending on her background, may have been aware of or affected by these tensions.

- Economic Challenges: The end of the war had brought some economic relief, but widespread poverty, especially in rural Ireland, persisted. If Sarah lived in a rural community, she likely witnessed the struggle of local farmers and laborers who faced declining wages and harsh living conditions.

2. Agrarian Unrest and Social Conditions:

- Agrarian Societies: During the years leading up to 1819, secret agrarian societies, such as the "Ribbonmen," were becoming more active in rural Ireland. These societies fought against the exploitation of tenant farmers by landlords, as well as high rents and evictions. If Sarah or her family lived in an agricultural community, they may have experienced or heard about these social uprisings.

- Living Standards: For many people in Ireland during this time, life was challenging. Poor living conditions, lack of access to education, and limited economic opportunities were common. Depending on her social class, Sarah could have faced these difficulties or may have lived in relative comfort if her family was more affluent.

3. Religious Environment:

- Religious Tensions: Religion played a central role in the lives of many Irish people, and by 1819, the push for Catholic emancipation was becoming a major political issue. The Penal Laws, which had placed restrictions on Catholics, were still in effect, though some had been relaxed. Sarah, whether Protestant or Catholic, would have lived in a society where religious identity heavily influenced one's social and political standing.

- Church Influence: Churches, both Protestant and Catholic, played a major role in community life, providing moral guidance, social support, and education. Sarah may have been an active member of her local church, which would have been a central part of her daily existence.

4. Technological and Cultural Developments:

- Technological Changes: The early 19th century saw the rise of new technologies that were slowly transforming society. The first commercial steamships had been introduced, and new forms of transportation were making travel easier. Additionally, the Industrial Revolution was well underway in England, and its effects were beginning to be felt in Ireland, though more so in urban areas. These developments might not have directly affected Sarah in a rural area, but they would have been part of the broader context in which she lived.

- Cultural Shifts: The early 19th century was also a time of cultural change. Enlightenment ideals had spread across Europe, and the Romantic movement in literature and the arts was growing. Sarah may have been exposed to these ideas through newspapers, books, or local social circles.

5. Personal Life and Family:

- Marriage and Family: By the age of 44, Sarah was likely married and may have had children. Life for women at the time revolved largely around family, home, and community. As a mother, Sarah would have been responsible for managing the household, raising children, and maintaining social ties within her community. If she came from a wealthier family, she might have had help from servants; if not, her daily life would have involved hard domestic work.

- Health and Mortality: Life expectancy in Ireland during this time was relatively low, and Sarah's death at 44 would not have been considered particularly unusual. Illnesses such as tuberculosis, typhus, and other infectious diseases were common and could quickly claim lives. Access to medical care was limited, especially in rural areas, meaning that health problems often went untreated.

Conclusion:

At the time of her death in 1819, Sarah Barry's life would have been shaped by the economic and social conditions of post-Napoleonic Ireland. She likely experienced or witnessed the hardships faced by many people, including economic struggles, social unrest, and religious tensions. Her daily life would have been centered around family and community, with religion playing an important role. Although the world was beginning to change due to technological advancements and cultural shifts, much of rural Ireland remained deeply traditional, and Sarah's life would have reflected the challenges and values of that era.

[1] https://www.wikitree.com/wiki/McLeese-86
[2] https://www.wikitree.com/wiki/McAleese-37
[3] https://www.wikitree.com/wiki/Unknown-695671
[4] https://www.wikitree.com/wiki/Adams-73029
[5] https://www.wikitree.com/wiki/Adams-73028
[6] https://www.wikitree.com/wiki/Adams-73019
[7] https://www.wikitree.com/wiki/Allen-73483
[8] https://www.wikitree.com/wiki/Higginson-1329
[9] https://www.wikitree.com/wiki/Allen-73484
[10] https://www.wikitree.com/wiki/Benning-453
[11] https://www.wikitree.com/wiki/Benning-425
[12] https://www.wikitree.com/wiki/Ellis-31232
[13] https://www.wikitree.com/wiki/Benning-454
[14] https://www.wikitree.com/wiki/Benning-426
[15] https://www.wikitree.com/wiki/Boyd-23281
[16] https://www.wikitree.com/wiki/Boyd-23282
[17] https://www.wikitree.com/wiki/Gordon-22674
[18] https://www.wikitree.com/wiki/Anderson-88724
[19] https://www.wikitree.com/wiki/Dunlop-3559
[20] https://www.wikitree.com/wiki/Unknown-695705

Don't miss out!

Visit the website below and you can sign up to receive emails whenever Angeline Gallant publishes a new book. There's no charge and no obligation.

https://books2read.com/r/B-A-QGSI-UMCCF

BOOKS2READ

Connecting independent readers to independent writers.

Also by Angeline Gallant

A Dragon's Diary
Dreaming of Dragons

Calling Her Heart
Whisper of the Heart
No Turning Back
Forsake Me Not
Hear My Cry

FORGET ME NOT
Victoria, Ontario's Babies 1894 - 1895

Guardian of the Heart
Fallen Petals

Keeper Of Secrets
A Lady's Secret

Midnight's Awakening
Heart of the Storm
Walking Through The Storm
Walking Through The Storm
Heart of the Storm

Secrets of the Underworld
Deklan's Dragons

Tell My Story Collection
Tell My Story: Germany 1851
Tell My Story: England 1852

The Dervock Legacy
Echoes of Dervock

The Grave Whisperer
Cataraqui United Church Cemetery
Wedding Bells in Kingston, Ontario, Canada 1923
St. Paul's Anglican Churchyard Kingston, Ontario, Canada A-B
St. Paul's Anglican Churchyard, Kingston, Ontario, Canada C - D
St. Paul's Anglican Churchyard, Kingston, Ontario, Canada G - H
St. Paul's Anglican Churchyard, Kingston, Ontario, Canada J - N
St. Paul's Anglican Churchyard, Kingston, Ontario, Canada O - R

St. Paul's Anglican Churchyard, Kingston, Ontario, Canada S - T
St. Paul's Anglican Churchyard, Kingston, Ontario T - Z
Small Graveyards & Burial Grounds: Kingston, Ontario, Canada
Cataraqui United Church Cemetery 1
Cataraqui United Church Cemetery 2
Cataraqui United Church Cemetary 3
Cataraqui United Church Cemetery 4
Cataraqui United Church Cemetery 5
Beth Israel Cemetery
Cataraqui United Church Cemetery 6

The Wolf Whisperer Series
Journey of the Heart
Cry of a Warrior
Wolf Whisperer volumes 1 & 2
The Wolf Whisperer volumes 1 & 2

Timeless Whispers of Dervock Saga
Secrets of Dervock

Standalone
Winds of Change vol 1-3

Watch for more at https://www.goodreads.com/author/show/19703964.Angeline_Gallant.

About the Author

Angeline Gallant is a Geneology addict who loves to work on her family tree and help others with theirs. This passion for history plays a huge role in her books as well.

An Old Stock Canadian and a homeschooling mother living in Canada, Angeline is determined to leave her own special mark on the world through her work, her child, and her writing.

Angeline is an author on Goodreads. If you follow her account on Goodreads, she will follow back.

Read more at https://www.goodreads.com/author/show/19703964.Angeline_Gallant.

Milton Keynes UK
Ingram Content Group UK Ltd.
UKHW020053181024
449757UK00011B/606